Sport Management

Now available in a fully revised and updated fifth edition, *Sport Management: Principles and Applications* tells you everything you need to know about the contemporary sport industry. Covering both the professional and nonprofit sectors, and with more international material than any other introductory sport management textbook, it focuses on core management principles and their application in a sporting context, highlighting the unique challenges of a career in sport management.

The book contains useful features throughout, including conceptual overviews, guides to further reading, links to important websites, study questions, and up-to-date case studies showing how theory works in the real world. It covers every core functional area of management, including:

- Strategic planning
- Financial management
- Organizational culture and design
- Human resource management
- Leadership and governance
- Marketing and sponsorship
- Performance management
- Sport and the media

The fifth edition includes expanded coverage of sport for development, analytics, monitoring and evaluation, ethics, risk management, sport and health, social media, sustainability, and other contemporary management issues. Complemented by a companion website offering additional resources for students and instructors, this is an ideal textbook for first and second-year students in sport management degree programs and for business students seeking an overview of applied sport management principles.

Russell Hoye is Pro Vice-Chancellor (Research Development) at La Trobe University, Australia. He is the editor of the Sport Management Series published by Routledge, a member of the editorial board for *Sport Management Review*, *International Journal of Sport Policy and Politics*, and *Journal of Global Sport Management*; past President of the Sport Management Association of Australia and New Zealand (SMAANZ); and a graduate of the Australian Institute of Company Directors.

Aaron C.T. Smith is Professor of Sport Business in the Institute for Sport Business at Loughborough University, UK. Aaron has research interests in the management of psychological, organizational, and policy change in business and sport and health. Recently he has focused on the impact of commercial and global sport policy, the ways in which internal cultures shape organizational conduct, the role of social forces in managing change, and the management of social policy changes such as those associated with health and drug use.

Matthew Nicholson is an Associate Professor and Director of the Centre for Sport and Social Impact at La Trobe University, Australia. His research interests focus on sport policy and development, the contribution of sport to social capital, and the relationship between sport and the media.

Bob Stewart is a former Professor of Sport Studies at Victoria University, Australia. Bob has been teaching and researching the field of sport management and sport policy for 20 years, and has a special interest in cartel structures, social control, and player regulation in elite sports and the ways in which neoliberal ideologies shape sport's governance and management practices.

Sport Management Series

Series Editor: Russell Hoye, La Trobe University, Australia

This **Sport Management Series** has been providing a range of texts for core subjects in undergraduate sport business and management courses around the world for more than 10 years. These textbooks are considered essential resources for academics, students, and managers seeking an international perspective on the management of the complex world of sport.

Many millions of people around the globe are employed in sport organizations in areas as diverse as event management, broadcasting, venue management, marketing, professional sport, community and collegiate sport, and coaching as well as in allied industries such as sporting equipment manufacturing, sporting footwear and apparel, and retail.

At the elite level, sport has moved from being an amateur pastime to one of the world's most significant industries. The growth and professionalization of sport have driven changes in the consumption and production of sport and in the management of sporting organizations at all levels.

Managing sport organizations at the start of the 21st century involves the application of techniques and strategies evident in leading business, government, and nonprofit organizations. This series explains these concepts and applies them to the diverse global sport industry.

To support their use by academics, each text is supported by current case studies, targeted study questions, further reading lists, links to relevant web-based resources, and supplementary online materials such as case study questions and classroom presentation aids.

Available in this series:

Managing People in Sport Organizations
A Strategic Human Resource Management Perspective (Second edition)
Tracy Taylor, Alison Doherty and Peter McGraw

Introduction to Sport Marketing (Second edition)
Aaron C.T. Smith and Bob Stewart

Sport Management
Principles and Applications (Fourth edition)
Russell Hoye, Aaron C.T. Smith, Matthew Nicholson and Bob Stewart

Sport and the Media
Managing the Nexus (Second edition)
Matthew Nicholson, Anthony Kerr and Merryn Sherwood

Sport Management
Principles and Applications (Fifth edition)
Russell Hoye, Aaron C.T. Smith, Matthew Nicholson and Bob Stewart

Sport Management
Principles and Applications

FIFTH EDITION

Russell Hoye, Aaron C.T. Smith,
Matthew Nicholson, and
Bob Stewart

Routledge
Taylor & Francis Group

LONDON AND NEW YORK

First published 2018
by Routledge
2 Park Square, Milton Park, Abingdon, Oxon OX14 4RN

and by Routledge
711 Third Avenue, New York, NY 10017

Routledge is an imprint of the Taylor & Francis Group, an informa business

British Library Cataloguing-in-Publication Data
A catalogue record for this book is available from the British Library

Library of Congress Cataloging-in-Publication Data
Names: Hoye, Russell, – author.
Title: Sport management : principles and applications / Russell
    Hoye, Aaron C.T. Smith, Matthew Nicholson, and Bob Stewart.
Description: Fifth Edition. | New York : Routledge, 2018. |
Series: Sport Management Series | Includes bibliographical
    references and index.
Identifiers: LCCN 2017042161 | ISBN 9780815385172 (Hardback) |
    ISBN 9780815385165 (Paperback) | ISBN 9781351202190 (eBook)
Subjects: LCSH: Sports administration.
Classification: LCC GV713 .S6775 2018 | DDC 796.06/9—dc23
LC record available at https://lccn.loc.gov/2017042161

ISBN: 978-0-8153-8517-2 (hbk)
ISBN: 978-0-8153-8516-5 (pbk)
ISBN: 978-1-351-20219-0 (ebk)

Typeset in Berling and Futura
by Apex CoVantage, LLC

Visit the companion website: www.routledge.com/cw/hoye

Contents

Figures

Images

Tables

In Practice Examples

Case Studies

Preface

The success of the previous four editions of this textbook point to a continued need for *Sport Management: Principles and Applications* to fill the gap for an introductory text in sport management that provides a balance between management theory and the analysis of the highly dynamic context of the sport industry. As we said in the preface to the previous edition, this textbook continues to get this balance right, as evidenced by its adoption in many educational institutions across Australia, Canada, New Zealand, the United Kingdom, Europe, and increasingly other countries as a core undergraduate textbook, as well as being reprinted in five other languages. As with the original text, our intention with this edition is not to replace the ever-increasing number of excellent introductory texts on management theory, or to ignore the increasing volume of books that examine various elements of the global sport industry. Our aim continues to be the provision of a textbook that includes sufficient conceptual detail for undergraduate students to grasp the essentials of management, while highlighting the unique aspects of how management is applied to sport across the globe.

The book provides a comprehensive introduction to the principles of management and their practical application to sport organizations operating at the community, state/provincial, national, and professional levels. The book is primarily written for first- and second-year university students studying sport management courses and students who wish to research the nonprofit, government, and commercial dimensions of sport. It is especially suitable for students studying sport management within business-focussed courses, as well as students seeking an overview of sport management principles within human movement, sport development, sport science, or physical education courses.

As with previous editions, the book is divided into two parts. Part I provides a concise analysis of the evolution of sport, the unique features of sport and sport management, the current drivers of change in the sport industry, and the role of government policy and agencies, nonprofit organizations, and professional or elite sectors of sport. Part II covers core management principles and their application in sport, highlighting the unique features of how sport is managed compared to other industrial sectors with chapters on strategic management, organizational structure, human resource management, leadership, organizational culture, financial management, marketing, sport and the media, governance, and performance management.

We recognize that many instructors, lecturers, and course leaders have used the various iterations of this textbook in core courses over many years, and we wanted to maintain the basic structure but update the case materials, examples, and current issues within the existing structure of the book. To assist lecturers and instructors, all chapters include an overview, a set of objectives, a summary of core principles, a set of review questions, suggestions for further reading, and a list of relevant websites for further information. Chapters 2 through 14 each contain three substantial examples (dubbed "In Practice") that help illustrate concepts and accepted practice at the community, state/provincial, national, and international levels of sport. As with previous editions, the majority of these have been completely rewritten with new examples and the remainder extensively revised with updated information.

We have also written new case studies for Chapters 2 to 14 which can be used by lecturers and instructors for classroom discussion or assessment and also included some discussion questions for each chapter that can be used for facilitating in class interactions with the content. For those academics who prescribe the book as essential reading for students, a comprehensive website is available that contains an updated set of PowerPoint slides that summarize each chapter as well as teaching notes to accompany each of the case studies to guide instructors in their use for in class activities or assessment tasks.

We would like to thank our colleagues and students for their valuable comments on the previous editions of the book and the very valuable anonymous reviews provided on those editions. Once again, we are indebted to our longstanding Commissioning Editor Simon Whitmore for his belief in us to deliver a quality book. As always, we acknowledge and thank our respective partners and families for their support and patience while we developed this new edition.

Russell Hoye
Aaron C.T. Smith
Matthew Nicholson
Bob Stewart

PART I

The sport management environment

CHAPTER 1

Sport management

OVERVIEW

This chapter provides a brief review of the development of sport into a major sector of economic and social activity and outlines the importance of sport management as a field of study and employment. It discusses the unique nature of sport and the drivers of change that affect how sport is produced and consumed. A model that explains the public, nonprofit, and professional elements of sport is presented, along with a brief description of the salient aspects of the management context for sport organizations. The chapter also serves as an introduction to the remaining sections of the book, highlighting the importance of each of the topics.

After completing this chapter the reader should be able to:

- Describe the unique features of sport;
- Understand the environment in which sport organizations operate;

- Describe the three sectors of the sport industry; and
- Explain how sport management is different to other fields of management study.

WHAT IS SPORT MANAGEMENT?

Sport employs many millions of people around the globe, is played or watched by the majority of the world's population, and at the elite or professional level has moved from being an amateur pastime to a significant industry. The growth and professionalization of sport has driven changes in the consumption, production and management of sporting events and organizations at all levels of sport. Countries with emerging economies such as Brazil, hosts of the 2014 World Cup for football and the 2016 Olympic Games, as well advanced economic powerhouses such as Russia (host of the 2018 Olympic Games) and Japan (host of the 2020 Olympic Games), increasingly see sport as a vehicle for driving investment in infrastructure; for promoting their country to the world to stimulate trade, tourism, and investment; and for fostering national pride amongst their citizens.

Managing sport organizations at the start of the 21st century involves the application of techniques and strategies evident in the majority of modern business, government, and nonprofit organizations. Sport managers engage in strategic planning and performance management, manage large numbers of paid and voluntary human resources, deal with broadcasting contracts worth billions of dollars, and manage the development and welfare of elite athletes who sometimes earn 100 times the average working wage. Sport managers also work within a highly integrated global network of international sports federations, national sport organizations, government agencies, media corporations, sponsors, and community organizations that are subject to a myriad of regulations, government policies, and complex decision-making frameworks.

Students seeking a career as a sport manager need to develop an understanding of the special features of sport and its allied industries; the environment in which sport organizations operate; and the types of sport organizations that operate in the public, nonprofit, and professional sectors of the sport industry. The remainder of the chapter is devoted to a discussion of these points and highlights the unique aspects of sport organization management.

UNIQUE FEATURES OF SPORT

Smith, Stewart and Haimes (2010) provide a list of 10 unique features of sport which can assist us to understand why the management of sport organizations requires the application of specific management techniques. A unique feature of sport is the phenomenon of people developing irrational passions for sporting teams, competitions, or athletes. Sport has a symbolic significance in relation to performance outcomes, success, and celebrating achievement that does not occur in other areas of economic and social activity. Sport managers must learn to harness these passions by appealing to people's desire to buy tickets for events, become a member of a club, donate time to help run a voluntary association, or purchase sporting merchandise. They must also learn to apply clear business logic and management techniques to the maintenance of traditions and connections to the nostalgic aspects of sport consumption and engagement.

There are also marked differences between sport organizations and other businesses in how they evaluate performance. Private or publicly listed companies exist to make profits and increase wealth of shareholders or owners, whereas in sport, other imperatives such as winning championships, delivering services to stakeholders and members, or meeting community service obligations may take precedence over financial outcomes. Sport managers need to be cognizant of these multiple organizational outcomes, while at the same time being responsible financial managers to ensure they have the requisite resources to support their organization's strategic objectives.

Competitive balance is also a unique feature of the interdependent nature of relationships between sporting organizations that compete on the field but cooperate off the field to ensure the long-term viability of both clubs and their league. In most business environments the aim is to secure the largest market share, defeat all competitors, and secure a monopoly. In sport leagues, clubs and teams need the opposition to remain in business, so they must cooperate to share revenues and playing talent and regulate themselves to maximize the level of uncertainty in the outcome of games between them so that fans' interest will be maintained. In some ways such behaviour could be construed as anti-competitive but governments support such actions due to the unique aspects of sport.

The sport product, when it takes the form of a game or contest, is also of variable quality. Although game outcomes are generally uncertain, one team might dominate, which will diminish the attractiveness of the game. The perception of those watching the game might be that the quality has also diminished as a result, particularly if it is your team that loses! The variable quality of sport therefore makes it hard to guarantee quality in the marketplace relative to providers of other consumer products such as mobile phones, cars, or other general household goods.

Sport also enjoys a high degree of product or brand loyalty, with fans unlikely to change the team or club they support or to switch sporting codes because of a poor match result or the standard of officiating. Consumers of household products have a huge range to choose from and will readily switch brands for reasons of price or quality, whereas sporting competitions and their teams are hard to substitute. This advantage is also a negative, as sporting codes that wish to expand market share find it difficult to attract new fans from other codes due to their familiarity with the customs and traditions of their existing sport affiliation.

Sport engenders unique behaviours in people, such as emulating their sporting heroes in play, wearing the uniform of their favourite player, or purchasing the products that sporting celebrities endorse. This vicarious identification with the skills, abilities, and lifestyles of sports people can be used by sport managers and allied industries to influence the purchasing decisions of individuals who follow sport.

Sport fans also exhibit a high degree of optimism, at times insisting that their team, despite a string of bad losses, is only a week, game, or lucky break away from winning the next championship. It could also be argued that the owners or managers of sport franchises exhibit a high degree of optimism by toting their star recruits or new coach as the path to delivering them on field success.

Sporting organizations, argue Smith, Stewart and Haimes (2010), are relatively reluctant to adopt new technologies unless they are related to sports science or data analytics, where on-field performance improvements are possible, indeed, highly desirable. In this regard sport organizations can be considered conservative and tied to traditions and behaviours more than other organizations.

The final unique aspect of sport is its limited availability. In other industries, organizations can increase production to meet demand, but in sport, clubs are limited by season length and the number of scheduled games. This constrains their ability to maximize revenue through ticket sales and associated income. The implication for sport managers is that they must understand the nature of their business, the level of demand for their product and services (whatever form that may take), and the appropriate time to deliver them.

Collectively, these unique features of sport create some challenges for managers of sport organizations and events. It is important to understand the effects of these features on the management approaches and strategies used by sport managers; the next section explains how these unique features of sport influence the operating environment for sport organizations and their managers.

SPORT MANAGEMENT ENVIRONMENT

Globalization has been a major force in driving change in the ways sport is produced and consumed. The enhanced integration of the world's economies has enabled communication to occur between producers and consumers at greater speed and variety, and sport has been one sector to reap the benefits. Consumers of elite sport events and competitions such as the Olympic Games; World Cups for rugby, cricket, and football; English Premier League Football; the National Basketball Association (NBA); and Grand Slam tournaments for tennis and golf enjoy unprecedented access through mainstream and social media. Aside from actually attending the events live at a stadium or venue, fans can view these events through free to air and pay or cable television; listen to them on radio and the Internet; read about game analyses, their favourite players and teams through newspapers and magazines in both print and digital editions; receive progress scores, commentary, or video on their mobile phones or tablets through websites or social media platforms such as Twitter; and sign up for special deals and information through online subscriptions using their email address or preferred social media platform. The global sport marketplace has become very crowded, and sport managers seeking to carve out a niche need to understand the global environment in which they must operate. Thus, one of the themes of this book is the impact of globalization on the ways sport is produced, consumed, and managed.

Most national governments view sport as a vehicle for nationalism, economic development, or social development. As such, they consider it their role to enact policies and legislation to support, control, or regulate the activities of sport organizations. Most national governments support elite training institutes to assist in developing athletes for national and international competition, provide funding to national sporting organizations to deliver high-performance and community-level programs, support sport organizations to bid for major events, and facilitate the building of major stadiums. In return for this support, governments can influence sports to recruit more mass participants; provide services to discrete sectors of the community; or have sports enact policies on alcohol and drug use, gambling, and general health promotion messages. Governments also regulate the activities of sport organizations through legislation or licensing in areas such as industrial relations, anti-discrimination, taxation, and corporate governance. A further theme in the book is the impact that government policy, funding, and regulation can have on the way sport is produced, consumed, and managed.

The management of sport organizations has undergone a relatively rapid period of professionalization since the 1980s. The general expansion of the global sports industry and commercialization of sport events and competitions, combined with the introduction of paid staff into voluntary governance structures and the growing number of people who now earn a living managing sport organizations or playing sport, has forced sport organizations and their managers to become more professional. This is reflected in the increased number of university sport management courses, the requirement to have business skills as well as industry-specific knowledge or experience to be successful in sport management, the growth of professional and academic associations devoted to sport management, and the variety of professionals and specialists that sport managers must deal with in the course of their careers. Sport managers will work with accountants, lawyers, human resource managers, taxation specialists, government policy advisors, project management personnel, architects, market researchers, and media specialists, not to mention sports agents, sports scientists, coaches, officials, and volunteers. The ensuing chapters of the book will highlight the ongoing professionalization of sport management as an academic discipline and a career.

The final theme of the book is the notion that changes in sport management frequently result from developments in technology. Changes in telecommunications have already been highlighted, but further changes in technology are evident in areas such as performance-enhancing drugs, information technology, data analytics focused on both on-field and off-field elements, coaching and high-performance techniques, sports venues, sport betting and wagering, and sporting equipment. These changes have forced sport managers to develop policies about their use, to protect intellectual property with a marketable value, and generally adapt their operations to incorporate their use for achieving organizational objectives. Sport managers need to understand the potential of technological development but also the likely impact on future operations.

THREE SECTORS OF SPORT

In order to make sense of the many organizations that are involved in sport management and how these organizations may form partnerships, influence each others' operations, and conduct business, it is useful to see sport as comprising three distinct sectors. The first is the state or public sector, which includes national, state/provincial, regional and local governments, and specialist agencies that develop sport policy, provide funding to other sectors, and support specialist roles such as elite athlete development or drug control. The second is the nonprofit or voluntary sector, made up of community-based clubs, governing associations, and international sport organizations that provide competition and participation opportunities, regulate and manage sporting codes, and organize major championship events. The third sector is professional or commercial sport organizations,

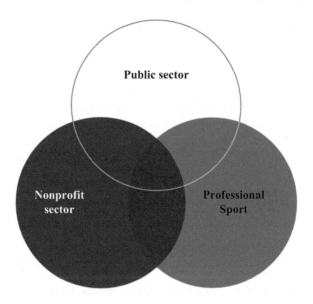

FIGURE 1.1 Three-sector model of sport

comprising professional leagues and their member teams, as well as allied organizations such as sporting apparel and equipment manufacturers, media companies, major stadia operators, and event managers.

These three sectors do not operate in isolation, and in many cases there is significant overlap. For example, the state is intimately involved in providing funding to nonprofit sport organizations for sport development and elite athlete programs, and in return non-profit sport organizations provide the general community with sporting opportunities as well as developing athletes, coaches, officials, and administrators to sustain sporting partic-ipation. The state is also involved in commercial sport, supporting the building of major stadia and other sporting venues to provide spaces for professional sport to be played, providing a regulatory and legal framework for professional sport to take place, and sup-porting manufacturing and event organizations to do business. The nonprofit sport sector supports professional sport by providing playing talent for leagues, as well as developing the coaches, officials, and administrators to facilitate elite competitions. Indeed, in some cases the sport league itself will consist of member teams which are technically nonprofit entities, even though they support a pool of professional managers and players. In return, the professional sport sector markets sport for spectators and participants and in some cases provides substantial funds from TV broadcast rights revenue. Figure 1.1 illustrates the three sectors and the intersections where these relationships take place.

WHAT IS DIFFERENT ABOUT SPORT MANAGEMENT?

Sport managers utilize management techniques and theories that are similar to man-agers of other organizations, such as hospitals, government departments, banks, mining companies, car manufacturers, and welfare agencies. However, there are some aspects of strategic management, organizational structure, human resource management, leadership, organizational culture, financial management, marketing, governance, and performance management that are unique to the management of sport organizations.

Strategic management

Strategic management involves the analysis of an organization's position in the competitive environment, the determination of its direction and goals, the selection of an appropriate strategy, and the leveraging of its distinctive assets. The success of any sport organization may largely depend on the quality of their strategic decisions. It could be argued that nonprofit sport organizations have been slow to embrace the concepts associated with strategic management because sport is inherently turbulent, with on-field performance and tactics tending to dominate and distract sport managers from the choices they need to make in the office and boardroom. In a competitive market, sport managers must drive their own futures by undertaking meaningful market analyses, establishing a clear direction, and crafting strategy that matches opportunities. An understanding of strategic management principles and how these can be applied in the specific industry context of sport are essential for future sport managers.

Organizational structure

An organization's structure is important because it defines where staff and volunteers 'fit in' with each other in terms of work tasks, decision-making procedures, the need for collaboration, levels of responsibility and reporting mechanisms. Finding the right structure for a sport organization involves balancing the need to formalize procedures while fostering innovation and creativity, and ensuring adequate control of employee and volunteer activities without unduly affecting people's motivation and attitudes to work. In the complex world of sport, clarifying reporting and communication lines between multiple groups of internal and external stakeholders while trying to reduce unnecessary and costly layers of management is also an important aspect of managing an organization's structure. The relatively unique mix of paid staff and volunteers in the sport industry adds a layer of complexity to managing the structure of many sport organizations.

Human resource management

Human resource management, in mainstream business or sport organizations, is essentially about ensuring an effective and satisfied workforce. However, the sheer size of some sport organizations, as well as the difficulties in managing a mix of volunteers and paid staff in the sport industry, make human resource management a complex issue for sport managers. Successful sport leagues, clubs, associations, retailers, and venues rely on good human resources, both on and off the field. Human resource management cannot be divorced from other key management tools, such as strategic planning or managing organizational culture and structure, and is a further element that students of sport management need to understand to be effective practitioners.

Leadership

Managers at the helm of sport organizations need to be able to influence others to follow their visions; empower individuals to feel part of a team working for a common goal; and be adept at working with leaders of other sport organizations to forge alliances, deal with conflicts, or coordinate common business or development projects. The sport industry thrives on organizations having leaders who are able to collaborate effectively with other organizations to run a professional league; work with governing bodies of sport; and coordinate the efforts of government agencies, international and national sport organizations, and other groups to deliver large-scale sport events. Sport management students wishing to work in leadership roles need to understand the ways in which leadership skills can be developed and how these principles can be applied.

Organizational culture

Organizational culture consists of the assumptions, norms, and values held by individuals and groups within an organization, which affect the activities and goals in the workplace and in many ways influence how employees work. Organizational culture is related to organizational performance, excellence, employee commitment, cooperation, efficiency, job performance, and decision making. However, how organizational culture can be defined, diagnosed, and changed is subject to much debate in the business and academic world. Due to the strong traditions of sporting endeavour and behaviour, managers of sport organizations, particularly those such as professional sport franchises or traditional sports, must be cognizant of the power of organizational culture as both an inhibitor and driver of performance. Understanding how to identify, describe, analyse, and ultimately influence the culture of a sport organization is an important element in the education of sport managers.

Financial management

Financial management in sport involves the application of accounting and financial decision-making processes to the relatively unique revenue streams and costs associated with sport organizations. It is important for sport managers to understand the financial management principles associated with membership income, ticketing and merchandise sales, sports betting income, sponsorship, broadcast rights fees, and government grants and subsidies. Sport managers also need to understand the history of the commercial development of sport and the ways in which sport is likely to be funded and financed in the future, in particular the move to private ownership of sport teams and leagues, sport clubs being listed on the stock exchange, greater reliance on debt finance, and public–private partnerships.

Sport marketing

Sport marketing is the application of marketing concepts to sport products and services and the marketing of non-sports products through an association with sport. Like other forms of marketing, sport marketing seeks to fulfil the needs and wants of consumers. It achieves this by providing sport services and sport-related products to consumers. However, sport marketing is unlike conventional marketing in that it also has the ability to encourage the consumption of non-sport products and services by association. It is important to understand that sport marketing means the marketing of sport as well as the use of sport as a tool to market other products and services.

Sport and the media

The relationship between sport and the media is the defining commercial connection for both industries at the beginning of the 21st century, and at the elite and professional levels sport is becoming increasingly dependent on the media for its commercial success. Managers of professional or commercial sport organizations and events need an understanding of the structure of the sport broadcast industry, the implications of media diversity and convergence, the valuation of media rights, and the restrictions that government policy and regulation has in some cases. The explosion in the use of social media platforms by consumers demands that sport managers know how to use these platforms to communicate, engage, and ultimately influence consumer decisions in relation to their product, service, or brand.

Governance

Organizational governance involves the exercise of decision-making power within organizations and provides the system by which the elements of organizations are controlled and directed. Governance is a particularly important element of managing sport organizations, many of whom are controlled by elected groups of volunteers, as it deals with issues of policy and direction for the enhancement of organizational performance rather than day-to-day operational management decision making. Appropriate governance systems help ensure that elected decision makers and paid staff seek to deliver outcomes for the benefit of the organization and its members and that the means used to attain these outcomes are effectively monitored. As many sport managers work in an environment where they must report to a governing board, it is important that they understand the principles of good governance and how these are applied in sport organizations.

Performance management

Sport organizations over the last 30 years have undergone an evolution to become more professionally structured and managed. Sport organizations have applied business principles to marketing their products, planning their operations, managing their human resource, and carrying out other aspects of organizational activity. The unique nature of sport organizations and the variation in missions and purposes has led to the development of a variety of criteria with which to assess the performance of sport organizations. Sport management students need to understand the ways in which organizational performance can be conceptualized, analysed, and reported and how these principles can be applied in the sport industry.

SUMMARY

Sport has a number of unique features:

- people develop irrational passions;
- differences in judging performance;
- the interdependent nature of relationships between sporting organizations;
- anti-competitive behaviour;
- sport product (a game or contest) is of variable quality;
- it enjoys a high degree of product or brand loyalty;
- it engenders vicarious identification;
- sport fans exhibit a high degree of optimism;
- sport organizations are relatively reluctant to adopt new technology; and
- sport often has a limited supply.

Several environmental factors influence the way sport organizations operate, namely globalization, government policy, professionalization, and technological developments.

The sport industry can be defined as comprising three distinct but interrelated industries: The state or public sector, the nonprofit or voluntary sector, and the professional or commercial sector. These sectors do not operate in isolation and often engage in a range of collaborative projects, funding arrangements, joint commercial ventures, and other business relationships.

Some aspects of strategic management, organizational structure, human resource management, leadership, organizational culture, financial management, marketing, the relationship between sport and the media, governance, and performance management are unique to the management of sport organizations. The remainder of the book explores the three sectors of the sport industry and examines each of these core management issues in more detail.

REVIEW QUESTIONS

1 Define sport management.
2 What are the unique features of sport?
3 Describe the main elements of the environment that affect sport organizations.
4 What sort of relationships might develop between sport organizations in the public and nonprofit sectors?

5 What sort of relationships might develop between sport organizations in the public and professional sport sectors?

6 What sort of relationships might develop between sport organizations in the professional and nonprofit sectors?

7 Explain the major differences between managing a sport organization and a commercial manufacturing firm.

8 Why does the sport industry need specialist managers with tertiary sport management qualifications?

9 Identify one organization from each of the public, nonprofit, and professional sport sectors. Compare how the environmental factors discussed in this chapter can affect their operation.

10 Discuss whether the special features of sport discussed in this chapter apply to all levels of sport by comparing the operation of professional sports league, an elite government sport institute, and a community sport club.

DISCUSSION QUESTIONS

1 Why do governments support sport through the use of taxpayer money to build facilities and stadiums?

2 Why have some professional sports, such as the English Premier League football competition or the NBA, become wildly more successful than others?

3 What are some of the unique attributes of sport that have attracted you (as students) to study this field?

4 Is sport still as popular as a leisure or active recreation activity as, say, 20 years ago? Why or why not?

5 What might be some of the emerging challenges that sport managers will have to face in the next decade?

FURTHER READING

Fort, R. (2011). *Sport Economics*. 3rd edn. Upper Saddle River, NJ: Prentice Hall/Pearson.

Hoye, R., Nicholson, M. and Houlihan, B. (2010). *Sport and Policy: Issues and Analysis*. Jordon Hill, UK: Elsevier/Butterworth Heinemann.

Hoye, R. and Parent, M. (eds) (2017). *Handbook of Sport Management*. London: SAGE.

Jarvie, G. (2013). *Sport Culture and Society: An Introduction*. 2nd edn. London: Routledge.

Sandy, R., Sloane, P. and Rosentraub, M. (2004). *Economics of Sport: An International Perspective*. New York: Palgrave Macmillan.

Smith, A., Stewart, B. and Haimes, G. (2011). *The Performance Identity: Building High-Performance Organizational Cultures in Sport*. New York: Nova Science Publishers.

RELEVANT WEBSITES

The following websites are useful starting points for general information on the teaching
   programs and research communities focussed on the management of sport:
Asian Association for Sport Management (AASM) at www.asianasm.wordpress.com
European Association for Sport Management (EASM) at www.easm.net
Latin American Association for Sport Management (ALGEDE) at www.algede.com
North American Society for Sport Management (NASSM) at www.nassm.com
Sport Management Association of Australia and New Zealand (SMAANZ) at www.
   smaanz.org
World Association for Sport Management at www.wasm2017.com

CHAPTER 2

Government influence on sport

OVERVIEW

This chapter examines the different ways in which governments and their agencies can influence the development of sport systems and practices. Particular attention is paid to the reasons why governments seek to intervene in the operation of sport and the different forms such intervention can take. A distinction is made between interventions that assist and promote sport, on one hand, and interventions that control and regulate sport on the other. A distinction is also made between government initiatives that aim to increase levels of community participation and those aimed at improving levels of elite athlete performance. Throughout the chapter, incidents and cases are used to illustrate both the concepts and theories that underpin government intervention in sport and the management implications that arise from this intervention.

After completing this chapter the reader should be able to:

- Explain the role and purpose of government;
- Understand why and how governments may want to intervene in a nation's economic, social, and cultural landscape;

- Distinguish between nations – and their governments – that operate from different ideological perspectives, which are first socialist, second, reformist, third, neo-liberal, and finally, conservative;
- Explain how each of these ideologies affect the way governments go about assisting sport on one hand, and regulating it on the other; and
- Critically compare and contrast strategies that aim to improve elite sport systems and standards with those that aim to build the participation base of sport.

DEFINING AND EXPLAINING GOVERNMENT

Government, by which we mean the structures and systems that govern, rule, and control societies, is pivotal in shaping the economic structure of nations and setting their social and cultural 'tone'. The government sector – or public sector, as it is sometimes called – includes all levels of government – federal, state, and local. These three levels intervene in the economy by collecting and spending tax revenue and by establishing and enforcing laws, rules, and other regulations. The government sector undertakes this intervention because society has deemed that the provision of some goods and services are better handled by the imposition of government than by market decisions involving the interaction of independent buyers and sellers. Government decisions thus affect the allocation of a nation's scarce resources, which means that it can, in line with its policies and goals, and hopefully with the interests of the broader community front and centre, either expand or contract a particular industry and the products and jobs they create. Sport is one such industry.

At the same time, government preferences and priorities can be markedly different across nations. Some governments put a lot of resources into health care and education on the grounds that they deliver greater levels of human productivity and happiness. Other governments have a commitment to manufacturing and will provide subsidies and assistance to businesses that manufacture, for instance, motor vehicles and computer hardware. Some governments also believe that it has a responsibility to protect its citizens from harm and risks, and especially if those harms and risks are likely to come from other nations. They consequently argue that too much spending on defence and security is never enough, which gets reflected in a massive level of spending on not only military hardware like fighter planes, tanks, drones, missiles, and battleships, but also surveillance and spy agencies. At the other extreme, some governments argue that society will be better off when fewer resources are spent on defence and more resources spent on arts, personal development, and leisure.

Leisure comes in various forms, but one critical element is sport. And, although many governments, have, in recent times, taken significant initiatives in the field of sport, they have always had some role to play in the provision of sport experiences to people. Take, for instance the ancient Olympic Games, which began around 700 BC. These games, and other related sport festivals were funded and organized by the various city states that made up ancient Greece. The same concern for sports was expressed by the ruling monarchs in Europe during the Middle Ages, who organized tournaments and combat games to hone the skills of their warrior classes (Mechikoff and Estes 1993). As the world became industrialized and modernized in the late 19th and early 20th centuries, governments expanded the provision of sport activities. In the United States, for example, many government-funded schools and colleges established sport facilities ranging from manicured playing fields and small indoor arenas to large stadiums seating anywhere from 10,000 to 80,000 spectators (Fort 2011).

Today, governments and their agencies provide a complex array of sport facilities and services. Many sport stadiums throughout the world were initially financed by government funds, and although subsequently controlled and operated by independent operators, are now subject to government legislation and policy guidelines (John and Sheard 1997). In most western nations the central government has funded both the establishment of training centres for elite athletes and their ongoing operation. As a result many thousands of coaches, sport scientists, and sport facility managers are now on the government payroll.

WHY SHOULD GOVERNMENTS ENGAGE WITH SPORT?

Sport, especially in western nations, is highly valued by government, even though many people – and even those with significant political clout – consider it to be a frivolous use of valuable time. It is often seen to be superficial, fleeting, anti-intellectual, and trivial (Stebbins 2007). Sport was summarized by the 1960s U.S. sport broadcaster, Howard Cossell as the 'toy department of life'. Be that as it may, millions of people around the world use sport to satisfy a number of drives and motives. One critic argued that "sport . . . is life . . . and the rest a shadow . . . To play sport, or watch others play, and to read and talk about is to uphold the nation and build its character" (Horne 1964). So, is there really a place for government involvement in sport, or is it there only because it feels obligated, and that it is the right thing to do?

The idea that sport can be used to build nations is something in which governments have a strong affinity. Governments have responsibility for creating the commercial and cultural space where people can not only build strong families, neighbourhoods, communities, and workplaces, but also healthy ones. The fact of the matter is that nearly all modern nations allocate a special space for sport, because sport is seen to be a practice that delivers a multitude of individual and social benefits. This is the case in Cuba, North Korea, and China as much as it is in the United States, Great Britain, and Germany. This is why, from a global perspective, governments have constructed so much infrastructure to service sport's needs and have given so much money to assist sport organizations deliver services to members. So, what are these 'things' that sport delivers, and that governments value so much? It is not all that difficult to identify the benefits and social utility that governments believe arise from the sport experience.

First, sport is supposed to contribute to the wellbeing of society by providing the context in which appropriate values, attitudes, and behaviours are learnt and perpetuated. It is claimed that sport participation allows young people to better fit into mainstream cultural and behavioural patterns of society. In this way it contributes to the stability, maintenance, and perpetuation of established society.

Second, sport is seen as character building, a principle that was the cornerstone of the British public school education system during the Victorian and Edwardian era. The popular 19th-century novel, *Tom Brown's Schooldays*, provided the most idealized and romanticized descriptions of the deep and culturally significant experiences that were supposed to come from playing sports. But, not only does sport build 'character', it also inculcates values which support and reinforce the central beliefs of modern industrial societies. These beliefs and attitudes are the ones that that industrial society holds so dear to their hearts, and the ones that drive the progress of these societies (Coakley et al 2009; Rigauer 1981).

So, what exactly are these values? First and foremost, they include a strong belief in the idea that success comes through hard work, self-discipline, and lots of initiative. They also include a respect for authority and adherence to rules and laws. Finally, they include all those traits and disposition that make for a compliant and diligent workforce, which include leadership, hierarchy, cooperative behaviour, and the desire for success and goal achievement. These are exactly the sort of traits a modern 21st-century nation wants from its citizens, because they enable a fully functioning commercial system, and a strong sense of civic pride, to flourish. Moreover, these are the exact same values that characterized the newly industrialized 19th-century societies and strengthened their commitment to the 'Protestant work ethic', which is precisely what enabled them to progress out of feudalism. And, sport is the seen to be the ideal practice for building these values (Rigauer 1981).

But it doesn't end there for governments in the 21st century. They now also recognize that sport has many other functions that can strengthen the bonds between disparate communities and build a healthier and stronger society. For instance, sport participation it is increasingly viewed as a mechanism for the dissipation of stress and management of tension. Additionally, sport is seen as a socially approved outlet for otherwise unacceptable behaviour and attitudes. For example, mass spectator sports can channel hostile emotions into socially useful activities. Aggression can therefore be cathartically released by crowds of spectators cheering the players and jeering the umpires. Sport can also increase levels of excitement, which means participants use sport to actually increase tension and stress as an antidote to the routines of their work life and household chores (Coakley et al 2009).

Governments also understand that discipline and commitment are just one side of a productive community and that in order to sustain reasonable levels of mental health, there needs to be a means of escape from the restricted and bureaucratic world of contemporary work. Recreational sport is the perfect release, and wilderness sports like bushwalking, snow skiing, and bicycle touring reflect this urge to balance the automated banality of urban life. It provides peak experiences by taking people out of their comfort zones and removing them from the safe realities of everyday life. Sport consequently becomes a 'sacred' time, full of excitement, exhilaration, and sometimes peace (Stebbins 2007).

Governments also recognize the capacity of sport to deliver a sense of deep spirituality, because it emanates from a natural impulse for freedom, symbolic meaning, and the pursuit of perfection. In this sense, sport is a 'natural' religion. It involves asceticism, a sense of awe and fate, a quest for community, a desire for participation in the rhythms of nature, and a respect for the mystery and power of one's own being. Sport is also a religion in the liturgical aspect of sport spectacles, where the vestments, rituals, and pageantry bespeak a sacred type of celebration involving a tremor of anticipation and reverence.

With the recognition that sport delivers healthy bodies and fresh minds, most governments around the world are left with no doubt about sport's capacity to build better societies. As a result, governments that do not invest in sport are actually denying its citizens the opportunities to not only find their ideal sports space, but to also find themselves. So, when faced with the demand to explain itself, and its apparent obsession with sport, governments can, with confidence, say that they have a duty to properly resource sport, because to deny sport any assistance is to undermine a nation's capacity to grow and prosper commercially, socially, and spiritually (Mannell and Kleiber 2013).

So, how does all of this discussion sound to you? And, having been exposed to a list of benefits that comes from sport participation, are you convinced that government has a major role in sports planning and delivering sport to all member of society? At the same time, not all sport practices are seen as socially valuable. Some sports have the capacity to undermine social cohesion, and even legitimize conduct that is socially undesirable. Take, for instance, boxing.

In practice 2.1 The problem of boxing

In some sports, there are very few rules that govern the conduct of its activities. The relatively gentile sport of lawn bowls is a case in point. Apart from having to abide by the laws of the land, lawn bowlers are not externally regulated in any additional ways by government regulations. At the same time it has to be said that players in lawn bowls clubs are sometimes highly regulated internally, particularly when it comes to dress-codes for the playing rink.

At the other extreme, combat sports like boxing are highly regulated, particularly at the professional level (Hoye, Nicholson and Houlihan 2010). Many countries have legislation which sets up government-controlled agencies that both issues licences to promoters and participants, and monitors the conduct of the sport. Although the degree of control varies from country to country, the most severe controls are in Norway, where professional boxing is banned. Any Norwegian boxer who wants to enter the professional ranks must relocate to another country.

The basic reason why boxing has such problematic status is because it not only provides community benefits, but also imposes community costs. The community benefits include an opportunity to engage in a vigorous sport that requires both extreme physical fitness and mental toughness. There is also some evidence that boxing is an effective means of channelling the energies of disadvantaged youth into socially constructive activities and subjecting them to a valuable form of personal discipline. On the other hand, boxing is highly combative and has high injury rates. In particular there is a high risk of brain damage, which brings with it enormous personal and social costs. Therefore, in order to minimize the risk of physical damage to the participants, strict regulation is required (Hoye, Nicholson and Houlihan 2010). More generally, boxing is seen as a brutal sport that has little relevance to a civilized society where there are rules against physical assault in everyday life. There are a number of medical associations and groups whose aim is to ban competitive boxing on the grounds that it has a net social cost to the community, and that as a result we would all be better off without it. However most national governments do not agree, and at the amateur level in particular, it is supported by an enthusiastic congregation of volunteer officials and coaches. In addition, it is still an integral part of the Olympic Games schedule. And, in recent times women's boxing has been added to the list of Olympic sports. This initiative may be good for women's rights but not so good for their long-term health.

REASONS FOR GOVERNMENT INTERVENTION

Governments have always intervened in the affairs of its society for the fundamental reason that it enables it to set the nation's economic and political direction. More specifically, governments believe through various interventions it can improve the wellbeing of society (Braithwaite and Drahos 2000). For example, by providing rail and road infrastructure it can improve transport systems and thereby increase the levels of overall efficiency in industry and commerce. Similarly, by funding the establishment of schools, universities, and hospitals, it can go a long way to not only improving the educational abilities of its citizens, but also enhancing their capacity to work more productively and more vigorously participate in the cultural and commercial affairs of the nation. The same sort of logic underpins government's goal of having a fit and healthy people that can defend the nation's sovereignty in times of war and generate international kudos and prestige through the success of its elite athletes.

At the same time, governments may wish to more directly control the behaviour if its citizens by establishing laws that prohibit things like industry pollution and anti-competitive behaviour by businesses, and various forms of discrimination and anti-social behaviour of individuals. The aim here is to reduce the negative "market externalities" (Braithwaite 2008, p. 27). In this context the state has a history of regulating sport to ensure the safety of its participants. One of the best examples is motor racing, where the risk of injury is very high, and externally imposed regulations are essential to ensure a lower chance of sustaining acute injury.

Thus, because of sport's potential to deliver significant social benefits, there are a number of sound reasons for governments wanting to invest in it. However, government resources and taxpayer funds are always scarce, and sport is one of many institutions that want to claim part of the government budget. As a result, sport assistance cannot always be guaranteed, and it must compete with defence, health, policing, social welfare, and education. Additionally, in capitalist economies at least, sport has also traditionally been seen as outside the scope of government responsibility on the grounds that it is far removed from commerce and more in the territory of volunteer amateurs. However, it is not that difficult to mount a case for government intervention in sport. For example, it is now appropriate to argue that not only will society be better off with more sport facilities and services, but that without state support, the resources invested in sport will be far less than optimal.

Market failure and the supply of sport services

In capitalist nations like Australia, Canada, Great Britain, New Zealand, and the United States, resources are in the main allocated in markets through the interaction of demand, supply, and prices. However, there are often cases where markets do not operate in the best interests of the community or nation. This is known as market failure (Gratton and Taylor 2000). Market failure can occur when the full benefits of markets are not realized because of an under-supply of socially desirable products, or alternatively, an over-supply of less desirable products. Market failure and under-supply arises in situations where there are significant external or social benefits in addition to private benefits. Private benefits are the value consumers obtain from the immediate purchase of a good or service and are measured by the prices people are prepared to pay for the experience. In sport, private benefits arise from a number of activities and practices. They include attending a major sport event, working out at a gymnasium, playing indoor cricket, or spending time at a snow resort. Social benefits, on the other hand, comprise the additional value communities obtain from the production of a good or service. These social benefits are over and above the private benefits. In those cases where social benefits can be identified, society would be better served by allocating additional resources into those activities. However, private investors will not usually do this because of a lack of profit incentive. Consequently, it will be left to government to fill the breach and use taxpayers' money to fund additional sporting infrastructure and services.

In other words, because sport provides significant social benefits, it deserves state support to ensure that the welfare of the whole community is maximized. According to the proponents of sport assistance, social benefits can arise from both active participation and spectator sport. In the case of active participation, the benefits include improved community health, a fall in medical costs, a reduction in the crime rate, the inculcation of discipline and character, the development of ethical standards through the emulation of sporting heroes, greater civic engagement, and the building of social capital. Research into social capital building suggests that sport not only expands social networks, but also produces safer neighbourhoods and stronger communities (Productivity Commission 2003). Moreover, the social benefits linked to social capital are extended when sport groups and clubs look outward and encompass people across diverse social cleavages. This bridging or inclusive social capital can be contrasted with bonding social capital, which characterizes sport groups and clubs with a narrow ethnic, social, or occupational base (Putnam 2000, p. 22). Either way, sport is seen to be a great builder of social capital.

In the case of elite and spectator sports, the social benefits include tribal identification with a team or club, social cohesion, a sense of civic and national pride, international recognition and prestige, economic development, and the attraction of out-of-town visitors and tourist dollars (Gratton and Taylor 1991). When these social benefits are aggregated the results are quite extensive, as can be seen in Table 2.1. At the same time, they are often

TABLE 2.1 Social benefits of sport development

Arising from active participation	Arising from elite athlete successes
Improvement in community health and productivity	Tribal identification and belonging
Fall in medical costs	Social cohesion
Reduction in juvenile crime rate	Civic and national pride
Development of 'character' and sense of 'fair play'	International recognition and prestige
Building of social capital, social cohesion, and civic engagement	Economic development and tourism

Adapted from Stewart et al (2004)

difficult to quantify, and in some cases the evidence to support the claimed benefit is soft and flimsy.

Sport as a public good

A case can also be made for the state's involvement in sport on the grounds that sport is often a public or collective good (Li, Hofacre and Mahony 2001). Public goods are those goods where one person's consumption does not prevent another person's consumption of the same good. For example, a decision to visit a beach, or identify with a winning team or athlete, will not prevent others from doing the same. Indeed, the experience may be enhanced by others being in proximity. This is the non-rival feature of the good. Public goods are also goods where, in their purest form, no one can be prevented from consuming the good. Again, a visit to the beach and identifying with a winning team meet this criterion. This is the non-excludable feature of the good. Public goods can provide substantial benefits throughout the whole of society and are usually not rationed through high prices. However, they are not attractive to private investors because there is no assurance that all users will pay the cost of providing the benefit. As the number of so-called free riders increase, there is a shrinking incentive for private operators to enter the public good market. In this instance it is argued that government should provide for this higher demand by increasing its funding to ensure an appropriate infrastructure and level of service.

Sport equity and inclusiveness

Finally, it can be argued that government should be funding sport on equity grounds. For example, if the whole community benefits from being fit and healthy, then no one should be excluded because of low income or lack of facilities. In these cases, the optimal community benefit can only be realized if everyone has access to appropriate sport and recreation services help them to improve their health and fitness, enhance their self-image, and build the community's social capital. In order to improve accessibility, and ensure equality of opportunity, governments can establish their own low-cost sport facilities, subsidize existing sport activity providers, and design targeted programs for disadvantaged groups.

This raises the question of just how much assistance government should provide to sport to ensure ease of access, equality of participation, and a diversity of experiences. Local and city governments have a long tradition of using taxpayers' money to build sport facilities for the use of their constituents. In some cases, however, this tradition can get out of control, as the following discussion reveals.

In practice 2.2 Local government stadium funding in the United States

In the United States, American football is the king of professional sports. Its television ratings are consistently high, and it draws the largest average crowd size – in excess of 60,000 – of any team sports league in the world. The annual Super Bowl – the grand finale to end all grand finales – is the high point of the American spectator sport calendar, where the mix of high-quality sport and Hollywood-style entertainment delivers uniquely memorable experiences to fans.

It is also an expensive sport to mount, especially when it comes to the construction of stadia to house the home team. At the same time, local government authorities – specifically, the city councils and their mayors – have been prepared to lead the construction of football stadia in the belief that having a stadium that accommodates an NFL franchise is not just good for local football fans, but also good for the local economy. There are many recent examples where local government authorities have provided subsidies – often in the hundreds of millions of dollars – to build stadia to house the local franchise and keep them there for the long haul.

Take, for instance, the accommodation of the Dallas Cowboys American football team. Its USD 1.2 billion-dollar stadium, which opened in 2009, would not have been completed without taxpayers' subsidies. As it turned out, the city of Dallas contributed USD 325 million (around 30% of the total cost) to the construction of the stadium. The Atlanta Falcons' new Mercedes-Benz Stadium – not to be confused with the Mercedes-Benz Superdome in New Orleans, was also heavily subsidized by the local city. It opened in 2017 with a price tag of USD 1.5 billion, with the public – that is, local tax-payers – contributing around USD 600 million. The recently constructed U.S. Bank Stadium in Minneapolis, where the Minnesota Vikings now play, was also generously underwritten by the local authorities. At last count, city taxpayers' funds accounted for roughly half the cost – an estimated USD 498 million – of the total $1.06 billion construction bill. Although the city of Minneapolis initially required a public referendum to approve funding for the stadium, a supposedly independent 'stadium authority' was able to override the referendum process and authorized the stadium budget without taxpayers' consent. And, in Buffalo, where the Bills stadium recently received a thorough makeover to ensure its suitability for NFL games into the future, a lazy USD 130 million came from public funding.

These subsidies would be quite reasonable if there is evidence to support the claim that investing in a football franchise – and the stadium that goes with it – is good for the city. Unfortunately, the evidence in support of this claim is very shaky indeed. After extensive independent research on the subject, the conclusion is that using public funds to subsidize wealthy sports franchises makes zero economic sense and is a waste of taxpayer money. Most studies have shown that professional football teams added virtually no net additional income to local economies, and in some cases, the opposite occurred. That is, large subsidies sometimes have a negative effect by taking money out of the local economy. It was also found that the job creation outcomes were less impressive than first thought. Aside from the jobs generated by actually building the stadium, most jobs inside the stadium – selling food and beer, and providing security services – were casual and low-paying.

EXTENT AND FORM OF GOVERNMENT INTERVENTION

In general, there are a broad array of arrangements by which governments can fund, develop, and deliver sport facilities and programs. At one extreme, governments can distance themselves from sport development by claiming that sport is a private matter for individuals and communities, and is therefore best left to the market and voluntary sectors to run. This arrangement was a primary feature of Australian sport until the 1970s when the national government resolved to fund sport facilities and programs (Stewart et al 2004). In the United States the national government has also adopted an arms-length approach to sport, and has left the funding and development of sport to the market, schools, and university sectors (Chalip, Johnson and Stachura 1996).

As noted earlier, governments can intervene in sport in all sorts of ways. The extent of the intervention, and the form it takes, is strongly influenced by the ideology, values, and overall philosophy of governments and their agencies (Gardiner, Parrish and Siekman 2009). There are a number of different ideologies to choose from, but when implemented, they become difficult to completely erase at a later time.

The first ideology is conservatism. A conservative ideology values tradition and customary ways of doing things. Conservative governments have a tendency to regulate the social lives of people, and therefore want to censor works of art and literature they find offensive. They also want to control the distribution of legal drugs like alcohol, and generally act to protect people from themselves. On the other hand, they believe that business should be left to its own devices, where the combination of individual self-interest, the profit motive, and market forces will ensure a favourable outcome. However, because conservative governments believe a strong private sector is the key to progress, they are prepared to assist and protect industry when the need arises. On one hand they recognize sport as an integral part of the social life of most people, but they do not want to assist or protect it because it is not part of the world of business. Indeed, for many conservatives, it is another world altogether that should be best kept at a distance from business. This sport world is underpinned by the belief that sport fulfils its function best when it is done for its own sake, played by amateurs, managed by volunteers, and generally left to look after its own affairs.

The second ideology is reformism, or as it is also known, welfare statism, or social democracy. Reformism is primarily concerned with social justice and equity. Although reformists recognize the necessity of a strong private sector, they believe it cannot be trusted to deliver fair and equitable outcomes. It therefore needs to be strictly managed. This could take the form of additional government-owned enterprises or tight regulations on business behaviour. Reformists share the conservative view that assistance and protection may be necessary in the public interest. Unlike conservatives, though, reformists believe primarily in social development, which not only means legislating for social freedom, but also for social justice. Income redistribution to disadvantaged groups is important, and is done by ensuring that wealthy individuals and corporations are taxed most heavily. State spending is also crucial to reformists, because it is used to stimulate the economy when demand and spending is low. Reformist governments tend to be more centralist, and aim to use this centralized power to engineer positive social outcomes. Reformists consequently see sport as a tool for social development and aim to make sport more accessible to the whole community. In these cases programs are established to cater for the needs of minority groups like the indigenous, the disabled, migrants who speak another language, and women. In short, reformist government policy focuses more on community and less on elite sport development.

The third ideology is neoliberalism. Neo-liberals believe that society is at its most healthy when people can run their daily lives without the chronic intrusion of the state. The rule of law is important, but beyond that, people should be free to choose how they organize their social lives, and businesses should be free to organize their commercial lives as they see fit. Neo-liberals see little value in government-owned enterprises, and argue that the privatization of government services produces greater efficiency and higher-quality outcomes. Moreover, deregulated industries are seen to run better than tightly controlled ones. In short, neo-liberals believe government should not engage directly in most economic activity, but rather provide only base level infrastructure, and legislative guidelines within which private business can thrive. Within this philosophy, sport is valued as an important social institution, but should not be strictly controlled. However, neo-liberals also believe sport can be used as a vehicle for nation building and economic development, and should be supported in these instances. This produces a sport policy that tends to focus on elite sport at the expense of community sport.

The final ideology is socialism. Socialists believe that a combination of privately owned and unregulated markets will produce severe levels of inequality and alienation. As a result, capitalist modes of production and distribution need to be replaced by a strong government where resource allocation is centrally controlled. Like neo-liberals, socialists agree that sport is an important social institution, but unlike neo-liberals, go on to assert that sport should be controlled from the centre to ensure a fair spread of clubs and facilities throughout society. To this end, a socialist system of sport development will be driven by a central bureaucracy that sets the sport agenda. In this type of setting, governments provide most of the funds and resources by which to develop sport at both the community and elite levels.

TABLE 2.2 Links between political ideology and sport development

Ideological type	Features	Implications for sport development
Conservatism	Private ownership of business Regulation of social practices	Arms-length association with sport. Sport is seen as a private activity that grows out of the community, and is managed by the volunteer sector
Reformism	Mixed economy Regulation of both social and economic affairs	Direct involvement in sport facility construction and community sport participation
Neo-liberalism	Emphasis on the market De-regulation of industry	Most resources go to the elite end of sport development and its commercial outcomes.
Socialism	Limited scope for the market Central planning Bureaucratic control over resource allocation	Direct involvement in all aspects of sport development. Often tightly regulated. Both community and elite sport are resourced.

Each of these four ideologies not only contains quite different assumptions about the proper role of government, but also different ideas about what sport can do to improve the welfare of society. As a result, each ideology will produce different sport development outcomes, and the ideology often overrides the claims of interest groups like sport scientists, coaches, and officials. The four ideologies described provide a simplified typology, and in practice, governments will often take bits and pieces of each ideology when forming its position on a particular sport issue or problem. At the same time, most governments will be characterized by more of one and less of another ideology. Table 2.2 outlines the different ideologies and indicates how they can shape a government's views on sport development, regulation, and assistance.

REGULATION AND CONTROL

There are also many situations where the state may want to regulate and control the provision of sport activities and limit the resources devoted to some activities (Baldwin, Cave and Lodge 2012). For example it may be necessary to enact laws and rules that safeguard public order when a large number of people are spectators of or are playing in a sport event. In most countries there are laws that clearly define the parameters within which sport grounds are to be constructed. These laws will cover things like design specifications, the provision for seating, the number of entry and exits points, and fire prevention facilities (Frosdick and Walley 1997). There may also be rules that govern the behaviour of spectators. Most commonly these laws will relate to the consumption of alcohol and disorderly and violent behaviour (Greenfield and Osborn 2001).

One of the most highly regulated activities is horse racing. It is not just a case of ensuring the animals are treated humanely, but of also making sure the gaming and gambling practices that surround the sport are tightly controlled so that corrupt practices are minimized. There are many cases around the world where horses have not been allowed to run on their merits. This can involve doping activities where stimulants will be given to horses to make them run quicker and depressants administered to make them go slower. In both instances the aim is to undermine the betting market, and through the use of inside information to back the horse that has been advantaged, and avoid the horse that has been slowed. Similar incidents are now happening more frequently in a number of professional team sports around the world (Muller, Lammert and Hovemann 2012). Crime syndicates and bookmakers have bribed sport officials, players, and even referees to provide confidential information on the game, deliberately play poorly, and make decision that favour one team and not another. Two recent cases involved Italy's premier football competition and the Pakistan cricket team. In each instance government action was immediately taken to more strictly regulate the competitions.

Another form of regulation involves the media in general, and TV in particular. In both Australia and England there are anti-siphoning rules that effectively give free-to-air television stations privileged access to major sport events at the expense of pay and cable television providers (Brown and Walsh 1999). This means that a major sport event like the Australian Football League (AFL) Grand Final must initially be offered to free-to-air stations before being offered to pay TV stations. This is done on the grounds that a sport of national significance should be made as widely available as possible. In Australia the pay TV subscriptions cover less that 50% of all households, and is consequently argued that it is inequitable to give exclusive rights to a pay TV station only.

But, as noted earlier, regulation is just one way of improving the sport experience for members of the community. Governments also have a history of assisting sport, and, in particular, funding initiatives that might get people more active and improve their quality of life. Take, for example, the following programs.

In practice 2.3 Government assistance to sport: the case of 'active living' promotion in England and Ireland

Most developed nations around the world recognize the value of sport. They consequently use sport a means of generating civic pride, national identity, and international recognition (Stewart et al 2004). This is why so many nations are prepared to spend a lot of money on facilities and programs that take talented young athletes and transform them into elite level champions (McDonald 2011). However, sport development is about much more than just winning medals at international sport events. The state has a responsibility to provide the community with rewarding sport experiences, and to make sure disadvantaged groups especially have open and easy access to facilities (Houlihan 1997). The problem of low participation is being addressed in many and varied ways.

In the 2013 document titled *Creating a sporting habit for life: A new youth sport strategy*, Sport England expressed concern that when people leave school they often stop playing sports, and thus neither fulfil their sporting potential, nor ensure a healthy lifestyle. As a result the goal is to get more people playing sport regularly and safely throughout their life, no matter what their economic or social background. These concerns led to the development of a 'Youth Sport Strategy' that aims to increase the number of young people developing sport as a 'habit for life' by undertaking the following initiatives:

- Sport England will invest 1 billion pounds to assist young people to more regularly play sport, and help break down barriers that make participation difficult at the moment.
- Sport England will work with schools, colleges, and universities, as well as local County Sports Partnerships, the National Governing Bodies for sport, local authorities and the voluntary sector to improve the sporting 'offer'.
- Sport England will seek a consistent increase in the proportion of people regularly playing sport, and especially the 14- to 25-year-old age group.
- Sport England will work to build links between schools and community sports clubs and work with sports such as football, cricket, rugby union, rugby league, and tennis to establish at least 6,000 partnerships between schools and local sports clubs by 2018.
- Sport England will invest 160 million pounds on new and upgraded sports facilities, on top of the 90 million already invested via Sport England's Places, People, Play program.

Like many nations around the world, Ireland is dealing with an ageing population. Research shows that a physically active older population is a healthy population. As a result the Irish government has resolved to assist older age groups to engage more strongly with sports and physical activity. This has many benefits. The benefit to the individual is a more productive and vigorous lifestyle. The benefit to the community and society in general, is a healthier population that contributes to the community, engages productively with local neighbourhoods, spends less time under medical care, and spends less money on prescription medicines.

The Irish Sports Council has consequently introduced a *Go for Life* program that aims to increase participation among older people in recreational sport activities. The program is administered by the Age and Opportunity agency, and is guided by a steering group comprising representatives of the Irish Sports Council, Age and Opportunity, the Federation of Active Retirement Associations, the Irish Senior Citizens Parliament, and the National Council on Ageing and Older People.

In 2007, the Irish Sports Council provided 700 000 EUR to drive the program, and more than 620 community groups nationwide shared the initial allocation of 350 000 EUR under phase seven of the *Go for Life* National Grant Scheme for Sport and Physical Activity for Older People. The national grant scheme comprises one important element of the *Go for Life* program, and complements the other main strands in the program, which are (1) the Active Living program and (2) the Sports Participation program.

SUMMARY

Governments have the capacity to significantly shape the structure and scope of sport through a number of mechanisms. First, it can construct sport facilities; second, it can fund the day-to-day operations of sporting associations and clubs; third, it can deliver sport programs to the community directly; fourth, it can establish training facilities for elite athletes to assist their ongoing development; and finally, it can control the operation of sport by introducing various laws, regulations, and rules that shapes the delivery of sport events, programs, and services (Hylton et al 2001). However, the scale of government support, and the form it takes, will vary between nations depending on the dominant political ideology and the overall cultural importance of sport to society. In some cases governments will directly control and manage sport, whereas at the other end of the political spectrum, governments will step back from the sport system and encourage the commercial and volunteer sectors to take up the slack.

At this point in time the evidence suggests that governments have a pivotal role to play in supporting both the community participation and elite-sport ends of the sport development continuum. Through the establishment of sports infrastructure, and facilities, and the funding of sport programs, it enables greater levels of community participation, creates all sorts of health and social benefits, improved international sport performance, and enhances a country's international status and prestige. It now seems as if some governments believe 'too much sport is never enough'.

REVIEW QUESTIONS

1 What comprises government, and what is its role?

2 How do governments go about shaping the political and economic landscape of a nation?

3 Apart from the state, what other social forces contribute to national development?

4 Explain how the state may contribute to sport development.

5 How might local investment in sport stadia assist local development and job creation?

6 In the case of big football stadia in the United States, what do the economic studies tell us?

7 What can the state do to increase the level of sport participation and sport club membership?

8 What can the state do to increase the level of elite sport performance?

9 Why should the state want to intervene in sport?

10 Would sport development be best left to the voluntary and commercial sectors?

11 Is there any evidence that a centralized model of elite sport development is any more effective than a market-based sport development model?

12 How might the state go about increasing the scale of sport participation at the community or 'grassroots' level?

DISCUSSION QUESTIONS

1 In modern industrial society, what is the role of government?

2 In what areas of society are government assistance and regulation most evident, and why?

3 How can governments shape the structure and conduct of the sports sector, and why does it now have such an influential role to play?

4 What strategies can government initiate to improve elite sport systems and standards?

5 How might government go about building the participation base of sport?

FURTHER READING

An excellent introduction to the crucial role of government and the public sector in managing a nation's affairs is provided in Stiglitz (2000) *Economics of the Public Sector*. 3rd edn. New York: W.W. Norton. For a thorough analysis of the ways in which government can go about regulating a nation's economic, social and cultural affairs, see Baldwin, Cave and Lodge (2012) and Braithwaite and Drahos (2000).

There are now a number of publications that examine the ways in which the state has intervened in a nation's sport development. To get a detailed picture of the Australian experience you should read Bloomfield (2003) and Stewart et al (2004). The British experience is nicely reviewed in Green, M. and Houlihan, B. (2005). *Elite Sport Development*. London: Routledge, Houlihan and White (2002) and Hylton et al. (2001).

For some comparative analysis of state involvement in sport the most comprehensive treatment is contained in Chalip, Johnson and Stachura (1996). Houlihan (1997) provides an excellent comparative study of Australia, Canada, Ireland, and the United Kingdom (UK).

The most definitive account of sport in socialist Cuba, although now a little dated, is Pattavino, P. and Pye, G. (1994). *Sport in Cuba: The Diamond in the Rough*. Pittsburg: University of Pittsburg Press.

A deep analysis of sport stadia and urban development is contained in Delaney, K. & Eckstein, R. (2003). *Public Dollars, Private Stadiums: The Battle Over Building Sports Stadiums*. New Brunswick: Rutgers University Press. See also Coakley, J., et al. (2009). *Sport in Society*. Sydney: McGraw Hill; Horne, D. (1964). *The Lucky Country*. Ringwood: Penguin Books; Rigauer, B. (1981). *Sport and Work*. New York: Columbia University Press; Stebbins, R. (2007). *Serious Leisure*. New Brunswick: Transactions Publications.

RELEVANT WEBSITES

To find out more about the relationship between government and sport in Australian sport go to the Australian Sports Commission site at www.ausport.gov.au

To get more details of the English experience go to the Sport England site at www.sportengland.org

For a comprehensive review of the state's involvement in NZ sport go to the New Zealand Government Sport and Recreation site at www.sparc.org.nz

For more details on the Irish sport-participation policy experience go to www.irishsportscouncil.ie/Participation/Go_for_Life/#sthash.ORQFNbu5.dpuf

A detailed analysis of how cities in the USA go about subsidising the construction of sport stadia is found in www.citylab.com/equity/2015/09/the-never-ending-stadium-boondoggle/403666/

A detailed critique of city subsidies for stadium construction is available in: http://news.stanford.edu/2015/07/30/stadium-economics-noll-073015/ See also https://medium.com/concentrated-benefits/the-hidden-costs-of-stadium-subsidies-fbc079f335f3

CASE STUDY 2.1

Government influences over sport: the Cuban experience

Governments around the world increasingly understand that allocating resources into sport can deliver significant benefits to society. Some governments believe that the delivery of sport activities is best left to the private sector, where people pay for the experience, and businesses make a profit in making it happen. Other governments take the opposite approach and argue that the provision of sport participation opportunities should not be in the hands of profiteers. It is too important for that. Rather, government should intervene, and in effect be the sole – that is, monopoly – provider of sport. In this way, it can accommodate everyone's desires and expectations, and always deliver on its promises. The Cuban government, and its relationship with sport, is a case in point.

Cuba is a small Caribbean nation of 11 million people. It is less than 100 kilometres from the American coastline. It calls itself the Republic of Cuba, and under its

Constitution, which was reshaped in 1976, views itself as an independent, sovereign, and socialist state. Within its socialist aspirations, it calls for the centralized control of markets, it aims to provide citizens with free education, and delivers a fully government managed universal health care system. Several amendments have been made to the Constitution since the 1970s. They include the declaration that Cuba is a secular state, and the pronouncement that its socio/political system is permanently and irrevocably socialist, where all the important industries including core manufacturing, agriculture, communications, health, education, and security, are owned and controlled by the national government.

At the same time, Cuba is not a wealthy nation when measured by its national output of goods and services. In addition, growth stagnated around 25 years ago, and as a result household spending on things like domestic appliances, flat screen television sets, and late model motor vehicles is low. Most Cubans live very frugally. On the other hand, Cuba has a very well-resourced education and health care system, which is entirely funded by government. Sport is also supported by the national government, which has not only delivered a range of inclusive and low cost community sport programs, but also trained up many elite athletes, some of whom became Olympic champions.

As any loyal Cuban will argue, there are many good reasons for allowing government to set the sport agenda, spending money on sport facilities across the nation, and funding the management of their operations. This approach to sport development was exemplified in the programs of most communist nations during the 1970s and 1980s. In the Soviet Union (USSR) and the German Democratic Republic (GDR), a national sport program was integrated into the school curricula, and sport schools were used to identify and nurture talented young athletes. In addition, sports that had a strong civil-defence and para-military flavour were conducted in factory and trade union facilities.

Cuba built a similar sport development model in which a government bureaucracy managed the whole sport experience for both the sport-for-all participant and the Olympic athlete. The government effectively controlled the structure and conduct of sport throughout the nation. Like China, Cuba ran a sophisticated talent identification program, and was, with the support of a broad based, if often run-down infrastructure and highly trained coaches, able to take talented young athletes – both male and female – and mold them into elite-level players.

However, in 1961, unlike China and the Soviet Union, the Cuban government banned professionalism in sport, but it also looked after its sporting heroes by giving them government jobs or enrolling them in college and university courses that they could complete at their convenience. In Cuba, like the USSR and GDR, sport success was not just a sporting victory, but was also a 'psychological, patriotic and revolutionary' one as well.

For the next 50 years Cuba continued its march along the road to an anticipated socialist utopia, But, despite all the talk about revolution, nationalism, patriotism, and the transformative power of socialism, Cuba's economy was floundering during the early part of the 21st century, and 'citizen frugality' was the order of the day. There were growing concerns that even with its impressive health care and education systems still intact, some of the nation's old values and beliefs, and especially its obsession with self-sufficiency, the nation was beginning to stagnate. A symbol of a change in its political direction was the decision in 2014 to reclaim relations with the United States, and the subsequent reopening of the American embassy in Havana. In addition, travel restrictions for locals were eased, and Pope Francis made an historic visit.

However, even more surprising was the Cuban government decision to relax its 1961 ruling that made it illegal to conduct professional sporting contests. For nearly half a century, a succession of gifted Cuban athletes – with the enthusiastic support of the Cuban government – shunned the opportunity to make money from sport by electing, instead, to become national icons in their homeland. The idea that money tainted the purity of sport, and that amateurism was the only authentic pathway to idealized sporting practice, became a national catch-cry. This honourable, romantic, but ultimately anachronistic view of sport, was exemplified in the attitudes of the legendary amateur heavyweight boxer Teofilo Stevenson, winner of three Olympic gold medals between 1972 and 1980. Boxing promoters in the United States dreamed of luring Stevenson to their stadia, where a bout with Muhammad Ali would have been among the most lucrative fights of all time. Stevenson, who died aged 60 in 2012, snubbed all attempts to persuade him to defect to America, and turn professional. As a *Sports Illustrated* article noted in 1974, Stevenson remarked that "I will not leave my country for USD 1 million dollars". However, Stevenson's views have now become obsolete. Legendary Cuban high-jumper Javier Sotomayor welcomed the changes, saying they would serve as an incentive for athletes, giving them greater motivation, and pushing them to higher levels of performance. In addition, in 2014, Cuba's national baseball league became professional, while its track and field competitors were allowed to retain 100% of prize money from overseas sporting competitions. Previously athletes were only allowed to pocket 15% of their earnings, with 85% going to the government's consolidated revenue account.

The fact of the matter was that the hardships faced by many Cuban athletes, and the steady flow of defectors overseas forced Havana's communist rulers to rethink the decades-old resistance to professional sport. Under the new 2013/2014 policy, Greco-Roman wrestling hero Mijain Lopez, a gold medallist at the 2008 and 2012 Olympics, and baseball star Yulieski Gourriel, widely regarded as the best player in Cuba, now had the opportunity to realize their true value on the professional sports stage. According to many Cuban sport fans, that was only a good thing.

CASE STUDY QUESTIONS

1   Provide a brief overview of the Cuban nation, paying particular attention to its government and its relation to the wider society.

2   How important was Cuba's socialist government in the production and distribution of goods and services in Cuba? Give examples of how Cuba's government affected the production and distribution of goods and services.

3   What role does the Cuban government play in developing and managing sport?

4   To what extent does the Cuban government promote community sport over elite sport?

5   To what extent can the Cuban government take credit for the nation's international sporting successes between 1970 and 2013?

6   How important was the concept of amateurism to the management of sport in Cuba, and why?

7   What reasons did the Cuban government give for discarding the amateur model of sport and giving space to professional sport in 2014?

8   To what extent has the professionalization of sport initiative in Cuba affected the quality of sport experiences for athletes on one hand, and the Cuban community on the other?

ADDITIONAL READING

The changing face of Cuba

www.economist.com/blogs/gametheory/2013/10/sports-cuba

The reintroduction of professional sport

www.abc.net.au/news/2013-11-02/professional-sport-returns-to-cuba-after-50-year-ban/5065602

www.nytimes.com/2016/11/27/sports/under-fidel-castro-sport-symbolized-cubas-strength-and-vulnerability.html

CASE STUDY 2

Government controls over horse racing in the UK, Canada, and Australia

There is widespread agreement that sporting contests will secure unconditional legitimacy only when they are well organized, run smoothly, and do it all in fair and transparent ways. There is also growing concern that some sports have become corrupted by the intrusion of gambling syndicates who have manipulated the results by bribing officials and players. This presents a serious problem for sport, because once it is understood that matches and contests have been tampered with, credibility will be destroyed. Once the belief in the integrity of sport is lost, its sustainability is placed under serious threat.

This is especially true in horse racing, where its capacity to attract dodgy 'personalities' and incorporate controversial – and even corrupt – practices, is legendary. It is also a high risk sport, where injury to jockeys and horses are probable and race-goer anxiety is inevitable. At the same time, governments around the world have also understood that horse racing is vulnerable to corruption, and thus needs protection.

Horse racing has been heavily controlled by government for most of its 200-year history, which in large part is due to its close connections to gambling and the potential for corrupt activities to emerge. The challenges that horse racing faces were highlighted in 2002 when the British Broadcasting Corporation (BBC) presented a documentary on race-fixing. In a BBC Panorama program a recently retired race official said that while "I wouldn't say it was bent . . . I would say it is institutionally corrupt". Similar problems were addressed in Australian horse racing in 2011, and police subsequently charged a number of trainers and jockeys with not only corruptly influencing the outcome of races, but also corruptly betting on them. In the United States horse racing authorities were also dealing with corrupt practices. In 2013 they investigated claims that trainers and riders were using electronic buzzers to 'stimulate' horses during races, while also attending to allegations that well-known trainers had been 'doping' horses with banned substances.

Ironically, this conduct occurred in sporting spaces awash with rules and regulations. In the UK horseracing must comply with the rules and regulations of the British Horseracing Authority (BHA). The BHA controls help to ensure that races are run fairly, that jockeys are adequately trained, and that the health and welfare of racehorses and jockeys are protected. Similar controls operate in Australia, although there are no over-riding national controls. Instead, there are different regulations for each of the six states. In the State of Victoria, for example, horse racing is regulated through the *Racing Act 1958*. This government legislation has wide raging powers and sets the operational parameters for the organization and conduct of race meetings. It accredits and licences race clubs and the tracks they managed. It sets appropriate safety conditions, and it also registers bookmakers and their clerks. Finally, it operates an appeals tribunal whose job it is to hear appeals – especially to do with fines and suspensions – against decisions taken by race clubs.

The regulation of horse racing in Canada is similar to Australia. That is, each province – the Canadian equivalent of an Australian state – has detailed legislation which sets out what horse racing participant can and cannot legally do. For example in the British Columbia province horse racing is controlled through the *Rules of Thoroughbred and Standardbred Horse Racing*, which is authorized under section 53 of the *Gaming Control Act and Gaming Control Regulation 2002*. The rules are both detailed and wide ranging. They begin with the licencing requirements, which covers more than 40 jobs and positions, and ranges from owners, trainers, and jockeys to veterinarians, farriers, and track superintendents. They go on to specify the roles of stewards and judges, the responsibilities of veterinarians, procedures for entry nomination and weight allocations, the use of supplements and substances, drug testing regimes, prohibited conduct for licenced participants – which includes penalties for being intoxicated, being cruel to horses, and using offensive language – rules for jockeys, handlers, and starters, and finally, the rules for the race itself.

Horse racing is heavily regulated by government on the grounds that without external controls the sport of kings – as it is sometimes known – it would plunge into a crevasse full of fixed races and illegal betting. It is thus argued that society would be better off with controls than without them. It also means that horse racing has many benefits – including the breeding and racing of high-performing trained thoroughbreds, the jobs the industry creates, and the pleasure it gives large segments of the sporting public – and that these need to be protected.

In most countries where horse racing is popular, the government controls are detailed, and the operational parameters are tight. This is not surprising in the light of its history and traditions. It has always been associated with gambling, and it has always been vulnerable to race fixing. This means that self-regulation is not enough. Given the social complexity of this sport, and its frequent contamination by a mix of secrecy, rumour, money laundering, and massive betting plunges, it demands close external scrutiny on an ongoing basis.

CASE STUDY QUESTIONS

1   How old is the sport of horse racing, and where did it begin?

2   What attracts people to horse racing?

3   What makes horse racing susceptible to corruption?

4   How prevalent has race fixing been in horse racing?

5   If horse racing is so easily corrupted, then why shouldn't governments just ban the sport outright?

6   How does government go about regulating the horse racing industry?

7   What do government controls focus on?

8   Do government controls on horse racing enhance its attractiveness to the public, or actually diminish its importance?

9   Would there be more resources allocated to horse racing if government actually removed itself from the industry?

ADDITIONAL READING

Regulation of horse racing in Britain

http://rules.britishhorseracing.com/

Regulation of horse racing in Victoria, Australia

https://rv.racing.com/racing-and-integrity/rules-of-racing

Regulation of horse racing in British Columbia, Canada

http://www2.gov.bc.ca/gov/content/sports-culture/gambling-fundraising/
gambling-in-bc/laws-regulations-policies

CHAPTER 3

Nonprofit sport

OVERVIEW

This chapter examines the role of the nonprofit sector in the provision of sport participation and consumption opportunities and explores the reasons why the nonprofit sector plays such a large part in the delivery of sport participation opportunities. The scope of the nonprofit sector's involvement in sport around the world is examined, with a particular emphasis on the role of volunteers in administration, officiating, and coaching and the role of nonprofit sport organizations in facilitating people's enjoyment of sport as active participants, supporters, or consumers. The chapter also provides a summary of the relationship between nonprofit sport organizations and the state and with commercial providers.

After completing this chapter the reader should be able to:

- Describe the scope of the nonprofit sector's involvement in sport;
- Understand the differences in the roles performed by the state and nonprofit sport organizations;

- Understand the ways in which nonprofit sport organizations provide sport participation and consumption opportunities around the world;
- Understand some of the challenges facing the nonprofit sector in delivering these opportunities; and
- Understand the field of sport development versus sport *for* development.

INTRODUCTION

The model presented in Chapter 1 presents the sport industry as comprising three distinct but overlapping sectors: the state or public sector, the commercial or professional sport sector, and the nonprofit or voluntary sector. This chapter focuses on the nonprofit or voluntary sector of the model; the various sport organizations that would be classified as nonprofit. Many terms have been used to refer to nonprofit organizations that operate in a variety of industry sectors and countries around the world. These terms include voluntary, not for profit, nongovernment, community, club based, associations, co-operatives, friendly societies, civil society, and the third sector. For our purposes we have chosen to use the term nonprofit organizations to describe those organizations that are institutionally separate from the state, do not return profits to owners, are self-governing, have a significant element of voluntary contribution, and are formally incorporated as separate legal entities.

The nonprofit sport sector comprises organizations that are markedly different from state organizations discussed in Chapter 2, and also profit-seeking organizations that are discussed in chapter 4. Nonprofit organizations vary in size, focus, and capability and include groups as diverse as community associations, chambers of commerce, private schools, charitable trusts and foundations, religious groups, welfare agencies, and sporting organizations. Nonprofit organizations are a major part of many industries in health services, education, housing, welfare, culture, and sport. Describing these organizations as nonprofit does not mean they run at a financial loss or do not generate a surplus of revenue over costs; the term nonprofit refers merely to the fact they do not exist for the primary purpose to make profits to reward their owners.

NONPROFIT SECTOR AND SOCIETY

Nonprofit organizations exist to develop communities, meet the needs of identifiable and discrete groups in those communities, and work for the benefit of public good rather than create wealth for individuals. Nonprofit organizations have evolved to fill gaps in the provision of services such as welfare assistance that are not provided by the state or market sector, and are driven largely by the efforts of volunteers with the occasional support of paid staff.

A succession of reviews of nonprofit organizations in western economies such as Canada and Australia (Statistics Canada 2004; Productivity Commission 2010) consistently point out that these organizations are vehicles for citizen engagement. Nonprofit organizations enable individuals to contribute their talent, energy, and time to engaging in group activities and causes that are not otherwise provided by the public or private sectors. Nonprofit organizations are self-determining; in general they are governed by volunteers, run on the time and money contributed by volunteers, and enable volunteers to contribute to enhancing their local, regional, national, and global communities in ways that volunteers have chosen. In Canada there are more than 161,000 nonprofit organizations that collectively utilize more than 2 billion volunteer hours and receive more than $CAN 8 billion in donations to deliver their services. According to Statistics Canada (2004) Canadians take out 139 million memberships in these organizations, an average of four per person. Similar rates of involvement are found in other westernized, developed economies and illustrate that the nonprofit sector represents a major part of the economic activity of many nations and plays a pivotal role in encouraging people to engage in social, religious, charitable, philanthropic, and sport-related activities.

Nonprofit organizations usually focus on delivering services to very specific population groups or within defined geographic areas. Many of them provide services to targeted groups, and only a few focus solely on providing services to members. The variety of activities carried out by nonprofit organizations is very broad and ranges from providing sporting opportunities to funding hospital and medical services. As a result, the revenue sources, cost base, numbers of paid staff and volunteers, and the sophistication of management systems also vary markedly between nonprofit organizations.

The nonprofit sector is not without its problems. The larger organizations such as independent schools, colleges, and hospitals receive the majority of funding and almost half the funding for most nonprofit organizations comes from government. The resourcing of nonprofit organizations in some sectors continues to be inadequate as they struggle to keep up with demand, particularly organizations providing welfare, housing, or other general charitable services. By far the biggest problem facing nonprofit organizations is the inability to fulfil their missions due to problems securing adequate numbers of volunteers, finding board members, and attracting enough sustainable funding (Cuskelly 2004), a problem that persists more than a decade after this research was published. As governments around the world seek to decrease their costs and devolve responsibility for service delivery to the private and nonprofit sectors without adequately funding such delivery, nonprofit organizations will find it increasingly difficult to operate.

In practice 3.1 Volunteers in Canada

The most recently published report on volunteers in Canada was produced in 2015 using the results from the General Social Survey of volunteering and charitable giving in 2013 (Turcotte 2015). The highlights from the report about volunteering trends were:

- In 2013, 12.7 million Canadians, or 44% of people aged 15 years and older, did volunteer work. They devoted about 1.96 billion hours to their volunteer activities, a volume of work that is equivalent to about 1 million full-time jobs.

- The volunteer rate in 2013 (44%) was lower than that recorded in 2004 (45%), in 2007 (46%), and 2010 (47%). However, the total number of hours Canadians volunteered remained stable between 2010 and 2013.
- Just like the general population, the population of volunteers is aging. In 2013, 28% of all Canadian volunteers were aged 55 and older, compared to 23% in 2004.
- Older volunteers are more likely to do certain types of activities. For example, in 2013, 42% sat on a committee or board, compared to 34% of volunteers aged 35 to 54 and 26% of volunteers aged 15 to 34. Older volunteers are also more likely to provide health care or support, such as companionship, through an organization.
- Also mirroring the overall population, volunteers are becoming more and more educated. From 2004 to 2013, the percentage of volunteers aged 25 to 64 with a university degree rose by 4 percentage points to 39%.

Turcotte (2015, p. 17) concluded that:

> Both volunteers and donors are getting older and more educated: more and more volunteer hours are contributed by seniors and older Canadians, and a greater proportion of all donations come from that demographic group. This changing profile could have many consequences for the voluntary and philanthropy sector in terms of the type of volunteer activities, the types of organizations benefiting from volunteerism and charitable giving, and the dollar amount of monetary contributions.

Source: Turcotte, M. (2015). *Spotlight on Canadians: Results from the General Social Survey Volunteering and Charitable Giving in Canada*. Ottawa: Statistics Canada.

NONPROFIT SECTOR AND SPORT

The International Classification of Nonprofit Organizations (ICNPO) has a designated category for sports and recreation organizations. This category includes three broad groups: (1) sports including amateur sport, training, fitness and sport facilities, and sport competition and events; (2) recreation and social clubs such as country clubs, playground associations, touring clubs, and leisure clubs; and (3) service clubs such as Lions, Rotary, Kiwanis, and Apex clubs. Of particular interest are those organizations that operate on a nonprofit basis in sport including professional service organizations, industry lobby groups, sport event organizations, and sport governing bodies.

Nonprofit professional service organizations operate in sport in similar ways to professional associations like accrediting medical boards or associations for lawyers and accountants. These organizations assist in setting standards of practice in their respective industries, provide professional accreditation for qualified members, and offer professional development opportunities through conferences, seminars, or training programs. They operate in a business-like fashion but the aim is to return surpluses to members through improved service delivery rather than create wealth for owners.

In Australia, the Australian Council for Health, Physical Education and Recreation (ACHPER) is a national professional association representing people who work in the areas of Health Education, Physical Education, Recreation, Sport, Dance, Community Fitness, or Movement Sciences. The roles of ACHPER include advocating for the promotion and provision of sport opportunities, providing professional development programs for teachers, and accrediting and training people wanting to become community fitness instructors. Similar groups operate in Canada (Canadian Association for Health, Physical Education, Recreation and Dance), the United States (American Alliance for Health, Physical Education and Dance), the UK (British Institute of Sports Administration), and New Zealand (Physical Education New Zealand).

A number of industry lobby groups, representing the interests of nonprofit sport organizations, also operate throughout the world. A leading example is the Central Council of Physical Recreation (CCPR) in the UK, the representative body for national sports organizations. They act as the independent umbrella organization for national governing and representative bodies of sport and recreation in the UK to promote their interests to government and other players in the sport industry. This role is undertaken by Sport Industry Australia, a similar nonprofit organization in Australia.

Some of the largest and most influential sport event organizations in the world operate on a nonprofit basis, including the International Olympic Committee (IOC) and the Commonwealth Games Federation (CGF). The IOC was founded in 1894 by Baron Pierre de Coubertin, and is an independent nonprofit organization that serves as the umbrella organization of the Olympic Movement. The IOC's primary role is to supervise the organization of the summer and winter Olympic Games.

The IOC has come under much criticism in recent years for poor governance practices, corruption allegations against some officials, and for not doing enough to share the proceeds of Olympic Games with those nations in most need. In reaction, the IOC has greatly improved its reporting to member organizations, providing far greater transparency for how revenues are distributed to National Olympic Committees and through a variety of sport development programs around the globe.

Similar to the IOC, the role of the CGF is to facilitate a major games event every four years but it also provides education assistance for sports development throughout the 53 Commonwealth countries. There are more Commonwealth Games Associations (CGA) (71) than countries (53) because some countries like the UK have seven CGAs (Scotland, England, Northern Ireland, Wales, Isle of Man, Jersey, and Guernsey) that all compete in the Games as separate nations (www.commonwealthgames.com). Both the IOC and CGF fund their operations through contributions from governments that host the games and the sale of international broadcasting rights, corporate sponsorship, ticket sales, licensing, and merchandising sales.

There is also a range of specialist nonprofit organizations that focus on discrete community groups. Foremost among these is the International Paralympic Committee (IPC) that is the international representative organization of elite sports for athletes with disabilities. The IPC organizes, supervises, and coordinates the Paralympic Games and other multi-disability sports competitions at elite level (www.paralympic.org). Other similar nonprofit organizations include the Cerebral Palsy International Sports and Recreation Association and the International Blind Sport Federation that facilitate major events for athletes.

Our focus for the remainder of the chapter is on those nonprofit sport organizations that provide sporting competition or event participation opportunities for their members and other members of the public – sport governing bodies and sports clubs. In countries such as Australia, the UK, Canada, New Zealand, Hong Kong, and other others with club-based sporting systems, almost all sporting teams and competitions are organized by nonprofit sport organizations (Lyons 2001). These organizations take many forms. They include small local clubs that may field a few teams in a local football competition; regional associations that coordinate competitions between clubs; and state or provincial organizations that not only facilitate competitions, but also manage coach development, talent identification, volunteer training, marketing, and sponsorship. They also comprise national sporting organizations that regulate the rules of competition in a country, coordinate national championships between state or provincial teams, manage elite athlete programs, employ development officers to conduct clinics, and undertake many other tasks that facilitate participation in sport. Finally, there are international sports federations that coordinate the development of sport across the globe and facilitate rule changes and liaison between countries on issues like international competitions.

The common element amongst all these sport organizations is their nonprofit focus – they exist to facilitate sporting opportunities for their members who may be individual athletes, coaches, officials or administrators, clubs, associations, or other sport organizations. They are also interdependent, relying on each other to provide playing talent, information to access competitions, resources for coach, official and player development and funding to support their activities. It is important to note that volunteers are at the heart of these organizations, playing significant roles in service delivery and decision making at all levels of nonprofit sport organizations. At the same time though, many of the larger nonprofit sport organizations contain a significant number of paid staff who support their ongoing administration and service delivery to member associations and clubs.

GOVERNING BODIES OF SPORT

Sport clubs compete against other clubs in competition structures provided by regional or state/provincial sporting organizations. State-based teams compete in competitions facilitated by national sporting organizations, and nations compete in leagues or events provided by international federations of sport, such as the Fédération Internationale de Football Association (FIFA), or major competition organizations such as the International Olympic Committee or the Commonwealth Games Association. These organizations are known as governing bodies for sport and have the responsibility for the management, administration, and development for a sport on a global, national, state/provincial level, or regional level.

The structure of the International Netball Federation Limited (IFNA) typifies the relationships between these various governing bodies of sport. The members if IFNA comprise 39 national associations from five regions: Africa, Asia, Americas, Europe, and Oceania.

Each region elects two members to direct the activities of the world governing organization who are responsible for setting the rules for netball, running international competitions, promoting good management in the regions, striving to seek Olympic accreditation for netball, and increasing participation levels around the globe.

Netball Australia, one of the 39 members of IFNA, has almost 500,000 registered players who participate through a variety of programs delivered by eight state/provincial associations. They in turn have a total of more than 550 affiliated associations. Each of the state/provincial associations has a delegate to the national board who, along with the staff of Netball Australia, are responsible for communicating rule changes from IFNA to their members, managing a national competition, promoting good management in the state/provincial organizations, increasing participation nationally, and bidding to host world events.

One of the largest members of Netball Australia, Netball Victoria, has 115,000 registered players who compete in 225 affiliated associations, organized into 21 regions and 6 zones across the state. Netball Victoria's role differs markedly from Netball Australia and IFNA, with responsibility for coach, official and player development, managing state competitions, promoting good management in the clubs, providing insurance coverage for players, assisting in facility development, trying to increase participation in the state, bidding to host national events, and managing two teams in the national competition. Finally, netball clubs field teams, find coaches and players, manage volunteers, conduct fundraising, and may own and operate a facility.

It is important to remember that these sport governing organizations are volunteer based, with volunteers involved in decisions at every level from clubs to international federations. As discussed in Chapter 12, nonprofit sport organizations do not operate as top-down power hierarchies, with clubs always abiding by regional directives, or national governing bodies agreeing with international policy initiatives. Communication and agreement can be difficult between these organizations that may have competing priorities and localized issues. A spirit of cooperation and negotiation is required to make the nonprofit sport system operate effectively. The simple exerting of authority in a traditional organizational hierarchy is not appropriate for most nonprofit sport organizations.

THE SPORTS CLUB ENVIRONMENT

At the centre of sport development in countries such as Canada, New Zealand, Australia, and the UK is the local or community sports club. It is worth taking some time to reflect on the role of the sports club, how volunteers and staff work in the club environment, and how clubs contribute to sport development.

A background report initially prepared in 2001 and updated in 2002 for Sport Scotland provides a snapshot of sport clubs in Scotland (Allison 2002). The most striking thing about local sport clubs is their diversity. Sport clubs have many functions, structures, resources, values, and ideologies and they provide an enormous range of participation opportunities for people to be involved in sport. Most clubs provide activity in a single sport and have as their focus enjoyment in sport, rather than competitive success.

Sport clubs in Scotland come in various sizes, with an average membership size of 133, and most tend to cater for both junior and adult participants. They operate with minimum staffing, structures, income and expenditure, and often rely on a small group of paid or unpaid individuals to organize and administrate club activities. The majority of club income comes from membership payments, so they tend to operate fairly autonomously. The management of local sport clubs in Scotland is regarded as an "organic and intuitive process based on trust and experience rather than formal contracts and codes of practice" (Allison 2002, p. 7).

The characteristics of local sport clubs in other countries are similar. The vast majority of sport clubs rely almost exclusively on volunteers to govern, administer, and manage their organizations and to provide coaching, officiating and general assistance with training, match day functions, and fundraising.

Administrators

Administrators who fill roles as elected or appointed committee members have the responsibility for the overall guidance, direction, and supervision of the organization. According to the Australian Sports Commission (2000, p. 2) the responsibility of the management committee of a sports club extends to:

- Conducting long-term planning for the future of the club
- Developing policy and procedures for club activities
- Managing external relations with other sport organizations, local governments, or sponsors
- Managing financial resources and legal issues on behalf of the club
- Carrying out recommendations put forward by members
- Communicating to members on current issues or developments
- Evaluating the performance of officials, employees (if any), and other serviced providers
- Ensuring adequate records are kept for future transfer of responsibilities to new committee members
- Acting as role models for other club members

Although governance is covered in detail in Chapter 12, it is important to note here that the ability of clubs to carry out these tasks effectively will vary according to their resources, culture, and quality of people willing to be involved. The important administrative roles within local sports club are the chairperson or president, secretary, treasurer, and volunteer coordinator. Other committee roles might involve responsibility for coaching, officiating, representative teams, match day arrangements, fundraising, or marketing.

The chairperson or president should be the one to set the agenda for how a committee operates, work to develop the strategic direction of the club, chair committee meetings, and coordinate the work of other members of the committee. Club secretaries are the administrative link between members, the committee, and other organizations and have responsibility for managing correspondence, records, and information about club activities. The treasurer has responsibility for preparing the annual budget; monitoring expenditure and revenue; planning for future financial needs; and managing operational issues such as petty cash, payments, and banking. The position of volunteer coordinator involves the development of systems and procedures to manage volunteers such as planning, recruitment, training, and recognition.

Coaches

Coaches working in the sport club system may be unpaid or paid, depending on the nature of the sport and the resources of individual clubs. The role of the coach is central to developing athlete's skills and knowledge, in helping them learn tactics for success, and enjoy their sport. Coaches also act as important role models for players and athletes.

Most sports provide a structured training and accreditation scheme for coaches to develop their skills and experience to coach at local, state/provincial, national, or international levels. In Australia, for example, the National Coaching Council established a three-tier National Coaching Accreditation Scheme (NCAS) in 1978. Coaches can undertake a Level 1 introductory course, Level 2 intermediate course, and Level 3 advanced courses in coaching. NCAS training programs comprise three elements: (1) coaching principles that cover fundamentals of coaching and athletic performance; (2) sport-specific coaching that covers the skills, techniques, strategies, and scientific approaches to a particular sport; and (3) coaching practice where coaches engage in practical coaching and application of coaching principles.

Officials

Sports officials include those people who act as referees, umpires, judges, scorers, or time-keepers to officiate over games or events. The majority of officials are unpaid, but some sports such as Australian Rules Football, basketball, and some other football codes pay officials at all levels, enabling some to earn a substantial salary from full-time officiating. Other sports such as netball, softball, or tennis rarely pay officials unless they are at state or national championship level. Sports officials are critical to facilitating people's involvement in sport but are the hardest positions to fill within the nonprofit sport system because they absorb a lot of time and often have low status.

All sports provide a structured training and accreditation scheme for officials in much the same way as coaches to develop their skills and experience at local, state/provincial, national, or international levels. The Australian National Officiating Accreditation Scheme (NOAS) was established in 1994, modelled on the NCAS, but does not prescribe formal levels of officiating as these vary greatly between sporting codes. The NOAS aims to develop and implement programs that improve the quality, quantity, leadership, and status of sports officiating in Australia through training programs that comprise three elements: (1) general principles of officiating and event management; (2) sport-specific technical rules, interpretations, reporting, and specific roles; and (3) practice at officiating and applying the officiating principles.

General volunteers

Sports clubs also depend on people to perform roles in fundraising, managing representative teams, helping with match day arrangements such as car parking or stewarding, or helping to market the club. The majority of general volunteers have an existing link to a sports club through being a parent of a child who plays at the club, having some other family connection, or through friends and work colleagues involved in the club.

The Statistics Canada 2012 publication, *Volunteering in Canada*, provides the most recent detailed picture of volunteer involvement of Canadians in a range of activities, including sport. This report uses the results from 2010 Canada Survey of Giving, Volunteering and Participating, and states:

> In 2010, about one-half of Canadians contributed their time, energy and skills to groups and organizations such as charities and nonprofits. They provided leadership on boards and committees; canvassed for funds; provided advice, counselling or mentoring; visited seniors; prepared and delivered food; served as volunteer drivers; advocated for social causes; coached children and youth. In short, they shaped their communities and enabled nonprofit organizations to deliver programs and services to millions of their fellow Canadians.
>
> (Vezina and Crompton 2012, p. 37)

Sport and recreation was the sector attracting the most volunteers; in 2010, 12% of people aged 15 and over did volunteer work for sports and recreation organizations and organizations associated with sports and recreation accounted for 19% of volunteer hours.

Volunteers dedicated more than 120 hours, on average, to sports and recreation organizations, and unsurprisingly, those people with school-aged children were among those most likely to volunteer. Vezina and Crompton (2012, p. 48), concluded that:

> Without question, lack of time is the biggest barrier to people becoming involved in volunteering. About two-thirds of Canadians aged 15 and over who had not done any formal volunteering in 2010 said that their key reasons were not having enough time (67%) and the inability to make a long-term commitment (62%) (Chart 12). This does not mean people who don't volunteer don't value the work done by nonprofit and charitable organizations; in fact, over one-half (52%) of this group said they preferred to give dollars instead of hours.

These figures, along with those provided in the In Practice 3.3, illustrate the enormous contribution volunteers make in roles such as coaches, officials, and administrators in order to facilitate people's involvement in sport. However, there are some worrying signs that such voluntary involvement may be on the wane in some age cohorts of the population and that in order to sustain current levels of involvement in sport, the management of sport volunteers needs to improve.

GOVERNMENT INTERVENTION

The substantial funds allocated to nonprofit sport organizations by governments to support their activities in areas of mass participation or elite performance has meant that governments are increasingly trying to influence the way in which the nonprofit sector of sport operates. Examples of these attempts include the Australian Sports Commission Volunteer Management Program and the policy of Sport England to have national organizations develop 'whole of sport' plans. These are briefly reviewed below to highlight the increasingly interdependent nature of government and sport organizations in seeking improvements in nonprofit sport.

The Australian Sports Commission developed the Volunteer Involvement Program in 1994 in partnership with the Australian Society of Sports Administrators, the Confederation of Australian Sport, and state departments of sport and recreation. The program aimed to improve the operation of nonprofit sport clubs and associations by providing a series of publications on sport club administration. In 2000, the Volunteer Management Program (VMP) and the Club and Association Management Program (CAMP) resources were published, and the ASC encouraged all clubs to join a Club Development Network and engage in strategic planning and other management techniques.

Another example is the policy developed by Sport England to require national sport organizations to develop 'whole of sport plans'. In 2003 Sport England identified 30 priority sports, based on their capability to contribute to Sport England's vision of an active and successful sporting nation and is now working with the national sport organizations to develop and implement these plans. The plans are designed to outline how a sport from grass roots right to the elite level will attract and keep participants and improve their sporting experiences. The plans will drive decisions by Sport England to provide funding to national organizations based on clearly articulated ideas of the resources they need to drive their sport. The plans will also provide for measurable performance results and assist Sport England evaluate the benefits that accrue from funding nonprofit sport organizations.

The CLUBMARK program developed by Sport England is indicative of the approach many governments have taken toward trying to enhance the capacity of the nonprofit sport sector at the community club level. Because approximately 60% of young people in England belong to a sports club outside of school (where government can influence delivery standards via the education system), the government sought to improve the standard of service delivery that young people receive from community sport clubs by creating CLUBMARK, a cross-sport quality accreditation for clubs with junior sections run by Sport England. The main purpose of CLUBMARK was to encourage sport clubs to seek accreditation as a CLUBMARK club. National governing bodies of sport (NGBs) and county sport partnerships (CSPs) award CLUBMARK to proven high-quality clubs. The national scheme has been in place since 2002 and midway through 2011 there were more than 10,750 accredited clubs in the CLUBMARK scheme.

CLUBMARK accreditation is awarded to clubs that comply with minimum operating standards in four areas: the playing program, duty of care and child protection, sports equity and ethics, and club management. Clubs working towards accreditation can receive support and advice from their NGB and other partners such as county sports partnerships (CSPs). Circumstances vary between clubs and sports, but the process of accreditation is the same. The benefits of implementing a single, national standard for sport club operations gives sports clubs of all types structure and direction, specifically in areas such as:

- Club development – The foundation for any club is its youth structure. By encouraging and attracting young members, it is building a strong future.
- Increased membership – Addressing issues like equity and child protection gives parents confidence when choosing a club for their children.
- Developing coaches and volunteers – As part of CLUBMARK, clubs receive help in developing the skills of those involved in their organization.
- Raised profile – Once CLUBMARK accredited, clubs are listed on a national database and in other directories, to help them attract new members and grow.

The CLUBMARK program provides sports clubs a framework for volunteer management as well as a series of templates that they can adapt for their specific circumstances. CLUBMARK is managed by Knight, Kavanagh & Page (KKP) on behalf of Sport England. It is responsible for validation of NGBs and CSPs, for moderation of its impact on clubs, and for the marketing and promotion of the program throughout England (Sport England 2011a).

In practice 3.2 Sport England Sport Makers

One of the more ambitious government intervention programs aimed at influencing the direction and capacity of the nonprofit sport sector is the Sport Makers program, an initiative tied to the legacy of the London 2012 Olympic Games. According to the Sport England website before the 2012 Games, the intention was the Sport Makers program would recruit, train, and deploy 50,000 new sports volunteers aged 16 years and over to organize and lead community sporting activities across England. The program was designed to grow the volunteer base who would have:

> A positive and inspiring introduction to the world of sport volunteering via a series of workshops delivered locally through a training provider and in conjunction with a county sports partnership. We anticipate that many volunteers will continue to give of their time, further increasing sport participation long after the 2012 Games are held in the UK. These Sport Makers will organise and support hundreds of thousands of new hours of grassroots sport, creating new opportunities across the country. While doing so, they will bring the Olympic and Paralympic values to life in every community. Sport Makers will be fully inclusive and target participants including people who have a disability, both males and females and participants from BME groups (Sport England 2011b).

The Sport Makers program was originally scheduled to run from April 2011 until September 2013 with a budget of £4 million drawn from National Lottery Funding, with approximately half delivered via county sport partnerships. The outcomes were planned to include (Sport England 2011b):

- 50,000 new Sport Makers recruited and invited to an orientation workshop delivered locally through a CSP and by an inspirational trainer.
- 40,000 Sport Makers are provided with deployment opportunities to increase participation for a minimum of 10 hours each by their CSP. Of those deployed, we anticipate 20,000 will continue to volunteer in sport beyond these 10 hours.
- Olympic and Paralympic values are brought to life for the Sport Makers through their orientation workshop so that they feel part of the Olympic movement and role model these values in raising participation.
- As a result of their deployment, thousands of new opportunities for people aged sixteen and over to participate will be created.

This ambitious program involved the British Olympic Association, London Organising Committee of the Olympic Games, national governing bodies, county sports partnerships, local authority sports development teams, local governments, and a range of national and county/sub-regional voluntary partners.

A review published in March 2013 (Nichols et al) concluded that although it had assisted the work of county sports partnerships, it had failed to meet its original targets. A further review published in 2014 by CFE Research (Adamson and Spong 2014) found that about 25% of people who registered to be a Sport Maker failed to attend any workshops or undertake any activities and that Sport Makers tended to recruit people they already knew to participate in sport activities. They also found that overall Sport Makers themselves benefitted from being involved in the program. Such a centralized, target-driven approach highlights the complexities of achieving significant sustainable change in the nonprofit sport sector where partnerships and collaboration across all the stakeholders involved in delivering sport is required.

Source: Sport England. (2011b). *Sport Makers Factsheet*. London, UK: Sport England; Nichols, G., Ferguson, G., Grix, J. and Griffiths, J. (2013). *Sport Makers: Developing Good Practice in Volunteer and Sports Development*. University of Sheffield; Adamson, J. and Spong, S. (2014). *Sport Makers Evaluation*. London: CFE Research.

ISSUES FOR THE NONPROFIT SPORT SECTOR

A range of challenges exist for the nonprofit sport sector around the globe. Foremost among these is the dependence on volunteers to sustain the sports system in areas such as coaching, administrating, and officiating. As highlighted earlier in this chapter there is evidence to suggest that the rate of volunteerism is declining for roles such as officiating and administration in sport. Governments and nonprofit sport organizations will need to address this issue if their mutually dependent goals of increasing participation in organized sport are to be achieved.

The increasingly litigious nature of society and the associated increase in costs of insurance for nonprofit sport organizations directly affects the cost of participation. In Australia fewer insurers are providing insurance cover for sporting organizations, and insurance premium prices have risen significantly in recent years. For example, the public liability insurance premium for the Australian Parachute Federation increased from $127,000 to $1.1 million in two years. Public liability insurance is vital to run sport events and programs, and these costs are passed onto participants for no additional benefits, which raises the question of whether people can afford to keep playing sport in traditional nonprofit systems.

A further issue for nonprofit sport organizations is the trend away from participating in traditional sports, organized through clubs and associations, to a more informal pattern of participation. Some people are unwilling to commit to a season of sporting involvement and are seeking ways to engage in sport and physical activity on a more casual basis, either through short-term commercial providers or with friends in spontaneous or pick-up sports (Stewart et al 2004). The increase in options available to young people to spend their discretionary leisure dollars, euros, or pounds has also presented challenges for nonprofit sport organizations to market themselves as an attractive option.

As highlighted earlier, nonprofit organizations, including nonprofit sport organizations, face significant capacity problems. They are often constrained by the size of their facilities or venues and may struggle to attract enough quality people to manage the operations of their organization. They are also constrained by the interdependent nature of sport – they require other clubs, teams, and organizations to provide competition – so they need to work cooperatively with other nonprofit sport organizations to expand their 'product'.

The very nature of nonprofit sport organizations requires adherence to frequently cumbersome consultative decision-making processes, often across large geographic areas and with widely dispersed and disparate groups of stakeholders. The additional complexity of the governance and management requirements of these organizations present their own set of challenges in terms of making timely decisions, reacting to market trends, being innovative, or seeking agreement on significant organizational changes.

Lyons (2001) also suggests that nonprofit organizations are unique because they have difficulty in judging performance relative to their commercial counterparts, have to be accountable to a wide range of stakeholders, and must deal with tension and possible conflict between paid staff and volunteers. These tensions are due to a lack of clarity about paid staff and volunteer roles and are exacerbated by the lack of clear performance measures. Nonprofit sport organizations are particularly susceptible to these problems, especially where there is a coterie of paid staff in senior administrative positions. In Practice 3.3 explores a recent attempt to understand the market for sport volunteers in order to address this growing problem of recruiting and retaining volunteers.

In practice 3.3 Market segmentation of sport volunteers

The following summary of the market segmentation project from the Australian Sports Commission has been sourced from the Clearing House for Sport at www. clearinghouseforsport.gov.au/knowledge_base/sport_participation/community_ participation/volunteers_in_sport

The ASC conducted research on volunteer involvement in the sport sector to gain insights that may help sports organizations develop targeted and effective volunteer recruitment and retention strategies. The primary purpose of the Market Segmentation for Volunteers study was to identify the core set of attitudes, motivators, needs, and barriers that underpin Australians' decisions to volunteer in sport, including at the club level and other types of sports-related volunteering, as compared to other (non-sport) voluntary activities. The information was used to develop a needs-based market segmentation model of Australian sports volunteers.

This ASC research identified segments of the Australian community with the greatest potential for recruitment as sports volunteers, as well as assessing best practices and strategies for the recruitment and retention of current volunteers. Attitudinal segmentation is a useful means of grouping people within the broader population into groups or segments with similar dispositions towards volunteering. Segmentation across the Australian population, aged 14 to 75 years, resulted in 10 identified types of persons, based on characteristics related to their attitudes to volunteering and current volunteering behaviour.

- Happy Helpers – volunteers who support their family in their activities by volunteering in club sport. These volunteers are likely to be involved in multiple activities.
- Community Committed – these volunteers are motivated by the social interaction and enjoyment that volunteering offers. They have a feeling of identity and commitment to a community organization and its future.
- Opportunists – this group of persons volunteers to gain a personal benefit, such as practical skills or work experience. They also enjoy being part of the atmosphere of a sporting environment or having the chance to meet elite athletes or sporting personalities.
- Altruists – these volunteers have a desire to help others, to give back to the community, and to help the disadvantaged.
- Overcommitted – these persons volunteer because they feel it is expected of them. They often feel they could use their time elsewhere.
- Occupied Observers – this group is not averse to volunteering for club sport, but they simply have other priorities and most likely to volunteer if their own child is directly involved.
- Sidelined – persons who are open minded about volunteering, but injury, lack of time, or some other personal reason becomes a barrier.

- Self Servers – this group is yet to find a cause they feel passionate about. They may be motivated if they perceive a personal benefit.
- Well Intentioned – this group has no real reason to volunteer within the sport sector. They are unlikely to be sports participants themselves.
- Uninvolved – this group has little interest in either sport or volunteering in general.

Each segment has its own set of challenges and opportunities that sports organizations must recognize and address if they are to recruit and then retain volunteers with a particular mind-set. For example, both Happy Helpers and Overcommitted persons are likely to volunteer, but the challenge for club sport is to retain them as a volunteer across different life stages, particularly once their child has moved on from being a sport participant. Likewise, Community Committed individuals are easily recruited, but the challenge for the club is to manage their enthusiasm to ensure their loyalty and commitment to the organization does not intimidate new volunteers.

Self Servers, Sidelined, and Occupied Observers are likely segments for clubs to attract new volunteers from. Clubs may be able to attract Self Servers if they can offer volunteer experiences that are tangible and provide personal benefit of some kind, such as learning useful skills or gaining valuable work experience. Because the Sidelined segment likes sport, they may be encouraged to volunteer if they can occupy a role that fits within their capabilities and other commitments. The Occupied Observer may be encouraged into volunteering if their role can be shaped to accommodate their overall time commitments.

Sources: Australian Sports Commission. (2017). *Market Segmentation Research*. Sourced at www.clearinghouseforsport.gov.au/knowledge_base/sport_participation/community_participation/volunteers_in_sport.

THE RISE OF SPORT *FOR* DEVELOPMENT

One area of nonprofit activity related to sport has been the enormous growth of the field of sport for development. In contrast to sport development (the player development pathways and structures for the delivery of sport), sport for development is the use of sport to deliver other non-sport outcomes for individuals or communities. One of the more widely cited definitions of sport for development is:

the use of sport to exert a positive influence on public health, the socialisation of children, youths and adults, the social inclusion of the disadvantaged, the economic development of regions and states, and on fostering intercultural exchange and conflict resolution.

(Lyras and Welty Peachey 2011, p. 311)

In the most recent comprehensive review of sport for development, Schulenkorf, Sherry, and Rowe (2016, p. 22) stated that

> As a consequence of growing political and institutional support, the number of sport-based projects aimed at contributing to positive development in these areas has been constantly increasing (Coalter 2007, 2013; Levermore and Beacom 2009; Schulenkorf and Adair 2014). The popularity of SFD stems from its ability to capture or "hook" a large number of people – particularly those interested in sport and physical activity – and use the momentum in and around sport as a strategic vehicle to communicate, implement, and achieve nonsport development goals.

The sport for development field is dominated by work in Africa, Asia, and Latin America where sport is used as a focal point to attract participants to programs aimed at youth development, tackling poverty, increasing retention rates in education programs, or overcoming social disadvantage. Programs are supported by individual philanthropists, corporations, governments, charitable organizations, and international and national sport federations, and is an increasing area for employment and volunteering for people skilled in sport management, as well as community development, international relations, or social work. This area will increasingly become a significant employer of sport management graduates, as well as a focal point for voluntary efforts of people seeking to facilitate community outcomes associated with sport activities or programs.

SUMMARY

Nonprofit organizations were defined as those organizations that are institutionally separate from the state, do not return profits to owners, are self-governing, have a significant element of voluntary contribution, and are formally incorporated. Nonprofit organizations exist to develop communities, meet the needs of identifiable and discrete groups in those communities, and work for the benefit of public good rather than wealth creation for individuals. The majority of nonprofit organizations are driven largely by the efforts of volunteers rather than paid staff.

Sport organizations that operate on a nonprofit basis include professional service organizations, industry lobby groups, sport event organizations, and sport governing bodies. By far the greatest number of nonprofit sport organizations is those that provide sporting competition or event participation opportunities for their members and other members of the public – sport governing bodies and sports clubs. The common element amongst all these sport organizations is their nonprofit focus – they exist to facilitate sporting opportunities for their members who may be individual athletes, coaches, officials or administrators, clubs, associations, or other sport organizations. They are also interdependent, relying on each other to provide playing talent; information to access competitions; resources for coach, official, and player development; and funding to support their activities.

Sport governing bodies and clubs rely almost exclusively on volunteers to govern, administer, and manage their organizations and to provide coaching, officiating, and general assistance with training, events, and fundraising. The substantial funds allocated to nonprofit sport organizations by governments to support their activities in areas of mass participation or elite performance has meant that governments are increasingly trying to influence the way in which the nonprofit sector of sport operates. Finally, a number of challenges exist for the nonprofit sport sector, including the dependence on volunteers to sustain the sports system, the increasingly litigious nature of society, and the associated increase in costs of insurance for nonprofit sport organizations. There is also a trend away from participating in traditional sports, significant capacity problems, and the additional complexity of the governance and management requirements of these organizations.

REVIEW QUESTIONS

1 What is the role of the nonprofit sector in relation to sport?

2 What are the unique aspects of nonprofit sport organizations that set them apart from profit oriented or privately owned sport organizations?

3 Describe the role of a local community sport club.

4 Explain how the state and the nonprofit sector may contribute to sport development.

5 In what ways are volunteers important to the delivery of sport?

6 What are the important management roles in nonprofit sporting clubs?

7 Explain the role of a national governing body for a sport.

8 Why does the government attempt to intervene in the management of nonprofit sport organizations? Explain how governments do this in your own country.

9 How can nonprofit sport organizations reduce the costs to participants?

10 Explain how nonprofit sport organizations have to work cooperatively with each other but still compete on the playing field.

DISCUSSION QUESTIONS

1 Why is sport an attractive vehicle to assist the delivery of other development programs aimed at overcoming poverty or another social disadvantage?

2 How could sport change its delivery model to better recruit and retain volunteers?

3 Should sport continue to rely on volunteers to support its delivery, or should we move to a more user pays model with more paid employees delivering sport?

4 Where do you sit within the ASC's market segmentation of sport volunteers? Do the categories make sense? How could a sport manager make use of this segmentation model?

5 Why is it important for sport organizations to remain self-determining?

FURTHER READING

Cuskelly, G., Hoye, R. and Auld, C. (2006). *Working with Volunteers in Sport: Theory and Practice*. London: Routledge.

Houlihan, B. and Green, M. (2007). *Comparative Elite Sport Development. Systems, Structures and Public Policy*. London: Elsevier.

Hylton, K. and Bramham, P. (eds) (2007). *Sports Development: Policy, Process and Practice*. 2nd edn. London: Routledge.

May, T., Harris, S. and Collins, M. (2013). Implementing community sport policy: Understanding the variety of voluntary club types and their attitudes to policy. *International Journal of Sport Policy and Politics*, 5(3): 397–419.

Misener, K. and Doherty, A. (2013). Understanding capacity through the processes and outcomes of interorganizational relationships in non-profit community sport organizations. *Sport Management Review*, 16(2): 135–147.

Productivity Commission. (2010). *Contribution of the Not-for-Profit Sector*. Canberra: Commonwealth of Australia.

Schulenkorf, N., Sherry, E. and Rowe, K. (2016). Sport for Development: An Integrated Literature Review. *Journal of Sport Management*, 30: 22–39.

Sport England. (2011a). *Clubmark Factsheet*. London, UK: Sport England.

Sport England. (2011b). *Sport Makers Factsheet*. London, UK: Sport England.

Vezina, M. and Crompton, S. (2012). *Volunteering in Canada*. Ottawa: Statistics Canada.

RELEVANT WEBSITES

The following websites are useful starting points for further information on nonprofit sport organizations:
Australian Sports Commission at www.ausport.gov.au
Sport New Zealand at www.sportnz.org.nz
Sport Canada http://pch.gc.ca/eng/1266246552427
Sport England at www.sportengland.org
Sport Scotland at www.sportscotland.org.uk

CASE STUDY 3.1

Quality accreditation push by England Netball

This case study explores the challenges faced by nonprofit sport organizations in delivering sport through a network of volunteer controlled community-based organizations. A standard approach taken by many sports is to create an accreditation or quality framework for clubs to meet in order to improve the standard of sport delivery throughout a sport.

The All England Netball Association Ltd (England Netball) is the national governing body of netball in England. England Netball develops programs, encourages new participants in netball, and guides existing participants through their netball journey as well as carrying out administrative, regulatory, and sanctioning functions to the game. The head office deals with the day-to-day administration of the association through its employees but a large portion of their work is carried out by a network of full- and part-time staff working for the association in the counties and regions, carrying out specific roles to ensure continued growth and development of the sport.

The country is divided into nine geographical regions, each sub-divided into 55 counties and three Armed Forces Associations. Within the 55 affiliated counties, there are approximately 400 leagues spread across England. England Netball's membership consists of approximately 3,000 registered clubs made up from approximately 90,000 individual players. Approximately 2,600 schools are also affiliated. The regions and counties are autonomous and have their own constitutions.

One of many programs run by England Netball is the Club Action Planning Scheme (CAPS), a program designed to help clubs deliver a quality netball development program and operate in line with best practice. CAPS is aligned to the Sport England CLUBMARK accreditation scheme which is the only national cross-sports quality accreditation scheme for clubs with junior sections. It is built around a set of core criteria which ensure that accredited clubs operate to a set of consistent, accepted, and adopted minimum operating standards across Bronze, Silver, and Gold levels.

England Netball has developed a toolkit to help a club compile the evidence needed to gain the accreditation and identify areas where further work may be required. The aim is to assist clubs increase the numbers of netballers in their local community, ensure they are providing a safe environment for members, and make sure important aspects of club management are applied. The following CAPS program is information rich (to say the least!) with a number of criteria for club operations to meet, informed by downloadable guidance notes and templates. England Netball deploys a team of Netball Development Officers in every county to assist clubs undertake the CAPS program.

The aim of clubs working through the CAPS are to:

• Increase membership numbers and retain them in clubs
• Ensure clubs deliver the right amount of duty of care for its members
• Address important aspects of the club management
• Develop coaches, umpires, and volunteers
• Develop links with local schools in the community
• Raise the profile of clubs

- Plan how you to improve clubs and help delegate those actions amongst its members

CAPS has three levels of accreditation: Bronze, Silver, and Gold. Bronze CAPS is the first level, incorporating the CLUBMARK criteria covering the areas of safeguarding and protecting children and young people, quality coaching and officiating, competition, talent development, sports equity, and good management. Bronze must be achieved before Silver or Gold. Silver and Gold CAPS are about demonstrating further quality across the areas of coaching, officiating, and developing volunteers. If clubs achieve Silver or Gold, they are demonstrating they have met the minimum operating standards required for CLUBMARK but have also demonstrated a further commitment to ensuring a club environment which provides a higher quality of coaching, officiating, leadership, and volunteering opportunities for the young people at a club. All accredited CAPS clubs are entered in prize draws throughout the season. Achieving accreditation is promoted, as clubs are able to claim national recognition as a well-run club which is active and accessible, helping get the best out of young people, and giving everyone a sporting chance.

The CAPS program website has almost 40 separate documents to download, including checklists, policy statements, templates, and assessment tasks. The program covers all aspects of club management, coaching delivery, athlete pathway development, facility requirements, volunteer workforce matrix, role descriptions for key club officials, model constitutions for clubs to adopt, and codes of conduct for players' parents and volunteers, as well as risk management checklists and procedures.

In their 2014–2015 Annual Report, England Netball reported that 25 new clubs had received Bronze accreditation, 18 clubs had upgraded to Silver or Gold, and 57 clubs renewed their existing level of accreditation. Clearly getting all 3,000 clubs to buy into the CAPS program will take some time and lots of resources.

Source: The material for this case study is based on the contents of the England Netball website that can be found at www.englandnetball.co.uk

CASE STUDY QUESTIONS

1 Visit the England Netball website and document all the roles where volunteers are involved in the governance, management, and operations of netball.

2 Explain the difference between the Gold, Silver, and Bronze CAPS levels.

3 What are the roles of volunteers versus paid staff in the CAPS system?

4 Identify the strengths and weaknesses of the CAPS system used by England Netball to ensure good quality in service delivery.

5 What alternative structures or systems could be used to improve the experience of people wanting to be involved in netball in England?

CASE STUDY 3.2

Inside the prestigious Melbourne Cricket Club

This case study explores the operations of one of the most famous sport clubs in the world, the Melbourne Cricket Club (MCC), a private membership club started in 1838 and incorporated under the Melbourne Cricket Club Act 1974, boasting by far the biggest membership of any sporting club in Australia. In 2017, the MCC had more than 230,000 people on a waiting list to become a member, and although there is no definitive waiting period, the most recent intake of members had been on the waiting list for more than 18 years!

The MCC has the public responsibility of managing the iconic sporting arena, the Melbourne Cricket Ground (MCG), home of many an Ashes defeat by Australia over the old enemy England, and home to one of the world's great sporting events, the Australian Football League Grand Final each September. It has also hosted the 1956 Olympic Games, the 2006 Commonwealth Games, Bledisloe Cup games between Australia and New Zealand, music events, and opera.

The MCG also houses the National Sports Museum within the Olympic Stand. The museum has a number of exhibitions focused on Australian football, basketball, boxing, cricket, cycling, golf, netball, Olympic and Paralympic Games, rugby union, rugby league, soccer, and tennis. It also tells the MCG story and includes an extensive interactive area that reinforces the MCG's traditional role as the spiritual home of Australian sport and curator of some of the finest sports-related memorabilia and interactive technology in the world.

The MCG is built on Crown land and is a significant asset of the Victorian community. The Melbourne Cricket Ground Trust, established by the Melbourne Cricket Ground Act 1933, is responsible for the ground management of the MCG. Section 7(1) of the Act states "the function of the Trust is to manage and control and make improvements to the Ground at its discretion". In 2003, following the signing of the Management and Indemnity Deed between the Melbourne Cricket Club, the Melbourne Cricket Ground Trust, and the Treasurer of Victoria, the MCC is contracted to manage the MCG until 2042. Under the terms of the deed the MCC has the exclusive rights to manage the MCG in accordance with the terms of the Management and Indemnity Deed.

The business and affairs of the MCC are overseen and controlled by a committee. The committee comprises members of the club elected to honorary office bearer positions, namely, a president, three vice-presidents, a treasurer, and nine other club members elected to the committee. To assist in the execution of its responsibilities, the committee has established a number of sub-committees to which the president appoints committee members. Committee members are also involved in the following additional sub-committees and related funds or corporate bodies: MCC Sporting Sections, Cricket, Legal, AFL, MCC Foundation, and MCC Nominees.

Additionally, the committee reviews the performance of the club's management team in consultation with the chief executive officer (CEO), measuring results against the business plan objectives, ensuring compliance with legal requirements, and monitoring the strategic and operational risk management plan. The MCC manages the ground through seven departments responsible to the CEO: Membership and Heritage, Events, Executive, Facilities, Finance and Information Systems, Commercial Operations, and People and Culture. There are about 140 permanent club employees, and event staff are drawn from a pool of 1,000-plus for match day duties at the ground.

One of the unique things about the MCC is that it is a private, not-for-profit club with public responsibilities in relation to managing the MCG. It also has created the MCC Foundation to further the purposes of the MCC. The foundation promotes some of the key assets of the MCC, namely the library and the museum, seeks and secures sponsorships and donations, and engages in capital development projects for MCC members. One of these is the development of the MCC Kew Sports Club, a joint venture between the Kew Heights Sports Club and the MCC Foundation. It has created a satellite sports club for members to enjoy a limited range of sports, events, and functions away from the MCG itself. Members can also play sport through more than 12 different affiliated sporting sections, including baseball, golf, hockey, tennis, and target shooting.

CASE STUDY QUESTIONS

1 Visit the MCC website and document all the roles where volunteers are involved in the governance, management, and operations of the MCC.

2 What comparable not-for-profit sports clubs are there around the world? What has been the secret to the success of the MCC since 1838?

3 Why does the MCC retain the right to manage the MCG? Why does the Victorian state government allow this to continue?

4 How could the MCC make better use of the huge demand it has for membership, with more than 230,000 people on a waiting list?

Source: MCC website at www.mcc.org.au

CHAPTER 4

Professional sport

OVERVIEW

This chapter examines the key features of professional sport organizations and provides examples of the unique features of professional sport leagues and clubs. The chapter does not examine community, state, or national sport organizations, but does comment on the relationship between these organizations and professional sport, as well as the impact professional sport has on the sport industry in general.

After completing this chapter the reader should be able to:

- Identify the ways in which professional sport dominates the global sport industry;
- Understand and explain the ways in which the media, sponsors, and professional sport organizations engage in corporate synergies to market and sell their products and services; and
- Understand and explain the roles of players, agents, sponsors, leagues, clubs, and the media in professional sport.

WHAT IS PROFESSIONAL SPORT?

Professional sport, wherever it is played, is the most expensive, most visible, and most watched sporting activity. It captures the lion's share of media coverage, as well as almost all sponsorship revenue and corporate support that is offered. Professional sport is played in cities all over the world, from Kolkata, India, to Rio de Janeiro, Brazil, to Melbourne, Australia, in the very best stadiums (Eden Gardens, Maracana Stadium, Melbourne Cricket Ground) by athletes who often earn, depending on the size of the market, millions of dollars. Professional sport, and the industry that surrounds it, dominates world sport and those who play it are cultural celebrities on a global scale. Local, regional, state, and national sport organizations are often geared around feeding professional sport leagues by developing player talent or spectator interest. These same organizations are also often forced, somewhat ironically, to compete in vain with professional sport for media coverage, sponsorship, and general support (from fans, governments, and communities). At its best, professional sport is the peak of the sports industry that supports those organizations below it by generating financial resources and cultural cache. At its worst, it is a rapacious commercial animal with an insatiable appetite for financial, cultural, and social resources.

Professional sport leagues, such as the National Football League (NFL) in the United States, dominate weekly media and social interests within the cities in which they are popular, with fans attracted to plots and sub-plots each week in the form of winners and losers, injuries and scandals, player or coach sackings, player transfers, and crisis events (financial, human, and organizational). In the late 19th century American college football games were played on an ad hoc basis, largely special events that captured the attention of some football followers and some media outlets. College football only became a part of the U.S. national psyche and identity when games were organized around seasons, when media outlets and fans alike could plan their sport production and consumption around a weekly routine. The constancy and consistency of professional sport leagues have been the foundation upon which their popularity has been built. In many cities around the world, professional sport leagues have become an ingrained part of what it means to belong to a cultural or social group. In other words, professional sport leagues and their clubs have become, for many fans, an essential way of understanding and defining who they are.

Professional sport events, such as the football, rugby union, or cricket world cups have also become part of our cultural and commercial consumption. They are held periodically (usually every four years) and capture audience attention because they provide out-of-the-ordinary sport action and are typically fuelled by nationalism. At a lower level, we are also exposed to annual events, such as world championships, and to circuits, such as the world rally championship, which hosts rounds in countries such as Sweden, Mexico, and Finland. Each day of our lives we are bombarded by saturation media coverage of sport events through television, radio, magazines, newspapers, and the Internet. There is no escaping the reach of professional sport in contemporary society.

Professional sport is now big business. It is not simply about what happens on the field of play, like it once was (in broad terms prior to the commercialization of sport in the 1970s), but is also about what happens in the boardroom and on the stock exchange. Table 4.1 lists *Forbes* magazine's estimation of the football/soccer teams with the highest

TABLE 4.1 Highest value football/soccer teams 2017

Team	Country	Value (US$)
Manchester United	England	3,689,000,000
Barcelona	Spain	3,635,000,000
Real Madrid	Spain	3,580,000,000
Bayern Munich	Germany	2,713,000,000
Manchester City	England	2,083,000,000
Arsenal	England	1,932,000,000
Chelsea	England	1,845,000,000
Liverpool	England	1,492,000,000
Juventus	Italy	1,258,000,000
Tottenham Hotspur	England	1,058,000,000

Adapted from: www.forbes.com

value in the world in 2017. The list demonstrates that many of these teams are significant corporate entities – all of the top 10 have estimated annual revenues in excess of US$300 million, with the top four recording estimated annual revenues in excess of US$650 million across three different leagues (Spain's La Liga, England's Premier League, and the German Bundesliga), a clear indication that sport is an established global business.

In the first chapter of this book you were introduced to the three-sector model of sport: public, nonprofit, and private. In Chapters 2 and 3 the public and nonprofit sectors were examined, and this fourth chapter examines professional sport. It would be a mistake, however, to assume that the terms private and professional are synonymous in the context of sport organizations and their operations. Rather, in this chapter we are examining those sport organizations in which competitive commercial revenue is used to sustain their operations, as opposed to organizations that are funded by the state or almost exclusively through membership fees or subscriptions. It is important to recognize that many of the organizations featured in this chapter are actually nonprofit and are not privately owned. Professional sport organizations have two important features that define them. First, they share a scale of operations (particularly commercial and financial) that means they exist at the apex of the sport industry, and second, all the players or athletes are 'professionals' – sport is their job and they are paid to train and play full time. Sports in which the players or athletes are required to find additional employment to supplement their income cannot be considered professional.

The example of the Australian professional football landscape is useful for illustrating and understanding the distinction between private and nonprofit organizations within professional sport, as well as the differences that exist between sports. In the Australian Football League (AFL) all the clubs are essentially member based organizations (in which supporters or fans who buy memberships are entitled to attend games, as well as vote to elect a board of directors to govern their club). AFL clubs have annual revenues of up to AUS$80 million, but they are nonprofit organizations – all the money is used on club operations (e.g. to pay players and staff, maintain facilities, or promote the club) and none of the money earned by the clubs is returned to an owner or to shareholders. Although it is essentially a collection of nonprofit organizations, the AFL is the wealthiest and most popular professional sport organization in Australia, which captures the greatest share of sponsorship and broadcast rights revenue. Like the AFL, Australia's National Rugby League (NRL) consists of many member based clubs, but there are also some which are privately owned. In the instances where a club is privately owned, the annual profit or loss is either returned to or borne by the private owner. For example, if the Melbourne Storm, one of the NRL's most successful and controversial clubs in the first decade of the 21st century, secures a profit, it is returned to its owners, headed up by New Zealand businessman Bart Campbell, who bought the club from multinational media conglomerate News Corporation in 2013. In contrast to the AFL and NRL, all eight clubs in the Australian A-League (soccer) are privately owned, but the governing body, Football Federation Australia, is a nonprofit organization. In this case the responsibility for ensuring a healthy and viable professional league is shared between private and nonprofit organizations. Throughout this chapter, and the remaining chapters of the book, it is important to keep in mind that both nonprofit and private organizations compete in professional sport leagues.

In practice 4.1 Dallas Cowboys

The National Football League (NFL) is the most popular sporting league in the United States and by extension the most popular and profitable sporting league in the world. The league consists of 32 teams, divided into two conferences (the American Football Conference – AFC – and the National Football Conference – NFC), each of which is divided into four divisions of four teams each. Of these 32 NFL teams, the following 29 were ranked in the *Forbes* top 50 most valuable sporting teams of 2017:

- Dallas Cowboys (1)
- New England Patriots (6)
- New York Giants (8)
- San Francisco 49ers (9)
- Washington Redskins (11)
- Los Angeles Rams (12)
- New York Jets (13)
- Chicago Bears (16)
- Houston Texans (20)

- Philadelphia Eagles (22)
- Denver Broncos (24)
- Miami Dolphins (25)
- Green Bay Packers (26)
- Baltimore Ravens (27)
- Pittsburgh Steelers (28)
- Seattle Seahawks (29)
- Minnesota Vikings (30)
- Indianapolis Colts (32)
- Atlanta Falcons (33)
- Oakland Raiders (34)
- Los Angeles Chargers (36)
- Carolina Panthers (37)
- Arizona Cardinals (38)
- Tennessee Titans (39)
- Jacksonville Jaguars (42)
- Kansas City Chiefs (44)
- Cleveland Browns (45)
- Tampa Bay Buccaneers (47)
- New Orleans Saints (50)

Only the Buffalo Bills, Cincinnati Bengals, and the Detroit Lions missed out on making the top 50 in 2017, meaning that more than half of the world's most valuable sporting teams are in the NFL. The Dallas Cowboys were number 1 with an estimated value of US$4.2 billion and the New Orleans Saints were in 50th position with an estimated value of US$1.75 billion. In 2017 there were an additional 36 sporting teams that didn't make the list but had an estimated value of more than US$1 billion.

In 2013, 2014, and 2015, Spanish football team Real Madrid was ranked by *Forbes* as the most valuable team, but in 2016 and 2017 the Dallas Cowboys were ranked as number one. The Dallas Cowboys joined the NFL as an expansion team in 1960, and in 1989 Jerry Jones purchased the team, in the same year that the Cowboys acquired quarterback Troy Aikman with the number one pick in the draft; Aikman would go on to play 12 consecutive seasons with the Cowboys, including leading them to three Super Bowl victories in 1992, 1993, and 1995. Jerry Jones purchased the Cowboys for US$140 million in 1989 and its value grew steadily through the 1990s and early 2000s. In 2005 the Cowboys were valued at approximately US$1 billion, but as the NFL signed larger broadcast rights agreements the value of all NFL teams, including the Cowboys, increased rapidly. The value of the Cowboys and other NFL teams is surprising given that the regular season in only 16 games long, with each team playing only 8 home games a year (compared to 41 in the NBA and 81 in Major League Baseball). The Cowboys play at AT&T Stadium in Arlington, Texas, which set the record for attendance at an NFL game when 105,121 attended a Cowboys game in 2009, the first year the stadium was open to the public.

Sources: Dallas Cowboys website at <www.dallascowboys.com>; Forbes website at <www.forbes.com>; NFL website at <www.nfl.com>

CIRCUITS OF PROMOTION

In order to describe and explain the interconnections between professional sport, the media, advertisers, and business, Whitson (1998) used the concept of 'circuits of promotion'. The key premise that underpins the circuit of promotion concept is that the boundaries between the promotion of sports and the use of sport events and athletes to promote products, which were previously separate, are now being dissolved. In other words, it is becoming increasingly more difficult to see where the sport organization ends and where the sponsor or media or advertiser begins. They are becoming (or have become) one, where one part of the professional sport machine serves to promote the other, for the good of itself and all the other constituent parts.

The relationship between Nike and former Chicago Bulls and Washington Wizards player Michael Jordan is a perfect example of a circuit of promotion at work. The Nike advertising campaigns that featured Jordan contributed to building the profile of both the company and the athlete, while Jordan's success in winning six NBA championships with the Bulls enhanced the corporate synergy between the two 'brands' and helped to increase the return on Nike's investment. Furthermore, the success of Jordan and the global advertising campaigns developed by Nike increased the cultural, social, and commercial profile of the National Basketball Association (NBA) in America. In turn, the global promotion and advertising by the NBA, that either did or did not feature Jordan, helped to promote both Jordan, as the league's most visible and recognizable player, and Nike, as a major manufacturer of basketball footwear and apparel, either by direct or indirect association. Lastly, any advertising undertaken by Jordan's other sponsors, such as Gatorade, served to promote Jordan, but also the NBA and Nike through their association with Jordan. At its best, a sporting circuit of promotion is one of continuous commercial benefit and endless leveraging opportunities for the athletes and organizations involved.

SPORT CIRCUITS

Sport circuits involve a league or structured competition. NASCAR has been one of the most popular sports in the United States for over 50 years. It is broadcast on the FOX and NBC television networks and stations (such as Fox Sports 1). Like some other professional sports such as the National Hockey League (NHL) in America, the Bundesliga in Germany, and the National Rugby League (NRL) in Australia, NASCAR operates on the basis of a seasonal calendar, with races in different American cities and towns each week, from

February through to November at race tracks such as the Texas Motor Speedway (Texas; 191,000 seating capacity), Daytona International Speedway (Florida; 168,000 seating capacity), and the Talladega Superspeedway (Alabama; 175,000 seating capacity). Scheduling races at different venues ensures good live attendances, but also enables NASCAR and its competing teams and drivers to capitalize on an array of sponsorship opportunities.

The European Champions League is an example of a global sport circuit that is based around a league model, whereby teams play in different cities depending on who qualifies for the tournament and teams are progressively knocked out until a winner is determined. The men's and women's professional tennis tours are examples of a global circuit in which a series of events represent the structured competition. Each event or tournament on the tour may be entered by ranked players (who may have qualified through a lesser 'satellite circuit'), who compete for prize money, as well as points that go towards an overall ranking to determine the world's best player. In both these cases, the circuit is managed or overseen by a governing body, although in the case of tennis the responsibility for managing and running individual tournaments is devolved to the host organization. For example, the Australian Open, the grand slam of the Asia-Pacific region, is managed and run by Tennis Australia, the sport's governing body in Australia.

The locations of events or tournaments that are part of national and global sport circuits are often flexible and cities or countries are able to bid for the right to host the event. In the case of the European Champions League the teams that qualify for the tournament are entitled to host their home games (a performance based flexibility), whereas in tennis the grand slam tournaments of the Australian Open, the U.S. Open, the French Open, and Wimbledon are the only marquee events (no flexibility). In other circuits, such as the World Rally Championship (WRC), the location of the events on the yearly calendar can change as cities and nations bid for the rights to host rounds. From 2014 to 2017 the WRC held a round in the European nation of Poland, which had only hosted two rounds in the previous 35 years. Similarly, Cyprus, Greece, and Turkey hosted rounds at various times between 2000 and 2014, but not in the 2017 season. Bidding for these types of events can often be very competitive, as cities and nations seek to secure the prestige, status, tourism, and potential economic benefit that are associated with popular global sport circuits.

The biggest global sport circuits are the Olympic Games and the FIFA World Cup, which are also the biggest events of any type staged in the world. Both events are held every four years and have a complex arrangement whereby countries and cities can bid to host the event. For a city to win the right to host the summer or winter Olympic Games it must go through a stringent two-phase selection process. In the first phase – the 'candidature acceptance procedure' – national Olympic committees may nominate a city, which is then evaluated during a 10-month process in which an International Olympic Committee (IOC) administrative committee examines each city based on technical criteria such as venue quality, general city infrastructure, public transport, security, and government support. Five cities applied to host the 2020 Olympic Games: Istanbul (Turkey), Tokyo (Japan), Baku (Azerbaijan), Doha (Qatar), and Madrid (Spain). Three cities were accepted as candidate cities: Tokyo, Istanbul, and Madrid. These cities were required to submit a comprehensive candidature file to the IOC and were visited by the IOC's evaluation commission. The evaluation commission's report on the candidate cities is made available to all IOC members, who subsequently elect a host for the Games at a full session of the

IOC (for the election of the 2020 Games the IOC session was held in Buenos Aires in September, 2013, at which it was announced that the Tokyo bid had been successful).

There are also global sport circuits in which participation in the event is dependent almost entirely on money, which situates them at the peak of the professional sport apex. Like the Olympic Games, the America's Cup is held every four years, but unlike the Olympic Games, a team can only enter if it has enough financial support to mount a challenge. For example, Oracle Team USA, the racing team which was formed in 2003 and won the 33rd and 34th America's Cups in 2010 and 2013 (but was defeated by Emirates Team New Zealand in 2017), is supported by Oracle, one of the world's largest software companies, which had revenues of US$37 billion in the 2016 fiscal year. It is estimated that Oracle's owner, Larry Ellison, spent $300 million on winning the Cup in 2013.

In practice 4.2 Women's Tennis Association

Founded in 1973, the Women's Tennis Association (WTA) is the peak body for women's professional tennis; its membership consists of more than 2,500 players who represent almost 100 nations. In 2017, these players competed for US$139 million in prize money across 55 events and four Grand Slams (Wimbledon, U.S. Open, French Open, and Australian Open), staged in 31 countries. Unlike sporting circuits such as Formula 1, which have 20 races that the same drivers and constructors compete in, the WTA essentially consists of a series of sporting circuits based on level of prize money and player ability/ranking.

Grand Slam

Each year the Grand Slam events are the Australian Open (January), the French Open (May–June), Wimbledon (July), and the U.S. Open (August–September). Each of these Grand Slams is conducted over a two-week period and nominally 104 of the top-ranked female tennis players in the world compete for the title, in addition to 24 players who qualify for the tournament by winning a qualifying tournament in the weeks leading up to the event, or who are given wild cards by the tournament organizers. Wimbledon, the French Open, and the U.S. Open all started towards the end of the 19th century, with the Australian Open first played in 1905. The so-called 'open era' of tennis began in 1968 when professionals were allowed to compete with amateurs in the Grand Slam events. In terms of the operations of the global tennis circuit, there is no flexibility in the location or scheduling of the four Grand Slams and no capacity for nations or cities to bid to host a Grand Slam, as there is in other sports.

WTA Finals and WTA Elite Trophy

The WTA Finals are held at the end of the season in Singapore, and the WTA Elite Trophy is held in the last week of the season in Zunhai (China). In 2017 the prize money for the WTA Finals was US$7 million, making it the most lucrative event after the four

Grand Slam events. Throughout the year players compete in WTA tournaments and Grand Slam events, earning ranking points as they do so. The top eight players in the world qualify for the WTA Finals, which is played as a round-robin event with two groups of four players. Unlike the Grand Slams, the WTA Finals has been played in a variety of countries since it was launched in 1972; prior to Singapore the Finals were played in Istanbul (Turkey) from 2011–2013, Doha (Qatar) from 2008–2010, Madrid (Spain) from 2006–2007, and Los Angeles (USA) from 2002–2005. The location of the WTA Finals is awarded through a competitive bidding process, which was won by Singapore for the period 2014 to 2018.

Premier Mandatory

In the 2017 WTA calendar there were four events in the 'premier mandatory' category that were staged in Indian Wells (USA), Miami (USA), Madrid (Spain), and Beijing (China). In comparison to the Australian Open Grand Slam, which offered more than US$16.5 million in prize money, these four premier mandatory events offered between US$5.4 million and US$6.99 million (i.e. less than the WTA Finals). The WTA is obliged to provide all 10 of the top 10 ranked female players in the world for these events, as well as all players who qualify by ranking for acceptance into the main draw. In this way, the WTA and the event organizers are able to ensure that the premier mandatory events are a success for tournament organizers, sponsors, and media. If seven or fewer of the top-ranked players play in the premier mandatory events, the WTA pays the tournament US$500,000 in compensation.

Premier 5

The Premier 5 events, of which there are five, are held in Dubai (United Arab Emirates), Rome (Italy), Toronto (Canada), Cincinnati (USA), and Wuhan (China). In 2017 the prize money for these events was between US$2.37 million and US$2.8 million. The WTA is obliged to provide 7 of the top 10 ranked female players in the world for these events. If four or fewer of the top-ranked players play in the premier mandatory events, the WTA pays the tournament US$350,000 in compensation.

Premier 700

The Premier 700 events, of which there are 12, are held in Australia (2), Russia (2), Qatar (1), Germany (1), United States (3), Great Britain (2), and Japan (1). In 2017, the prize money for these events ranged from US$710,000 to US$890,000, but unlike the premier mandatory and premier events, the premier 700 events are not entitled to any level of player commitment from the WTA.

There are also 32 'International' events and seven '125K Series' events held all over the world each year.

Sources: WTA website at <www.wtatennis.com>

MEDIA

Media organizations have become essential partners for professional and nonprofit sport organizations alike. The breadth and depth of coverage that media organizations provide their professional sporting partners is of such significance that it has the capacity to influence the social and commercial practices of millions, if not billions, of people. The scale and scope of the financial relationship they enjoy are also important, so much so that sport and the media are often regarded as interdependent (Bellamy 1998; Nicholson 2015). The impact of sport news on the popularity and profitability of new media forms has only been equalled by the transformation that sport has undergone as a result of its interplay with the media. It might have been possible in the 1890s to think about sport and its social and commercial relevance without reference to the media, but by the 1990s the task was impossible. It is now as if "one is literally unthinkable without the other" (Rowe 1999, p. 13).

Whereas sport organizations once relied on ticket sales as their primary source of income, they now rely on the sale of broadcast rights (and to a lesser extent sponsorship revenue). For example, in 1930, 85% of FIFA's income was derived from ticket sales and subscriptions from its member associations, yet at the beginning of the 21st century these revenue sources are dwarfed by broadcasting and marketing. During the period 2007 to 2010, FIFA's revenue was US$4,189 million, of which the 2010 World Cup in South Africa provided US$2,408 million in television broadcast rights, and US$1,072 in marketing rights, which were largely dependent on media coverage. During the period 2011 to 2014, FIFA's revenue grew to US$5,718 million, of which US$5,137 was classed as event-related revenue; US$2,484 was from the sale of television broadcast rights and US$1,629 million from the sale of marketing rights. Clearly, sport is effective in attracting both audiences and advertisers. Importantly, the relationship between professional sport and the media has reached a point where professional sport would not survive in its current form without the media. More information about the relationship between sport and the media is provided in the media chapter of this book.

SPONSORSHIP

The amount of money available to professional sport organizations through sponsorship arrangements or deals is directly related to the return on investment that the sponsor is able to achieve. In broad terms, the return on investment is dependent on an increase in sales or business, which a sponsor achieves through increased awareness or direct marketing. Sport organizations with large supporter bases, such as Manchester United, are able to secure significant sponsorship deals because the sponsor is able to market its product directly to a large number of supporters, as well as increase its awareness through media coverage of the club and the league. Sport organizations with global, regional, or strong national profiles have a distinct advantage in the sponsorship market.

Sponsors want to be involved with a club or league that has very good network television coverage, which reaches a broad audience. This is most often achieved through exclusive broadcast rights arrangements. However, the general 'news' media coverage that a club or league receives in a variety of media forms and outlets, including television, radio, newspapers, magazines, and the Internet, can also influence its attractiveness to sponsors. This media coverage promotes the club or league and generally encourages fans to consume the sport, either by attending the game live or by accessing a mediated version. The club or league that is able to attract a greater amount of this 'news' media coverage is more likely to be embedded in the commercial consciousness of audiences and consumers. Thus, the amount of media coverage received is a measure of the audiences that can be reached by advertisers (or sponsors) through a commercial association with a professional sporting club or league and is directly proportional to the worth of the sponsorship.

The value of sponsorships differs between sports, between leagues, between clubs, and across countries. At the highest level the IOC created 'The Olympic Partner Program' (TOP) in 1985 in order to provide companies with exclusive worldwide marketing rights to the Games. The Top VIII partnership program, which included the 2014 Winter Olympic Games in Sochi and the 2016 Olympic Games in Rio de Janeiro, comprised the following companies: Coca-Cola, Atos, Bridgestone, Dow, GE, McDonalds, Omega, Panasonic, P&G, Samsung, and Visa. TOP I, from 1985 to 1988, raised US$96 million in revenue for the IOC, which increased to US$579 million for TOP IV, from 1997 to 2000, and to US$1,003 million for TOP VIII, which represented 18% of IOC revenue during the period 2013–2016. At other levels of professional sport the sponsorship or marketing arrangements may go further, as clubs and leagues are willing to enter into sponsorship arrangements whereby commercial organizations are able to acquire naming rights or enter into arrangements that give them either exclusive or increased access to fans. The development of the Internet and online marketing has been particularly instrumental in this respect.

The English Premier League (EPL) provides an example of the proliferation of sponsors within professional sport leagues and clubs. EA Sports, the maker of video games such as the popular FIFA and Madden NFL products, is the 'Lead Partner'; Barclays Bank, a United Kingdom–based financial services group engaged in banking, investment banking, and investment management, is the 'Official Bank' and prior to the 2017/2018 season was the naming rights sponsor of the league for 15 years; confectionary company Cadbury is the 'Official Snack' of the EPL; Carling is the 'Official Beer'; global sports brand Nike provides the 'Official Ball'; and watchmaker Tag Heuer is the 'Official Timekeeper'. Furthermore, the clubs that play in the Barclays Premiership have significant sponsorship deals. The primary sponsor of each club is entitled to place its brand prominently on the front of the playing strip: Arsenal is sponsored by Emirates, one of the world's leading airlines (previous sponsors of Chelsea), and Puma, a global sports brand; Manchester City is sponsored by Etihad, another of the world's airlines and competitor to Emirates; Chelsea is sponsored by Yokohama Tyres, a Japanese tyre manufacturer; Liverpool is sponsored by Standard Chartered, a bank; Everton is been sponsored by SportPesa, a Kenyan gaming company; and Tottenham Hotspur is sponsored by AIA, a pan-Asian life insurance company based in Hong Kong.

Like broadcast rights revenue, sponsorship revenue within professional sport has grown exponentially. In the early 1960s, NASCAR driver Fred Lorenzen's sponsorship, from a Ford dealership, was US$6,000 for an entire season. By the late 1980s, it was estimated that approximately US$3 million in sponsorship was required for a NASCAR team to break even over the course of the season. In 2000 UPS announced its sponsorship of the Robert Yates No. 88 team driven by Dale Jarrett, which was estimated to be worth US$15 million per year. The cost of sponsoring an elite NASCAR team is now between US$20–30 million per year.

The sponsorship of professional sport goes further than commercial agreements between clubs and leagues. Individual athletes also have sponsorship agreements that provide them with additional income to supplement their playing contracts (for team sports) or prize money (for individuals). Well-chosen brands with a global profile can enhance an athlete's overall image and in the case of more popular athletes a sponsor can establish the athlete as a brand in their own right. Sponsorship of professional athletes is not restricted to superstar athletes like David Beckham (formerly of football teams Manchester United, Los Angeles Galaxy, Real Madrid, and Paris Saint-Germain), Tiger Woods (golf), or Kobe Bryant of the Los Angeles Lakers (basketball). Rather, sponsorship of professional athletes exists wherever there is a market, whether it a mass market in the case of global athletes or a niche market in the case of small or cult sports.

PLAYER MANAGEMENT

As sport has become increasingly professional and the amount of money secured through broadcast rights and sponsorship deals has increased, the salaries of players and athletes have also increased. The growth in player and athlete income has been mirrored by a concurrent rise in the expectations of clubs and leagues, an increase in the complexity of contract negotiations and greater off-field commercial opportunities for prominent 'sport stars'. These developments in the world of professional sport have led to the evolution of an industry focussed on player and athlete management, which is essentially geared towards providing players and athletes with services in return for a share of their income.

One of the most prominent player and athlete management companies is the International Management Group (IMG), which was formed in the 1960s and employs in excess of 2,000 staff in 70 offices in 30 countries. What began exclusively as a player management business has evolved into a complex commercial operation that includes television and publishing divisions. Golfer Arnold Palmer, winner of the U.S. Masters golf tournament in 1958, 1960, 1962, and 1964, the U.S. Open in 1960, and the British Open in 1961 and 1962, was the first athlete in the world to be branded by Mark McCormack, the creator and head of IMG. Back in the 1960s the 'brand-name' principle by which Palmer and McCormack approached sport was the first attempt to transform the business activities of leading athletes. Sport and business were previously related, but the scale of their operation was unique. The level of vertical and horizontal integration was essential to what became known as 'Sportsbiz' (Boyle and Haynes 2000). McCormack took the relationship of the agent further than before, and began to handle contract negotiations, proactively sought business opportunities, and planned the sale of the Palmer brand on a long-term basis, rather than previous attempts that might be characterized as ad hoc. McCormack set an important precedent by selling people as marketable commodities.

Octagon is a global sport marketing company and competitor to IMG. It represents and promotes more than 800 athletes in 35 different sports across the world. Octagon provides a broad range of services for the athletes it manages, including the following:

- Contract negotiations
- Marketing initiatives and endorsements
- Public relations and charity involvement
- Financial planning
- Media management
- Property development
- Speaking engagements

Octagon claims that it generates annual marketing revenues of in excess of US$300 million by maximizing its athletes' off-field corporate relationships. The company states that it does this by developing a unique and individual marketing plan for each of its athletes. Octagon represents American swimmer Michael Phelps, winner of the most Olympic medals of all time (28), including 23 gold medals (6 in 2004 at Athens, 8 in 2008 at Beijing, 4 in 2012 at London, and 5 in 2016 at Rio). The company claims Phelps is a perfect case study in what successful sport marketing and management can provide for an athlete in the contemporary hyper-commercial sport environment. Octagon suggests that Phelps laid the foundation with his performances in the pool, but that Octagon enhanced the Phelps story with a targeted publicity campaign, which included appearances in *Time*, *People*, the *Wall Street Journal*, and *USA Today*. The result was what Octagon claims to be the creation of a connection between Phelps and corporate America, including the largest-ever endorsement deal in swimming with Speedo and subsidiary deals with Visa, Omega, and AT&T Wireless.

In many respects, athletes competing in individual sports are logical targets for both agents and sponsors; however, athletes in team sports are often as valuable, if not more so, particularly because they play often (weekly or more regularly) and in many cases across very long seasons (e.g. the English Premier League or the National Basketball Association and Major League Baseball in North America). High-profile team athletes who have the ability to attract significant media and endorsements, such as Le Bron James of the Cleveland Cavaliers, are extraordinarily valuable. These athletes' play on the field is at the highest level, they help to bring fans to the game, help the team to secure broadcast contracts or sponsorships deals, help the team in merchandising and licensing, and have the potential to increase the net financial worth of the organization. Thus, an athlete's commercial potential can be calculated in individual earnings (through the team or an agent), but also in terms of the growth of the club or league of which they are a part.

Professional sport stars are well paid by any measures. Importantly, their salaries are relative to revenue of the clubs, leagues, tournaments, and events of which they are a part. In fact, in some professional sports with strong player unions, the level of remuneration for players is set as a percentage of league revenue. Table 4.2 is an estimate of the highest-paid football/soccer players in the world in 2017. Their annual earnings are indicative of their on-field worth and the significant investment made by their respective teams, as well as their commercial worth off the field. Until 2014 David Beckham was by far the

TABLE 4.2 Highest value football/soccer players 2017

Player	Team	Annual Earnings (US$)
Cristiano Ronaldo	Real Madrid	93,000,000
Lionel Messi	Barcelona	80,000,000
Neymar Jr	Barcelona	37,000,000
Gareth Bale	Real Madrid	34,000,000
Zlatan Ibrahimovic	Manchester United	32,000,000
Wayne Rooney	Manchester United	23,600,000
Luis Suarez	Barcelona	23,300,000
Sergio Aguero	Manchester City	22,600,000
James Rodriguez	Real Madrid	21,900,000
Paul Pogba	Manchester United	21,200,000

Adapted from: www.forbes.com

world's highest-paid soccer player, with annual earnings of US$50 million, but since his retirement Cristiano Ronaldo and Lionel Messi, both of who play in Spain's La Liga, have taken over as the highest-paid and best-known football/soccer players in the world.

In practice 4.3 Be like Mike

Michael Jordan is perhaps the most famous basketball player of all time, winning 6 NBA championships with the Chicago Bulls between 1991–1993 and 1996–1998, including the finals MVP in each of the championship years, 5 League MVP awards, and 10 league scoring titles. Jordan retired from basketball after his third NBA championship in 1993 in an attempt to play professional baseball, then retired again after his sixth championship in 1998, prior to returning briefly for a two-year career with the Washington Wizards. Jordan also won two gold medals with Team USA at the 1984 and 1992 Olympic Games, the first time as a college player and the second time as part of the celebrated 'Dream Team' that included Magic Johnson and Larry Bird. Continuing his influence on basketball in retirement, Jordan is now the majority owner of the Charlotte Hornets. His most significant influence, however, might not be his exploits on the court, but rather his relationship with Nike, which began in 1984 and has been an extraordinary commercial success.

Famous for its iconic swoosh logo, Nike is a global sports brand with a mission to 'bring inspiration and innovation to every athlete in the world' (they note that if you have a body, you are an athlete, meaning that this inspiration and innovation extends to everyone living on planet Earth). In its 2015 annual report, Nike reports that it focuses its business in eight key areas: running, basketball, football (soccer), men's training, women's training, action sports, sportswear (sport-inspired lifestyle products), and golf. The basketball offerings include the 'Jordan Brand', which "designs, distributes and licenses athletic and casual footwear, apparel and accessories predominantly focussed on Basketball using the Jumpman trademark". In 2015, Nike's revenue was US$30.6 billion, of which US$18.3 million was in footwear, US$8.6 million in apparel, and US$1.6 billion in equipment. Of the eight key business areas, sportswear was US$6.6 billion, running US$4.9 billion, and basketball US$3.7 billion.

In its 1984 annual report, a year in which its revenue was US$919 million and it signed Jordan, Nike wrote that "extensive promotional programs, tailored for each sport, are aimed at having athletes wear NIKE products. Shoes and equipment are provided to outstanding athletes and teams, athletes are hired as consultants, and product endorsements are obtained from leading professional athletes". Upon signing Jordan, Nike made the first Air Jordan shoes, which reportedly made the company US$70 million in their first two months on the market. Since then, Nike has employed a very successful strategy of using athletes to endorse its products, although the scale of its operations in this area grew exponentially during the 1980s, 1990s, and into the 21st century. According to the 2015 annual report, the payments due to athletes, teams, and leagues as part of endorsement contracts was US$1 billion in 2016, US$919 million in 2017, US$882 million in 2018, US$706 million in 2019, and US$533 million in 2020, although the figures for 2017 and beyond are likely to exceed US$1 billion as contracts are renewed and new athletes and teams signed. In 2017, Nike was sponsoring the following athletes (including four of the top five in *Forbes* 2017 list of the highest-paid athletes):

- LeBron James
- Cristiano Ronaldo
- Kevin Durant
- Tiger Woods
- Roger Federer
- Neymer Jr
- Rafael Nadal

Both James and Ronaldo have followed in Jordan's footsteps, signing 'lifetime' endorsement deals with Nike, a marker of their on-field success, global popularity, and media saturation.

Sources: Nike website at <www.nike.com>

OWNERSHIP AND OUTCOMES

Professional sports utilize different ownership and governance models in order to regulate and manage their businesses effectively. Some of the models have strong historical traditions, whereas others have been selected or adapted for their utility. One of the key distinctions is between professional sport teams and leagues that can be considered 'profit maximizers' and those that are 'win maximizers'. There is some debate as to whether these terms accurately reflect the practice of professional sport teams and franchises, but they are useful for broadly categorizing operational and financial priorities. Profit-maximizing teams, such as those in the major American professional sport leagues, are typically owned by individuals or businesses who seek to maximize the financial return on investment. In some sports, however, such as English, Scottish, and Australian football and cricket (Quirk and Fort 1992), the need to win is a greater priority than the need to make a profit. In fact, in some instances win-maximizing teams will place the club in financial jeopardy, particularly by purchasing players they cannot afford.

In some cases, the ownership model has adapted to meet specific conditions brought about by commercial change. In the J-League, Japan's professional football (soccer) competition, teams like the Kashiwa Reysol are privately owned. The Reysol is owned by the Hitachi corporation that specializes in the manufacturing of electrical goods and equipment. Originally established as an amateur team of the Hitachi corporation, the Reysol was professionalized in order to participate in the inaugural J-League season in 1993.

Whether teams are win maximizing or profit maximizing, they must cooperate with each other at some level to ensure that fans, sponsors, and the media remain interested and involved with the sport. Sport leagues that are dominated by one or two teams are often perceived to be less attractive to fans than leagues in which the result of games is uncertain. There is, however, a long history of leagues in which strong rivalries have maintained interest in the game (Los Angeles Lakers versus Boston Celtics in the NBA and Rangers versus Celtic in the Scottish Premier League, for example), although often the teams that are part of the rivalry benefit at the expense of teams that perform poorly. A league that is not dominated by only a couple of teams and in which there is an uncertainty of outcome (of a game or season) is said to have 'competitive balance' (Quirk and Fort 1992). Leagues across the world have instituted a range of measures to try to achieve competitive balance, which is often elusive. Perhaps the most obvious and publicized measure is the draft system that operates in football leagues such as the National Football League in America or the Australian Football League. The draft allows the league to allocate higher draft preferences (the best athletes on offer) to poorer performed teams, in order to equalize the playing talent across the league and create more competitive games.

SUMMARY

This chapter has presented an overview of professional sport and some of the central relationships that are essential to its ongoing prosperity and survival. The media, sponsors, agents, owners, advertisers, leagues, clubs, and athletes are part of a self-sustaining commercial alliance, in which each of the partners promotes and supports the activities and interests of the others. Commercial networks are the binding forces that are holding professional sport together in the 21st century. Since the middle of the 20th century, professional sport leagues and clubs have increasingly become willing partners in the promotion of their activities (sports and events), as well as the promotion of subsidiary products and services, and in the process have become major players in a multi-billion-dollar industry.

REVIEW QUESTIONS

1 Use the circuit of promotion concept to explain the role of sponsors and the media in the professional sport industry.

2 Explain the rationale behind a company sponsoring a professional sport club, league, or athlete.

3 Is the media important to the survival of professional sport? Why?

4 Identify an international and a domestic professional circuit and examine its operation. What are the special features that attract fans and media?

5 Choose a professional sport league and identify the fees paid by television broadcasters over the previous 20 years for the broadcast rights. Has it increased or decreased over the period? Explain why.

6 Choose a sport in which the location of events or tournaments is not fixed. Imagine that the city you live in is going to bid for the right to host the event and create a list of potential benefits – consider such features as the economy, environment, transportation, public services, and housing.

7 Choose a high-profile athlete and identify what companies or products sponsor the athlete. Is the athlete presented by an agent, or did they secure the sponsorships or endorsements themselves?

8 Choose a sporting league of the world and identify whether it should be classified as 'win maximizing' or 'profit maximizing'. Provide a rationale for your answer that includes a commentary on the ownership of teams in the league.

9 Create a list of the top five paid sportspeople in the world. What does the list tell you about the size of the commercial markets that the sports are played in and the popularity of the sports?

10 Create a fictional international sport circuit. What cities of the world would host your events and why?

DISCUSSION QUESTIONS

1 Does the diversification of media, and the increasing importance of social and digital media, mean that sports outside the football codes will have opportunity for more

growth and might challenge the dominance of football in terms of popularity and profit? Why?

2   Does the circuit of promotion concept work for all levels of sport, or does it only apply to high-level professional leagues and athletes? Why might this be the case?

3   Some sport circuits have been criticized because of the amount of money that cities and nations have to pay to gain entry or access to the circuit. Are these circuits worth the money that cities and nations invest, and what criteria might be used to make such a determination?

4   Companies and businesses previously paid sport organizations to have their name attached to a league, team, or athlete, which was called 'sponsorship'. Contemporary professional sport appears to have transitioned to 'partnerships', in which the relationship is about much more than simply associating one organization or brand with the other. What are the ways in which sport and business now partner to gain mutual benefit?

5   Many of the world's highest-profile football teams are owned by some of the richest people in the world. Why do these people want to invest in sport, and what are the implications of having a collection of the world's richest people owning sport teams, which are often concentrated in a selection of high-profile leagues?

FURTHER READING

Bellamy, R. (1998). The evolving television sports marketplace, in L. Wenner (ed). *MediaSport*. London: Routledge, pp. 73–87.

Boyle, R. and Haynes, R. (2000). *Power Play: Sport, the Media and Popular Culture*. London: Longman.

Cousens, L. and Slack, T. (2005). Field-Level Change: The Case of North American Major League Professional Sport. *Journal of Sport Management*, 19(1): 13–42.

Euchner, C. (1993). *Playing the Field: Why Sports Teams Move and Cities Fight to Keep Them*. Baltimore: John Hopkins University Press.

Fielding, L., Miller, L. and Brown, J. (1999). Harlem Globetrotters International, Inc. *Journal of Sport Management*, 13(1): 45–77.

Nicholson, M., Kerr, A. and Sherwood, M. (2015). *Sport and the Media: Managing the Nexus*. 2nd ed. London: Elsevier Butterworth-Heinemann.

O'Brien, D. and Slack, T. (2003). An analysis of change in an organizational field: The professionalization of English Rugby Union. *Journal of Sport Management*, 17(4): 417–448.

Shropshire, K. (1995). *The Sports Franchise Game*. Philadelphia: University of Pennsylvania Press.

Smith, A.C.T. and Stewart, B. (2015). *Introduction to Sport Marketing*. 2nd ed. Oxon: Routledge.

Stewart, B. (ed.) (2007). *The Games Are Not the Same: The Political Economy of Australian Football*. Melbourne: Melbourne University Press.

Wenner, L. and Billings, A. (eds) (2017). *Sport, Media and Mega-Events*. Oxon: Routledge.

RELEVANT WEBSITES

Americas
National Football League – www.nfl.com
National Basketball Association – www.nba.com
Women's National Basketball Association – www.wnba.com
Major League Baseball – www.mlb.com
National Hockey League – www.nhl.com
Ultimate Fighting Championship – www.ufc.com
NASCAR – www.nascar.com
Professional Golfers' Association – www.pga.com
Ladies Professional Golf Association – www.lpga.com

Australia and New Zealand
Australian Football League – www.afl.com.au
Cricket Australia – www.cricket.com.au
National Rugby League – www.nrl.com
Super 15 Rugby Union – www.superxv.com

Great Britain
English Premier League – www.premierleague.com
British Rugby League – www.superleague.co.uk/

Asia
J-League – www.j-league.or.jp/eng/
Japanese Sumo Association – http:// www.sumo.or.jp/en/
Chinese Professional Baseball League – www.cpbl.com.tw/html/english/cpbl.asp

Europe
European Champions League – www.uefa.com/
Serie A (Italy) – www.legaseriea.it
La Liga – www.lfp.es/en
Bundesliga (Germany) – www.bundesliga.de
European Professional Golfers' Association Tour – www.europeantour.com

Global
Olympics – www.olympic.org
World Cup – www.fifa.com
America's Cup – www.americascup.com
Tour de France – www.letour.fr/indexus.html
Formula One – www.formula1.com
Association of Surfing Professionals – www.aspworldtour.com
Association of Tennis Professionals (men) – www.atptennis.com/en
Women's Tennis Association – www.wtatour.com/
World Rally Championship – www.wrc.com

Take one big breath: the Pro Kabaddi League

This case explores the organization and operations of the Pro Kabaddi League (PKL), based in India. India is known internationally as a great cricketing nation; cricket is the national sport and has one of the largest participation levels in the world, which is not surprising given its ever expanding population, which in 2017 was just over 1.2 billion people. As a point of reference, two other cricketing nations, Great Britain and Australia, have populations of just under 60 million and 24 million, respectively. Despite the huge success of cricket tournaments such as the Indian Premier League and the individual popularity of individual cricketers such as Sachin Tendulkar and Virat Kholi, which appears to dwarf all other competitors, there is room in India for other professional sports. One of these sports is not only played at the community level, but is also now played at the highest professional level. But, unlike cricket, it does not have a strong international presence, having confined itself to the Indian sub-continent and surrounding regions. The game is called Kabaddi and it has managed to transform itself from a popular, but mainly regional, game into one that now supports a massively popular professional sports league.

Kabaddi is a high-intensity, contact team sport. It is played by seven players on each side over two 20-minute halves, with a five-minute half-time break. The two teams each occupy a half of the court, and the purpose of the game is to score points by having the offensive team's players 'raid' the opposing team's court and touch as many defensive players as possible without getting caught. Points are scored by the touching of the opposition players. In addition, the game also demands that this incursion is enacted while the raider takes only a single breath. In order to demonstrate to the referee that they have not inhaled a second breath, the raider will chant 'kabaddi, kabaddi, kabaddi', as they charge into the opponent's court and try to touch the opponent closest to them, while all seven members of the opposing team will aim to catch and restrain the attacker.

Players on the defensive side are called 'antis' and players in the offence are called 'raiders'. Any antis touched by raiders during an attack are declared 'out' and sent off the field of play. In addition, raiders who are caught are also outed. A point is earned if a raiding team member manages to touch an opposing team member and return to the home half without being caught, all while taking only a single breath. If, however, a raider is tackled and prevented from returning home, the opposing team earns the point. The team with the most points at the end of the game wins.

This 'game of struggle', as it is often called by Indian 'locals', has its origins in the playing out of inter-tribal rivalries in traditional Indian societies. Today, of course, it is a fiercely competitive sport which requires speed and agility to perform at the highest level. It also supported by a strong administrative infrastructure which had its beginnings in the formation of the All India Kabaddi Federation in 1950 to manage the coordination and promotion of the game. The Senior National Championship commenced in 1952, and a new national governing body, the Amateur Kabaddi Federation of India (AKFI) was established in 1972. AKFI subsequently affiliated with the Indian Olympic Association (IOA) with a view to popularizing the game in India and neighbouring countries of Asia, and securing its international credibility. This led to the establishment of national-level competitions for junior boys and girls and the Federation Cup, an elite competition for men and women.

Kabaddi became a regular sports discipline at the 1990 Asian Games, where India won a gold medal. The Indian Kabaddi team also secured gold medals at each succeeding Asian Games: Hiroshima 1994, Bangkok 1998, Busan 2002, Doha 2006, Guangzhou 2010, and Incheon 2014. Kabaddi also established a global presence, played not only in south East Asia, but also in Europe and North America.

Although Kabaddi was traditionally viewed as an amateur sport and the game embedded in the rural regions of India, this all changed in 2014, when a professional league centred in India was established. The Pro Kabaddi league (PKL), modelled on the highly successful Indian Premier League (IPL) of Twenty20 cricket, was established by Marshal Sports, which entered into an agreement with the Kabaddi Federation, with a focus on popularist marketing and saturation television broadcasting. PKL secured the backing of local Indian broadcaster *Star Sports*, and, like most commercialized sports, the rules and presentation of the game were changed to make it more suitable for television audiences. For example, by contrast to traditional amateur kabaddi – which was played in a rectangular court – PKL-style kabaddi is played inside a circular playing area as a way of giving the game even greater focus and intensity.

The league began in 2014 with a season that lasted five weeks between July and August, following the intensive format of cricket cousin the IPL, which was repeated in 2015. In 2016, as a result of the popularity of the league and a desire to further expand, the PKL was offered as two seasons of five weeks, one during January and February and one in June and July. From 2014 to 2016 the PKL featured the following eight teams:

- Bengal Warriors (Kolkata)
- Bengalaru Bulls (Bengalaru)
- Dabang Dehli (Dehli)
- Jaipur Pink Panthers (Jaipur)
- Patna Pirates (Patna)
- Puneri Paltan (Pune)
- Telegu Titals (Hyderabad)
- U Mumba (Mumbai)

In season 5 of the PKL in 2017, the league was expanded to 12 teams, with the following four expansion teams added:

- Gujarat Fortunegiants (Ahmedabad)
- UP Yoddha (Lucknow)

- Tamil Thalaivas (Chennai)
- Haryana Steelers (Haryana)

Like the IPL, players are purchased by the teams in an auction. The most expensive player purchased at the auction was Nitin Tomar, who will play for the new franchise UP Yoddha; Tomar was purchased for the US$145,000. Like the IPL, there are also international players in the PKL, with South Korean Jang Kun Lee the most expensive import for the 2017 season. In the first season of PKL in 2014 the league had no sponsors, whereas only three years later in 2017 the league has nine sponsors, including title sponsor Vivo, as well as associate sponsors such as Gillette, TVS Motors, Bajaj Electricals, Indo Nissan, and Castrol. The increasing popularity of the PKL resulted in Star India purchasing a 74% stake in Marshal Sports in 2015, meaning that they are the majority owner of the league.

Unlike many professional sporting leagues around the world in which teams play a series of home and away games or matches, the PKL has a somewhat unusual caravan or circus format, in which all the teams travel to each of the team locations. For the 2014–2016 seasons this meant that all eight teams would travel together to all eight locations over the course of the season. For the 2017 season, in which there was an expanded format of 12 teams, the teams were divided into zone A and B, which matches played from late July until late October. The season started in Hyderabad, at the Gachibowli Indoor Stadium, the home of the Telugu Titans, with 11 matches conducted over the course of a week. This caravan or circus format means that the entire league travels to different regions of India, and the resources required to stage, promote, and market the matches are concentrated. This format works particularly well for a league in relative infancy, attempting to ensure the long-term financial viability of the teams involved. Were the season to be played like other professional leagues, the teams and the league could be crippled by the costs of travel, as well as the need to stage and promote matches in six different locations every three to four days.

CASE STUDY QUESTIONS

1   What are the positives and negatives of the caravan or circus format of a league as identified in the case?

2   Are there other leagues in the world that could adopt the caravan or circus model? Which ones and why?

3   Explore the broadcast ratings for the PKL and compare these to the IPL. What does this tell you about the popularity of the PKL, and do you think that the players are underpaid relative to the IPL?

4   What does the process of professionalizing Kabaddi suggest are the underpinning commercial requirements for a viable sports league?

Sources: Pro Kabaddi website at <www.prokabaddi.com>

CASE STUDY 4.2

The kings of Cleveland and Jamaica: LeBron James and Usain Bolt

This case explores two of the most prominent athletes in world sport, LeBron James and Usain Bolt, one from a team sport, basketball, and the other an individual competitor in athletics. The 'circuit of promotion' concept referred to in the chapter explains the ways in which media, sponsors, athletes, teams, and leagues are intertwined, and in particular, that these 'actors' have intersecting commercial interests. James and Bolt, both of whom have huge global reach, have not only accumulated significant personal wealth for themselves, but have also delivered significant benefits to the other actors in their 'circuit'. It is, in effect, a win-win situation where each member of the circuit of promotion benefits from the other. However, the nature of their relationships with the other partners in their circuit, and the circuits themselves, are not the same. The most obvious difference, as noted earlier, is that James is a team athlete who plays basketball, whereas Bolt is an individual athlete who is a track sprinter. Additionally, James plays in a sports league with a massive global audience throughout the season, whereas Bolt, apart from the Olympic Games and, to a lesser extent, the World Athletic Championships, participates in track and field meetings that have significantly smaller audiences.

LeBron James is a professional basketball player, who plays with the Cleveland Cavaliers in the National Basketball Association (NBA). The NBA consists of 30 teams, 29 of which are located in the United States and one of which is located in Canada. The NBA is split into the Eastern and Western conferences, and each conference is split further into three divisions. James and the Cavaliers play in the Central division of the Eastern conference. James has won three NBA championships, two with the Miami Heat and one with the Cavaliers, and four NBA most valuable player awards. James played for the Cavaliers from 2003 to 2010, winning two of his NBA MVP awards in the final two seasons. In 2010 James became an unrestricted free agent, which led him to being courted by a range of teams in the NBA and culminated in a live ESPN special titled 'The Decision', in which James announced he would be joining Miami. In response, Cavaliers' owner Dan Gilbert published an open letter to Cavaliers' fans in which he wrote:

> As you know, our former hero, who grew up in the very region that he deserted this evening, is no longer a Cleveland Cavalier. This was announced with a several day, narcissistic, self-promotional build-up culminating with a national TV special of his 'decision' unlike anything ever 'witnessed' in the history of sports and probably the history or entertainment.

He went on to reference a "cowardly betrayal", a "shameful display of selfishness", and a "shocking act of disloyalty". It is clear that Gilbert was hurt by James' decision, but he was correct in identifying that there had not been anything like 'The Decision' in sport previously, made possible by James' play on the court, but also his significant appeal off the court, which has made him one of the most recognizable athletes in world sport. In a twist, James became a free agent after four years with the Heat and chose to go back to Cleveland. In an essay explaining his decision, this time published in *Sports Illustrated*, James wrote that "the letter from Dan Gilbert, the booing of Cleveland fans, the jerseys being burned" had been hard on his family and that he had met with Gilbert "face-to-face, man-to-man" and that they had "talked it out". Although James wrote in the essay that he was not promising a championship in Cleveland, he delivered for the city and its fans. James led the Cavaliers to three NBA Finals in a row in the 2014–2015, 2015–2016 and 2016–2017 seasons, winning in 2015–2016 and losing on the other two occasions to the Golden State Warriors.

James' achievements on the court for the Cavaliers (and prior to that, the Miami Heat for four seasons) have resulted in a significant global public profile, media coverage, product endorsements, personal sponsorships, and a range of business ventures. In 2016 it was reported that James had re-signed with the Cleveland Cavaliers, on a three-year contract worth US$100 million, and that in the third year of the deal he would receive the highest single season salary in the history of the League. According to *Forbes*, James is the second highest earning athlete in world sport, behind Real Madrid and Portuguese superstar Cristiano Ronaldo, with salary of US$31.2 million per year and endorsements of US$55 million per year. Global footwear and clothing company Nike is a major sponsor, and James has also been sponsored by major brands such as Coca-Cola, McDonalds, Samsung, Intel, and KIA Motors. At the end of 2015 it was reported that James and Nike had signed a lifetime endorsement agreement, similar to the best basketball player of all time, Michael Jordan, and it was speculated that this was worth more the US$30 million per year.

James' off-court endorsements can in part be explained by his significant social media presence, but also the interaction between himself, the Cavaliers, the NBA, and Nike in the James circuit of promotion. In 2016, it was estimated that a LeBron James tweet on Twitter was worth US$165,000, or more than US$1,000 per character, assuming each of the 140 possible characters is used. In 2017, the following figures were evident on Facebook and Twitter, which indicate why LeBron James is such an important commercial property for the NBA, Cavaliers, and Nike, the reach of which are unable to compete with James on social media:

- James has 37.3 million followers on Twitter (@KingJames), the 24th most popular Twitter handle in the world, with an average of 14,000 new followers every day

- The NBA has 26 million followers on Twitter (@NBA), the 50th most popular Twitter handle in the world
- Nike has 7.11 million followers on Twitter
- The Cavaliers has 2.39 million followers on Twitter
- James has more than 23 million likes on his Facebook page
- The NBA has 34 million likes on its Facebook page
- The Cavaliers has 9 million likes on its Facebook page
- Nike has almost 29 million likes on its Facebook page

Usain Bolt, a Jamaican, is also a professional athlete. He is a sprinter who runs predominately 100-metre and 200-metre events and is recognized as the greatest short-distance runner in track and field history. He rose to prominence in July 2002 at the IAAF World Junior Track and Field Championships in Kingston, Jamaica, when he won the host nation's only individual gold medal, winning the 200 m in 20.61 seconds. Bolt went on to win two IAAF Rising Star awards, but like many young sporting prodigies, his career was slowed down by injuries. In 2004, soon after breaking the Word Junior Record in the 200 m with a time of 19.93 seconds, he suffered a severe hamstring tear, which effectively put his career on hold for the next two years. He realized his massive potential in 2007 when he broke the 30-year-old Jamaican 200-m record, with a time of 19.75, seconds before travelling to the 2007 IAAF World Track and Field Championships in Osaka, where he won two silver medals in the 200 m and 4 × 100 m relay.

According to the Usain Bolt website, Bolt is "arguably the most naturally gifted athlete the world has ever seen", and his record from 2008 to 2016 gives credence to the claim. At the 2008 Olympic Games in Beijing, Bolt won three gold medals in the 100 m, 200 m, and the 4 × 100 m relay. In all three events he (and his teammates in the relay) broke the world record. At the 2012 Olympic Games in London Bolt repeated the feat, with another three gold medals, and at almost 30 years of age did it again at the 2016 Olympic Games in Rio. Bolt's six individual Olympic Games sprint gold medals was a feat that had never been achieved before and is likely never to be achieved again. In addition to his highly successful Olympic campaigns, Bolt won multiple gold medals in the IAAF World Track and Field Championships, in Berlin in 2009 (three gold medals in the 100 m, 200 m, and 4 × 100 m relay), in Daegu in 2011 (won two gold medals after he was sensationally disqualified in the 100 m), in Moscow in 2013 (three gold medals), and Beijing in 2015 (three gold medals). In 2017 Bolt announced that the IAAF World Track and Field Championships in London in 2017 would be his final competitive event. As of 2017, Bolt held world records in the 100 m (9.58 seconds), 200 m (19.19 seconds), and the 4 × 100 m relay (36.84 seconds). Bolt has been awarded the Laureus World Sportsman of the Year on four occasions (2009, 2010, 2013, and 2017) and the IAAF Male Athlete of the Year six times (2008, 2009, 2011, 2012, 2013, and 2016).

Usain Bolt is not only a gifted athlete, but also projects a larger-than-life personality. He is gregarious, smart, articulate, and a super salesperson. His 'lightning bolt' salute to the crowd has become an iconic and worldwide trademark as part of his victory celebrations. Bolt not only sells himself to fans, sponsors, and media enterprises, but also sells the sport of track and field to the widest possible audience. Outside the Olympic Games and the World Championships the sport of track and field depends on the Diamond League for its annual appeal, and it is fair to say that Bolt has kept the sport of athletics in the spotlight at a time when it has been dogged by poor publicity as a result of performance-enhancing drugs and speculation about whether particular athletes are 'clean'.

In 2017, *Forbes* ranked Bolt as the 23rd highest-paid athlete in the world, with US$2.2 million in salary/winnings and US$32 million in endorsements, a year in which he was the only track and field athlete in the top 100. It is estimated that Bolt's endorsements are 10 times any other track and field athlete, an indication of his sheer dominance of the sport, as well as the sport's reliance on Bolt for its popularity. Like James, Bolt is sponsored by a global footwear and apparel company in Puma, which reportedly pays Bolt US$10 million per year in a deal that runs until 2025 and markets a Bolt-themed clothing line. Bolt is also sponsored by other high-profile brands such as Hublot watches, which has made the Bolt watch, and Gatorade, which is a natural synergy given the lightning bolt in the company's logo. Bolt's global appeal is evident in his sponsorships with Australian telecommunications company Optus and Japan's All Nippon Airways.

CASE STUDY QUESTIONS

1   How do the circuits of promotion differ between James and Bolt, and how are they similar?

2   What explains the difference in the money earned via endorsements by James and Bolt?

3   What is the relative importance of James and Bolt to their respective sports in terms of the circuit of promotion concept?

4   Both James and Bolt have created charitable foundations. How much are their foundations built around service to the community, and how much is about enhancing their public image and/or personal brand?

Sources: NBA website at <www.nba.com>; ESPN website at <www.espn.com>; Sports Illustrated website at <www.si.com>; LeBron James website at <www.lebronjames.com>; Usain Bolt website at <www.usainbolt.com>; Forbes website at <www.forbes.com>

PART II

Sport management principles

CHAPTER 5

Strategic sport management

OVERVIEW

This chapter explains the processes and techniques of strategic management. Specifically, it focuses on the analysis of an organization's position in the competitive environment, the determination of its direction and goals, the selection of an appropriate strategy, the leveraging of its distinctive assets, the evaluation of its chosen activities, and the relationship to organizational change. These processes are reviewed within the context of a documented plan.

After completing this chapter the reader should be able to:

- Understand the difference between strategy and planning;
- Appreciate why strategic management should be undertaken;
- Differentiate the steps of the strategic management process;

- Identify the tools and techniques of strategic management;
- Specify the steps involved in the documentation of a strategic plan;
- Explain how the nature of sport affects the strategic management process;
- Consider the relationship between strategy and organizational change.

PRINCIPLES OF STRATEGIC MANAGEMENT

In the simplest terms possible, strategy is the match or interface between an organization and its external environment. Looking at strategy in this way is a helpful start because it reinforces the importance of both the organization itself and the circumstances in which it operates. At the heart of strategy is the assumption that these two elements are of equal importance. Furthermore, strategy concerns the entirety of the organization and its operations as well as the entirety of the environment. Such a holistic approach differentiates the strategy management process from other dimensions of management.

One troublesome aspect of strategic management relates to its complex, multi-facetted nature. Johnson et al (2017); for example, note several important features associated with strategic decision making:

1   Strategy affects the direction and scope of an organization's activities;

2   Strategy involves matching an organization's activities with the environment;

3   Strategy requires the matching of an organization's activities with its resource capabilities;

4   The substance of strategy is influenced by the views and expectations of key stakeholders;

5   Strategic decisions influence the long-term direction of the organization.

With these points in mind, it is easily concluded that the management of strategy requires a keen understanding of the organization, the environment, and the consequences of decisions. But these points miss one vital outcome in the strategy process. The central purpose of strategy is to become different to the competition. From this viewpoint, strategy should help explain how one football club is different from the next, or why a customer should choose to use a recreation facility over another in the same area. The match between an organization and its environment should result in a clear competitive advantage that no other organization can easily copy.

Before we proceed, it is necessary to make several important distinctions in definition and terminology. First, strategy and planning are not the same. Strategy can be defined as the process of determining the direction and scope of activities of a sport organization in light of its capabilities and the environment in which it operates. Planning is the process of documenting these decisions in a step-by-step manner indicating what has to be done, by whom, with what resources, and when. In short, strategy reflects a combination of analysis and innovation; of science and craft. Planning identifies in a systematic and deductive way the steps and activities that need to be taken toward the implementation of a strategy. Strategic management marries strategy and planning into a process.

Second, the term strategy can be legitimately used to explain three levels of decision making. At the first identity level, a sport organization is faced with the task of establishing clarity about what business it engages in. For example, is the core business providing sport competitions, managing facilities, developing players, winning medals, championships and tournaments, selling merchandise, making a profit, or improving shareholder wealth? At the second level, the term strategy is commonly used to identify how the organization will compete successfully against others. Strategy here offers an explanation of how competitive advantage is going to be created and sustained. Strategy can also be used at an operational level to identify how regular activities are to be undertaken and how resources are to be deployed to support them. For example, a broader strategy to improve player scouting methods might be supported by an operational strategy specifying the purchase of some computer software. Keep in mind that strategic management forms both a process and way of thinking that can be applied to multiple levels of a sport organization. Moreover, even when using a common method for formulating strategy, two sport organizations in the same local environment (such as a league) will rarely end up with similar models (Monroe Olson et al 2016).

WHY PRACTICE STRATEGIC MANAGEMENT?

The need for management of the strategy process is not always considered necessary. Some managers believe that the fast-paced nature of the sport industry precludes the use of a systematic strategic management process. Strategy for these managers is developed 'on the run' and in response to emerging circumstances and events. However, this approach contradicts the principles of strategic management, which emphasize the importance of actively shaping the future of one's own sport organization rather than waiting for circumstances to prompt action. Pro-activity drives good strategy because it helps to reduce the uncertainty that accompanies chaotic and changeable industries like sport, where on-field performance can have such a radical effect on an organization's success.

Those versed in the concepts of strategic management would argue that with more uncertainty comes the need for greater strategic activity. Thus, a sport club that can generate a sizable surplus with a performance at the top of the ladder, but a dangerous deficit with a performance at the bottom of the ladder, should engage in the strategy process in order to seek new ways of managing its financial obligations. In addition, those who favour reactive approaches to strategy assume that opportunities are always overt and transparent. This is seldom true. Identifying new opportunities that have not already been leveraged by competitors rarely proves easy and requires thorough analysis and innovative thinking. Neither of these can be achieved easily without the investment of time and energy on strategy development.

Allied to the notion of pro-activity is the importance of coordination. Without a broad approach to the strategy process, different parts of the organization are likely to pursue their own agendas. Scarce resources need to be deployed in a coordinated and integrated manner consistent with an overarching strategy. Such a coordinated approach to strategy ensures that new strategy represents change. In many sport organizations for which change is a necessary condition for survival, strategy represents the intellectual part of management that can be planned. The result of this process should be a coordinated attempt to achieve goals that have been agreed upon by organizational stakeholders that takes into account a balance between the achievement of goals and the resources required to do so. Efficiency arrives as an important benefit from sound strategic management.

SPORT AND STRATEGIC MANAGEMENT

One of the biggest issues in sport strategy comes in finding the balance between two or more divergent obligations. For example, sport organizations commonly seek both elite success and improved participation levels. Deploying resources to both of these commitments may be troublesome from a strategic viewpoint because they are not necessarily compatible. International success for a particular sport can motivate people to participate. However, the retention of new participants in sport tends to be poor in the medium term and negligible in the longer term. To make matters more complex, the choices of direction inherent in sport can be distracting, including the necessity to develop players or increase participation, the pressure to make more money or win at all costs, and the need to accommodate the parochial emotional identification of loyal supporters (Rodriguez-Pomeda et al 2017).

In practice 5.1 A strategic 'manifesto' for the International Table Tennis Federation

Recently re-elected International Table Tennis Federation (ITTF) President Thomas Weikart revealed in mid-2017 a comprehensive plan for his forthcoming term at the head of world table tennis. Weikart's entitled his so-called 'manifesto', 'Delivering Value and Growth for Global Table Tennis', which proclaimed an ambitious vision for the sport outlined in seven foundational 'pillars'. These pillars, according to the newly reinstalled president, will expand the sport by pushing its global reach and improving its accessibility. Weikart observed, "Our sport will enter an exciting new phase of global growth that sees the creation of more table tennis players and fans".

The seven key pillars in Weikart's manifesto comprise fuelling the development of table tennis and empowering national associations; setting the highest standards of governance, integrity, and transparency; ensuring stability, continuity, and positive Olympic/IOC relations; maximizing commercial and marketing opportunities; enhancing the presentation of the sport; engaging audiences digitally and attracting younger fans; and developing para-table tennis.

As the seven pillars demonstrate, Weikart places a high value on a more aggressive commercial focus in order to secure additional revenues that can be used to bolster improved access, reach, and scale for the sport. Included will be the vigorous pursuit of technology, digital engagement through social media, and product innovation. In a nod to the political support needed to enact the manifesto, Weikart made special note of the close relationships with national associations he believes is critical to global success. He commented,

> The Federations are the rightful owners of the sport – it belongs to them so they know the opportunities and challenges best. That's why I believe in working in

full partnership with Federations with a consultative approach to leadership and ensuring regular dialogue.

In many ways, the new strategic manifesto builds further upon the ITTF's accomplishments over the last few years. The governing federation has worked hard to stay competitive amidst the clutter and competition of sporting opportunities for potential new players. For example, it launched 'Table Tennis X' (TTX), a fast-paced, modified version of the game, with the ambition of attracting a new cohort of time-poor participants who perhaps have never contemplated a 'conservative' sport like table tennis. TTX arrived to coincide with the Rio Olympics in the hopes of capitalizing on a potential new generation of followers and participants. To that end, the new version employs a larger, heavier ball to be used with racquets less likely to impart spin. Games are also shortened with 'wildcard' rules allowing for extra points to be scored.

Weikart's team has also pushed up marketing revenue over the last four years, shifting up a gear from around US$7m to more than US$10m for 2017. It came largely thanks to the most significant commercial sponsorship deal in the sport's history, a partnership with Seamaster, a Chinese shipping firm, and now the chief sponsor of the ITTF's world tour and the exclusive sponsor of the new TTX competition. In addition, the ITTF managed to attract a record four major sponsors to support their latest world championship. The biggest news, however, came when table tennis was elevated to 'Group C' of International Olympic Committee funding. Now the emphasis will shift to acquiring approval to increase the number of Olympic medal categories from four to six, introducing mixed doubles and men's and women's doubles for the 2020 Tokyo Games. With Japan a major market for table tennis, the Olympics opportunity seems significant indeed.

With a stakeholder imprimatur for the new strategy in place, Weikart moved quickly to seize momentum in transitioning the Manifesto to reality. Accordingly, he announced the enactment of a 10-point plan detailing the first 100 days of the new term of office, establishing a sense of prioritization as well as urgency:

1 Develop a comprehensive ITTF Strategic Plan that maps out how to develop and grow the sport further around the world.
2 Re-evaluate ITTF's finances to increase the prize money for athletes and improve development opportunities for all National Federations.
3 Complete the Commercial Strategic Continental Agreements – with the long-term goal to make the entire Table Tennis economy greater for all National Federations and Table Tennis stakeholders.
4 Finalize the new ITTF Ethics and Governance Code to ensure the organization is fully transparent, applies governance best practice, and acts with complete integrity.
5 Establish the ITTF Ethics Commission, which will act independently to the ITTF structures, the Executive Committee, and the President's Office.
6 Introduce further digital and communication innovations to the ITTF so that great Table Tennis content can be shared and reaches many more people.

> 7 Work closely with the ITTF development department to dramatically increase the number of more flexible National Federation projects relating to growth.
>
> 8 Establish the ITTF Constitution Working Group to review organizational structures and practices with the key recommendations to be adopted in 2018.
>
> 9 Review the tender process for future ITTF IT management projects – ensuring the organization has best-in-class services for database and results management and a fit-for-purpose main events calendar.
>
> 10 Introduce a new dedicated digital portal that is effective for different Table Tennis stakeholders – so each group can source tailored content and information according to their individual needs.

THE STRATEGIC MANAGEMENT PROCESS

Strategic management is a process designed to find the intersection of preparation and opportunity. This way of thinking has emerged from the first uses of the strategy concept, which came from the military. On the battlefield, the importance of imposing conditions that disadvantage the enemy in combat is paramount. For example, one of the key principles of military strategy is to manoeuvre an adversary into a position where they are outnumbered at the point of conflict. Variables like terrain and the opportunity to outflank, or attack the enemy from both the front and side simultaneously, make strategic decisions more complicated. These principles are also applied in the strategic sport management process, which is illustrated in Figure 5.1.

Like an army general, the sport manager must first make an assessment of the 'battle' conditions. They do this by studying the capacities and deficiencies of their own organization, competing organizations, stakeholder groups, and the business environment or 'battlefield'. This first stage in the strategic management process is known as *Strategy Analysis*.

Next, and in light of the information obtained from the first stage, the sport manager must make some decisions about the future. These are typically concentrated into a 'mission' statement recording the purpose of the organization, a 'vision' statement of the organization's long-term ambitions, and a set of objectives with measures to identify the essential achievements along the way to the vision. This second stage of the strategic management process is called *Strategy Direction*.

Setting a direction only determines what an organization wants to achieve. In the next step, the sport manager must consider how the direction can be realized. This is the most creative part of the strategic management process. Here, the sport manager, and his or her team, must work together to imagine the best methods or strategies for the organization. At this time, sport manager's attempt to match the unique circumstances of the organization to its unique environmental conditions. When undertaken well, opportunities are found. This stage is called *Strategy Development*.

With a clear direction and a sharp idea of how that direction can be achieved, the task of the sport manager becomes one of implementation. At this point the range of products, services, and activities that the organization engages with, and the systems that support

Strategy Analysis	**Internal Analysis** (capabilities, deficiencies, and stakeholders)	Strengths Weaknesses
	External Analysis (environment, competitors, and customers)	Opportunities Threats
Strategy Direction	**Mission** **Vision** **Objectives**	Performance Measures
Strategy Formulation	**Strategic Options**	Generic Strategies *Cost Leadership* *Differentiation* *Focus*
Strategy Implementation	**Deployment of Strategy**	Products Services Systems Structure Culture
Strategy Evaluation	**Performance Measurement**	Corrective Action

FIGURE 5.1 The strategic management process

them, are adjusted in line with the overarching strategy that was developed in the previous step. This is known as the *Strategy Implementation* stage.

Finally, strategy is rarely perfect the first time around. Modifications are always essential. Mostly this means a minor adjustment to the way in which the strategy has been implemented. However, sometimes it does require a re-think about the suitability of the strategy itself. Neither of these can be successfully undertaken without some feedback in the first place about the success of what has been done. That is why the final stage in the strategic management process, *Strategy Evaluation*, is necessary. In this stage, the organization reviews whether objectives have been achieved. Most of the time, some corrective action will need to be taken. Typically, the catalysts for these changes are unexpected events that affect the environment in which the sport organization operates, necessitating a return to strategy analysis. In this sense, the strategic management process never stops. In fact, moving back and forth between the stages in order to develop the best outcomes is normal. The strategy process works best when management takes the view that it is not linear or discrete but rather a circular and continuing activity.

STAGE 1: STRATEGIC ANALYSIS

One of the biggest challenges facing sport managers lies with combating the desire to set strategy immediately and to take action without delay. Although a call to action is a natural inclination for motivated managers, many strategies can fail because the preliminary work has not been done properly. This preliminary work entails a comprehensive review of the internal and external environments. The tools for doing this include 1) SWOT analysis; 2) stakeholder and customer needs analysis; 3) competitor analysis; and 4) the five forces analysis.

SWOT analysis

One of the basic tools in the environmental analysis is called the SWOT analysis. This form of analysis helps to examine an organization's strategic position, from the inside to the outside. The SWOT technique considers the strengths, weaknesses, opportunities, and threats that an organization possesses or faces.

There are two parts to the SWOT analysis. The first part represents the internal analysis of an organization, which can be summarized by its *strengths* and *weaknesses*. It covers everything that an organization has control over, some of which are performed well, and can be viewed as capabilities (strengths), whereas others are more difficult to do well and can be seen as deficiencies (weaknesses). The second part of the SWOT technique is concerned with external factors; those which the organization has no direct control over. These are divided into *opportunities* and *threats*. In other words, issues and environmental circumstances arise that can either be exploited or need to be neutralized.

The SWOT technique helps sport managers to find the major factors likely to play a role in the appropriateness of the organization's direction or the success of its strategy. With this in mind, the sport manager should be looking for overarching issues. A good rule of thumb is to look for no more than five factors under each of the four headings. This way the more important issues receive higher priority.

Given that the strengths and weaknesses part of the analysis concerns what goes on inside the organization, it has a time orientation in the present; what the organization does right now. Strengths can be defined as resources or capabilities that the organization can use to achieve its strategic direction. Common strengths may include committed coaching staff, a sound membership base, or a good junior development program. Weaknesses should be seen as limitations or inadequacies that will prevent or hinder the strategic direction from being achieved. Common weaknesses may include poor training facilities, inadequate sponsorship, or a diminishing volunteer workforce.

In contrast, the opportunity and threats analysis also has a future-thinking dimension, because of the need to consider what is about to happen. Opportunities are favourable situations or events that can be exploited by the organization to enhance its circumstances or capabilities. Common opportunities tend to include new government grants, the identification of a new market or potential product, or the chance to appoint a new staff member with unique skills. Threats are unfavourable situations that could make it more difficult for the organization to achieve its strategic direction. Common threats include inflating player salaries, new competitors, or unfavourable trends in the consumption of leisure such as the increased popularity of gaming consoles with young people over playing traditional sports.

Stakeholder and customer needs analysis

Before an analysis of the environment is complete, an assessment of the organization's stakeholders and customers remains essential. Stakeholders are all the people and groups that have an interest in an organization, including its employees, players, members, league or affiliated governing body, government, community, facility owners, sponsors, broadcasters, and fans. The constant question that a sport manager has to answer is concerned with whom they are trying to make happy. Either deliberately or inadvertently serving the interests of some stakeholders in preference to others has serious implications for the setting of strategic direction, and for the distribution of limited resources. For example, some professional sport clubs tend to focus on winning to the exclusion of all other priorities, including sensible financial management. Although this may make members and fans happy in the short term, it does not reflect the interests of governing bodies, leagues, and employees, for whom a sustainable enterprise is fundamental.

Sponsors and government sport funding departments sometimes withdraw funding if their needs are not met. A careful analysis of the intentions and objectives of each stakeholder in their affiliation with the sport organization must therefore be completed before a strategic direction can be set. The substance of strategy is influenced by the beliefs, values, and expectations of the most powerful stakeholders. Often these conflict and will necessitate a strategy that does not fit neatly with the generic strategic categories offered by non-sport models.

Competitor analysis

Opportunities and threats can encompass anything in the external environment, including the presence and activities of competitors. Because the actions of competitors can greatly affect the success of a strategic approach, *competitor analysis* ensures that an investigation is conducted systematically.

There are many forms of competitor analysis, and they can range in detail considerably. However, most competitor analyses consider the following dimensions, as summarized in Table 5.1. For each competitor, these eight dimensions should be considered. Time and care should be taken in assessing competitors' strategies, their strengths, vulnerabilities, and resources, as well as their next likely actions.

Five forces analysis

An extension of the competitive environment analysis is the *five forces analysis*, which was developed by Michael Porter. It is the most commonly used tool for describing the competitive environment. The technique does this by focusing upon five competitive forces (Porter 1980) (see Figure 5.2).

The threat of new entrants: Every organization is faced with the possibility that new competitors could enter their industry at any time. In some forms of professional sport, this is unlikely as the barriers preventing entry are very high. For example, it would be extremely difficult for a private independent league to enter the market against any of the

TABLE 5.1 Competitor analysis dimensions

Dimension	Description
Geographic Scope	Location and overlap
Vision and Intent	Ranges from survival to attempts at dominance
Objective	Short- to medium-term intentions
Market Share and Position	From small player to virtual monopolist
Strategy	Methods of gaining a competitive advantage
Resources	Volume and availability
Target Market	To whom the products and services are directed
Marketing Approach	The products, services and promotions, pricing, and distribution behind them

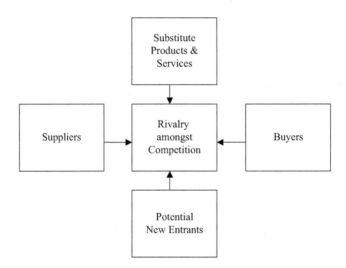

FIGURE 5.2 Five forces competitive analysis

professional football leagues in Europe. On the other hand, new sport facilities, events, sport apparel companies, and new equipment manufacturers are regular entrants in the sport industry.

The bargaining power of buyers: Buyers are those individuals, groups, and companies that purchase the products and services that sport organizations offer. The nature of the competitive environment is affected by the strength, or bargaining power, of buyers. For example, most football fans in the UK hold little power, if the price of football tickets is any indication. When there is buying power, prices are lower. Despite some extravagant sums paid by broadcasters for the media rights of certain sports, the bargaining power of media buyers should be relatively strong. For most sport organizations, however, the chief buyers – fans – do not work together to leverage their power, and therefore the bargaining power of buyers is limited.

The bargaining power of suppliers: When suppliers of raw materials essential to sporting organizations threaten to raise prices, or withdraw their products or services, they are attempting to improve their bargaining power. This may come from suppliers of the materials necessary in the building of a new facility or from sporting equipment suppliers. The most important supplier issue in sport has come about with the unionization of professional players in an attempt to increase their salaries and the salary caps of clubs. Where player groups have been well organized, their bargaining power has proven significant.

The threat of substitute products and services: Increasingly, the traditional sport industry sectors are expanding, and it is more common for different sports to compete against each other. When this threat is high, a sport organization is faced with the problem of being out-competed by other kinds of sports, or worse, by other forms of leisure activity.

The intensity of rivalry among competitors in an industry: The more sport organizations offering virtually identical products and services, the higher the intensity of rivalry. For example, in the sport shoe marketplace, the rivalry between Nike and Adidas is extremely intense. Rivalry is more ambiguous between sport clubs in the same league that share a general geographical region. London football clubs, Melbourne Australian football clubs and colleges in the same state in the United States, are examples. In these cases, it is unlikely that one club would be able to 'steal' supporters from another local club. Nor is the alumnus of one college likely to start attending home games of another college team. However, these clubs do intensely compete for media exposure, corporate sponsorship, players, coaches, managers, and management staff. Of course, they also compete with the most intense rivalry imaginable for the championship.

STAGE 2: STRATEGIC DIRECTION

Once the strategic analysis has been completed, the strategic direction can be set. Four conventional tools are used to clarify and document this direction: 1) mission statement, 2) vision statement, 3) organizational objectives, and 4) performance measures.

Mission statements

A *mission statement* identifies the purpose of an organization. Although it may seem strange to need to put this in writing, such a statement reduces the risk of strategic confusion. For example, players, members, spectators, staff, coaches, media, sponsors, and government representatives may all hold different interpretations of the purpose of a sport organization. The mission statement should define why an organization was set up, what services and products it provides, and for whom it provides them. When reduced to a single statement, this mission is a powerful statement of intention and responsibility. It usually does not exceed one paragraph.

Vision statements

It goes without saying that behind the idea of setting a strategic direction is the need to be visionary: to look into the future and form a clear mental image of what an organization could be like. Thinking in this manner means being able to interpret the information collected during the analysis stage and find the opportunities they present. A *vision statement* represents the culmination of this kind of thinking. It is a statement that declares the medium- to long-range ambitions of an organization. The statement is an expression of what the organization wants to achieve within a period of around three to five years. The statement is normally no longer than a sentence.

Organizational objectives

Given that the vision statement is a reflection of the medium- to long-term ambitions of an organization, *organizational objectives* serve as markers on the way to this destination. Objectives reflect the achievements that must be made in order to realize the vision. For example, if a club is situated at the bottom of the championship ladder, their vision might be to finish in the top three. However, achieving this vision inside a single season is unrealistic, so an objective might indicate the ambition to improve by three places by next season, as a progression toward the overarching vision. Objectives are normally set in each of the major operational areas of an organization, such as on-field performance, youth development, finances, facilities, marketing, and human resources. However, it is essential that objectives stay measurable.

Performance measures

Key Performance Indicators (KPIs) are used in combination with organizational objectives in order to establish success or failure. KPIs are therefore inseparable from objectives and should be created at the same time. Each time a performance measure is used, care should be taken to ensure that it can indeed be measured in a concrete way. For example, a marketing objective of 'improving the public image' of an organization is meaningless unless it is accompanied by something quantifiable. It is worth noting that measures do not have to focus exclusively on outputs like volumes, rankings, and trophies. They can also be used to measure efficiency; that is, doing the same with less or doing more with the same resources.

STAGE 3: STRATEGY FORMULATION

Strategic analysis reveals the competitive position of a sport organization and setting the strategic direction plots a course for the future. The next question is how to get there. In the strategy formulation stage of the strategic management process, the sport manager and his or her team face the task of positioning their organization in the competitive environment. This necessitates a combination of imagination and scenario thinking. In other words, they must consider the implications of each potential strategic approach. To help matters, however, from a strategic positioning viewpoint a finite number of strategies are available to the sport manager. These are called *generic competitive strategies*.

In practice 5.2 Planning the Olympic dream with Tokyo 2020

When it comes to the Olympic Games, expectations run high. Perhaps the most ambitious plan in recent history is currently being formulated by the Tokyo 2020 Summer Olympic Games Organising Committee. Organizers have steadfastly linked the Games with the promise of a powerful post-event legacy. Not only can the event leave behind a lasting suite of world-class venues and local regeneration, it has also been conferred with the power to 'change the world' along with Tokyo's future. With such lofty ambitions already committed in print, it is unsurprising that the organizers further claim that the mega event will deliver the most innovative Games ever. Delivering 'positive reform to the world' will, according to the official plan, be built upon three foundational concepts: achieving personal best, unity in diversity, and connecting to tomorrow. In terms of the first concept, personal best athletic performance will be realized through cutting-edge venues, world-leading technologies, and unmatched hospitality. Towards the second, diversity will be celebrated by recognizing differences and by providing a culture of respect and unity. The third concept promises a future-oriented perspective, where equal consideration is afforded to venue utility for the Games and for the longer-term future. It is clear that the Games custodians believe that the 2020 version can augment the economic, political, and social progress of Tokyo and the nation to a level equivalent to that which the 1964 event yielded.

Several other aspects of the Tokyo strategy warrant mention as critical success factors in achieving the sweeping legacy the organizers declared in their vision. A first factor concerns plans to build or develop a total of 39 venues, comprising eight new constructions, 22 existing sites, and 9 temporary structures. Of these, 20 will also host Paralympic Games events. Paramount amongst the new constructions is the strikingly designed National Stadium, which broke ground in December 2016. An 'Athletes' Village' comprises another massive project.

Second, attuned to the legacy goals was the promise of venue sustainability. For the Tokyo organizers, this incorporates the 'entire concept' of sustainability, built upon the principle of waste avoidance and environmental sensitivity, the consideration of human rights, labour, and working practices, and the management of supply chains. A 'High-level Sustainability Plan and Fundamental Principles for the Sustainable Sourcing Code' articulates the commitment to achieving a 'minimal impact' Games. It also aims to raise awareness for the importance of sustainability in sporting events. One practical example will see the prominent use of hydrogen energy in buses used in the city during the Games.

A third critical success factor, according to Games organizers, will be the role of technology as a core feature in all aspects of event delivery, from fan engagement to venue management. Examples include multi-lingual translation devices, enhanced real-time performance data, and the latest mobile media viewing packages and social engagement platforms. Games organizers have announced that they are working closely with local industry on novel innovations to enhance the viewing experience, whether live or distant.

In addition to the so-called 'hard' legacy of infrastructure, regeneration, and new technologies, the Tokyo Games organizers have identified a range of 'soft' legacy impacts accompanying the event. To that end they are currently planning around five themes: Sport and Health; Urban Planning and Sustainability; Culture and Education; Economy and Technology; and Recovery (from the 2011 earthquake and tsunami), Nationwide Benefits, and Global Communication. It still remains to be seen whether such broad, 'soft' legacy goals can be made tangible through an actionable and realistic plan.

Generic competitive strategies

Porter (1985) contended that there are only three fundamental or generic strategies that can be applied in any organization, irrespective of their industry, products and services, environmental circumstance, and resources. Generic competitive strategies answer the most basic question facing a sport manager while forming a strategic choice: What is going to be our source of *competitive advantage*? To put it another way, every sport organization must take a position somewhere in the marketplace. The challenge is to find a position that is both opportune *and* advantageous. As a result, some sport organizations try to out-compete their adversaries because they can provide their products and services cheaper; others compete on the basis of a unique product or service that is hard for others to replicate; others still attempt to position themselves as the exclusive supplier to a small but loyal niche in the marketplace. These three strategic positions are described next:

Cost leadership: To become a cost leader by supplying products and services at the lowest possible cost to as many customers as possible. The logic of this strategic approach is driven by volume and market share where more sales than any other competitors lead to greater profitability. Essential to this generic competitive strategy is efficiency and the ability to keep costs to a minimum. Although this approach is common in consumer products like shampoo, it is less common in sport. However, some equipment and sport apparel manufacturers do provide their products at the cheap end of the market in the hope that they can significantly outsell their more expensive competitors. Similarly, many leisure facilities try to attract customers on the basis of their lower prices.

Differentiation: To provide a differentiated set of products and services that is difficult for competitors to replicate. The logic of this strategic approach is underpinned by an assumption that consumers will place a high value on products and service that are unique. Typically, this approach is supported by an attempt to build a strong brand image, incorporate regular innovations and new features, and provide responsive customer service. Many sport organizations are thrown into this position almost by default because of the nature of their offerings. A tennis club, for example, offers a range of services that are by definition differentiated, at least when compared to other sports or leisure activities. However, when two tennis clubs compete in a similar area, it may become necessary for one to take a new strategic position. One option is to further differentiate their services, perhaps by offering something new or innovative like a creche for mid-week players or a gym for conditioning the more seriously competitive players.

Focus: To provide a set of products and services to a niche in the market with the intention of dominating market share. The logic guiding this strategic approach is that being dominant in a small section of a larger market allows an organization to have early success, without having to compete with much larger and better resourced organizations. To succeed with this strategic approach it is necessary to choose the market segment very carefully, aware that the products and services provided must fill particular needs in customers very well. Many sport organizations take this approach. Examples include specialist sport equipment and less mainstream sport clubs and associations like rock climbing and table tennis.

The key to making a decision between these three alternatives returns to the analysis and direction stages of the strategic management process. A strategy-savvy sport manager is always looking for a way to position the organization in a cluttered market. Part of the choice is in determining what the sport organization is likely to be able to do better than others; their competitive advantage (like keeping costs low or delivering great customer service). The other part is in finding the opportunity in the environment that is worth exploring. Where there is a match between these factors consistent with strategic direction, strategic formulation is born. It is worth remembering that the worst place to be is 'stuck in the middle' between strategies, but that combining strategic options can be advantageous if managed effectively.

STAGE 4: STRATEGY IMPLEMENTATION

Strategy implementation represents the introduction of the organization's choice of competitive strategy. For example, if a differentiation strategy has been selected, the implementation stage considers how it can be brought about across the organization's products, services, and activities. There is an important distinction to be made here between the strategic level of decision making and the implementation level. To return to the military analogy, strategy concerns how an entire army is deployed. At the implementation level, tactical and operational decisions are made as well. These are like the choice of what each battalion, unit or platoon does. Always the overarching goal is a reflection of the army's objectives, but each smaller part of the army works towards bite-sized achievements that will eventually bring about success in the battle.

Once decisions have been finalized concerning the strategy that will be employed to achieve organizational objectives, the task of converting them into action begins. This means that representatives from each major area or department of the organization must become involved in deciding how they can contribute towards the generic strategy. For example, if one objective in a club is concerned with on-field performance, it is likely that the leaders of the developmental programs will play a role in planning. Equally, an objective associated with financial performance will require marketing staff responsible for sponsorship to become involved. As a result, the strategy implementation process should permeate the organization including junior development, community liaison, coaching, facilities, governance, marketing, finance, and human resources, for example. In each of these areas a plan should be developed that illustrates the set of activities that will be performed at the tactical and operational levels to support the generic strategy. Like objectives, each of these actions requires a measure or KPI of some sort. Often the implementation process also requires changes to resource allocation, organizational structure, systems for delivering products and services, organizational culture, and leadership. These areas are considered in subsequent chapters.

In practice 5.3 A cautionary tale from the Irish Athletic Boxing Association

German military strategist Helmuth von Moltke postulated that, "No battle plan survives contact with the enemy". And, sometimes, that's how it is with strategic plans. No matter how well crafted or well designed a plan might be, there is no guarantee of success. Few things in life go totally as planned. Reality has a way of constantly interrupting one's ideas. External forces can intervene, plans can be too optimistic, and there is always the threat of the unknown. Of course, that is no reason not to plan; time spent in planning is seldom wasted. It does suggest, however, that any strategic plan needs constant fine-tuning and updating.

Take, for example, the case of the Irish Athletic Boxing Association (IABA). Established in 1911, the IABA is the national governing body for amateur boxing in Ireland. Boxing has been Ireland's most successful Olympic sport having produced 16 medallists. None, however, were won at the 2016 Rio Olympics.

The strategic plan, formulated primarily in house, that preceded the 2016 Olympics was generally acceptable, but somewhat lightweight in concept and lacking in specific detail. It was certainly sufficient for the Irish Institute of Sport to offer individual grants to three boxing coaches to allow them to access key performance support. It was also sufficient for Sport Ireland to provide a 900,000 Euro grant to the overall high-performance program in boxing – the highest for any sport. The result was a world-class, eight-person boxing squad that travelled to Brazil.

What went wrong? Several things. For a start, the high-performance system was not as effective as believed and the position of High Performance Director, never clearly spelt out in terms of responsibility and authority, had been left vacant since 2008. Then, the head coach defected to the United States team 10 months before the games and was never adequately replaced. Nor was another senior coach. Furthermore, the strategic plan did not recognize the fact that the national titles were held at the wrong time or that the national stadium was too cramped to successfully do its job. Unfortunately, once written, no individual had overall control of the strategic plan and little, if any, updating occurred.

When the team arrived in Rio, fortunes failed to improve. One boxer was sent home in disgrace after failing a drug test, another had difficulty making the correct weight, and others failed to perform as expected. To make matters worse, some controversial judging decisions delivered unfavourable outcomes.

The IABA recognized its failures and in early 2017 produced a new strategic plan acknowledging nine key areas for major changes. The plan was this time formulated following extensive consultation with stakeholders and member clubs. It contains specific and detailed vision, mission, aims, goals, and action statements, and a commitment has been made to ensure that it is continually updated. A clear timetable has been provided and a way forward detailed. Equally importantly, the CEO of the IABA has clear responsibilities for the plan's implementation.

The 2012 plan failed for many reasons but the underlying cause was undoubtedly the failure of the IABA to sufficiently detail the plan, to monitor it, provide updates both in the plan and in practice, and to have in place a structure that constantly supported implementation. Planning never corresponded with reality.

STAGE 5: STRATEGIC EVALUATION

One of the more difficult aspects of strategic management is the control or evaluation of what has been done. In sport there are numerous issues that make this process more complicated including the obvious one that on-field performance can have a tendency to overwhelm the other elements of strategy. Chapter 13 considers these important issues in detail.

The *strategic evaluation* stage requires an assessment of two related aspects of the strategy. First, the KPIs associated with each organizational objective need to be compared with actual results, and second, the success of the implementation actions needs to be ascertained. It is also build upon a strategic 'perspective', upon which a view of how strategy and change intersect is founded. In some cases, this perspective can itself change over time, either in response to environmental conditions or leadership transitions.

STRATEGY AS CHANGE

For managers taking a strongly strategic perspective, organizational change requires a coherent framework in which to manage the process. From this viewpoint, successful organizational change remains intractably connected to strategy implementation, as change should materialize as an outcome. Strategy and change are therefore often conflated and treated as the same thing. Confronted by a deteriorating bottom line, a bad run on the field, an unexpected shift in technology, underwhelming merchandise sales, or one of a hundred other possibilities, strategists confront organizational change problems that previously seemed too difficult or too entrenched. Unfortunately, many sport organizations get side-tracked or distracted by the minutia of how to come to grips with the need for change without considering the simple need to plan for it.

Strategic change is typically seen as a difference in the form, quality, or state over time in an organization's alignment with its external environment. Yet most change leaders scarcely have time for definitions when it comes to strategy. Strategy feels like great art in that we know it when we see it. Assuming a strategic approach to change assumes that the idealized final destination shapes change attempts in the same way that the top of a mountain defines the end of a climb. A strategic method requires a sport organization and its leaders to apply both logic and honesty to define a current position and then to determine precisely where it would like to be at the end of the change process. The difference between the two positions then dictates the requirements for change. Although an oversimplification, the gap method characterizes strategic change because the inspiration for action focuses on bridging the difference between the current and desired state. Of course, traversing a gap in performance leads to decisions about the deployment of scarce resources, taking into account the complexities of environmental boundaries and the relative importance of different objectives. A strategic perspective also assumes that organizations behave with purposeful, adaptive proactivity. Change occurs because senior managers and other change agents deem it necessary, proceeding in a rational and linear fashion with leaders as the pivotal instigators and arbiters. As a result, a strategic approach maintains that sport managers wield the ultimate control of their organizations. Leaders introduce various processes, structures, and products until they either reveal the most successful recipe, or catastrophe strikes. Conversely, unsuccessful change must be due to managerial or leadership inadequacy, or poor strategy selection in the first place. Strategic change takes a managerial, interventionist approach. It emphasizes the manipulation of organizational parts by strategically aware leaders in response to environmental circumstances. Such thinking remains obvious in sport organizational leaders today whose use of strategic language and methods uncovers a certainty about the cause and effect relations between strategic decisions and performance consequences.

When change emanates from the formulation of an organizational strategy it presumes the sequential, planned pursuit of optimal solutions to clear and well-understood problems. Sport managers believe that they optimize their organization's performance by finding the fit between a vision and the environment. In this respect, change relies on the conventional interpretation of strategy outlined in this chapter in that it reflects an alignment between organizational objectives, internal capabilities and environmental opportunities. Repetitive sequences of goal formulation, implementation, evaluation, and modification always feature as stalwarts. Although unfair to suggest that a conventional model does not attempt to accommodate the complexities of organizational change, it does present it in a linear fashion. Change can be controlled because everything in a sport organization should be subservient to the will, vision, and action of its leaders.

Notwithstanding the presumption that strategic change operates as a clearly determined process envisioned at the outset, often sport organizational change exhibits emergent properties. Change programs change. Leaders and commentators tend to offer neat and systematic reconstructions after the event, implying a careful calculation behind every move. In counterpoint, the personal experiences of observers and employees within sport organizations can depict a lot of muddling and messiness. A strategic presentation of change might be clean and neat, but few operational sport managers and employees experience change as anything but fuzzy. Original plans seldom come to fruition in exactly the way they were conceived. Although plans can go wrong and unanticipated issues can arise in the environment, disconnections between strategic planning and strategic thinking are probably inevitable. In addition, it may be argued that the need for organizational change in the first place demonstrates a failure of organizational planning and strategy. The proper response, of course, means proceeding with some more strategic change.

No matter how well planned, how strongly agreed by the majority of staff, how well led, or how important the strategic change plan, someone or some group of individuals within, or, occasionally outside the organization, will attempt to derail it. This may occur because an individual or group feels that the proposed strategy will adversely affect them, because they misunderstand the requirements of the plan, because they genuinely lack the capability to readily accept change, or because they believe the plan flawed. When faced with change not everyone reacts with the same rationality supposedly driving the change process. Almost all commentaries on strategic change will acknowledge the prospect of possible obstruction from some element of the workforce. Most will provide sensible suggestions for improvement, but it remains problematic to plan for resistance while employing a strategic mind-set.

It should also be noted that the strategic change model does not perform equally well for all sport organizations or for all levels of change. However, for substantive change across a large sport organization, the strategic model offers a powerful organizing framework. Given committed leadership together with a clear impetus for change, we think that the concepts associated with strategic change offer a useful, if sometimes too rigid, initial guide. Sport organizations are not always rational actors in the change process. Their fate is not exclusively determined by a leader's ability to make correct analyses and to formulate appropriate plans to meet predetermined objectives.

Strategic change methods suggest that change works in a one-dimensional way. However, change occurs at different levels, and with varying magnitudes and directions. Moreover, although not an immutable force, the external environment cannot always be mitigated with clever tactics. Sport organizations contribute to, and interact with their environments, in a way that makes choices about responses far more ambiguous and complex than a strategic plan can always capture. In some cases, change managers find that more analysis leads to more complexity as the subtle idiosyncrasies of various possibilities become apparent. Another obvious limitation of the strategic approach to change accompanies its treatment of management decision making as a 'black-box' that produces the correct outputs when the correct inputs are computed. For example, in sport, it is especially difficult for organizations to gain objective distance from their socio-historical circumstances. In practice, the result is that organizational change can be messy and non-linear due to environmental turbulence and historical baggage, not to mention the unpredictable 'human factor'. Despite the wisdom of conducting environmental analyses and establishing clear goals, the future often runs contrary to expectations based on linear trends. The challenge for sport managers is not just about planning for change but in knowing when to change the plan.

STRATEGY AS PRACTICE

An emerging issue in strategy emphasizes the blurred line between strategy and the practice of management, particularly where organizing forms are considered an integral part of the strategizing process. This position is reflective of the wider strategy-as-practice trend in strategic management, which is concerned with how managers 'do strategy', or strategize. The view that organizing forms within structures remain subservient to strategy may be considered old-fashioned, as it demands a sharp distinction between the two as different properties and processes. However, strategy and organization are not necessarily distinct states. Organization does not follow strategy. Instead, the more contemporary view holds that organization *is* the strategy. For example, investment in sophisticated IT infrastructure may be instrumental in enabling a sport organization to enter new markets and reach more fans. The assumption here is that a change to organizing forms is a strategic change. In addition, the use of the terms organizing and strategizing lies central to this proposition. As verbs, the terms impart the importance of continuous rather than static change processes. Organization and strategy therefore become organizing and strategizing.

From the standpoint of a sport manager, success is not so much a function of getting strategy and structure right in the first place, but rather is about having the capability to adjust them continuously alongside shifts in competitive and market forces. A sport organization's knowledge – its know-how – relies on managers' abilities to think about strategy and organizing decisions at the same time. Like a sport team without designated playing positions, strategizing without organizing is limited in scope. The strategizing-organizing way of thinking also suggests that middle- and lower-level managers need to engage in the strategy-making process.

SUMMARY

This chapter is concerned with the process of strategic management. This process is founded on the principle that opportunity is discovered by analysis rather than luck. Strategic management, we have argued, is therefore at the heart of the success of a sport organization.

Five stages in the strategic management process have been identified. The first stage is strategy analysis, which demands the assessment of both internal organizational capacities as well as external environmental conditions. The second stage is strategy direction, which sets the vision and objectives of an organization. The third stage is strategy formulation, where a definitive strategic position is selected for an organization. The fourth stage is strategy implementation, where the strategy is directed to action across organizational areas. The final stage, strategy evaluation, involves the control and measurement of the process so that improvements can be made.

Strategic management in sport organizations requires preparation, research and analysis, imagination, decision making, and critical thinking. It demands an equal balance of systematization and innovation. This chapter is weighted heavily toward the system side, but that is simply a necessity to convey the principles and techniques of strategic management. It is up to the readers to provide the imagination in their own strategic management activities.

REVIEW QUESTIONS

1 Why is strategic management important in the turbulent world of sport?

2 What is the basic principle that underpins strategic management?

3 Name the five stages of strategic management.

4 What is the relationship between a SWOT analysis and competitor analysis?

5 How do stakeholders influence the setting of strategic direction?

6 Explain the differences between the three generic strategies.

7 What is the relationship between KPIs and strategy evaluation?

8 Select a sport organization that has a strategic plan on its website. Conduct an analysis of this plan, and comment on its approach to each of the five steps of strategic management explained in this chapter.

9 Select a sport organization that you know well and that does not have a strategic plan available. Based on your background knowledge, make point form comments under the headings of the five steps in strategic management to illustrate your approach to forming a plan.

10 Provide an example where a new kind of organizing method in a sport organization could impart a strategic effect.

DISCUSSION QUESTIONS

1 Discuss the relationship between the processes of strategy and of planning.

2 Some commentators argue that strategic plans are outdated tools given the rapid pace of today's sport business environment. Do you think this is a fair observation?

3 Sport enterprises tend to serve stakeholders with diverse, even contradictory, agendas. Discuss how balancing these divergent needs can be managed through the strategy process.

4 Is the structure-strategy relationship in sport organizations old-fashioned? How could new, more innovative organizing forms be employed for strategic effect?

5 How are new developments in technology affecting sport strategy? Discuss examples.

FURTHER READING

Anagnostopoulos, C., Anagnostopoulos, C., Byers, T., Byers, T., Kolyperas, D. and Kolyperas, D. (2017). Understanding strategic decision-making through a multi-paradigm perspective: The case of charitable foundations in English football. *Sport, Business and Management: An International Journal*, 7(1): 2–20.

Heinze, K.L. and Lu, D. (2017). Shifting responses to institutional change: The National Football League and player concussions. *Journal of Sport Management*, 1–44. doi: 10.1123/jsm.2016–0309

Johnson, G., Whittington, R., Regner, P., Scholes, K. and Angwin. (2017). *Exploring Strategy*. 11th edn. London: Prentice-Hall.

Juravich, M., Salaga, S. and Babiak, K. (2017). Upper echelons in professional sport: The impact of NBA General Managers on team performance. *Journal of Sport Management*, 1–38. doi: org/10.1123/jsm.2017–0044

Monroe Olson, E.M., Duray, R., Cooper, C. and Monroe Olson, K. (2016). Strategy, structure, and culture within the English Premier League: An examination of large clubs. *Sport, Business and Management: An International Journal*, 6(1): 55–75.

Porter, M. (1985). *Competitive Strategy: Creating and Sustaining Superior Performance*. New York: Simon & Schuster.

Rodriguez-Pomeda, J., Casani, F. and Alonso-Almeida, M.D.M. (2017). Emotions' management within the Real Madrid football club business model. *Soccer & Society*, 18(4): 431–444.

RELEVANT WEBSITES

www.botswanatourism.co.bw/ – Botswana Tourism Organisation
www.bcfc.com/ – Birmingham City Football Club
www.cbssports.com/ – CBS Sports Network
http://img.com/ – International Management Group
www.ittf.com/ – International Table Tennis Federation
http://iaba.ie/ – Irish Athletic Boxing Association
www.inter.it/en/hp – Inter Milan Football Club (F.C. Internazionale Milano)
www.suningholdings.com/cms/snSports/ – Suning Sports Group
https://tokyo2020.jp/en/ – Tokyo 2020 Summer Olympic Games Organising Committee
www.theworldsstrongestman.com/ – World's Strongest Man

CASE STUDY 5.1

The Chinese takeover of European football

Travel back in time a couple of thousand years or more and you would likely find large portions of the Chinese youth playing what we would recognize as an early version of football. In the Han Dynasty (206 BC–220 AD) football was called Tsu' Chu or cuju, and was played with a round ball frequently made of leather and filled with feathers or animal hair. The aim was to kick the ball through a small opening into a net tied to a long bamboo cane. The game became so prevalent that it lasted throughout several Chinese dynasties and even hosted professional players and teams. It was probably the earliest form of the game.

The modern version of (association) football, together with its complexity of rules and regulations, germinated in Victorian Britain, predominantly within selective and rich private schools. With its emergence, China's role in the formation of the game was severely diminished if not almost entirely forgotten. That was until fairly recently.

In more recent times, China has sought to reassert her dominance over the sport – not on the playing field, but rather in the board room. Its somewhat inelegant origin began in 2007 with an aborted attempt by Hong Kong resident Carson Yeung to take over then Premier League side Birmingham City Football Club. His purchase of 29.9% of the club from their millionaire owners, David Sullivan and brothers David and Ralph Gold, achieved little other than ridicule. They rejected Yeung's attempt for a seat on the Birmingham Board and ignored his attempts to influence the club. It took a further two years before Yeung, with the aid of a substantial loan from Best China Ltd, a company owned by business friend Pollyanna Chu, secured complete control of the club at a cost of £81 million, a figure more than three times the £24m value at which Birmingham had been trading during the preceding six-month period.

The shell company, Grandtop International Holdings registered in the Cayman Islands tax haven, which Yeung used to buy Birmingham City, recorded interests in investment, entertainment, sports clothing, media, energy, water, and property, as well as an indirect interest in a Macau casino. It had also recorded an almost zero profit during its existence.

Yeung was not an ex-player and despite having served for a year in 2005–2006 as the chairman of Hong Kong Rangers Football Club, he was not considered to possess any serious knowledge of the game.

From the moment Yeung took control of the club his declared aim was to profit from guanxi, the intermix of obligations, understandings, and dealings within Chinese business, and to utilize guanxi to promote his own interests. To achieve this, he set out six observable, though not clearly overt, strategic objectives:

1   To make Birmingham City the centrepiece around which all other aspects of his business empire would revolve.
2   To promote the values and activities of Birmingham City within China.
3   To make Birmingham City a leading club within Britain and Europe.
4   To promote both Chinese football and Chinese players.
5   To utilize the acquisition of Birmingham City as leverage to enter the sports market.
6   To use Yeung's newfound exposure both with China and Britain to increase his own personal standing and wealth.

Yeung took several initial steps to progress his strategies. During the initial close season after purchase, Yeung took Birmingham to China to play matches against up and coming Chinese sides. The reaction was mixed. Football fans attended but not in the numbers Yeung sought. After all, Birmingham did not have the name recognition of a Manchester United, Liverpool, or Arsenal.

Next, Yeung changed the name of the company on the Hong Kong Stock Exchange from Grandtop International Holdings Ltd to Birmingham International Holdings Ltd to better reflect the overwhelming value of the football club to his company.

Yeung further completed a five-year kit deal with clothing company Xtep worth a baseline fee of £7.2 million, a deal that eventually saw the club pay more to the clothing company than it received in the initial kit supply deal.

Although an initial amount of money was provided to the club to buy new players, the amount was nowhere near the sum that Yeung had originally stated. Although Yeung ostensibly instructed his scouting team to search China for the best player in the country with the aim of recruiting him, no player was ever found.

Yeung, however, continued his primary aim, and in one of his first official interviews stated that as he was the first man from mainland China to get involved in European football, he was well placed to profit from guanxi and that he could manipulate that positioning to build any necessary repertoire with Chinese partners. Nevertheless, Yeung neglected any further opportunities to translate his strategies into reality, and time became his enemy. Two years after buying Birmingham City Football Club, Yeung was arrested in Hong Kong in connection with alleged money laundering, and in March 2014 was convicted on five counts of money laundering and sentenced to six years in jail. Birmingham City has now been purchased by another Chinese company, Trillion Trophy Asia Ltd, and its future remains unclear. The club is still relatively unknown in China.

China's serious attempt to become a major player in the European football arena had at its foundation a political imperative. In October 2014, the State Council of the People's Republic of China issued a document which sought to 'Accelerate the Development of the Sports Industry [and] Promote Sports Consumption' in China. In May 2016, China's 13th five-year plan directed that the sports industry should comprise 1% of gross domestic product (GDP) by 2020, an increase from its then-estimated 0.6%. The eventual goal was for sport to be a US$750–800 billion industry by 2026, a figure far exceeding that in the United States. China's desire is a reflection of Chinese President Xi Jinping's aspirations, who is a keen football fan and who anticipates that China will one day host, and win, the World Cup.

In pursuing the five-year plan directive, Chinese companies and individuals have purchased, in total or in part, a number of European football teams. One of the largest initial investments occurred in June 2016 for 68.55% of the giant Italian football club Inter Milan by Chinese retail entity Suning Holdings Group Ltd, for the sum of 270 million euros (US$307 million). In addition to the initial cost, Suning took on a large, but undisclosed, portion of the loss-making club's debt.

Suning comprises six vertical industries. Its multi-faceted entity includes Suning Sports, which has interests in e-commerce sports media and owns a top club in the Chinese league, Jiangsu Suning. According to a Suning Sports Group document, the aim of the sports division is club ownership, sports media rights, player agencies, training institutions, broadcast platforms, content production, and sports related e-commerce. The document indicates that through strategic expansion and acquisitions Suning would establish a "sporting ecosystem along the whole supply chain." As one of the first mainland Chinese businesses to have a controlling interest in a major European club, Suning's strategy in sport appears to have been an important first step.

Unlike Carson Yeung's earlier foray in European football, Suning's involvement seems to have a more thoughtful, unified, and integrated strategic approach. When announcing the purchase of the club, Zhang Jindong, the billionaire chairman of Suning Holdings and a man with noted connections to President Xi Jinping, acknowledged Inter Milan's 'glory of the past', and sought 'the glory of the future'. He carefully avoided announcing the purchase as a Chinese takeover of the club, instead declaring that "Inter Milan firstly belongs to Italy, Europe, [and] definitely to the whole world". Suning's purchase of Inter Milan, he stated, "was the integration of Suning in Italy . . . rather than a Chinese takeover of the club". He noted that, "Our experience in entering more than 600 cities in the world teaches us that only by integrating into the local area and becoming a local enterprise can an enterprise become successful". This carefully formulated comment underlies, perhaps, the strategic positioning of the group. In his initial speech, Zhang Jindong also stated that having a majority interest in the Italian club "helps Suning to capture the trend of sports and fitness interest in China, raise the standards of local football and also raises Suning's profile as it expands globally".

While emphasizing the importance of Inter Milan restoring its leading position in Serie A, under-written by the financial assistance of Suning, Mr Zhang promised fans that Suning would adhere to three basic principles. First, that the club would retain professional management; second, that the prime aim of the club would be to win the Serie A competition and enter and win the European Champions League; and third, to ensure that the club followed the road of steady development, including the development of a professional youth training system and the cultural expansion of the club.

Suning is more fortunate in their choice of club than was Yeung. Unlike Birmingham, Inter Milan is acknowledged for its top-class professional management and its rich 100-year history, studded as it is with European and domestic success including winning the Italian League title no fewer than 18 times. The club's fans are legion and distributed throughout the world; the team can also boast world-renowned football stars and coaches.

Equally, Inter Milan is more fortunate in its choice of owner than was Birmingham. Yeung was ostensibly a one-man owner with visibly limited financial resources. Suning, by comparison, is reported to employ 180,000 people across China and has, as a minority investor, the giant Alibaba Group.

Suning's strategy in sport generally contains the air of genuineness. In 2015, Suning Sports paid La Liga US$270 million for its video site PPTV to have the Spanish football league's exclusive media rights. Suning's initial steps have built a foundation beneath their declared and assumed strategies. In addition to having taken over a goodly proportion of Inter Milan's debt, much of which occurred after running afoul of UEFA Financial Fair Play in 2015, Suning has indicated that they will inject a steady stream of capital investment into the club in order to attract more talented players. Suning is both willing and able to part with cash for players, as witnessed by their Chinese team Jiangsu Suning, which has recently outlaid 28 million euros for Chelsea player Ramires, and an even more staggering 50 million euros for Shakhtar Donetsk's Alex Teixeira.

Deals for multi-year naming rights, including for the club's first team and youth training centres, have been secured, as well as rights agreements concerning the official training apparel partner for the senior and youth teams. Additionally, Suning has secured brand visibility via advertising boards and logo positioning throughout the stadium and on shirts. Suning's strategic task is not easy. Although established throughout China, Japan, the United States, and elsewhere, the company was only established in 1990, and the task of guiding a football team based so far away from its parent company will be challenging. It does, however, have both political and financial capital on its side along with a solid strategic outlook.

CASE STUDY QUESTIONS

1   Both Carson Yeung and Suning Holdings had/have nominated strategies to achieve their objectives. In what major way do those strategies differ? Discuss the difference between their approaches to undertaking those strategies.

2   To what extent was the political imperative to ultimately host, and win, the World Cup a factor in Suning Holdings' desire to purchase Inter Milan? Had that imperative been known earlier would it have assisted or hindered Yeung's takeover of Birmingham City?

3   Do you believe that Chinese ownership of a European club provides automatic access to commercial opportunities in China and elsewhere in the world? Why?

CASE STUDY 5.2

Bulging strategy with the World's Strongest Man Contest

With the 40th World's Strongest Man (WSM) decided in 2017 – with Englishman Eddie Hall edging out Hafthor Bjornsson (aka 'The Mountain' from the HBO series *Game of Thrones*) and four-time winner Brian Shaw – the contest reinforced its niche position as one of the most novel entertainment products in the global sporting calendar. A made-for-television production, the WSM is nothing short of an arresting visual spectacle, at its core a dramatic script mythologizing hyper-masculine ideals about body and power, framed in a breath-taking aesthetic that emphasizes the immense proportions of the contestants and their herculean tasks. In fact, to portray the athletes as behemoths seems rather banal given their stupendous size, the top three finishers all weighing over 200 kilograms. After completing events, these human tractors eventually sidle up to camera to reveal a handful of comments replete with self-bravado and a handful of blood-soaked ripped callouses.

In addition to the larger-than-life participants, the WSM's coverage is amplified by the nature of the events themselves, each one wielding objects well known to armchair viewers as prohibitively heavy or immobile. Gone are abstract barbells in exchange for refrigerators and awkward lumber or gigantic stones. Tugs of war between competitors give way to truck or plane pulls for time. With more than 50 event variations the competing titans complete suitably fantastic challenges, with car lifts, fire-engine pulls, 200 kilo tire flips, and keg tosses amongst the most popular. To support the theatrics, production is a unique collision of equal parts Olympics, professional wrestling, and action movie montage. Brief events are punctuated by pre-taped interviews, action replays featuring sweaty, puffed-out, vein exploding muscles, along with power music, and a few fist-pumping, chest thumping moments from each event's crazed winner.

WSM is organized by TWI, the events arm of International Management Group (IMG), with the culminating finals usually broadcast around Christmas. Participants have to qualify through a top three finish at one of the 'Giants Live' event series held in the month's leading up. Presently, the major sponsor is the Commerce Casino based in Los Angeles, California. Past sponsors have also reflected the expectation of a heavily male-oriented audience, such as DAF Trucks, Tonka, MET-Rx (sports supplement company), and PartyPoker.com.

As far-fetched as it might sound, the WSM invented the sport of 'strongman', which although far from mainstream, enjoys a solid and rapidly increasing following from a global cadre of YouTube-sharing muscle mass monsters. Presently, strongman competitions are commonplace worldwide, and in its most popular geographies like North America, western and eastern Europe, the United Kingdom, South Africa, Australia, and Scandinavia, contests are held at the club, local, regional, national, and international levels. At the heart of every competitor's ambition resides the dream of competing in, and securing the title of, the world's strongest man. Although not without its challenges, the WSM contest has become a mainstay of sport's most unique events. Its strategic positioning may also claim to have delivered a world first in sport: the only pinnacle world championship to found a sport, rather than the usual model where grassroots interest eventually tips into growing competition. As we shall see, the WSM has prospered by finding its own way in sport's immensely competitive landscape.

The initial WSM was based on the simple and intuitive desire to know who the strongest person in the world is. First staged in 1977, the hastily arranged tournament involved only eight invited competitors, comprising heavyweight National Football League players, field athletes, bodybuilders, weightlifters, and powerlifters who contested new and imaginative events involving lifting, carrying, throwing, and tugging. It was not barbell weight as with the more familiar strength sports, but refrigerators, stone balls, barrels, and wheelbarrows. Other events comprised bending steel, tossing tyres, pulling trams, shifting fridges, and hoisting live weight (girls in mock cages!). Amongst the American-only competitors was Ken Patera, a four-time United States national weightlifting champion turned professional wrestler; Lou Ferrigno, the Mr Universe who would later star on television as the green-skinned Incredible Hulk; Franco Columbu, a Mr Olympia bodybuilder renowned for inflating hot water bottles; Olympic hammer thrower George Frenn; NFL football player Bob Young; and the eventual winner, United States national superheavyweight Olympic weightlifter, Bruce Wilhelm. He won US$20,000, paid upon his retirement from 'amateur' sport.

WSM was conceived by two Scots, David Webster and Douglas Edmunds. The two event entrepreneurs had already established themselves as strong players in the Scottish Highland Games, Webster as a strategist and organizer and Edmunds as a former elite field athlete. Evidently the combination proved to be a formidable team, as the two men convinced American broadcaster CBS that staging an event to determine the strongest man in the world had both entertainment and profit potential. However, their challenge remained; creating what was effectively a whole new sport, 'strongman', intuitively linked to, but not based upon the strength based sports that existed at the time like Olympic weightlifting, powerlifting, the highland games, and athletic field events such as the shotput or discus.

A few years later in 1982, CBS sold the WSM rights to the British broadcaster BBC, who in turn sold it to TWI. But it was not all plain sailing. By 1995, Edmunds and Webster had become dissatisfied with the WSM concept and sought to reclaim the sport along with some influential competitors, including former event winner Jamie Reeves. Together they formed the International Federation of Strength Athletes (IFSA). Like in many sports that begin to find a market niche, the athletes felt marginalized and exploited, having little say in the sport or in the commercial dividends that it generated. In an attempt to wrestle some control back of the emerging strongman sport, the IFSA started to organize its own events, but nevertheless maintained a partnership with the BBC and TWI. The three entities worked collaboratively for almost a decade, but the relationship came to an end in 2004 when another entity, InvestGroup Sports Management, took a heavy equity position in the IFSA. Its strategy was to corner the strongman supply market by creating another event series, the IFSA Strongman. With a new series in place, the IFSA had effectively secured all the talent in strongman. Despite holding the old name, it was a completely new company and it had little intention of sharing the spoils.

Event owner TWI recoiled at the insider takeover attempt. Tension escalated between the two groups until the crack become an intractable division. TWI formed another series of qualifying contests, leading to its own WSM-branded premier events. In the process, athletes remaining in the original IFSA series were excluded from the TWI version of the WSM, which incidentally still had the broadcasting arrangements. Notwithstanding the absence of some big name strongman talent, the TWI's WSM emerged dominant on the back of its longstanding television reputation as the preeminent strongman contest and the legitimate world's strongest man contest. Although competition has come and gone, there have been and remains a handful of rival series including the Strongman Super Series, the now-defunct IFSA Strongman World Championships (run from 2005–2007 after the International Federation of Strength Athletes parted company with WSM in 2004), and Strongman Champions League. However, none of the non-WSM affiliated entities have secured more than a meagre share of the market, while the 'biggest' athletes naturally head for the WSM prize-money and exposure.

One of the enduring challenges facing the WSM competition has revolved around where to hold the event. After years of trying out various international locations in order to generate local spectator interest, including Los Angeles, China, Malaysia, France, Iceland, New Zealand, Finland, Spain, Hungry, and the Bahamas, WSM organizers finally concluded that the event is not a live spectator sport and that its host site should present a spectacular, iconic backdrop for a pre-packaged broadcast product, rather than become distracted with the needs of a real-time viewing audience.

The 40th anniversary WSM competition was held in Botswana for the second year in a row, hosted by the Botswana Tourism Organisation (BTO). Based in the country's capital, Gaborone, the event was able to capture some of the region's most breath-taking landscapes and vistas, providing quintessentially awesome natural spectacles to accompany the hyper-immense specimens delivering preternatural performances.

For a media-impoverished nation such as Botswana, which relies so heavily on a fickle natural tourism market, the WSM offers a powerful vehicle directly to the armchairs of the affluent western audience it seeks to attract. Botswana Minister Tshekedi Khama commented in a media interview that the awareness the WSM has created for the country's tourism has been unprecedented. He added, "Our main interest on this event, which is a film for television, is to create awareness about the country". Minister Khama was also keen to ensure that the event would showcase the fullest range of Botswana's indigenous features: "The choice of sites at which the various activities are held during this event is therefore very important as it forms the backdrop of the footage, which will later appear on television." As a result, the BTO had used the 2016 event to profile Chobe and the Okavango, but then shifted to Gaborone in order to display the city's emerging tourism opportunities. Minister Khama further observed, "Awareness of a country is very important and it forms a basis which is very important when selling packages to the various markets."

Botswana's WSM hosting strategy seems well considered, especially given that the event is televised in more than 70 countries to an estimated audience of nearly 500 million. Yet it is not the first time the continent has employed the event to highlight a marquee natural backdrop. In fact, Zimbabwe attracted intense interest when it staged the strongman competition at its Victoria Falls Zambian border, but failed to capitalize on the subsequent tourism interest due to political unrest.

Currently, CBS Sports Network (CBSSN), the 24-hour component of CBS Sports, holds the chief broadcasting partnership with WSM. The network delivers a significant distribution channel in concert with the prodigious sporting content the network already packages, including 350 live games and 2,200+ hours of original programming every year featuring live college football and college basketball. In the United Kingdom, the WSM rights are held by Channel 5, a 20-year veteran of public broadcasting through a suite of popular content, such as documentaries, entertainment, reality, sport, drama, and children's television.

Event and sport management specialists, IMG (via TWI), maintain the licensing ownership to WSM. IMG and CBS Sports Network secured a multi-year agreement for broadcasting as part of the network's 'Sports Spectacular' series. Following a fragmented broadcasting strategy, ten 30-minute pre-packaged episodes are created for each event, culminating in a 60-minute finals episode leading to the medals ceremony crowning the World's Strongest Man.

As a final strategic pillar, the WSM has also hit upon a comfortable cross-promotional relationship with the 'Arnold Strongman Classic', a prize-fuelled, entertainment-oriented contest created for live consumption. The event is one of many high-profile competitions held during the 'Arnold Sports Festival'. Named after Arnold Schwarzenegger, the festival originated with a bodybuilding contest in 1989 and has since expanded to include a myriad of fitness, bodybuilding, powerlifting, combat, strength, and sport events. However, instead of trying to replace the WSM, the Arnold Strongman Classic moved in another direction. Since 2002, the Arnold Strongman Classic has become a strongman institution due to the confluence of its eponymous sponsor, generous prize money, live audience demand, and its shortened, spectacle-driven composition. The Arnold Classic's focus on live entertainment means that the WSM remains the lengthier, more serious contest; the WSM is the strongman equivalent to earnest test cricket, whereas the Arnold Classic represents the sport's exhilarating twenty20. Meanwhile, the Arnold Strongman Classic generates attention for the participants, as well as a potentially handsome payday.

The WSM remains an undeniably niche event, but nevertheless enjoys considerable brand equity amongst a narrow but globally populous strength, bodybuilding, powerlifting, weightlifting, strongman, and even crossfit community. Having consolidated its position as the most coveted strongman contest in the world – and the only authentic equivalent of a world championship – the WSM has found a secure niche as a packaged television program. It is filmed in locations commensurate with the exotic and unconventional nature of the events and participants, and is positioned as a heroic, hyper-masculine ideal, aimed towards an affluent, western audience of bicep-admiring men. With a solid audience in place and a successful delivery channel, the WSM seems poised to capitalize on its equity through other commercial brand extensions.

CASE STUDY QUESTIONS

1   The WSM brand involves partnerships between the event owner (IMG), the event distributor (CBS Sports Network), and the event location (via Botswana Tourism Organisation). Explain the appeal of the WSM for:

    a   CBS Sports Network

    b   Botswana Tourism Organisation

2   Given the success of the WSM brand strategy, do you think there's room for IMG to consider some brand extensions to further commercialize their product? If so, what kinds of new products would you recommend they investigate?

CHAPTER 6

Organizational design

OVERVIEW

Organizational structure or design is a phenomenon that receives a significant amount of attention from managers as they seek to organize their staff and volunteers to optimize their impact on organizational performance and meet their strategic goals. Rather than replicate the myriad of existing material on this topic, this chapter highlights the unique aspects of the structure of sport organizations. Consequently, this chapter reviews the key concepts of organizational structure, provides examples of the unique features of sport organization designs, and summarizes the key research findings on the structure of sport organizations. The chapter also provides a summary of principles for managing organizational structures within community, state, national, and professional sport organizations.

After completing this chapter the reader should be able to:

• Describe the key dimensions of organizational structure;

- Understand the unique features of the structure of sport organizations;
- Understand the various models of organization design that can be used for sports organizations;
- Identify the factors that influence the structure of sport organizations; and
- Understand some of the challenges facing managers and volunteers involved in managing the structure of sport organizations.

WHAT IS ORGANIZATIONAL STRUCTURE?

An organizational structure is the framework that outlines how tasks are divided, grouped, and coordinated within an organization (Robbins, Judge, Millett and Boyle 2010). Every sport organization has a structure that outlines the tasks to be performed by individuals and teams. Finding the right structure for an organization involves juggling requirements to formalize procedures and ensuring accountability for tasks are clear whilst fostering innovation and creativity. The 'right' structure means one in which owners and managers can exert adequate control over employee activities without unduly affecting people's motivation and attitudes to work. It also provides clear reporting, accountability, and communication lines while trying to reduce unnecessary and costly layers of management.

An organization's structure is important because it defines where staff and volunteers 'fit in' with each other in terms of work tasks, decision-making procedures, the need for collaboration, levels of responsibility, and reporting mechanisms. In other words, the structure of an organization provides a roadmap for how positions within an organization are related to each other and what tasks are performed by individuals and work teams within an organization.

DIMENSIONS OF ORGANIZATIONAL STRUCTURE

When designing any organization's structure, managers need to consider six elements: work specialization, departmentalization, chain of command, span of control, centralization, and formalization (Robbins et al 2010).

Work specialization

Creating roles for individuals that enable them to specialize in performing a limited number of tasks is known as work specialization. This concept can easily be applied in organizations that manufacture things such as sporting goods, or need to process a large volume of resources such as distributing uniforms and information to volunteers for a large sporting event. The advantage of breaking jobs down to a set of routine repetitive tasks is an increase in employee productivity and reduced costs through the use of a lower skilled labour force. This advantage must be balanced against the risks of making work too boring or stressful for individuals which can lead to accidents, poor quality, lower productivity, absenteeism, and high job turnover.

The majority of sports organizations employ small numbers of staff who are often required to perform a diverse range of tasks over a day, week, or year. In these cases, the structure of the organization will require a low level of work specialization. For example a sport development officer within a state or provincial sporting organization would be involved in activities such as conducting skills clinics with junior athletes, designing coach education courses, managing a database of casual staff, or representing the organization to sponsors or funding agencies over the course of a season. These roles require very different skill sets and in such an organization the structure would benefit from a low level of work specialization.

Departmentalization

Departmentalization is the bringing together of individuals into groups so that common or related tasks can be coordinated. In essence, people are assigned to departments in order to achieve organizational goals. Organizations can departmentalize on the basis of functions, products or services, processes, geography, or customer type.

The most common form of departmentalizing is based on assigning people or positions to various departments according to the function a person may perform. For example, a state or provincial sporting organization might group their staff according to athlete development, competition management, special events, and corporate affairs departments, with each department having a very specific function to perform.

Alternatively, a sport organization that manufactures cricket equipment may group their staff according to the product line they produce, with groups of people handling the manufacturing, sales and service for cricket apparel, cricket bats, and training aids. In this case, the functions of marketing, human resource management, financial management, and production are all replicated in each department. These criteria can also be applied to service-based sport organizations. For example, an athlete management firm may offer a range of services under financial planning, career development, life skills, and public relations training. Again, each department would manage their own marketing, human resource management, and financial management systems.

Sport organizations can also design departments on the basis of geography. For example, the operations for a sports law firm may be split into departments for capital city offices or regions. Each of the offices or regions would have responsibility in regard to their operations in a designated geographical region. Finally, sport organizations can arrange their departments on the basis of their various customer types. This approach could be used by an organization like the Australian Institute of Sport, which might create departments that support individual athletes or team sports.

It is important to note that organizations may choose to use more than one criterion to devise departments and their choice will depend on organizational size, capabilities, and operational requirements.

Chain of command

The chain of command is the reporting trail that exists between the upper and lower levels of an organization. In essence it is the line of authority that connects each position within an organization to the chief executive. It encompasses the notions of establishing clear authority and responsibility for each position within the organization. Authority refers to the rights managers have to give orders to other members in the organization and the expectation that the orders will be carried out. If managers at certain levels of an organization are provided with the authority to get things done, they are also assigned a corresponding level of responsibility. Having a single person to whom an employee is responsible is known as the unity of command. Having a single 'boss' avoids employees having to deal with potential conflict when juggling the demands of two or more managers and it helps achieve clear decision-making.

Robbins et al (2010) argue that the basic tenets of the chain of command are less relevant today due to the increase in the use of information technology, and the corresponding ease with which most employees can communicate with each other at all levels of the organization and access information that was previously restricted to top level managers. Nevertheless, managers of sports organizations should be cognizant of the basic principle of the chain of command when designing their organizational structure.

Span of control

Span of control refers to the number of staff which any manager can directly supervise without becoming inefficient or ineffective. The exact number which any manager can effectively control is determined by the level of expertise or experience of the staff – the logic being that more experienced and skilled staff require less supervision. The complexity of tasks, the location of staff, the reporting mechanisms in place, the degree to which tasks are standardized, the style of managers, and the culture of an organization also play a role in determining what the ideal span of control might be for an individual manager in an organization. The span of control affects how many levels of management are required in any given organization. The wider the span of control, the more employees can be supervised by one manager which leads to lower management costs. However, this reduced cost is a trade-off with effectiveness, as this single manager must devote more of his or her time to liaison and communication with a large number of staff.

The trend over the past 10 years has been for organizations to introduce wider spans of control and a subsequent flattening of organizational structures. This must be done in conjunction with the provision of more employee training, a commitment to building strong work cultures, and assistance to ensure staff are more self-sufficient in their roles.

Centralization and decentralization

Centralization refers to the degree to which decision making is located at the top of an organization. An organization is deemed to be highly centralized when the majority of decisions are made by senior managers with little input from employees at lower levels. Alternatively, an organization is decentralized when decisions are able to be made by employees and lower-level managers who have been empowered to do so. It is important to understand that the concepts of centralization and decentralization are relative, in the sense that an organization is never exclusively one or the other. Organizations could not function if all decisions were made by a small group of top managers or if all decisions were delegated to lower level staff.

Nonprofit sport organizations tend to be more centralized than decentralized due to the influence of their traditional structures. Decision making is often concentrated at the board level, where volunteers make decisions related to strategy for paid staff to implement at an operational level. This can lead to problems (see Chapter 12) of slow decision-making or politics. On the other hand, the nature of nonprofit sport organizations that are often made up of disparate groups and spread over a wide geographical area, requires local level decision-making for clubs, events, and sporting competitions to operate effectively.

Formalization

Formalization refers to the extent jobs are standardized and the degree to which employee behaviour is guided by rules and procedures. These rules and procedures might cover selection of new staff, training, general policies on how work is done, procedures for routine tasks, and the amount of detail that is provided in job descriptions. Formalizing an organization increases the control managers have over staff and the amount of decision-making discretion individual staff may have. An organization such as a local sport club may have very few procedures or rules for how things are done, but the tribunal for a professional sports league will have a very detailed set of procedures and policies in regard to how cases are reported, heard, and prosecuted.

In practice 6.1 Netball Queensland

Netball is the largest female participation sport in Australia and has more than 52,000 registered participants in Queensland, one of the major states of Australia. Netball Queensland (NQ), the state sporting organization responsible for the management and development of netball across Queensland, uses a typical nonprofit sport organizational structure.

NQ was established in 1971 and incorporated in 1985 and provides a range of programs and services for netball players, coaches, umpires, administrators, associations, and clubs with the aim of increasing and enhancing participation experiences. More than 360 clubs affiliate with NQ, which provides access to netball events, programs, and services as well as a pathway to state, national, and international representation. These clubs are affiliated with one of 79 associations across the state that are geographically grouped into one of 12 regions.

Associations that choose to affiliate with NQ do so to receive a number of benefits:

- Insurance including public liability, professional indemnity, personal accident, property insurance (for associations), and association liability – including directors and officers.
- Coach development and pathways for grassroots to elite through the provision of courses, resources, workshops, accreditation, and networking opportunities.

- Umpire development and pathways from grassroots to elite through courses, accreditation, mentoring, testing, and resources.
- Player development and pathways from grassroots to elite through ANZ NetSetGO!, training, clinics, regional academies, state teams, and resources.
- Community development through the Inclusion Policy and the Quality Member Program (QMP).
- Management and administration support through the Netball Queensland constitution, policy and procedures advice, facility development advice, complaint handling, MyNetball support, member protection, QMP training, and support.
- Information and access to Netball Queensland sponsors and preferred supplier opportunities.
- Voting rights at the Netball Queensland annual general meeting, general meetings, and special general meetings.
- Representation and advocacy to Netball Australia and stakeholders such as local and state government, sponsors, and supporters.

The relationship between clubs, associations, regions, and the state governing body is often described as the governance structure of a sport, and is covered in more detail in Chapter 13 when we examine sport governance in detail.

In addition to facilitating participation opportunities, NQ holds the license for the Queensland Firebirds, the Queensland team that used to compete in the trans-national netball competition, the ANZ Championship, that was discontinued in 2016. NQ is responsible for the management and marketing of the Firebirds who now play in the new Australian elite competition, Suncorp Super Netball. NQ also stages the Suncorp Super Netball Games that are held in Queensland as part of the new eight-team competition. NQ also manages a second-tier elite team, the Queensland Fusion, that competes in the Australian Netball League.

A team of over 30 staff work with a board of management and an extensive network of volunteers to deliver these programs, services, and events across Queensland. The organizational structure for the NQ state office staff is based around the key functional departments of financial management, the high-performance sport program, communications and events, membership services for affiliated associations, and the sports participation and development functions. These functional departments broadly align with the main themes in the NQ strategic plan for 2017 to 2019; to increase participation as players, coaches, umpires, and bench officials through development programs and support services; to provide a comprehensive elite pathway for netballers, coaches, and officials; improve governance and delivery of services; to grow their commercial revenues and supporters through marketing; and to develop their state facility. The structure allows individuals to be appointed to carry out specialized tasks and for the establishment of clear communication between the lower levels of the organization and the chief executive. The six dimensions of organizational structure help us understand why an organization such as NQ is structured this way.

Source: Netball Queensland website at www.qld.netball.com.au

STRUCTURAL MODELS

The types of structure adopted by sports organizations can be categorized into four common types: the simple structure, the bureaucracy, the matrix structure, and the team structure. Let's examine each of these briefly and explore their relevance for sport organizations.

The simple structure (Figure 6.1) has a low degree of departmentalization and formalization, wide spans of control and would most likely have decisions centralized to a few people. Such a structure would be used by a small sporting goods retail store that might have 10 casual and full-time staff and an owner/manager. There would be no need for departments, as most decisions and administrative tasks would be performed by the owner/manager and all other staff on the sales floor. The majority of procedures would be executed according to a simple set of rules and the owner/manager would have all staff reporting directly to him or her. The advantages of the structure in this case are obvious: decisions can be made quickly, it ensures a flexible workforce to cater for seasonal needs and busy periods, and accountability clearly rests with the owner/manager.

If the owner/manager wanted to expand the operation and open other stores in other locations, he or she would require a different structure to cope with the added demands of controlling staff in multiple locations, making decisions across a wider number of operational areas, and ensuring quality products and services are provided in each store or location. The owner/manager might consider adopting a bureaucratic structure (Figure 6.2).

The bureaucratic structure attempts to standardize the operation of an organization in order to maximize coordination and control of staff and activities. It relies on high levels of formalization, the use of departments to group people into discrete work teams that deal with specific functions or tasks, highly centralized decision making, and a clear chain of command. An organization such as Sport England, the Australian Sports Commission, or a state or provincial government department of sport would be structured along these lines. Obviously, as an organization expands in size, increases the number of locations it delivers services, or diversifies its range of activities, the more likely it is to reflect some elements of bureaucratization.

The matrix organization structure reflects the organization of groups of people into departments according to functions and products (Figure 6.3). For example, an elite institute for sport might group specialists such as sports psychologists, biomechanists, skill acquisition coaches, and exercise physiologists into discrete teams. At the same time,

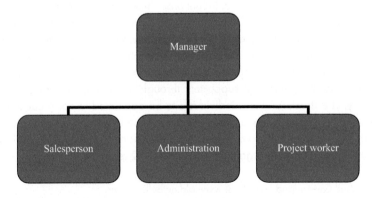

FIGURE 6.1 The simple structure

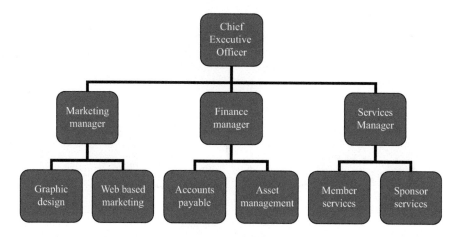

FIGURE 6.2 The bureaucratic structure

	Football operations division	Corporate services division	Marketing division
Team 1	Manager 1	Project worker 1	Worker 1
Team 2	Manager 2	Project worker 2	Worker 2
Team 3	Manager 3	Project worker 3	Worker 3

FIGURE 6.3 The matrix structure

individuals in these teams might be involved in providing services to a range of different sporting groups or athletes, effectively creating two bosses for them. This breaks the unity of command principle, but allows an organization to group specialists together to maximize sharing of expertise while facilitating their involvement in a number of projects or service delivery areas. The argument for this arrangement is that it is better to have the specialists work as a team than to appoint individuals to work in isolation to provide their services. Although this allows the organization to provide a range of services, it does increase the potential for confusion in regard to managing the demands from two bosses, which in turn may lead to an increase in stress.

A relatively new structural design option is the team structure (see Figure 6.4). The team structure requires decision making to be decentralized to work teams that are made up of people with skills to perform a variety of tasks. A football club franchise might employ such a structure with teams formed for club events or marketing campaigns as it will allow quick decision making in regard to finance, staffing, or impacts on players.

Although these generic structures can be applied to all types of organizations, there has been some research that has attempted to categorize the various structures that exist within nonprofit sport organizations. Kikulis et al (1989) developed a structural taxonomy

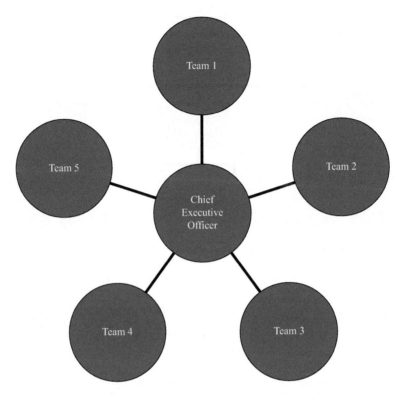

FIGURE 6.4 Team structure

for provincial (state) Canadian amateur sport organizations based on the organizational dimensions of specialization, standardization, and centralization. The evolution of Canadian sport organizations in the 1980s to a more professional and bureaucratized form prompted the researchers to attempt to establish exactly what form this evolution had taken. Kikulis et al (1989) identified eight structural designs for voluntary sport organizations, ranging in scale of complexity for the three structural dimensions. Theodoraki and Henry (1994), in a similar study defined a typology of structures for British sport governing bodies. They, too, utilized the structural elements of specialization, standardization, and centralization to distinguish between various structural designs.

Identifying design types for national-level sport organizations was the focus of a study by Kikulis et al (1992) in which organizational values and organizational structure dimensions were used to identify three distinct designs – kitchen table, boardroom, and executive office. Each design represents a distinct mix of organizational values comprising their orientation toward private or public interests; the domain of activities conducted (ranging from broad participation based to a focus on high performance results); the degree of professional involvement in decision-making; and the criteria used to evaluate effectiveness.

Now that we have explored the elements of structure and the various ways they can be used, we can examine the factors that influence the structure adopted by a sport organization.

WHAT INFLUENCES THE STRUCTURE OF A SPORT ORGANIZATION?

There are generally four factors that influence the structure of an organization: strategy, size, technology, and environmental uncertainty. Each of these is briefly reviewed.

Strategy

In a perfect world, an organization's structure would be designed purely around the requirement to maximize the chances of an organization's strategic goals being achieved. This is rarely possible, but strategy does play an important part in determining the structure adopted by a sport organization. Whether an organization is pursuing an overall strategy of innovation, cost minimization, or imitation will necessitate the design of a specific organizational structure.

An important trend to note in the development of structure for nonprofit sport organizations has been the impact of the introduction of paid professional staff, a very deliberate strategy in response to increases in government funding in sport in most club-based sporting systems around the world. The impact of such a strategy on the structure of Canadian provincial VSOs was explored by Thibault, Slack and Hinings (1991). They found that specialization and formalization increased after the introduction of professional staff, but that centralization, after initially increasing, actually decreased over time. It was suggested that centralization increased because volunteer board members sought to retain control over decisions, and then decreased as the relationship between board members and staff stabilized. Such resistance to changes in structure were noted by Kikulis, Slack, and Hinings (1995), who studied the changes in specialization, standardization, and centralization of Canadian NSOs over a four-year period. They found that incumbent volunteers resisted change across all three elements of organizational structure, highlighting the role of human agents and personal choice in determining organizational change outcomes.

Size

The size of an organization also plays an important part in determining its best possible structure. Larger organizations tend to be more formalized, with more specialist roles and departments and more levels of management than smaller organizations. This makes sense as managers need to implement greater control measures to manage the volume and communication of information in a large organization. Amis and Slack (1996) state that much of the research into the relationship between organizational size and degree of centralization suggest that as "organizations become larger, decision-making becomes more decentralized" (p. 83). In terms of nonprofit sport organizations they also found that with an increase in size of the organization, control over organizational decision making remains at the voluntary board level and concluded that a "central role of decision-making as a means of control and the desire for volunteers to retain this control" (Amis and Slack 1996, p. 84) meant that the boards of many sport organizations were reluctant to relinquish control to professional staff.

Technology

Technology does have an impact on organizational structure. Robbins et al. (2010) argue that if organizations predominantly undertake routine tasks then there is a high degree of departmentalization, and a high level of centralized decision making. This appears logical because non-routine tasks require decisions to be made at the level of organization where they actually happen. In regard to a sport organization such as a professional sport club, the increased use of information and communication technology means that it requires additional specialist staff such as video technicians, statisticians, and network programmers who may have replaced staff that used to perform tasks manually. The net effect is a higher level of departmentalization and specialization amongst the workforce.

Environmental uncertainty

Environmental uncertainty for sport organizations can be influenced by the actions of suppliers, service providers, customers, sponsors, athletes, volunteers, staff, stakeholder groups, and government regulatory agencies, as well as general changes in economic or market conditions. For example, if a group of professional athletes behave inappropriately, their actions can affect the ability of their club or team to maintain or develop sponsorships, which in turn may affect their ability to retain staff and hence require a structural adjustment. Similarly, a downturn in the economy can directly affect sales of sporting merchandise, and organizations may have to adjust their structure accordingly to reduce costs or change product lines.

There are some additional drivers of structural change in sport organizations that are worth noting. These include poor on-field performance, changes in personnel due to politics, competition and market forces, government policy changes, and forced change via mergers and amalgamations. Poor on-field performance by professional sporting teams or clubs can lead to an end-of-season purge of playing or coaching personnel, and may entail a review of how the group of staff involved in coaching, athlete support, or allied health services is organized. The political nature of some sport organizations that elect individuals to govern their activities can lead to structural change being implemented due to personal preferences of elected leaders or a mandate for change. Competition and market forces affect all organizations, but the interdependent nature of clubs operating within a league or competition necessitates them sharing information. Consequently, these organizations tend to be structured in similar ways, making structural change difficult. Governments may also change the way they fund high-performance programs or tie funding levels to the performances of international teams or individuals. Poor international performances may consequently reduce funding and therefore the capability of an organization to sustain their organizational structure. Finally, structural change may be forced upon sports organizations, either by economic conditions (such as population loss in rural areas forcing clubs to merge) or government policy (such as forcing single-gender sport organizations to merge). The example of Sport Scotland highlights how the four generic factors of strategy, size, technology, and environmental uncertainty can influence the structure of a sports organization.

In practice 6.2 Victorian Institute of Sport

The VIS is funded by the Victorian state government in Australia to "be the leading provider of high performance sports programs for talented athletes, enabling them to achieve national and international success". Their self-proclaimed core business is to select talented athletes and work to optimize all aspects of their preparation to achieve world class performances by:

- Providing a daily training environment with world-class coaching, management, and support services
- Enabling access to high-performance training facilities and equipment, and
- Supporting athletes to compete in national and international competitions

The VIS's organizational structure is directly linked to their strategy. The entire organization is based on a simple structure, with the CEO having four direct reports (or a span of control of four): a performance manager who works with a team of coaching specialists to deliver services to a range of sports; a performance services manager who works with a team of sport science providers (i.e. doctors, physiotherapists, nutritionists, psychologists, exercise physiologists); a corporate manager who works with a small team to provide finance, technology, and facility services to the organization; and a communication and marketing coordinator.

It is clear that each of the four contingency factors noted earlier in the chapter have affected the structure of the organization. The VIS has a very clear mandate to deliver professional services and support for elite athletes in a number of targeted sports. Accordingly the structure reflects these core functions or strategic foci. Any increase in the number of elite sports or athletes supported by the VIS would not necessarily lead to a change in structure; rather each of the existing teams would simply expand to cater for the increased service requirements. As a government-owned enterprise, its structure is in part determined by its mandate to deliver services to the Victorian sport industry, and is unlikely to be unduly affected by environmental uncertainty. The drivers of change in structure would include any significant shifts in funding support, strategy or government policy, such as a move to focus on a selected number of priority sports, which would perhaps require a redesign in organizational structure.

Source: Victorian Institute of Sport website at www.vis.org.au

CHALLENGES FOR SPORT MANAGERS

An ongoing challenge facing sport managers is the need to strike a balance between lowering costs by using fewer staff and increasing productivity. This can be achieved through a greater use of technology for communication, data management and analysis, the appointment of skilled staff able to use technology, and the development of semi-autonomous work teams that are able to make operational decisions quickly. This requires the use of a more flexible organizational structure than perhaps is the norm for the majority of contemporary sport organizations.

A further challenge for sport managers is to ensure that their organizations are flexible enough to quickly react to opportunities in the market or to the demands of their stakeholders, while at the same time maintaining adequate forms of control and accountability. Sport managers will need to establish clear guidelines for decision making and acceptable levels of formalization for standard procedures, without unduly constraining the flexibility to modify those guidelines and formal procedures.

An aspect of managing organizational structures that is relatively unique to sport is the presence of both paid staff and volunteers, often with volunteers directing the work of paid staff. Sport managers will need to be cognizant of the need to maintain close links between these two significant parts of their workforce and maintain a suitable structure that allows these groups to communicate effectively and work to achieve organizational outcomes.

Sport managers also need to ensure the structure can enable strategy to be realized. If strategic plans are devised, new markets identified, or new product and service offerings developed in the absence of concomitant changes to the organizational structure, then the ability of the organization to deliver such planned changes is questionable. It is imperative that sport managers pay attention to designing their structure to enable specific strategic directions to be achieved.

As illustrated in the previous chapters, organizations that work within the sport industry must work within a myriad of other organizations from the public, private, and non-profit sectors. Often, sport organizations have many stakeholders involved in setting the strategic direction of the organization. The organizational structure should therefore facilitate decision-making processes that engage all relevant stakeholders.

Finally, the interdependent relationships that exist between sports organizations that may be involved in a league, a collection of associations, a joint venture, or a funding agreement with multiple partners and sponsors necessitate organizational structures that reflect these connections. This may extend to establishing designated roles for external liaison within the structure or incorporating representation from members of external organizations on internal decision-making committees.

In practice 6.3 Working for The Blues: Carlton Football Club

Carlton Football Club is regarded as one of Australia's most famous sports clubs. It is also one of the world's oldest, having been founded in 1864. The club is known as 'The Mighty Blues' and has secured 16 Premierships (League Championships) since it joined the Victorian Football League, now the Australian Football League, in 1897.

Like many Australian Rules football clubs, its primary purpose is to win the Premiership and its structure reflects this singular focus. The club is organized around seven functional divisions: Consumer and Marketing (membership sales, branding, retails sales), Commercial Operations (sponsorship, partnership management, event management), Media (digital and social media content creation and dissemination, media liaison), Corporate Services (finance, venue management, technology), Community (programs in the community), Football (coaches, support staff, medical, analytics, players), and a new division for the AFL Women's team (coaches, support staff). This structure organizes the more than 120 staff and 75 contracted players into groups focused on playing their part in making the club a success.

An examination of the club's website, or any other major professional sport club in the world, shows the enormous range of roles that exist within professional sport clubs. These roles range from on-field coach or sport science roles, player recruitment, injury management, and other football-focused roles to the off field areas of membership sales, event delivery, and corporate hospitality. Having an effective structure that facilitates the delivery of the myriad of tasks need every week and over the course of a season is crucial for success but also for managing within a budget where clubs operate in a very competitive commercial marketplace.

Source: Carlton Football Club website at www.carltonfc.com.au

SUMMARY

Organizational structure was defined as the framework that outlines how tasks are divided, grouped, and coordinated within an organization. An organization's structure is important because it defines where staff and volunteers 'fit in' with each other in terms of work tasks, decision-making procedures, the need for collaboration, levels of responsibility, and reporting mechanisms.

Six key elements of organizational structure were reviewed: work specialization, departmentalization, chain of command, the span of control, centralization, and formalization. In addition, four basic models for how an organization may use these six elements to design an appropriate structure were reviewed: the simple structure, the bureaucracy, the matrix structure, and the team structure.

The generic contingency factors that influence organizational structure – size, strategy, technology, and environmental uncertainty – were reviewed as well as some unique drivers of change to the structure of sport organizations. Finally, a number of unique challenges for sport managers in dealing with structure were presented. Sport managers should be aware of these factors that drive structural change and the specific structural elements they can influence that are likely to deliver improved organizational outcomes and performance.

REVIEW QUESTIONS

1 Define organizational structure in your own words.

2 If you were to manipulate any of the six elements of structure, which do you think could have the most impact on the day to day role of the chief executive of a sports organization?

3 Do staff in small sports organizations have a low degree of work specialization? Why or why not?

4 Which structural model would suit a large sports event such as the Commonwealth or Olympic Games? Why?

5 How are organizational strategy and structure related?

6 How does a change in size affect the structure of a sports organization?

7 Compare the organizational structure of a sport manufacturing organization and a local community sports facility? How do each of the six elements of organizational structure differ? Which elements are similar?

8 Explain how environmental uncertainty can force change to the structure of a sports organization.

9 Interview the CEO of a medium-sized sports organization. What is their most significant challenge in managing their organizational structure?

10 Explore the structure of a small community sport club. Are the principles of organizational structure outlined in this chapter directly applicable? Why or why not?

DISCUSSION QUESTIONS

1 What are some of the important issues that affect the structure adopted by a sport organization?

2 Why do sport organizations sometimes look to restructure themselves?

3 What are some of the common structural elements in place for professional sport clubs across the world?

4 Should an organization's strategy drive its structure or the other way around?

5 Why do CEOs sometimes restructure an organization when they are appointed?

FURTHER READING

The use of organizational theory in the analysis of structures for nonprofit sport organizations is well established. Three broad questions have been addressed in these studies. These are first, investigating the relationship between organizational structure and organizational effectiveness; second, attempting to categories organizational types; and third, exploring the impact of professionalization on various elements of organizational structure.

Students interested in reading further should consult the following journal articles: Amis, J. and Slack, T. (1996). The size-structure relationship in voluntary sport organizations. *Journal of Sport Management*, 10: 76–86.

Kikulis, L.M., Slack, T. and Hinings, B. (1995). Toward an understanding of the role of agency and choice in the changing structure of Canada's national sport organizations. *Journal of Sport Management*, 9: 135–152.

Olson, E.M., Duray, R., Cooper, C. and Olson, K.M. (2016). Strategy, structure and culture within the English Premier League: An examination of large clubs. *Sport, Business and Management: An International Journal*, 6(1): 55–75.

Relvas, H., Littlewood, M., Nesti, M., Gilbourne, D. and Richardson, D. (2010). Organizational structures and working practices in elite European professional football clubs: Understanding the relationship between youth and professional domains. *European Sport Management Quarterly*, 10(2): 165–187.

Stevens, J. (2006). The Canadian Hockey Association merger and the emergence of the Amateur Sport Enterprise. *Journal of Sport Management*, 20: 74–101.

Theodoraki, E.I. and Henry, I.P. (1994). Organizational structures and contexts in British national governing bodies of sport. *International Review for the Sociology of Sport*, 29: 243–263.

Thibault, L., Slack, T. and Hinings, B. (1991). Professionalism, structures and systems: The impact of professional staff on voluntary sport organizations. *International Review for the Sociology of Sport*, 26: 83–97.

RELEVANT WEBSITES

The following websites are useful starting points for further information on the structure of sport organizations:

Australian Sports Commission at www.ausport.gov.au
Sport New Zealand at www.sportnz.org.nz
Sport Canada at www.pch.gc.ca/eng/1266246552427
Sport England at www.sportengland.org
Sport Scotland at www.sportscotland.org.uk

CASE STUDY 6.1

Design challenges for professional basketball in Britain

The top men's professional basketball league in the UK is the British Basketball League (BBL). The BBL is an independent company owned by its 12 member clubs, each with an equal shareholding in BBL. Each club has a representative on the BBL board of directors who oversee the operation of a central BBL office in Birmingham, which manages administration, marketing, and media functions. The interesting aspect of the structure of the BBL is that each club operates as a franchise in designated areas across the UK in order to maximize commercial and media value within their local community. In 2017, these franchises were:

- Bristol Flyers
- Cheshire Phoenix
- Glasgow Rocks

- Leeds Force
- Leicester Riders
- London Lions
- Manchester Giants
- Esh Group Eagles Newcastle
- Plymouth Raiders
- DBL Sharks Sheffield
- Surrey Scorchers
- Worcester Wolves

Unlike other sports where second-division champions are promoted to replace the bottom-ranked team in the top league, the BBL operates independently of the second-tier competition, the English Basketball League (EBL). There is no promotion and relegation between the BBL and the EBL, and EBL clubs cannot join the BBL based on their performances in official competition alone. However, EBL clubs and any other organizations can apply for a franchise from the BBL. Indeed, new franchise development is a cornerstone of the BBL strategy.

The organizational structure or franchise system used by the BBL is used because of the significant costs of running a team in the BBL compared to running any other team in the UK. The structure attempts to provide financial security and protect investment into clubs by removing the threat that comes with relegation. A salary cap and income distribution policy amongst BBL clubs also assists with competitive balance and financial management.

Clubs can apply to join the BBL by submitting a detailed business plan to the BBL Franchise Committee that specifies venue details, proof of an acceptable level of financial backing, and an explanation of how the club will be sustainable. Because government funding for basketball goes to England Basketball, the BBL receives no government financial support. Instead, it derives its income from sponsorship, media partnerships, merchandising, and ticket sales. Commercial and media rights generate the largest portion of income for the league and clubs.

The BBL has introduced player eligibility rules to provide more opportunities for British players, with each team allowed a maximum of five over-18 non-British players per game. There is no national draft system; players are recruited directly by clubs from their development programs or via direct application.

In 2014, the Women's British Basketball League (WBBL) was created along similar design principles. In 2017, there were 11 franchises in the WBBL, some operated by universities:

- Barking Abbey Crusaders
- Caledonia Pride
- Cardiff Met Archers
- Durham Palatinates
- Leicester Riders
- Manchester Mystics

- Nottingham Wildcats
- Team Northumbria
- Oaklands Wolves
- Sevenoaks Suns
- Westfield Health Sheffield Hatters

The challenge of organizing viable professional basketball leagues for men and women in a country dominated by football, rugby, and cricket is significant. Competition for sponsorship dollars, access to appropriate venues, securing media rights, and maintaining market share in a crowded professional sport market are all challenges for the directors of the BBL, WBBL, and the managers of their member clubs. The organizational structure adopted by the BBL and the WBBL in using the U.S.-style franchise system is an attempt to combat these challenges. The structure allows the league and clubs to plan for future expansion, manage income and costs across all elements of the organization, and ensure equitable decision making amongst the member clubs.

CASE STUDY QUESTIONS

1   Access the BBL and WBBL websites at www.bbl.org.uk and www.wbbl.org.uk and read about the history of the leagues. Why do you think professional basketball has evolved to this structure in Britain?

2   Why is one of the key strategies for both leagues to increase the number of franchisees and therefore change the structure?

3   What are the barriers or constraints that might limit the effectiveness of the structure adopted by the BBL and WBBL?

4   What are some of the economic and market forces that both leagues need to be mindful of in order to ensure its structure meets its needs?

5   Do you think the leagues would be able to quickly modify their organizational structure? Why or why not?

Source: British Basketball League website at www.bbl.org.uk and WBBL website at www.wbbl.org.uk

CASE STUDY 6.2

Biscuits, buckets, and barn burners: Hockey Canada

Hockey Canada, the sole governing body for amateur ice hockey in Canada, claims that more than 4.5 million Canadians are associated with it as players, coaches, officials, trainers, administrators, or volunteers. Its mission is deceptively simple – lead, develop, and promote positive hockey experiences.

The organization works in conjunction with 13 provincial branches, the Canadian Hockey League, and Canadian Interuniversity Sport in growing the game at all levels. Hockey Canada oversees the management of programs in Canada from entry-level to high-performance teams and competitions, including world championships and the Olympic Winter Games. Hockey Canada is also Canada's voice within the International Ice Hockey Federation. Hockey Canada has offices in Calgary and Ottawa and operates regional centres in Ontario and Quebec.

Hockey Canada exists to:

- Foster and encourage the sport of amateur hockey throughout Canada;
- Foster and encourage leadership programs in all areas related to the development of hockey in Canada;
- Recognize and sanction the establishment of governing bodies in Canada in accordance with the principles, philosophy, and practices of the association;
- Support and encourage branches and other members in the development of amateur hockey within their jurisdictions and areas of responsibility;
- Establish and maintain uniform playing rules for amateur hockey;
- Maintain national insurance programs;
- Affiliate with and co-operate with other national or international amateur hockey organizations;
- Conduct inter-branch and international contests of amateur hockey;
- Provide representation for international open hockey competition.

More than 636,000 registered players and another 1.5 million casual or unregistered participants play hockey at more than 3,000 arenas throughout Canada through the efforts of more than 3,500 minor hockey associations. Hockey Canada employs over 75 staff and has offices in most Canadian provinces. In conjunction with these member organizations, Hockey Canada facilitates participation in amateur hockey leagues, teams, and games through player, coach, and referee development; grading of competitions; and establishing appropriate rules and regulations for amateur hockey across Canada. Each year more than 32,000 paid staff and unpaid volunteers officiate at hockey games, where more than 93,000 largely volunteer coaches ply their trade.

An important element of the structure of Hockey Canada is the large size of the board of directors which comprises officers (8), branch presidents (13), council representatives and directors (8), and special advisory council members (5). Each of these positions represents a specific constituent group within Hockey Canada. In addition, the board of directors receives reports from a Hockey Development Council of 24 members, again made up of individuals representing the specific interests of regional affiliates, or membership types (i.e. coaches, officials). The board of directors has a number of policy sub-committees (five) that deal with areas such as elite competitions, women's programs, policy development, programs of excellence, and junior development. Finally, there are 10 standing sub committees that report to the board on issues such as insurance, marketing, finance, management, and other areas of activity. This appears to be a very cumbersome way to manage the affairs of a relatively simple activity like facilitating games of ice hockey, but the sheer scale and geographic spread of its constituents require Hockey Canada to maintain a comprehensive governance structure that facilitates decision making and communication amongst its 4.5 million participants.

The most recent annual report from Hockey Canada highlights the reach of this organization through its web page and social media platforms. In the 2015/2016 season there were more than 17 million page views on the Hockey Canada website, including 4 million views of videos. Hockey Canada had more than 460,000 Twitter followers and 130 million Facebook impressions. Hockey is clearly the national sport of a nation obsessed with hockey. A whole language has evolved to describe hockey: the biscuit (the puck), buckets (players' helmets), and barn burners (a fast-paced, high-scoring game) amongst the colloquialisms. Having a good governance system as well as an effective structure to support the delivery of hockey participation opportunities is crucial.

CASE STUDY QUESTIONS

1   Access the Hockey Canada website at www.hockeycanada.ca and read about the history of hockey in Canada. Is there are simpler structure possible to support hockey across the country?

2   Does the strategy for Hockey Canada drive its structure or is it subject to the history of provincial organizations being created to deliver hockey in each province? Is this a positive or negative for Hockey Canada?

3   What are some of the economic and market forces that Hockey Canada needs to be mindful of in order to ensure its structure meets its needs?

4   What is the relationship of Hockey Canada to the National Hockey League? If hockey is such a dominant sport in Canada, why are there so many teams based in the United States? Does the structure of Hockey Canada limit its ability to act more commercially and leverage the NHL brand?

Sources: Hockey Canada (website www.hockeycanada.ca) and Hockey Canada. (2014). *Annual Report 2014*. Calgary, CA: Hockey Canada.

CHAPTER 7

Human resource management

OVERVIEW

This chapter reviews the core concepts of human resource management, provides examples of the unique features of human resource management within sport organizations, such as volunteer and paid staff management, and summarizes the key phases in the human resource management process. The chapter examines human resource management within community, state, national, and professional sport organizations in order to illustrate core concepts and principles.

After completing this chapter the reader should be able to:

• Identify the key concepts that underpin human resource management within sport organizations;

- Explain why human resource management in sport organizations can be different from non-sport organizations;
- Identify each of the phases within the human resource management process; and
- Explain the ways in which each of the human resource management phases would be implemented in different sport organization contexts.

WHAT IS HUMAN RESOURCE MANAGEMENT?

Human resource management, in business or sport organizations, is essentially about first, finding the right person for the right job at the right time, and second, ensuring the organization has an appropriately trained and satisfied workforce. The concepts that underpin effective human resource management are not particularly complex. However, the sheer size of some organizations, as well as the difficulties in managing unusual organizations in the sport industry, make human resource management a complex issue to deal with in practice. Successful sport leagues, clubs, associations, retailers, and venues all rely on good human resources, both on and off the field, to ensure they achieve their objectives. Conversely, organizations with staff that lack motivation, are ill suited to their work, are under-paid, or are under-valued will struggle to perform.

Human resource management is a central feature of an organization's planning system. It cannot be divorced from other key management tools, such as strategic planning, financial planning, or managing organizational culture and structure. Human resource management can both drive organizational success, and is a consequence of good management and planning. Importantly, human resource management is a process of continual planning and evaluation and is best viewed as part of a cycle in which an organization aims to meet its strategic goals. Human resource management, therefore, is a holistic management function in that it can be "both person-centred and goal-directed" (Smith and Stewart 1999).

Human resource management can mean different things to different organizations, depending on their context and outlook. For professional sport organizations that are profit driven, such as the American National Basketball Association (NBA), Major League Baseball (MBL), or National Hockey League (NHL), successful human resource management is equated with profitability, long-term growth, and success (on and off the court, diamond and rink). This is not to suggest that these things are pursued at the expense of employees, but rather that the success of the employees is measured by dispassionate business indicators and human resource management is a tool for driving the business towards its goals. For example, some player welfare and development programs within professional sport organizations are designed to produce socially, morally, and ethically responsible citizens. This is viewed as a good human resource strategy, not only because of the intrinsic value to the athletes, but for the extrinsic value that comes from better public relations and sponsor servicing. In other words, better behaved athletes mean greater profitability and overall success for professional sport teams and franchises.

For nonprofit sport organizations, successful human resource management is not always about bottom-line financial performance. Rather, it can encompass a range of strategies and outcomes depending on the organizational context. A local sporting club that has had a problem with alcohol consumption among its junior players may develop a range of programs to educate its players, coaches, and administrators (who may be paid or volunteer staff), in order to encourage a more responsible club culture. This player welfare program may actually be part of a human resource management strategy, as the inappropriate club culture may have been making it difficult to attract and retain volunteers with expertise and commitment. In the case of the professional team context the player welfare program can be used to manage image and maintain brand credibility. In the case of the local community sport club the player welfare program can be used to retain volunteers who were being driven away from the club by poor behaviour and a dysfunctional culture. From these two examples it is clear that human resource management can be both person centred and goal directed at the same time.

One of the significant challenges of implementing effective human resource management within sport organizations is that not all sport organizations are alike. As Taylor, Doherty, and McGraw (2008) have illustrated, different types of sport organizations have different staffing profiles. These staffing profiles are dependent on an organization's type, as well as its purpose or reason for being. For example, a professional sport organization, such as a club in the Spanish La Liga, will have an extensive staff of full-time paid professionals engaged in marketing, coaching, sport science, and general administration, whereas a voluntary organization, such as local cricket or rugby club, is likely to have no paid staff. Other sport organizations might have a mixture of paid and voluntary staff who work together in the day-to-day operations of the organization, or work together in their capacities as staff and members of a committee of management or board of directors. We will investigate the governance of sport organizations later in the book, but at this point it sufficient to note that in many sport organizations paid staff are answerable to a voluntary board of directors. This relationship can be a challenge for the overall management of the organization and the practice of human resource management more specifically.

Many of the functions of professional and voluntary sport organizations are similar, such as event management, promotion, fundraising, membership services, and financial management; however, the scale of the organizations is different. Although it is true that the scale and type of organization have an impact on the human resource management practices that can and need to be put in place, in many respects sport organizations are increasingly adopting human resource management practices that are underpinned by the notion of professional and standard practice. Indeed, the implementation of specific human resource management practices has been viewed as an important catalyst in the professionalization of voluntary or community sporting organizations. For example, in the early 1990s the Australian Sports Commission, in conjunction with the Australian Society of Sports Administrators, the Confederation of Australian Sport and state departments of sport and recreation, developed the 'Volunteer Involvement Program'. The original program was designed to encourage sport organizations to adopt professional volunteer management practices, which was viewed as essential given the large numbers of volunteers involved in sport organizations and the increasing professionalization of the industry.

The program has since been revised and improved to provide sporting clubs and associations with resources and training modules for volunteer management ('recruiting volunteers', 'retaining volunteers', 'volunteer management: a guide to good practice', 'managing event volunteers', 'volunteer management policy', and 'the volunteer coordinator'). These modules encourage Australian sporting clubs and associations to develop systematic processes and practices, although it should be acknowledged that the diversity of club-based sporting system, such as that which is in operation in Australia, means that the capacity to professionalize varies considerably.

IS HUMAN RESOURCE MANAGEMENT IN SPORT SPECIAL?

Many of the core concepts that underpin human resource management apply to all organizations, whether they are situated in the world of business, such as soft drink manufacturer Coca-Cola or mining company BHP Billiton, or in the world of sport, such as the South African Rugby Football Union or the Canadian Curling Association. This is not surprising, given that all these organizations employ staff who are expected to execute a range of designated tasks at an appropriate level of performance. These staff will manage finances, undertake strategic planning, and produce products like Fanta, iron ore, coaching clinics, and national championships. There are, however, significant differences between business and sport organizations, which result in modifications to generic human resource management practices.

In particular, professional sport organizations have special features which present a unique human resource management challenge. Sport organizations, such as the Cincinnati Bengals in America's National Football League, revolve around three distinct types of employees. First, the Bengals employ people in what they call 'the front office', such as the director of business development or the director of corporate sales, marketing, and broadcasting. Second, the Bengals employ people in what can be referred to as the 'football department', such as the coaches, trainers, and scouts. Finally, the Bengals employ people who comprise 'the team', the players, who are the most visible people within any professional sport organization. It could be argued that non-sport businesses operate in the same way, with different levels of management, from the chief executive officer all the way through to the employee on the factory floor. The obvious difference in the sporting context is that the human resources at the bottom of the staffing pyramid are the highest paid employees in the entire organization. The difference between sport and non-sport organizations is illustrated in Figure 7.1. It should be noted that sport organizations have employees that could be considered 'the lowest paid', but relative to non-sport organizations they are not equivalent, and as such a light blue arrow has not been included for the sport organization pyramid (sport organizations are not completely unique in this respect, however, for in many forms of entertainment, such as film or television drama, the actors are the highest paid).

In non-sport organizations, chief executive officers, general managers, and other senior executives often receive performance bonuses and have access to share options that allow them to share in the wealth and profitability of the company. The workers producing the product (at the Fanta bottling plant or the iron ore mine, for example) do not have access to performance schemes and bonuses that might be worth millions of dollars. In professional sport organizations the situation is reversed and the performance bonuses are typically available to those who produce the product, the players. It is important to keep this special feature of sport in mind when considering the human

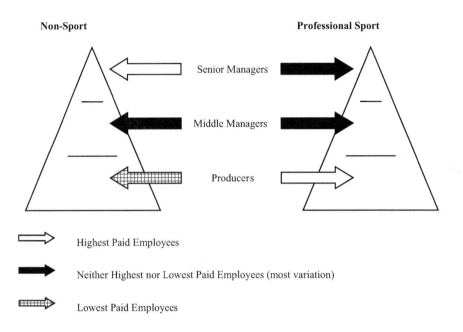

FIGURE 7.1 Pay and organization levels in professional sport and non-sport organizations

resource management needs of professional sport organizations specifically and sport organizations more generally.

Additionally, a significant proportion of staff in semi-professional and nonprofit sport organizations are volunteers. The distinction between volunteers and paid staff in the effective management of these groups is a challenge for human resource management in sport organizations. Because sport is often played in a community environment (at a state, regional, or local level), it necessarily requires the support of volunteers to maintain services, facilities, and events. Some national sport organizations, like the South Africa Rugby Football Union or the Canadian Curling Association mentioned earlier, have paid staff at the national level, whose job it is to coordinate and develop programs, events, championships, and national teams. Equivalent state or regional associations for sports like these might, depending on the size, popularity, and government funding afforded the sport, also have paid staff in key management, development, and coaching positions. In some instances these state or regional associations will have more staff than the national body because of the requirement to deliver programs and services, as well as manage and provide strategic direction for the sport. Local associations, again depending on the size and popularity of the sport, might also have some paid staff; however, at this level sports are supported by a significant core of volunteers. In Australia it has been estimated that sporting activities are supported by 1.5 million volunteers who collectively contribute in excess of 150 million volunteer hours per year, whereas in the United Kingdom it has been estimated that volunteers contribute in excess of 1 billion hours of labour (www.sportengland.org).

A significant proportion of sport is played on a weekly basis within leagues and associations across the world. Depending on whether the sport is played indoor or outdoor, the sport might have a winter season (football or ice hockey), a summer season (baseball), or might be played all year (basketball). The regularity of the season and the competition, whether at the elite or community level, means that the staffing requirements of sport organizations are predictable and remain relatively stable. There are, however, a range of sporting events and championship for which staff planning is difficult and staffing levels fluctuate greatly. These events are either irregular (a city might get to host the Olympics once in 100 years) or big enough that they require a large workforce for an intense period of time (the annual Monaco Grand Prix). The staffing for major annual sport events can be referred to as 'pulsating' (Hanlon and Cuskelly 2002), as illustrated in Figure 7.2.

In essence, major events need a large workforce, often composed primarily of volunteers or casual workers, for a short period of time prior to the event, during the event, and directly following the event, and a small workforce of primarily paid staff for the rest of the year (events such as the Olympic Games or world championships will require a permanent paid staff for many years prior to the event, but most staffing appointments will conclude within six months of the event finishing). The rapid increase and decline in staffing within a one- or two-week period is a complex and significant human resource management problem. It requires systematic recruitment, selection, and orientation programs in order to attract the staff, and simple yet effective evaluation and reward schemes in order to retain them.

Large organizations with a large workforce have both the capacity and responsibility to engage in sophisticated human resource management. Often there is a dedicated team or department that manages human resources, led by a senior member of staff. In small to medium sized organizations, however, there is not always the human or financial capacity to devote to human resource management practices in a formal system. Human resource

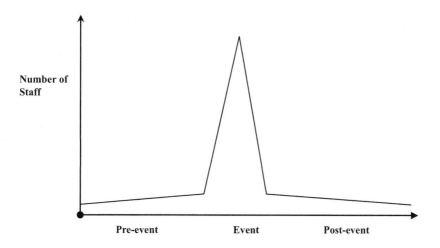

FIGURE 7.2 'Pulsating' sport event staffing

management in small to medium sized organizations is often the responsibility of the most senior staff member, such as the chief executive or general manager or is combined with roles performed by another senior manager responsible for finances, planning, or marketing, for example.

Sport leagues, clubs, associations, and venues rarely have enough staff to warrant employing someone to be responsible solely for human resource management. Often the other key management roles, such as marketing, events, or sponsorship are considered essential and human resource management is considered either as a luxury or peripheral to the core management functions. Furthermore, human resource management can be confused with personnel management, which encompasses more mechanistic functions such as payroll and record keeping (leave, sick pay, etc.).

THE ESSENTIALS OF HUMAN RESOURCE MANAGEMENT

Human resource management in sport organizations aims to provide an effective, productive, and satisfied workforce. Human resource management refers to the design, development, implementation, management, and evaluation of systems and practices used by employers use to recruit, select, develop, reward, retain, and evaluate their workforce. The core elements of the human resource management process are represented in Figure 7.3. The following phases are considered the core functions of human resource management, although it is important to keep in mind that these functions will differ significantly

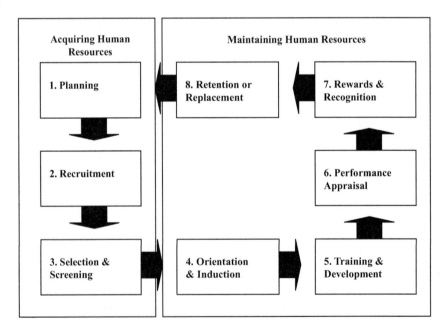

FIGURE 7.3 The traditional human resource management process

depending on the size, orientation, and context of the sport organization in which they are implemented.

Phase 1: human resource planning

Human resource management planning is essentially about assessing and forecasting the staffing needs of the organization and is often referred to as the most important phase for effective human resource (Smith and Stewart 1999). The planning phase of human resource management is short and fairly static for organizations in which the staffing levels remain fairly constant and the types of jobs performed by staff members vary little. For organizations that are dynamic or in a state of flux (as a result of economic pressures or opportunities for example), human resource planning is a cycle of ongoing development.

In the planning phase an organization must assess whether current staffing needs will be adequate to meet future demand (or alternatively, whether fewer staff will be required), whether staff turnover is predictable and can be accommodated, whether the ratios of paid, full-time, part-time, casual, and volunteer staff are appropriate or adequate, whether there are annual or cyclical fluctuations in staffing that need to be met and managed, and whether specific capabilities will be required in the future that the organization is currently lacking.

Once an organization decides that a new staff member is required or a new position is to be created, the organization must undertake a job analysis in order to determine the job content (primary and implied tasks), requirements (skills, competencies, qualifications, and experience), and context (reporting relationships and job characteristics). Once the job analysis has been completed in as much detail as possible, the organization is ready to develop a job description (a document that covers the job content and context) and a job specification (a document that covers the job requirements, especially skills and knowledge base).

Four management principles can be applied to job design. They are most useful for considering how a job might be positioned within an organization, as well as for identifying different types of organizations. These themes are job simplification, job rotation, job enlargement, and job enrichment (Chelladurai 2006). Job simplification refers to the process in which a job (and the organization) is broken down into a series of simplified and specialized tasks. This simplification is intended to increase the specialization of employees, thereby increasing efficiency and productivity. Job simplification can be viewed as a positive management tool, particularly when it comes to evaluating the performance of an individual employee; however, job specialization, depending on the context, can lead to workers becoming bored and subsequently dissatisfied with their work.

The second principle, job rotation, is partly a remedy to the boredom and dissatisfaction that can result from simplification. Job rotation involves workers swapping jobs on a periodic basis in order to keep fresh and stimulated, although clearly a sport organization will only have a finite range of jobs through which employees can rotate.

Job enlargement refers to a process in which employees are encouraged to enlarge the scope of their work and add tasks, even if they are simplified and specialized. The benefit of this approach is a happier workforce, but the downside is the perception of overwork.

Finally, job enrichment refers to the structuring of the job so that it maximizes employee motivation and involvement. This process relies on being able to design jobs that are flexible and have the capacity for growth and change, as well as the employment of people that can work autonomously. According to Chelladurai (2006), the greater levels of responsibility and challenging work that are available through job enrichment means that it is a superior method of job design.

Phase 2: recruitment

Recruitment refers to the process by which an organization tries to find the person most suited to the job that has been designed. The greater the pool of applicants, the greater the chance the organization will find a suitable candidate. Generating a pool of applicants is not always simple, however, particularly if the job requires specific skills, knowledge, qualifications, or experience that are in demand or short supply. Thus, for the chief executive position in a major professional club with responsibility for a multi-million-dollar operation, the search might be extensive and costly. However, recruiting an attendant to check membership tickets at home games of the professional club might only require a small advertisement in a local newspaper. Finally, recruiting 10,000 people to act as volunteers for a major hallmark event might require a nationwide or international advertising campaign across various media forms. Increasingly, recruitment processes are becoming more sophisticated as organizations take advantage of rapidly developing communication technologies.

In practice 7.1 Tough job?

Co-founded by Will Dean and Guy Livingstone, Tough Mudder is an endurance event that has gained popularity under the motto 'probably the toughest event on the planet'. Based on a series of obstacles that use fire, water, electricity, and heights, Tough Mudder events challenge participants both physically and psychologically. Tough Mudder started in the United States in 2010 and has grown quickly, expanding to the UK and Australia in 2012, Germany in 2013, and Mexico in 2016. According to the company, by 2015 more than 2 million people had participated in a Tough Mudder event; by 2016 the company had grown to 150 employees in three international offices, and participants have raised more than US$10 million for charity through their participation in more than 150 events since 2010.

In 2017, Tough Mudder advertised for an 'Operations Supervisor' at their UK head office. The job advertisement noted that Tough Mudder's "mission is to grow a global tribe that lives courage, personal accomplishment, teamwork and fun", that the "opportunity ahead of us is vast, and we continue to look for the best, brightest and most badass to join us" and that "as a member of TMHQ, you'll be given an opportunity to push your boundaries and find out what you're capable of, to work with and learn from incredibly smart colleagues, and to enjoy the journey of building a world-class company".

The job advertisement was divided into four sections: 'The Job', 'The Work', 'The Traits', and 'The Experience'. A selection of each of these sections is provided here in order to provide an example of the way in which a job analysis is transformed in the recruitment phase.

The Job

The job was described as follows:

> The primary responsibility of the Operations Supervisor is to create and manage an exceptional event experience within the Mudder Village area – focusing on maximizing customer satisfaction whilst delivering a seamless, cost effective operation. The role holder will report into the Operations Manager, and will work closely with the Course & Construction Manager, Mini Mudder & Workforce Associate, and other central event service functions.

The Work

The description of the work was detailed enough for prospective candidates to get a very clear indication of what they would be doing should they be successful in securing the position:

- Assist the Operations Manager with all event planning requirements
- Own the planning and delivery for all front of house aspects of the event. Specifically focus on design, set up, and management of the Mudder Village area
- Identify, negotiate terms, and contract external vendors and service providers
- Identify and deliver revenue enhancing activities to drive on site participant spend
- Identify and deliver opportunities to enhance customer satisfaction through the Mudder Village experience
- Ensure effective partner servicing and management
- Create event specific briefing documents for both internal and external use
- Manage up to 120 staff on event weekends
- Create purchase orders and ensure financial control documents are up to date and accurate
- Assist in post-event budget reconciliation

The Traits

Many of the traits identified are common to many job advertisements for jobs within the sport, recreation, and leisure industries, such as critical thinking, communication skills, teamwork, and problem solving:

- Strong critical thinker and communicator
- Ability to thrive in a fast-paced environment

- Team player with strong organizational skills and attention to detail
- Creative problem solver and conflict manager
- Focused on meeting objectives and delivering results
- Willing to be based in London and travel 30–40% of the time

The Experience

The job required a degree from 'a leading university', a minimum of three to four years of "work experience in event planning, operations, project management or outdoor industry", as well as preferred experience in mass participation event planning.

Sources: Tough Mudder website at <www.tmhq.com>; globalsportsjobs website at <www. globalsportsjobs.com>

Phase 3: selection

Selection and screening is the process of condensing the candidates that applied for the position during the recruitment phase to a short-list and then selecting the best candidate for the role. The selection phase will usually include at least one interview of the short-listed candidates, which will supplement the application form and curriculum vitae submitted by the applicants. These selection tools will be used to determine whether the applicant is appropriate in light of the job analysis and which of the applicants is the best person for the job. Depending on the geographic location of the applicants, the interview might be conducted in person, via telephone, via video conferencing, or via the Internet. Industrial relations legislation covers a range of organizational and employment issues in most countries. It is important to comply with these laws and regulations throughout the human resource management processes, such as the recruitment and selection phase, so that the organization is not exposed to claims of discrimination or bias (on the basis of race, colour, country of birth, ethnicity, disability, religion, sex, age, marital status, pregnancy, or sexual preference). In this respect Smith and Stewart (1999) refer to the types of questions *not* to ask in an interview:

- How old are you?
- Do you have a problem working with younger people?
- Are you married?
- Do you have any children?
- How will you care for your children when at work?
- How long have you been a single parent?
- Do you intend to have any more children?
- Where do you attend church?
- Do you have a Christian background?
- What are your views on taking prohibited drugs?
- Please send a recent photo with your application form.

- What are you going to do about your weight problem?
- Do you have a communicable disease?
- What clubs do you belong to?
- Do you belong to a trade union or professional association?
- Tell us about your political affiliations?
- Have you undertaken any military service?

An interview is the most common way of determining whether a prospective employee will be best suited to the organization and the position. However, other techniques, such as sophisticated personality and intelligence tests, are increasingly being used to determine whether the applicant has the job requirements identified in the planning phase (skills, competencies, qualifications, and experience). For example, the Myers-Briggs Type Indicator (MBTI) is a personality test which, based on questions about psychological processes such as the way people like to interpret information or make decisions, categorizes people into one of 16 personality types. Based on the psychological theories of Carl Jung, the MBTI can be used by sport organizations to determine whether an applicant not only has the appropriate skills and educational qualifications for the job, but also whether their personality, attitudes, and values will be a good 'fit' for the organization.

In practice 7.2 USA Taekwondo coach selection

The sport of taekwondo is a Korean martial art, which was included as a demonstration sport at the 1988 Olympic Games in Seoul, South Korea, and became an official sport at the 2000 Olympic Games in Sydney. The United States is one of the many nations that have been successful, winning gold, silver, and bronze medals. USA Taekwondo (USAT) is the governing body responsible for the sport in the United States, charged with ensuring high-performance outcomes at the Olympic Games; it has jurisdiction over junior and senior taekwondo events, junior and senior athlete selection, and the national coaching pool, which is divided into various sections (such as senior, junior, cadet). In order to select coaches, USAT has developed a set of procedures in order to "create a more objective process by which the USAT High Performance team can select a staff that will work to maximize the potential of athletes on a given team".

The USAT coach selection procedure has 16 criteria and each coach is rated as 'limited', 'below average', 'average', 'above average', or 'outstanding':

- Technical acumen
- Sport-specific experience
- Contemporaneous: Currently active and involved with the athletes, organizations, and officials
- Certification
- Licensing

- Team work
- Rules and regulations adherence
- Rules and regulations enforcement
- Knowledge of international rules and procedures
- Positive contributor
- Communication skills
- Motivational skills
- Organization/Institutional merit
- Coaching merit
- Knowledge and understanding of athletes
- Talent and skills integration with tactical planning and adjustments

Some of the selection criteria are based on qualifications, such as 'certification' (whether the coach is level 2 certified) or 'licensing' (currently licensed with the world federation); some are based on experience, such as having experience working with high-performance athletes or having athletes on the national team; and other criteria are what might be considered 'soft skills', such as communication skills, teamwork, and ability to motivate. Some of the criteria, therefore, are able to be assessed or measured objectively, whereas others require a subjective evaluation of the candidate.

Sources: USA Taekwondo website at <www.teamusa.org/usa-taekwondo/>

Phase 4: orientation

Once the employee has successfully navigated the recruitment and selection processes, they are ready to begin work in their new job within the sport organization. Before they start, however, they need to be orientated and inducted. This phase of human resource management is important, as a good quality orientation and induction program can make an employee feel both welcome and empowered, but a poor program, or no program, can make a new employee feel as if they have travelled to a foreign country, in which they can't speak the language, don't know where to go, and can't read any of the signs. In short, being in a new organization can be a daunting and frightening experience. The implementation of successful orientation and induction programs can ameliorate some of the difficulties, concerns, and anxieties. Potential problems are compounded if the employee is a volunteer and can be exacerbated further if the volunteer does not have any direct supervision from a paid employee of the organization. This is a recipe for disaster, both for the organization and the employee. Table 7.1 outlines some of the orientation and induction steps that the Australian Sports Commission recommended as part of a series of volunteer management modules.

Once an athlete has been selected to play for a team in a major professional sport league (passed the recruitment and selection processes), they are invariably faced with the completely new world of professional sport and all the demands that accompany it. The National Basketball Association (NBA) in the United States recognized that this was

TABLE 7.1 Australian Sports Commission volunteer orientation

Orientation Program Checklist

☑	Provide an orientation guidebook or kit
☑	Provide copies of current newsletter, annual report, and recent marketing/promotional material
☑	Provide a copy of the constitution
☑	Enter the name, address, and contact details of each volunteer into database
☑	Gather and file copies of qualifications and accreditation certificates from each volunteer
☑	Introduce the organization's culture, history, aims, funding, clients/members, and decision-making processes
☑	Introduce key volunteers and/or staff (and organization chart)
☑	Outline the roles and responsibilities of key volunteers and staff
☑	Detail the roles and responsibilities and accountabilities of the volunteer in their new position
☑	Familiarize volunteers with facilities, equipment, and resources
☑	Explain and 'walk through' emergency and evacuation procedures
☑	Familiarize volunteers with the organization's day-to-day operations (safety and risk management, telephone, photocopier, keys, filing system, tea/coffee making, office processes, and procedures, authorizing expenditure)

Adapted from: Australian Sports Commission website at <www.ausport.gov.au>

a difficult time for many young athletes and developed a comprehensive orientation and induction program. Since 1986, the rookie players of the forthcoming season have been required to participate in a week-long training and development camp in the month prior to the season's start. The rookie transition program is designed so that these young athletes can develop better life skills, which in turn will hopefully prepare them for the particular and peculiar stresses of a professional athletic career. Through the transition program, which includes a diverse range of topics such as sexual health, nutrition, and anger management, the NBA hopes that its young players will be able to make better decisions.

Successful orientation and induction programs revolve around forthright and effective communication of information about the organization and its operations. This information might include a general overview, policies and procedures, occupational health and safety regulations, industrial relations issues, a physical tour of the organization's facilities, an overview of the training and development programs available to employees, or an explanation of the performance appraisal process (Slack 1997). The focus on orientation and induction is usually magnified when a large number of volunteers are required by the organization, such as at an Olympic Games. A total of 60,422 volunteers participated in running the Atlanta Olympics in 1996, 47,000 volunteers participated in Sydney in 2000, and the 2004 Athens Olympics received in excess of 160,000 volunteer applications from all over the world. At the 2008 Beijing Games, 74,615 volunteers provided services at Games venues, and another 400,000 volunteers provided information, translation services, and emergency aid at 550 street stalls throughout the city.

Phase 5: training and development

Training and development is at the heart of an organization that seeks continual growth and improvement. Sport organizations that do not engage in systematic training and development programs are destined to operate far below their optimum, not only because they will fall behind in current trends, practices, and skills, but because they will not see themselves as learning organizations (Senge 1990). At its most basic, training and development is a process through which new and existing employees learn the skills required for them to be effective in their jobs. At one end of the spectrum these skills could be associated with learning how to operate automated turnstiles at a professional sport arena (training for the novice employee), or learning how to creatively brand the organization in order to compete in a hostile marketplace (training for the experienced existing employee). Where training was once a fairly mechanistic activity, it now includes more generic organizational skills that require development and implementation, such as when a major league sport franchise ensures product or service quality, or when a national sport organization develops an organizational culture that encourages compliance from state or regional sport organizations.

Dressler (2003) outlines a five-step training and development process that is useful for sport organizations. Step one is to complete a 'needs analysis', in which the organization identifies the necessary skills for its employees, analyses the current skills base and develops specific training objectives. Step two involves developing the actual training program, which may be done internally or externally. Most sport organizations, as previously noted, are too small to have sophisticated human resource management departments that have the skill and experience to design, develop, and implement comprehensive training programs. Sport organizations will most often use external training providers, such as universities or consultancy firms, to provide tailored or standard programs, depending on the needs analysis. Step three, validation, is an optional step in which the organization is able to validate that the training program that has been developed or contracted satisfies the needs analysis. Step four is the implementation of the program, during which the staff are trained (this could be anything from a one-day short course to a two-year master's program). In the fifth and final step the training program is evaluated. The successful program might be expanded to include more employees or more skills, while the unsuccessful program needs to be discontinued or re-worked, which requires the organization to re-assess the needs analysis. Like the entire human resource management process, the training and development process is best viewed as cyclical.

Phase 6: performance appraisal

This phase of the human resource management process is potentially the most dangerous, as it has the inherent ability to pit 'management' against 'employees' at the macro level, and at the micro level cause managers to feel uncomfortable in judging others or cause employees to feel unworthy as part of a negative appraisal. The performance appraisal process must be approached carefully by sport organizations and human resource managers within an organization must seek to develop a collaborative process in which the employee, as well as the manager, feels empowered. As Chelladurai (2006) has noted, it is useful to think of performance appraisal in terms of its administrative and developmental purposes. The administrative purpose refers to the need within organizations to make judgements about performance that are directly related to rewards and recognition, such as promotions and salary increases. The administrative purpose often requires quantitative measures, so that employees can be appraised based on similar criteria. The developmental purpose refers to developing and enhancing the capabilities of an employee, which often requires a mix of quantitative and qualitative measures, and can be a catalyst for further training and development. The administrative and developmental purposes of performance appraisal demonstrate that the human resource management process is not always a neat cycle. Rather, there is a constant to and fro between the phases.

During the performance appraisal process, managers and leaders need the ability to review performance and suggest improvement, as a way of developing overall organizational capacity. On the other hand, employees need a forum in which they feel comfortable identifying the things they did well and the things they could have done better, as part of a process of ongoing professional and career development. In this respect the performance appraisal process within any sport organization, whatever its size or type, must be seen within the simple, but effective 'plan, do, review, improve' scheme, which is usually associated with the quality assurance agenda (Deming 1993, pp. 134–136).

In professional sports organizations in particular, the performance appraisal process is often very public, if at times convoluted. Athletes and coaches are constantly rated on their performance. In basketball the number of points, rebounds, assists, turnovers, steals, fouls, and blocked shots are recorded meticulously. From year to year, goals are set for athletes and their ability to meet targets in key performance indicators can result in an extended contract with improved conditions. On the other hand, not meeting the targets can mean a player in a sport like baseball has to return to the minor leagues, to return to form or to see out their playing days. For coaches, performance appraisal is often based on one statistic alone, the win-loss record. The fact that the coach is adept at making the players feel good about themselves or has a great working relationship with the administrative staff, will count for very little when it comes to negotiating a new contract if he or she has posted a losing record.

In practice 7.3 Measuring performance

For the 2017–2018 season, the National Basketball Association set the salary cap at US$99.093 million per team, with the minimum team salary set at

US$89.184 million, or 90% of the salary cap. This means that a minimum of US$2.7 billion will be spent on player salaries alone in a single season of the NBA. As a result, it is not surprising that monitoring and improving player performance has become an important industry. The performance appraisal of professional athletes is conducted privately by their employers, but also publicly by media organizations and fans.

Catapult is one of the organizations providing performance monitoring technology to sport organizations worldwide. Born out of the marriage between emerging micro-technology science and the desire of the Australian Institute of Sport to measure athlete performance, Catapult was formed in 2006 in order to fully commercialize the wearable sensor technology that had been developed since the early 1990s. Catapult provides athlete tracking and data analysis systems for indoor and outdoor venues, to over 1,100 teams and institutes in 35 sports across 57 countries. According to Catapult, sport organizations using their systems are able to reduce the risk of athlete fatigue, optimize performance, enable athlete's to peak at the right time, and reduce the risk of injury. The development of highly sophisticated athlete tracking and monitoring systems has meant that athlete performance appraisal is no longer a subjective assessment of performance during game time only, as it was in the 1980s and 1990s, but it now consists of a vast array of objective measures, often delivered 24 hours a day, 7 days a week.

The statistical analysis of players has also developed exponentially, in part driven by the rise of fantasy leagues, but also by intense media attention and analysis of professional sport in particular. In basketball, players were once assessed, in large part, on the basis of their number of points, rebounds and assists, which were joined by steals, blocks, and turnovers. These relatively simple performance measures were then calculated per 48 minutes in order to provide an assessment of whether some players were more productive than others based on the amount of time they spent on the court. The +/- statistic was created to assess the contribution of a player to the overall performance of the team, calculated by recording the number of points scored for or against the team while that player was on the court. In addition to the sophisticated software that can plot where and when players take shots, and how successful they are from all positions on the court, fans can now also track new 'hustle stats', such as deflections, loose ball recovered, screen assists, charges drawn, and contested shots. The performance of professional sport organization employees is able to be publicly scrutinized in a way that employees from non-sport organizations would never have to endure and at a level that was previously unimaginable only 20 years ago. The development and availability of sport statistics has meant that fans worldwide are the ultimate human resource managers, engaging in constant performance appraisals, passing judgement on whether employees should be rewarded and retained or dismissed.

Sources: Catapult website at <www.catapultsports.com>; NBA website at <www.nba.com>

Phases 7 and 8: rewards and retention

Once a sport organization has planned for, recruited, selected, orientated, trained, and appraised its staff, it makes good sense that it would try to retain them. Retaining high-quality staff, whether they are in a paid or volunteer capacity, means that the organization will be better off financially and strategically. Organizational knowledge and intellectual property are lost when a sport organization fails to retain its staff. Constantly losing staff will mean that the organization may have the opportunity to encourage and develop new ways of thinking, but the more likely scenario is that it will lead to wasted resources, unnecessarily diverted to rudimentary induction programs.

The first six phases of the human resource management process all contribute to retaining staff. Poor orientation, training, and performance appraisal programs in particular can all have a negative impact on staff retention. On the other side of the retention equation, rewards and compensation can encourage employees to remain with an organization. At a professional sport organization this may mean, rather than attempting to keep wage costs low, the senior managers will be prepared to pay the 'market rate' (Smith and Stewart 1999). In a primarily voluntary organization, the reward may take the form of a letter of appreciation for being part of a successful event and an invitation to participate next year. In other words, the reward and retention strategy will depend greatly on the context in which it is being implemented and the existing level of job satisfaction.

SUMMARY

Effective human resource management in sport organizations relies on the implementation of an interdependent set of processes. At one level this can be viewed as quite mechanistic, yet on another more positive level it can viewed as a blueprint for the successful management of people through a clearly delineated set of stages. Human resource management planning, recruitment, selection, orientation, training, performance appraisal, rewards, and retention strategies are essential for an organization to operate successfully in state, nonprofit, or commercial sport environments, because good people management is at the core of every successful sport organization, irrespective of the context. Good human resource management allows sport organizations to deal with some of their unique and particular challenges, such as the place of athletes in professional sport organizations, the large casual and semi-permanent workforces required by major events (annual or periodic), and the large volunteer workforce within club-based sporting systems. On the other hand, poor human resource management can result in a workforce that is not only uncommitted, but also subject to low levels of morale and job satisfaction. In short, effective and systematic human resource management should be seen as an important management tool in any sport organization, whatever the size or type.

REVIEW QUESTIONS

1 Which is the most important phase of the human resource management process? Why? Refer in your answer to organizations with primarily paid staff and organizations with primarily volunteer staff.

2 Is human resource management important for the effective management of sport organizations? Why?

3 Examine the human resource management processes of a local sport organization. Are the processes adequate?

4 Examine the staffing levels of a major annual event in your city/province/region. Are the staffing levels stable?

5 Should the human resource management role within sport organizations be combined with another functional division? Why?

6 Should different human resource management strategies be applied to volunteers and paid staff? Why?

7 Does the place of athletes in professional sport organizations make the need for effective human resource management practices more or less important?

8 Compare the orientation and induction processes of a sport organization and a non-sport organization. How and why do they differ?

9 Does the often public appraisal of employees in sport organizations diminish the integrity of the human resource management process?

10 Choose a small to medium sized organization without a human resource management specialist. Perform a job analysis for a new employee in the role of human resource management.

DISCUSSION QUESTIONS

1 Does the pay structure of professional sporting teams, in which the players are paid more than the CEO and the senior managers, mean that these administrative staff have less or more job security than their colleagues in non-sport organizations? Take into account who is considered responsible for organizational performance in both arenas.

2 Do volunteers need specific forms of human resource management within sport organizations, or could the same processes and practices that apply to paid staff simply be applied to volunteers? Consider the role of financial remuneration in your answer and how significant an influence you think it is on the ways in which people operate in the workplace.

3 Is asking candidates applying for a job in a sport organization to provide references or referees who can be contacted to provide information about the candidate worthwhile for making decisions about a prospective employee in the selection phase of human resource management? What components of the selection process are subjective and which are objective?

4　Coaches of sporting teams, particularly those that are high profile, often undergo a very public performance appraisal. What implications does this have for the practice of human resource management in sport organizations and how could any negative effects be minimized?

5　Professional athletes in team sport move from team to team, and from league to league in global sports, in search of better rewards and opportunities. What implications do professional sport team markets and international player migration have for the practice of human resource management within sport?

FURTHER READING

Chelladurai, P. (2006). *Human Resource Management in Sport and Recreation*. Champaign: Human Kinetics.

Cuskelly, G., Hoye, R. and Auld, C. (2006). *Working with Volunteers in Sport*. London: Routledge.

Doherty, A. (1998). Managing our human resources: A review of organizational behaviour in sport. *Journal of Sport Management*, 12(1): 1–24.

Robinson, L. (2004). Human resource management, in L. Robinson (ed). *Managing Public Sport and Leisure Services*. London: Routledge.

Taylor, T., Doherty, A. and McGraw, P. (2008) *Managing People in Sport Organizations: A Strategic Human Resource Management Perspective*. London: Elsevier Butterworth-Heinemann.

RELEVANT WEBSITES

The following websites are useful starting points for further information on the human resource management of sport organizations:

Australian Sports Commission Resources at <www.ausport.gov.au/supporting/clubs/resource_library/people_management>

Sport England's Running Sport Program at

Sport and Recreation New Zealand Resources at
<www.sportnz.org.nz/managing-sport/search>

CASE STUDY 7.1

Staffing the Slam: the Australian Open

This case explores one of the highest-profile tennis tournaments in the world, the Australian Open, held in January in Melbourne, Australia, each year. Tennis has always been one of Australia's most popular sports, producing a series of world champions, and hosting major international events for many years. For most of the 20th century it was second to the United States in terms of success. Tennis in Australia also has a large participation base and is a significant summer pastime, underpinned by the staging of the Australian Open Tennis Championship each year. During the 1950s and 1960s it was an integral part of the Grand Slam circuit, which included the French, American, and all England/Wimbledon events. However, during the 1970s it lost its premier status. The Kooyong stadium where the event was held had become tired and old, grass courts had lost their appeal, and many of the world's best players were not prepared to come to Melbourne just after the late December/early January Christmas break.

In 1981 the Lawn Tennis Association of Australia (LTAA), the national governing body for tennis, investigated the feasibility of designing a large-scale tennis complex to accommodate a world class event. The LTAA persuaded the Victorian state government to underwrite the development of a multi-purpose sport and entertainment centre, and construction began in 1986. In 1988 the Australian Open shifted to the new multi-purpose stadium adjacent to the city's downtown district. It was funded and built by the state government and managed by a stadium trust. It was initially called Flinders Park, which was later changed to Melbourne Park National Tennis Centre. The focal point of the Centre was a 14,000-seat centre court with corporate box facilities and a retractable roof. This venue was complemented by two large show courts, outside courts, and a large indoor facility. The all-weather playing surface consisted of a rubberized compound called rebound-ace. Since then, an additional AUD$800 million has been spent on facility upgrades, and the site now sets the international benchmark for elite tennis venues. The evolution of the Australian Open since the 1980s into a major international event has had significant human resource management implications.

The 1988 Australian Open at the newly opened Flinders/Melbourne Park venue was a major success, and the LTAA, which managed the event, felt vindicated in moving the tournament from inner suburban Kooyong to the new inner-city sport precinct. It attracted most of the world's best players and drew bigger crowds than Kooyong had ever achieved. The total attendance of 266,000 for the inaugural event was nearly 126,000 more than attended the 1987 Kooyong event. Thirty years later, the Australian Open had consolidated its position as one of four Grand Slam tennis tournaments in the world. In 2015, 704 players competed across all events and categories, representing 49 nations and 704,000 people attended the event.

The Australian Open was also good for tourism. In 2016, 48% of the 703,000 attendees came from outside of Melbourne. This included:

- 9% of attendees from regional Victoria
- 26% of attendees from interstate

- 13% of attendees from overseas
- 650 journalists, photographers, and videographers – mostly international – provided coverage of the event

These out-of-town visitors helped fill Victorian hotels for a combined total of 513,882 nights during the tournament, with an average stay of 11 nights per visitor. In addition, each visitor had an average daily spend of $181 and 75% of tourists surveyed said they would happily recommend others to visit Victoria as a result of their stay in Melbourne during the event. It was clear that good people management at every level of the event was good for business. In 2017 the total attendance was 720,000, an all-time record. In addition, players competed for a total of AUS$50 million in prize money in what is now recognized as the premier tennis event for Asia-Pacific region. But it also meant that, from a human resource management viewpoint, the event was a complex logistical exercise.

By any measure the Australian Open presents a major staffing challenge for the event organizers, which in this case is Tennis Australia (TA), the national governing body for tennis in Australia. The recruitment, training, and supervision of staff are especially pertinent in this instance, since, like any big sporting event, the Australian Open must supplement its core operational staff with a massive injection of casual, but highly trained personnel for a three-week period. The following figures for the 2015 event illustrate the scope and scale of the tournament:

- 380 ball-kids worked at the Open, including 327 from Victoria, 25 from interstate, 20 from Korea, 20 from China, and 2 from Singapore
- 107 cars were used to transport players to and from Melbourne Park, which were driven by staff and volunteers
- 360 chair umpires, linespersons, and reviewers officiated matches during the Open
- 8,412 staff, contractors, and volunteers were employed
- 27,500 people were accredited as players, coaches, special guests, umpires, officials, and media

Most of these employees were casual staff or volunteers, but they all had to be closely managed, and all work within performance guidelines. In addition, there also had to be an exit plan for staff to ensure that the following year's event would be staffed and managed even more effectively. At the end of each year's event, the event management team reverts to being a small operational unit, the job of which is to initiate the planning and implementation cycle for the following year. The Australian Open uses a range of methods to recruit staff for the Australian Open, including contracting the services of global recruitment firm Adecco, which has more the 5,200 branches across 60 countries and employs more than 32,000 staff. The Australian Open contracts Adecco to assist in recruiting staff because the team of employees at Tennis Australia is not large enough to hire the number of people required each year prior to and during the tournament.

In July 2017 the Australian Open was advertising for casual courtesy car drivers for the 2018 event, indicative of the timeframe required to recruit, select, induct, and train staff. Drivers would be employed for a three-week period between January 5 and January 29, 2018. According to the job advertisement,

> Courtesy Car Drivers are responsible for providing a professional standard, customer focused transportation service to players, coaches, official media, and official guests. This includes transportation to and from Melbourne Airport, Melbourne Park and places of accommodation, amongst a vast range of other locations.

The following were the knowledge and skills required for the position:

- Advanced knowledge and previous experience of driving in Melbourne CBD and surrounds
- Aptitude to use in-car technologies to benefit passengers and your safety
- Outstanding customer services and communication skills
- Ability to build rapport and engage quickly with a diverse range of cultural backgrounds
- Must demonstrate the ability to respond efficiently and courteously to a range of requests and tasks
- Ability to speak languages other than English is desirable
- Previous experience in professional driving or transportation services at major events is desirable
- Holders of light rigid, medium rigid, or heavy rigid licenses types are desirable

Prospective applicants were required to submit a curriculum vitae and if successful were required to attended an Australian Open 2018 team rally, in addition to area specific training of a minimum of three hours and online induction. If the 2018 Australian Open was the first for the driver, they would also have to successfully complete the driver appraisal program. Although the courtesy drivers are an interface between the Australian Open and a range of important stakeholders, the knowledge and skills required for the position, as well as the induction and training requirements, provides an indication of the attention to detail required for international events of this type, as well as the complexity of the human resource management required to staff the entire event.

The expansion and contraction of staff at the Australian Open and during the rest of the year fits neatly within the concept of the 'pulsating organization', which was first promulgated in the early 1990s by social commentator and futurist, Alvin Toffler. He coined the term as a way of highlighting the ways in which organizations adjust their staffing arrangements to meet the shifting demand of their different stakeholders. This term has relevance for all major sport event organizations. They generally operate with a small core of personnel for much of the year, expand substantially in the lead up to an event, and afterwards, dramatically shrink in size. As noted above, this effect poses substantial challenges in delivering a quality recruitment, induction, and training process for major sport event organizations.

The Australian Open has an international reputation for its smooth organization and efficient operations. The Tennis Australia event management team prides itself on its ability to take a mix of paid and volunteer staff – more than 8,000 in total – and mould them into a co-ordinated and purposeful team. According to Tennis Australia, the key to its staffing success is not only its recruitment, induction, and operations training programs, but also its culture of cooperation, professionalism, and loyalty. But Tennis Australia also concedes that a lot of work needs to be done in making it all happen. For instance, new appointments – including ball-kids and drivers – all go through an interview process and are included into the culture of the event through an intensive induction process. The same methodical process is followed for the training programs, where performance benchmarks set the expectations for building appropriate skills and interpersonal conduct.

CASE STUDY QUESTIONS

1   Choose another major international sporting event that compares to the Australian Open and explore the types and number of staff and volunteers that are employed by the event. Are they similar or different to the Australian Open? Why? Is there scope for the same human resource management practices and procedures to be adopted worldwide by major sporting events?

2   Events like the Australian Open are often referred to as pulsating events. What other events at the international, national, and local level in your country could be considered 'pulsating'? Do all of these events have the same human resource management challenges as the Australian Open?

3   Which phases of the human resource management process are most important for each of the following staff/volunteer categories referred to in the case study: ball-kids, event drivers, accredited media, chair umpires and linespersons, and contractors?

4   What are the implications of casualization for staff recruitment and training for events like the Australian Open?

Sources: Australian Open website at <www.ausopen.com>; Victorian Government website at <www.economicdevelopment.vic.gov.au>; Tennis Australia website at <www.tennis.com.au>

CASE STUDY 7.2

Major events, major needs: volunteer recruitment, selection, training, and rewards – the 2016 Rio Olympics experience

This case study explores the operations of the 2016 Rio Olympic Games. One of the key elements in understanding the human resource management function is to frame the discussion within the eight-stage model discussed earlier in this chapter. Case studies are essential in bringing the model to life, because it enables readers to secure tangible information on the ways in which the stages are actually put into place, and as a result they become more than just abstract concepts. With this principle in mind, this case examines the ways in which volunteers were recruited, selected, trained, and rewarded for the Rio de Janeiro 2016 Olympic Games.

The Olympic Games brings together not just athletes, coaches, and spectators, but also an enthusiastic group known as 'Olympic Volunteers'. These aptly named individuals volunteer their time and skills in order to make the Games as successful as they can be, and according to Games officials, volunteering has now become an integral part of the ethos of the Games, and is central to the delivery of a quality experience for not only spectators, but also the athletes themselves.

Volunteers contribute in a number of ways. Most of the 70,000 Olympic volunteers in Rio, for example, worked in one of the four "clusters" in the neighbourhoods of Barra, Deodoro, Maracanã, and Copacabana. Their responsibilities ranged from interpreting and translating to setting up broadcast camera stands, and from guiding athletes to and from their events to ensuring the health and safety of participants. Candidates for the Rio volunteer positions were subjected to a careful selection process, which began in late 2014 (keep in mind that the Games were held in August 2016). More than 240,000 people from around the world applied for the 70,000 positions available, and although the majority (60%) of candidates were from Brazil, there was also a strong international presence, particularly from the United States (11,000 applicants), Russia (11,000), China (8,000), and Great Britain (8,000).

To narrow down this pool of candidates, a three-stage selection process was implemented. The first stage consisted of an online exercise. It was, in the words of the Volunteer Program Manager Flavia Fontes, "a way to engage the candidates, and help them understand what it would be like to work at the Rio 2016 Games". In addition to it being an interesting way of getting to know the Olympics, it allowed the selection team to learn more about the candidates themselves. The second stage was language evaluation. Whilst applying, many candidates had declared their fluency in a given number of languages. This stage was used to help verify these claims and to assemble a group of applicants who, when considered together, had a diverse range of language competencies. The third and final stage was the interviews of the applicants, which began in March 2015. Brazilians based near the newly constructed training centres in cities such as Rio, Curitiba, Belo Horizonte, and São Paulo had their interviews in person. Those who did not have access to the centres – such as most of the international applicants – had their interviews via video conferences. In total, more than 80,000 people were interviewed.

The successful applicants, representing 191 countries, received their letters of invitation in November 2015. However, the staffing process was far from complete, because they now had to undergo an intensive training program. The training program, like that of selection, had three main stages. The first stage was a general information session led by professional trainers. It was essentially a 'mega-lecture', commented a trainee who had volunteered as a venue protocol team member. However, the second stage of the training program was far more interactive, and by involving the trainees in group-centred conversations, and question and answer sessions, the roles and responsibilities of their jobs, together with expected interpersonal conduct, were explained. The third and final stage involved the trainees completing case studies and simulation exercises relevant to their roles at the Games. According to a volunteer in event services, these sessions made them feel both excited and prepared, while also making them feel part of the 'Olympic family'.

One of the innovations at the Rio Olympic Games were the volunteer training centres, which included a sensory tour for volunteers, in which they were spoken to by 'Olympic gods' and provided with an experience that attempted to simulate what it would have been like to be an athlete participating in the Games. These training centres were part of the infrastructure used to train the 70,00 strong volunteer workforce, but were also an important part of making the volunteers feel valued. As Fontes noted, "the goal of the centre is to train volunteers so that they perform focussed and efficient work", but that we also "want our candidates to learn new things, to have the opportunity to have unique experience and to be able to share with other people the experience of having worked on the world's largest sports event". Much of the human resource management associated with Olympic Games volunteers is striking a balance between ensuring the candidates are trained and ensuring a high quality environment that rewards and retains people who are providing their time and energy for free.

The IOC places enormous value on volunteers and see them as the 'spirit of the Games', recalling the time when athletes were unpaid amateurs and everything was done for the 'love of the sport'. Like all other Games before them, the Rio volunteers did a multitude of jobs – greet fans, escort athletes, and give directions around the city – while also delivering specialized services including paramedical and information technology. They become, in effect, the 'smiling faces of the host nation'. Thus, in many ways they set the tone for the event, and in the case of Rio, this was a crucial role, because a lot of the lead-up media commentary had dampened enthusiasm for the event and painted a gloomy picture of the quality of some venues. In the end, however, the Rio Games were rated as successful, which, in part, was the result of the friendly volunteer faces. They were praised at both the opening and closing ceremonies, and once again confirmed the claim that without the athletes and the volunteers, the Games can't happen. This regular praise for the work of volunteers also has a secondary effect of providing additional psychological rewards for the effort they generously provide.

There is, however, another side to role of the volunteer and the jobs they perform. They also saved the Games organizers more than $100 million in salaries, a massive benefit to the organizing committee. In this respect, the success of the Games depends on the goodwill of volunteers, and the preparedness to bear the cost of their involvement. Moreover, volunteers are not only unpaid, but they are also required to pay for their own accommodation and transportation to the host city, which is what happened in Rio. They did, however, receive transportation to and from venues, meals on the days they worked, work-related training, and uniforms to keep.

A conservative estimate suggests it would have cost at least $100 million to pay Rio's 70,000 volunteers at minimum wage rates for two weeks of Games-related work. The operating budget – the budget for simply running the games themselves – was just over $3 billion. Paying volunteers would thus have boosted the operating budget by about 3%, which is significant increase over the scenario of using an unpaid workforce. This 3% would be nearer 4% if highly skilled volunteers, such as doctors and other medical professionals, were paid at their professional and commercial rates. Rio utilized the services of about 1,000 medical volunteers.

CASE STUDY QUESTIONS

1   Given that none of the Rio 2016 volunteers were paid, what motivated them to be involved? Are these motivations the same for non-Olympic major and mega events? At which stage of the human resource management process should these motivations be considered in improving the volunteer experience?

2   What incentives did the Rio Organizing Committee provide to ensure a full pool of volunteers?

3   Which phase of the human resource management process is most important for managing volunteers at mega events such as the Olympic Games? Why?

4   How might the lessons learnt from volunteer engagement at the Olympic Games be translated into the improvement of practices related to volunteer management at local and community sports club levels?

Sources: IOC website at <www.olympic.org>;

CHAPTER 8

Leadership

OVERVIEW

Leadership is arguably the most researched yet least understood topic in the context of management. What we define as excellent leadership and who are great leaders remain points of serious and widespread academic debate. In the United States alone, more than 2,000 books on the topic of leadership are published every year. In this chapter we provide a broad outline of the different approaches that have been used to describe and analyse leadership. We will also use a number of examples and cases to explore leadership. Much of this discussion will take place in reference to the leadership challenges that confront sport organizations.

By the end of this chapter the reader should be able to:

- Describe the need for leaders and for leadership;
- Distinguish between leadership and management;

- Outline the different levels (in the organization) that leaders can work at and how this affects their approach to leadership; and
- Provide an overview of your personal leadership development needs.

WHAT IS LEADERSHIP?

It is not easy to find agreement among any group on a definition of leadership. Sometimes leadership is described as 'getting things done through people'. Others argue that leadership is about 'exercising power in order to influence others' or that true leadership is about 'envisioning a bright future and taking others by the hand towards it'. In other words, leadership can be many things to different people. Cotton Fitzsimmons, former coach of the Kansas City Kings argues that "if you're a positive person, you're an automatic motivator. You can get people to do things you don't think they're capable of" (Westerbeek and Smith 2005). Vince Lombardi, the famous coach of the Green Bay Packers of the 1950s and 1960s, once said that

> leaders are made, they are not born; and they are made just like anything else has been made in this country – by hard effort. And that's the price that we all have to pay to achieve that goal, or any goal.
>
> (Westerbeek and Smith 2005)

According to former U.S. President Theodore Roosevelt "the best executive is the one who has sense enough to pick good men to do what he wants done, and self-restraint enough to keep from meddling with them while they do it", and Lou Holts, a former coach of the Notre Dame football team, argued that "'all winning teams are goal-oriented. Teams like these win consistently because everyone connected with them concentrates on specific objectives. They go about their business with blinders on; nothing will distract them from achieving their aims" (Westerbeek and Smith 2005).

Harvard professor and leadership expert Linda Hill (2008) argues that in today's global, fast-changing, business environments with multiple stakeholders making decisions, we may well have to 'lead from behind' in order to let others take charge as leaders when it is most needed. According to these experienced, but very different leaders and leadership experts, leadership is:

- goal oriented;
- about influencing others;
- about empowering others;
- about seeing the big picture;
- about needing others; and
- about strength of character.

We can use these different components of leadership to construct a leadership definition. For the purposes of this book we define leadership as 'influencing and enabling others towards the attainment of aspirational goals'. We appreciate that there are many other definitions of leadership, but as an introduction to the topic in this book this definition will serve the purpose. In the next section of this chapter we will further outline the ways that leadership can be viewed.

In practice 8.1 Sepp Blatter and the importance of leadership

Sepp Blatter led the Fédération Internationale de Football Association (FIFA) for 17 years until he was dumped as leader in 2015 after the FIFA ethics committee banned him for 6 years. FIFA is arguably the second most powerful sport organization in the world (after the IOC) and is an association governed by Swiss law founded in 1904 and based in Zurich. It has 211 member associations and its goal, enshrined in its statutes, is the constant improvement of football.

Blatter's reign at FIFA had been beset by scandal. He was investigated by the ethics committee over allegations surrounding a 2005 TV rights deal between FIFA and Jack Warner, the former president of Concacaf, the governing body of football in North and Central America and the Caribbean.

His decision in June 2015 to resign came as a surprise, as only days before, he had been re-elected for an unprecedented fifth term and had insisted he was the man to lead reform at the organization. Blatter was banned for allegedly signing a contract 'unfavourable' to football's governing body and making a 'disloyal payment' to UEFA president Michel Platini, who has also been suspended for eight years. The ethics committee launched its investigation after the Swiss attorney-general began its own investigation into the disloyal payment.

Although Blatter himself was not found guilty of corruption, he was accused of standing idly by while corruption happened throughout the organization. His dumping from FIFA after so long at the helm highlights how leadership can affect an entire organization as FIFA struggles to recover its reputation on the world stage.

Sources: Sepp Blatter: End of era for FIFA boss at www.bbc.com/news/world-europe-32985553 and Sepp Blatter after the fall at www.theguardian.com/football/2017/jun/19/sepp-blatter-fifa-president-corruption-

---

THEORIES OF LEADERSHIP

Northouse (2010) separates leadership theories into categories that relate to traits of leaders, their skills, their styles, and the situation in which they have to lead or the contingency that they face. He also lists theories such as the path–goal theory, the leader member exchange theory, the transformational approach, the authentic approach, team leadership, and the psychodynamic approach as separate categories. As this is an introduction to the concept of leadership, the dominant theories have been conflated into four approaches: trait or personality approaches, the behavioral approach, the contingency approach, and the transformational approach.

Trait or personality approaches

Although the personality and trait approaches to leadership stem from the earliest of leadership research times, popular leadership literature continues to stress the importance of personality and innate ability in the demonstration of leadership. Locke (1991) argues that trait theories (or great man theories as they are also called) are incomplete theories of leadership, irrespective of traits and/or personality of the leaders being important contributors to or detractors from excellent leadership. Locke (1991) suggests that the possession of certain traits, such as energy and honesty, appear to be a vital for effective leadership. Basketball legend Michael Jordan, for example, has been credited with having an impressive range of innate leadership traits that will put him in good stead of being an excellent leader in many different contexts. Leaders must use their traits to develop skills, formulate a vision, and implement this vision into reality. This being the case, it appears that traits only form part of the picture.

Although empirical evidence linking the personality of leaders with their success is weak, much of the popular literature still focuses on leadership traits as a way to better understand leadership. In general, the trait theories are based on the assumption that social background, physical features, and personality characteristics will distinguish good leaders from poor leaders.

Behavioural approach

When it became clear that good leadership could not simply be explained on the basis of the innate characteristics of the leaders, organizational research began to focus on discovering universal behaviours of effective leaders. Behaviourists argued that anyone could be taught to become a leader by simply learning the behaviours of other effective leaders.

Behavioural strategy takes behaviours as signs of learned responses to contingencies. If research shows that to behave in a certain manner results in success for a leader, then one can learn to discharge those behaviours in particular leadership situations. The behavioural approach to leadership was also a response to early approaches to management as a whole. Frederick Taylor was an early champion of the idea that managers should use science to improve efficiency. This approach became known as Taylorism or scientific management, a philosophy in which there was limited attention for the human side of the mass production movement. Rather, under Taylorism, humans were simply 'part of the larger machines' and standardization of human labour would lead to great efficiency and higher profits. Managers, according to Taylor, should begin by studying the tasks workers performed, breaking jobs down by analyzing, measuring, and timing each separate element of the job in order to determine the most efficient manner of doing the job. The most efficient method for each job became both the standard method that workers were supposed to adopt and a means for measuring worker productivity.

In response to Taylor's ideas, behaviouralists demanded a new 'human relations' approach to management of organizations involving an examination of the interaction between managers and workers. In the Hawthorne experiments, which were originally designed to study the effects of lighting upon factory workers, Elton Mayo discovered that human relations between workers and between workers and supervisors was most important in ensuring efficiency. In other words, to focus on interaction between humans, and by studying the best ways of interacting, managers could better lead the people that worked for the organization. Another behavioural approach to the study of leadership is the so-called Theory X and Theory Y, developed by Douglas McGregor. The theories are formulated based on the assumptions that leaders have about individuals. Managers that have Theory X assumptions argue that the typical employee dislikes work and needs direction at all times. They also think that employees need to be coerced to perform their duties. Theory Y managers believe that employees are self-motivated and committed to work and to the company. They naturally seek responsibility for the work they perform As a result, Theory Y leaders would behave in quite different ways from Theory X leaders.

Another behaviouralist approach was formulated by Blake and Mouton (1964). They developed the managerial grid model along two dimensions: one with a concern for people and one with a concern for production. Blake and Mouton argued that differing levels of concern along those dimensions would lead to different styles of leadership. For example, managers with low levels of concern for people and production will have an impoverished style of leadership, whereas those leaders with high concern for people and production can be typified as having team-style leadership qualities. The Blake and Mouton approach has also been used to differentiate person-centred leaders from task-centred leaders. Ultimately it is important to conclude that the behaviouralist approach to leadership leads to the identification of different styles that can be described as more or less successful.

Contingency approach

It became increasingly clear to those studying leadership that traits and behaviours of leaders were often observed in relation to the situation at hand, or in other words, according to situational contingencies. Isolated behavioural and trait approaches failed to take account of how situational variables, such as task structure, the characteristics of the environment, or subordinate characteristics, could affect and moderate the relationship between the behaviour of a leader and the different outcomes.

In contingency theories of leadership, the core argument is that different leadership styles and approaches will apply to a range of possible management situations. This is why, for example, the on-field leadership brilliance of Diego Maradona with the Argentinean team resulted in winning the 1986 World Cup, but when Diego was required to achieve similar results with club teams in different cultures (Napoli in Italy and Barcelona in Spain) or even as the national coach of the Argentinean side at the 2010 World Cup in South Africa, he failed dismally, also resulting in the exposure of a number of personal leadership flaws. The centrality of leader behaviour and/or personality needs to be de-emphasized, and in the contingency approach we turn our attention to the leader in conjunction with circumstances that are specific to the situation at hand, including characteristics of the subordinates and the work setting. In the next section we will present three situational theories of leadership that have influenced the ways in which leadership is understood and practiced. They are:

- Fieldler's least preferred co-worker approach
- Hersey and Blanchard's situational leadership theory
- Path–goal theory

	Situational favourability			
Condition	Leader–member relations	Task Structure	Position Power	Effective leadership
1	Good	High	Strong	Low LPC
2	Good	High	Weak	Low LPC
3	Good	Weak	Strong	Low LPC
4	Good	Weak	Weak	High LPC
5	Poor	High	Strong	High LPC
6	Poor	High	Weak	High LPC
7	Poor	Weak	Strong	High LPC
8	Poor	Weak	Weak	Low LPC

Adapted from Fiedler, F.E. (1967), *A theory of leadership effectiveness*, New York: McGraw-Hill, p. 34.

FIGURE 8.1 Fiedler's situational favourability factors and leadership effectiveness

Fiedler's least preferred co-worker approach

Fiedler's (1967) model is based on the following three axioms:

1 The interaction between the leader's personal characteristics and some aspects of the situation determines the effectiveness of the leader,

2 Leaders are either 'task oriented' or 'person oriented', and

3 Effectiveness of the leader is determined by the leader's control of the situation.

Fiedler comes to his classification of task or person oriented leadership by the use of a measurement scale called the 'Least Preferred Co-worker' (LPC) scale. The instrument asks leaders to assess co-workers on a series of bi-polar descriptors including pleasant-unpleasant, cold-warm, and supportive-hostile in order to assess to what degree they think they would not work well together with that co-worker. A leader who obtains a low LPC is more motivated by task achievements and will only be concerned about relationships with subordinates if the work unit is deemed to be performing well. A leader who obtains a high LPC score will be more motivated to develop close interpersonal relations with subordinates. Task-directed behaviour is of a lesser concern, and only becomes important once sound interpersonal relations have been developed. According to Fiedler, if the least preferred coworker still scores relatively high it indicates that the leader derives a sense of satisfaction from 'working on good relationships', indicating a person oriented leadership style.

The model further suggests that control is dependent on three combined contingency variables:

1   The relations between the leader and the followers,

2   The degree of task structure (or the degree to which the followers' jobs can be specified clearly), and

3   The leader's position of power or amount of authority, yielding eight possible conditions presented in Figure 8.1.

Hersey and Blanchard's situational leadership theory

A theory claiming that as maturity of the group changes, leader behaviour should change as well, is known as the situational theory of leadership. Hersey and Blanchard (1977) argued that as the technical skill level and psychological maturity of the group moves from low to moderate to high, the leader's behaviour would be most effective when it changes accordingly. When low levels of maturity are enacted in relation to the tasks being performed, a high task-behaviour of the leader should be exhibited, or in other words, a 'selling' and 'telling' approach to communicating with the subordinates. At medium levels of maturity, leaders need to be more focused on relationship-behaviours and at the highest levels of subordinate maturity, the leader needs to offer little direction or task-behaviour and allow the subordinate to assume responsibilities, or in other words, a 'supportive' and 'delegation' driven style of leadership communication.

According to sport organization theory researcher Slack and Parent (2006), there have been few attempts to empirically test the concepts and relationships that Hersey and Blanchard (1977) have outlined in their work, even in the management and organizational literature. Some attempts have been made to apply the theory directly in sport settings, but results have been inconsistent.

The path–goal theory

The path–goal theory (House 1971) takes a behavioural and situational approach to leadership. There are many roads that lead to Rome, and therefore the path–goal theory suggests that a leader must select a style most appropriate to the particular situation. The theory in particular aims to explain how a leader's behaviour affects the motivation and satisfaction of subordinates.

House (1971) is cited in Wexley and Yukl (1984) arguing that

> the motivational function of the leaders consists of increasing personal payoffs to subordinates for work-goal attainment, and making the path to these payoffs easier to travel by clarifying it, reducing roadblocks and pitfalls, and increasing the opportunities for personal satisfaction en route.

> (p. 176)

In other words, characteristics of the subordinates and characteristics of the environment determine both the potential for increased motivation and the manner in which the leader must act to improve motivation. Subordinate preferences for a particular pattern of leadership behaviour may also depend on the actual situation in which they are placed (Wexley and Yukl 1984). Taking those different perspectives in consideration the path–goal theory proposes four styles of leadership behaviour that can be utilized to achieve goals (House and Mitchell 1974). They are:

- Directive leadership (leader gives specific instructions, expectations, and guidance);
- Supportive leadership (leader shows concern and support for subordinates);
- Participative leadership (subordinates participate in the decision making);
- Achievement-oriented leadership (leader sets challenges, emphasizes excellence, and shows confidence that subordinates will attain high standards of performance).

The theory is principally aimed at examining how leaders affect subordinate expectations about likely outcomes of different courses of action. Directive leadership is predicted to have a positive effect on subordinates when the task is ambiguous and will have a negative impact when the task is clear. Supportive leadership is predicted to increase job satisfaction, particularly when conditions are adverse. Achievement-oriented leadership is predicted to encourage higher performance standards and increase expectancies that desired outcomes can be achieved. Participative leadership is predicted to promote satisfaction due to involvement (Schermerhorn, Hunt, and Osborne 1994).

From transactional to transformational leadership

As already noted earlier in this chapter, the scientific approach to management (Taylorism) reduced the individual to performing machine-like functions. The human relations approach to management took into consideration the human part of the labour equation, appreciating that much better results can be achieved if people's individual needs are taken into consideration when leading them towards achieving certain work outputs.

One of the most recent thrusts in leadership research is that of transactional and transformational leadership. Transactional leadership encompasses much of the theories based on rational exchange between leader and subordinate, such as the theories presented earlier, but transformational leaders, according to Bass (1985), are charismatic and develop followers into leaders through a process that transcends the existing organizational climate and culture. The transactional leader aims to create a cost–benefit economic exchange, or in other words, to meet the needs of followers in return for 'contracted' services that are produced by the follower (Bass 1985). To influence behaviour, the transactional leader may use the following approaches:

- Contingent reward (the leader uses rewards or incentives to achieve results)
- Active management by exception (the leader actively monitors the work performed and uses corrective methods to ensure the work meets accepted standards)

- Passive management by exception (the leader uses corrective methods as a response to unacceptable performance or deviation from the accepted standards)
- Laissez-faire leadership (the leader is indifferent and has a 'hands-off' approach toward the workers and their performance).

However, leadership theorists have argued that transactional leadership merely seeks to influence others by exchanging work for wages. It fails to build on the worker's need for meaningful work and it does not actively tap into their sources of creativity. A more effective and beneficial leadership behaviour to achieve long-term success and improved performance therefore is transformational leadership. Sir Alex Ferguson, the long-time Manchester United manager, can be described as a transformational leader. He envisioned a future for the club, and the board repaid him with the trust of keeping him at the helm at Manchester United since 1986 for more than 1,400 games. Under his guidance and supervision the club became the most successful team in the new English Premier League and the team has also won multiple Champions League crowns. Sir Alex has prepared the likes of Eric Cantona, Ryan Giggs, Roy Keane, David Beckham, Ruud van Nistelrooy, Wayne Rooney, and Cristiano Ronaldo for the world stage of football leadership.

What is transformational leadership?

It has been argued by Bass and Avolio (1994) that transformational leadership is the new leadership that must accompany good management. In contrast to transactional models, transformational leadership goes beyond the exchange process. It not only aligns and elevates the needs and values of followers, but also provides intellectual stimulation and increased follower confidence. Bass and Avolio (1994) identified four 'I's' that transformational leaders employ in order to achieve superior results. These are:

- Idealized Influence: Transformational leaders behave in ways that result in them being admired, respected, and trusted, and ultimately becoming a role model. The transformational leader demonstrates high standards of ethical and moral conduct.
- Inspirational Motivation: By demonstrating enthusiasm and optimism, the transformational leader actively arouses team spirit and motivates and inspires followers to share in and work towards a common goal.
- Intellectual Stimulation: By being innovative, creative, supportive, reframing problems, and questioning old assumptions the transformational leader creates an intellectually stimulating and encouraging environment.
- Individualized Consideration: Transformational leaders pay special attention to each individual's needs for achievement and growth by acting as a coach or mentor.

Looking closer at the four it can be argued that charisma (the ability to inspire enthusiasm, interest, or affection in others by means of personal charm or influence) is an important component of transformational leadership. Purely charismatic leaders may be limited in their ability to achieve successful outcomes, due to their need to instill their beliefs in others which may inhibit the individual growth of followers. However, transformational leaders are more than charismatic in that they generate awareness of the mission or vision of the team and the organization, and then motivate colleagues and followers towards outcomes that benefit the team rather than merely serving the individual interest.

In practice 8.2 Investing in women's leadership in sport

Australia has developed a national program conducted by the ASC to support the development of women as leaders in their respective sport systems. In Canada, a similar development program is conducted by the Canadian Association for the Advancement of Women and Sport and Physical Activity (CAAWS).

The Women Leaders in Sport (WLIS) grant program (formally Sport Leadership Grants and Scholarships for Women) is an Australian government initiative that is managed by the Australian Sports Commission (ASC) in partnership with the Australian Government Office for Women. The WLIS website claims it has supported more than 23,000 women with development opportunities since it started in 2002.

The WLIS grant program in 2018 provided three types of support for female administrators, coaches, and officials to access opportunities for intermediate or advanced training within an existing pathway in the sport industry to reach their leadership potential.

As part of the Women Leaders in Sport (WLIS) grant program, the Australian Sports Commission (ASC) conducts a two-day residential sport leadership workshop for grant recipients. The workshop aims to develop the participant's leadership capabilities to progress within sport as an administrator, coach, or official and to enable them to effectively manage the challenges within their sport and life in general. All individual grant recipients are required to attend an allocated sport leadership workshop, and all organization recipients are required to nominate an aspiring female leader from within the organization who is participating in the proposed project to attend the workshop. Topics covered in the workshops include:

- Exploring leadership
- Leadership styles and functions
- Leadership and culture
- Leadership and performance
- Communication
- Coaching and mentoring
- Leadership challenges
- Emotional intelligence
- Driving vision and change management

CAAWS' Women and Leadership Program in Canada consists of a series of five professional development sessions that blend theory with practical applications, and provide an opportunity for women working or volunteering in the sport or physical activity sector to share experiences, reflect on ideas and apply specific techniques.

The sessions also allow for networking opportunities among participants. The Canadian Association for the Advancement of Women and Sport and Physical Activity (CAAWS) delivers the program through strategic partnerships within the Canadian sport and physical activity system to actively engage women as leaders (senior administrators, coaches, officials, board members, etc.). Collaboration through the Women and Leadership Program is intended to:

- Increase provincial/territorial and national sport and multi-sport commitment to taking action to engage women and girls as participants and leaders;
- Increase capacity to address the barriers limiting women's leadership throughout the system; and
- Integrate the workshops into ongoing professional development and support services delivered by partner organizations during the project period, and into the future.

The workshops are focused on five key themes as outlined on the CAAWS website:

Effective Communication: In the workplace, effective communication is the foundation for better job performance and relationship building. During this workshop participants will:

- Consider the importance of their personal brand
- Learn about four distinct communication styles, and identify your preferred style
- Discuss electronic communication and social media etiquette, and how to avoid common pitfalls

Conflict Resolution: Conflict, in its many forms, is an inevitable part of our personal and professional lives. This workshop will ensure participants can understand and resolve conflict professionally.

- Consider sources of conflict and the cost of leaving conflict unresolved
- Consider five styles for dealing with conflict, identify your preferred style, and discuss situations when each style should be employed
- Review tips for effective conflict management

Influencing Change: Whether influencing change in your organization, across the sport and physical activity system, or more broadly in society, this workshop will provide participants with theory and practical tools for success.

- Identify elements of effective change movements
- Discuss the (under)representation of women in society
- Review tips for being heard and improving your listening skills
- Discuss approaches on how to influence others

Life Balance: For many women, balancing the demands of work, family, friends, and personal time is a challenge. This workshop will provide participants with an opportunity to explore a variety of strategies to add more balance to their lives.

- Examine your priorities and what "balance" means to you
- Examine key dimensions that can help or hinder life balance
- Learn strategies and collect tips to help you experience balance

Effective Networking: Strong networking skills can be a valuable tool, both personally and professionally. From building organizational partnerships to knowing about upcoming events, building your network is a long-term investment with great payoffs.

- Explore the value of networking
- Discuss in-person and online networks
- Identify strategies to build and maintain your network

Sources: The ASC website at www.ausport.gov.au/participating/women, and the CAAWS website at www.caaws.ca/leadership/women-and-leadership-program/.

LEADERSHIP AND MANAGEMENT

At this stage of the chapter it will be useful to briefly consider the debate about the relationship between leadership and management and how to distinguish between the two. Kotter (1990) has conducted extensive research work in order to find out how to differentiate managers from leaders. He concluded that management effectiveness rests in the ability to plan and budget, organize and staff, and control and solve problems. Leadership, however, is principally founded upon the ability to establish direction, to align people, and to motivate and inspire. According to Kotter, leaders achieve change, whereas managers succeed in maintaining the status quo. Bass (1990), however, states that "leaders manage and managers lead, but the two activities are not synonymous" (p. 383). It goes beyond the scope of this book to further elaborate on the distinction between leadership and management. Suffice to say that in the context of discussing management principles in sport organizations, management without leadership is much less likely to be successful than a capable manager who can also provide excellent leadership. In the next section we will therefore put forward what can be described as the five key functions of leadership:

- To create a vision
- To set out strategy
- To set objectives and lead towards performance
- To influence and motivate people
- To facilitate change and nurture culture

To create a vision

A vision can be described as 'a state of the future that lies beyond the directly imaginable by most people'. This view of the future, in the context of an organization, is a positive and bright state of being that only the 'visionary' (one who is characterized by unusually acute foresight and imagination) can see at that time. In other words, the leader is responsible for envisioning a future for the organization that can become reality if the people working in the organization can be aligned towards achieving that 'envisioned state'. It is often said that good leaders distinguish themselves from good managers because they do have a vision, whereas managers do not. How to achieve the vision through strategy is the next function of the leader.

To set out strategy

The process of strategic planning is all about the different ways that a vision can be achieved. It constitutes two principal perspectives: that of the organization and that of the individuals making up the organization. Visionary leaders are not necessarily successful leaders if they are not capable in translating the vision into action strategies. The process of strategic management is therefore concerned with carefully managing the internal organization, including considering the individual needs of workers, and the external environment in which many opportunities and threats impact the ability of the leader to achieve the vision. To be better prepared for action, the leader needs to be involved in setting measurable objectives.

To set objectives and lead towards performance

Setting objectives is the next function of the leader. Once the broad strategies have been set out (and these strategies are never set in concrete, they need constant updating), it is time to link measurable outcomes to these strategies. In other words, what do we want to achieve in the short term in order to work towards our visionary objectives that lie ahead in the distant future. Stated differently, the leader often is involved in setting objectives at different levels of the organization, ranging from 'visionary' and strategic objectives to mostly delegating the responsibility to set more operational objectives at lower levels of the organization. Only when SMART (specific, measurable, achievable, resources available, time bound) objectives are set, the leader will be in a position to manage the performance of the organization and its employees effectively. An important part of the performance of an organization is achieved through the people management skills of the leader.

To influence and motivate people

In our overview of the different approaches to leadership, we have already commented on the different styles that leaders chose to develop (because they better fit their skill set) in order to influence groups of people and communicate with individuals or teams. Where setting objectives is important in making people aware of the targets of performance, the actual activation and application of people skills is critical when trying to steer people in a certain direction. This is where leaders with charismatic appeal will have an easier job. Their natural ability to inspire enthusiasm, interest, or affection in others by means of personal charm or influence will put these leaders in a favourable position in regard to achieving the objectives that were set.

To facilitate change and nurture culture

Finally it is important to acknowledge that in this day and age, change is constant. Leaders who are incapable of assisting others to understand why 'change' is needed and how this change can be achieved with minimal disruption and maximum outcomes will have a difficult time surviving in the organizations of the 21st century. Most organizations are required to keep close track of the market conditions that they are working under and the impact changes in market conditions will have on their structures and strategies. Often a rapid response to changing market conditions is needed, and this is where the interesting relationship with the organization's culture comes into play. Ironically, a strong and stable organizational culture can contribute to the need to constantly modify direction and changing the systems and structures of the organization. It is the leader's responsibility to create and nurture a culture in which change is accepted as part of the natural way of organizational life. A strong culture is the backbone of any successful organization and the maintenance of culture is therefore one of the primary areas of leadership responsibility.

In practice 8.3 Leading Teams

Leading Teams is a consulting firm specializing in facilitating change and improvement in organizations. Founded by Ray McLean, Leading Teams, according to their website, specializes in the delivery of culture change, leadership, and team development programs that create elite teams and improve performance. Leading Teams shot to prominence through its work with a number of leading Australian Rules Football Clubs, including many that have had a sustained period of success in the last decade such as Geelong FC, Sydney Swans FC, and Hawthorn FC.

The website for Leading Teams describes their approach:

> Our Performance Improvement Program (PIP) is the cornerstone of our work at Leading Teams. It is a values-based approach to leadership, teamwork and culture change. The PIP is generally delivered over a sustained period for maximum impact and typically encompasses an all-of organisation approach. It is a behaviours-based framework for managing the entire life-cycle of any given team, from a member's induction to their eventual retirement from the team. The program provides a structure that empowers team members to become leaders, be accountable, and participate in open and honest reviews of performance.

We provide teams with the necessary tools to develop functional dynamics within the group and create a shared vision, behaviours and expectations. The main areas that we address are:

– Leadership Development
– Team Development
– Culture Change

We work in a wide range of industries in organisations of various sizes. Our program can be rolled out with Board and Senior Executive teams, right through to entry-level teams. The Leading Teams program highlights the importance of functional team dynamics and builds a strong level of engagement, commitment and accountability within teams. Specifically the model centres on:

- *Building and strengthening current relationships within and across teams*
- *Identifying a common purpose for each specific team*
- *Defining the behaviours which are considered essential to the trademark of the team/organisation*
- *Developing leaders who behave in a manner that has a positive impact on their peers and the performance of the organisation*
- *Developing a framework for leaders to honestly assess their own performance as leaders and that of their staff. This enables them to make intelligent decisions around recruitment, retention and induction*
- *Further develop managers as leaders who model and drive the Trademark behaviours of the team/organisation*
- *Creating an environment where open and honest professional dialogue takes place in regard to behaviour and performance*

Leading Teams has not only been involved in AFL, it was also engaged by the Australian Netball Diamonds Head Coach Lisa Alexander in their ultimately successful quest to secure a Commonwealth Games Gold Medal at the 2014 Glasgow Games. Players were asked to provide feedback on their own performances and their training sessions. In an article by Chris Barrett of The Age at www.theage.com.au, he cited the Diamonds Captain, Laura Geitz, as saying

It's about creating an honest environment. 'We've probably not had that in the Australian netball team before and it's speaking volumes. It was implemented at the beginning of last year [2013] and we went on to have our most successful series against New Zealand in 15 years. 'I think there's definitely something to be said for creating that environment where a lot of research goes into each individual, that's for sure. We've seen great things because of it.

The Leading Teams approach has not been without its critics, with some saying it can be too confronting for some athletes and actually counterproductive to good performances. Although this case study is not an endorsement of the Leading Teams approach, there does seem to be some merit in sport organizations engaging in a conscious attempt to develop their culture, their communication, and ultimately their leadership capacity at all levels of their organization.

Source: Leading Teams website www.leadingteams.net.au and the Chris Barrett article from July 23, 2014 at www.theage.com.au/commonwealth-games-glasgow-2014/commonwealth-games-news/lisa-alexander-has-some-homework-for-the-diamonds-20140723-zvw3y.html

SUMMARY

In this chapter we described what it takes to be a leader. We argued that irrespective of leadership type or style, leaders are goal oriented; they influence others; they empower others; they need to remain focused on the big picture; they need others to achieve their goals; and they have strong characters. Based on these components of leadership we discussed a number of theoretical approaches to leadership including the trait/personality, behavioural, and contingency approaches, ultimately resulting in a discussion about transactional versus transformational leadership. We also highlighted the differences between managers and leaders by outlining what are the functions of leaders: the creation of a vision; the setting out of strategy; setting objectives and measuring performance; influencing and motivating people; and finally, to facilitate change and nurture organizational culture.

REVIEW QUESTIONS

1   Are leaders born or can they be made? Justify your answer by comparing the different leadership theories discussed in this chapter.

2   Does sport offer valuable leadership lessons to business? What are the specific characteristics of sport organizations that challenge leaders in sport organizations more than leaders in business, and how can this knowledge be transferred to a non-sport context?

3   'A good manager is also a good leader'. Do you agree or disagree with this statement. Justify your answer.

4   Explain how leadership is important for the performance of a sport organization.

5   Interview the leader of a small sport organization. How would you describe their leadership style?

6   Is there any difference in the leadership skills required to be the CEO of a major professional sport franchise versus the leader of community sports club?

7   What criteria would you use to evaluate the leadership skills of a sport manager?

8   Is it possible to compare the performance of leaders of two different sport organizations? Why or why not?

DISCUSSION QUESTIONS

1   Who do you consider to be a good leader of a sport organization? What information have you used to form your view?

2   Who do you consider to be a poor leader of a sport organization? What information have you used to form your view?

3   In professional sports, the CEO, coach, and sometimes chairman, president, or owner are seen as the leader of the organization. Who is the most important and why?

4   What sort of support do middle managers need to make the transition from middle manager to CEO?

5   What sort of behaviours do you like to see exhibited by leaders in sport?

FURTHER READING

Amar, A.D., Hentrich, C. and Hlupic, V. (2009). To be a better leader, give up authority. *Harvard Business Review*, 87(12): 22–24.

Bass, B.M. (1990). *Bass & Stogdill's Handbook of Leadership: Theory, Research, and Managerial Applications*. 3rd edn. New York: Free Press.

Hill, L.A. (2008). Where will we find tomorrow's leaders? *Harvard Business Review*, 86(1): 123–129.

Kotter, J.P. (1990). *A Force for Change: How Leadership Differs from Management*. New York: The Free Press.

Kouzes, J.M. and Posner, B.Z. (2006). *A Leader's Legacy*. Hoboken: Jossey-Bass.

Northouse, P.G. (2010). *Leadership: Theory and Practice*. 5th edn. Thousand Oaks, CA: Sage.

Thomas, R.J. (2008). *Crucibles of Leadership*. Boston: Harvard Business School Publishing Corporation.

RELEVANT WEBSITES

Leadership Victoria www.leadershipvictoria.org/

Sport Leaders UK www.sportsleaders.org/

Women Sport Australia www.womensportaustralia.com.au/leadership

Australian Sports Commission Centre for Performance coaching and leadership www.ausport.gov.au/ais/centre_for_performance_coaching_and_leadership

CASE STUDY 8.1

Ferran Soriano leading City Football Group

Ferran Soriano is the CEO of Manchester City FC, part of the increasing global network of clubs owned wholly or in part by the City Football Group. He has an MBA and business degree and speaks five languages: Catalan, Spanish, English, French, and Portuguese. As one of the leading architects of Barcelona's dominance of European football in the 2000s, Soriano is considered one of the best sport CEOs in the world. He started with Manchester City FC in 2012 and has transformed that club, rolling out a global strategy to lead that club to on-field and off-field success. The City Football Group has ownership stakes in six franchises across the globe: Manchester City FC, Melbourne City FC, Major League Soccer team New York City, Japanese side Yokohama F Marinos, Uruguayan team CA Torque, and La Liga side Girona.

Soriano's CEO message in the 2015/16 Annual Report for Manchester City FC highlights everything about what being a great CEO encapsulates. It outlines key achievements for the organization, sets out a clear strategy, recognizes contributions from other leaders in the organization, acknowledges its customer (fan) base, and points to his organization investing in its people and culture.

2015–16 was another eventful season for Manchester City and one which marked the end of one chapter and the beginning of a new one in the Club's journey.

On the pitch, we continued in our endeavours to play beautiful football. Our men's first team won the League Cup and reached the Champions League Semi-Final for the first time. They also ended the Premier League season in fourth place, a finish which, though disappointing for all of us, only encourages us to work harder and better in the future.

Our women's team qualified for the Champions League for the first time in its history and the Club's Academy squads won a record number of trophies across all age groups, signalling that there is a new generation of talented players that should play an important role in our Club's future. This form of sustainability – that of bringing through young talent via our Academy – has always been central to His Highness Sheikh Mansour bin Zayed Al Nahyan's vision of a flourishing Manchester City. We continue to work hard towards those goals and build on the many tangible successes that have already emerged in this area.

Long-term financial sustainability is another well-documented key objective for us and we are seeing consistent and continued evidence of this in our financial performance. In the 2015–16 season, we achieved record revenues of £391.8 million – an 11% increase on the previous season – and, once again Manchester City FC generated a profit (of £20.5 million). These positive results were achieved in the context of a zero debt operation and a wage/revenue ratio of 50%, a figure which is among the best in the football industry.

A year ago, we spoke about the opening of the City Football Academy as a single site for all of our teams as the hardware of our strategy. The software is our consistent coaching methodology, our style of play across all of our teams and our commitment to hard work and intensity at every level. We are already beginning to see some positive results from this integrated approach, not only with the success of our Youth teams in Manchester but also with the other teams of the City Football Group.

All of our Clubs are now well-established and delivering promising results. There is a network of support and openness and a culture of sharing best practice that helps us all improve. We are delighted with the progress we have made but there is clearly a lot more work to do and we must constantly adapt to new challenges and embrace fresh opportunities.

Our global network is providing unmatched benefits for our players, coaches, and staff. Patrick Vieira joined Manchester City as a player in 2010, graduated to coach the EDS team for three years and this year became Head Coach of New York City FC. In addition, three players from Manchester's EDS were loaned or signed to NYCFC and had successful experiences with the Club. Frank Lampard played for both Manchester City and NYCFC, whilst Aaron Mooy left Melbourne City to be signed by Manchester City. These are examples that the City Football Group's truly global approach is working to benefit the development both of the game and of our people.

The curtain rose on last season with the opening of the newly expanded Etihad Stadium. This expansion enabled us to post record crowds on multiple occasions during the season. We have seen a significantly enhanced atmosphere and fan experience, noticeable, for example when we played our Champions League games against Paris St Germain and Real Madrid. The renewed energy and atmosphere was very special.

Bringing our supporters closer to the Club and keeping our Cityzens family closer together is, and will always be, a key objective for us. Maybe the best example of this in the past twelve months was the consultation with our members on the possibility of changing the Manchester City badge, and their subsequent influence on its design. Tens of thousands took the opportunity to engage with us in creating a crest which would be most authentic to and reflective of the Club and the City of Manchester itself. What emerged was considered a 'modern original', representing both the Club's rich history and its exciting future.

China deserves a very special mention. This season, we were very happy to welcome our new investors, a consortium led by China Media Capital (CMC) which injected US$400m into CFG, leading to a new Group valuation of US$3 billion. Our new partners are instrumental in our ability to understand and foster the opportunities for our Group in China, at the same time as we work to help develop the game in such a vast and interesting country.

As our commercial structure continued to mature, we opened new offices in Singapore and Shanghai, taking the total number of regional offices to eight, and enabling us to serve our partners and fans around the world in more individual and localised ways.

We are confident that all these positives will make for an even better 12 months to come as we begin our next chapter. Our new manager, Pep Guardiola is an important part of this next stage, just as Manuel Pellegrini was before him. Pep brings rich experience, a new level of tactical sophistication and intensity, with a passion and vision that *will help move our Club forward with the energy and focus expected by our owners and all of the City family.*

We start from a solid base, we have committed owners and partners, world-class coaches and players, superb facilities, highly talented employees, and the most passionate and enduring supporters.

Together, I believe that we are in a great position to continue making history at Manchester City.

CASE STUDY QUESTIONS

1   Take a tour of the Manchester City FC website. What sense do you get of the global strategy being delivered by Ferran Soriano?

2   What sort of leadership qualities does a CEO like Soriano seem to possess?

3   The media coverage of City Football Group at times seems to emphasize the huge investment being made by His Highness Sheikh Mansour bin Zayed Al Nahyan, the owner of CFG, in this global strategy, suggesting money buys success. Do you think this sort of coverage is warranted, and does this diminish the contribution key leaders like Soriano can make in transforming a sport organization?

4   How crucial is having a leader like Soriano to ensuring an organization is able to successfully implement a strategy?

Sources: Manchester City FC website at www.mancity.com

CASE STUDY 8.2

NCAA leadership development

The National Collegiate Athletic Association (NCAA) invests in a leadership development program designed to provide education and training for college athletes, coaches, and administrators to assist with the transition to life after college sports. Their aim is to also foster the growth of the next generation of leaders and to encourage athletics administrators to translate lessons learned through competition. Their program offerings are comprehensive, offering everything from financial management, leadership training, and assistance in applying for graduate school entry.

One of their programs is focused on administrators, as their website attests:

This programming is developed for the athletics professionals who work each day to serve student-athlete needs on campus and at the conference office. Administrators learn about emotional intelligence and student-athlete welfare and diversity initiatives, improve as public speakers, enhance leadership abilities and identify the skills related to specific coaching assignments. The opportunity is also there to build a close-knit network of advisors and engage the decision makers in college sports.

In addition to exposure to university, conference and NCAA administrators, athletics professionals get real-time experience in budget management, strategic planning and fundraising, as well as university and NCAA compliance. Lessons include how to create comprehensive leadership curriculum for student-athletes and department staff; how to structure activities, facilitate discussions and build effective sessions; and create a leadership academy of your own on campus.

The Dr Charles Whitcomb Leadership Institute provides tailored programming to assist racial and ethnic minorities in strategically mapping and planning their careers in athletics administration.

They also offer a Leadership Academy Workshop that educates and trains athletics administrators on the ins and outs of developing effective, comprehensive leadership curriculum for student-athletes and department staff. Participants in the workshop learn how to structure activities, facilitate discussions and structure effective sessions.

As an organization focused on athletes, the NCAA also offers an Athlete Development Professional Certification Program. The rationale on the website is:

As student-athlete development professionals grow in importance to college sports, it is critical that you possess not just a passion for sports, but consistent, applicable management and leadership skills and relevant business acumen. The Athlete Development Professional Certification Program will provide you with the business skills to work more effectively with college athletes, their families and campus constituents and become a well-respected and valued member of your school's team. During the program you will:

Develop essential management and leadership skills, including critical thinking and decision making, negotiation, influence and persuasion, finance for the college athlete, and crisis and media communications.

Hone your personal and professional leadership skills to motivate and engage peers, players, staff and league decision-makers.

This program is a joint venture between the NCAA, the Wharton Executive Education and the National Football League developed in conjunction with the Wharton Sports Business Initiative

For more senior leaders, the NCAA also provides a pathway program designed to help people aspiring to reach the role of Director of Athletics. The summary from their website:

The Pathway Program is designed to elevate those currently in senior-level positions within athletics administration to the next step as a director of athletics. This year-long program is an intensive, experiential learning opportunity for selected participants representing NCAA Divisions I, II and III.

Since its inception in 1997, the Pathway Program (formerly the Fellows Program) has produced more than 100 alumni. Nearly 25% of the participants have gone on to become directors of athletics, while more than 60% have received promotions in their careers.

During the yearlong program, you as a participant identify how values fit into your philosophy and execution of leadership within college athletics and higher education. You also develop knowledge in areas such as budgeting, strategic planning and fundraising for both your current job responsibilities and while you transition to the role of director of athletics.

The Pathway Program kicks off for all divisions during a weeklong session in late June at the NCAA national office in Indianapolis. Throughout the year, program dates and locations will then cater to each division's needs, such as participating in governance meetings and media and interview training. Skill building will take place in the areas of values clarification, leadership, media training, diversity and inclusion, and you will get an in-depth look and introduction to search firms and the hiring process within college athletics.

In addition to the in-person programming throughout the year, you will be paired with both a presidential and director of athletics mentor to assist you in navigating the year.

To wrap up the year, all participants come together and are recognized at the annual NACDA convention luncheon.

The NCAA will cover the cost of travel to and from all in-person programming, including hotel accommodations, meals during the programs and any program materials. You will also receive an honorarium to be used during the year for professional development opportunities and mentor visits.

CASE STUDY QUESTIONS

1   Why does the NCAA invest so many resources into developing the next generation of leaders amongst its member universities?

2   Can you compare this program to any other league or sport organization that devotes some much attention and resourcing to leadership development?

3   How are other leadership programs structured in other sports? What are the similarities and differences to the NCAA?

4   Does having such a centralized program run the risk of creating leaders that are very similar? Why or why not?

5   Should the NCAA continue to invest in this program? Why?

Source: NCAA website at www.ncaa.org/about/resources/leadership-development

CHAPTER 9

Sport organizational culture

OVERVIEW

This chapter explores the influence organizational culture imparts upon sport organizations. It examines why organizational culture is pivotal, highlights its impact, and explains how it can be diagnosed. Several cases and numerous examples will be used throughout the chapter to help explain the role of culture in a sport organization's performance.

By the end of this chapter the reader should be able to:

- Define the meaning of organizational culture;
- Specify why culture is important to sport organizations;

- Explain how different contexts can affect an organizational culture;
- Connect organizational culture and organizational identity;
- Identify how sport organizational cultures can be diagnosed;
- Show the dimensions across which sport organizational cultures can be measured; and
- Discuss how sport organizational culture can be changed.

CULTURE AND THE SPORT MANAGER

This chapter explores the role played by organizational culture in sport and explains its development, expression, and potency. Moreover, this chapter is for readers who want to destroy the tyranny of tradition that keeps organizations in the managerial dark ages and transform clubs, associations, agencies, and businesses into something of greater value. It reveals how to understand cultures and helps to signpost how to create sport enterprises characterized by strong attachments and high performance. However, our task is not as simple as it appears, because culture and its mirror image, identity, present slippery concepts. Securing an early agreement on exactly what constitutes culture and how it works will help us to introduce the concept and its importance to sport managers. In short, organizational culture comprises the shared values, beliefs, and assumptions that influence the attitudes, habits, customs, and behaviour of an organization's members. The 'culture-proof' sport manager needs to be able to diagnose these shared ideas and determine how to use or adjust them to make a positive impact upon their organization.

Culture also reflects the internal and external perceptions of an organization. Examining an organization's culture and identity enables a better understanding of how groups, or subcultures within them, behave and work together, and consequently how others perceive them. The significance of culture has intensified since the 1980s, when the concept first flourished, because it offers a window through which organizational leaders can reflect upon how to adapt to or resist changes in the environment, and either enhance or squander any competitive advantage.

All sport organizations have become embedded with their own unique culture, even when dysfunctional or in disarray. In fact, under-performing sport organizations notoriously covet old traditions and customs, even when faced with marginalization at best, or irrelevance at worst. Culture operates as the underlying force preserving old ways of doing things. Culture is like the elephant in the room. Everyone knows it is there, everyone knows it is shaping the agenda, but no one wants to talk about it, much less try to change it. Culture can be a repository for crazy beliefs under the guise of historical truth and wisdom passed down through the ages. It can also be a recipe for redundancy and chronic failure. Not all cultures deliver good outcomes, even those renowned for their strength and resilience. In reality, old cultures can often be disastrous cultures. Moreover, dysfunctional cultures can be so embedded within an organization's identity – that is, the ways in which they see themselves – that nothing seems to be able to change them. For the outside observer, the amount of effort that some sport organizations invest into preserving old identities does not make sense.

On the other hand, appropriate cultures drive performance, leverage powerful histories, and change quickly in turbulent conditions. Sport organizations with great cultures find ways of winning because success lies at the heart of their identities. Organizational culture provides an understanding of how and why an organization does things, the way the people within the organization behave, and the perceptions held sovereign by stakeholders. Put another way, culture provides a means by which a sport organization's members interpret the way things are done and what happens in daily working life.

All sport organizations possess cultures, but some are stronger than others, and these cultures can exert a powerful influence on individual behaviour and organizational outcomes. Given the emergence of sport business as an independent discipline of theoretical study, in concert with a growing body of literature demonstrating sport's peculiar economies, an argument has developed suggesting that sport cultures may possess unique characteristics. We share this view and argue that the key to successful sport culture lies with understanding how it is created, transmitted, maintained, and challenged within a specific context.

THE IMPORTANCE OF SPORT AND ORGANIZATIONAL CULTURES

The notion of culture tends to receive only superficial treatment by practitioners and educators. Part of the reason lies with culture's social and anthropological background, which does not intuitively appeal to the commercially minded, market-oriented, number-crunching sport executive. Sometimes, interrogating culture may be seen as too distant from work-related outcomes or that too much arms-length 'critiquing' of sport and organizations fails to accommodate the commercial realities of business. These arguments can then be easily fused with the view that the examination of culture may create a chronic tension within an organization about its identity, strategic management, and commercial outlook. For some, the critical analysis of culture contains the inevitable danger that the organization will be declared socially or culturally 'flawed'. But our view remains that the history and tradition associated with any sport organization needs to be understood in order to achieve any subsequent improvement in performance. Furthermore, any attempt to diagnose and improve sport culture must also account for how sport is wielded as a tool for communication and shared understanding.

Sport simultaneously incurs global and local implications, rarely best described in absolute terms. It is within the texture and grain that the idiosyncratic features of sport and organizations should be explored. As a result, we caution against a view that constrains the analysis of sport or organizations to a single interpretive lens. Such an approach leaves little room for complexity in the relationships between sport fans, organizational members, and the sport enterprise, which can range from the rational cost–benefit appraisal of an entertainment experience to the subtle devotion of quiet mourning after a heavy loss. If sport were reducible to simple, one-dimensional cultural structures, then we would all be Manchester United and New York Yankees supporters. We should also be careful not to dismiss the realities of sport's context, from its commodification to its media impact.

DEFINING SPORT ORGANIZATIONAL CULTURE

Culture was originally defined by anthropologists as the values and beliefs common to a group of people. These researchers set themselves the task of investigating, interpreting, and translating the behavioural and social patterns of groups of individuals by trying to understand how they relate to their environment. From a sport perspective, although people in organizations run the technology and invent the processes, they in turn, as part of the process, have much of their behaviour determined by the systems they operate including an often rich and voluminous suite of traditional practices. In other words, there are underlying forces that impact upon behaviour. The concept of culture is a way of putting a name to these forces.

There is no single accepted definition of organizational culture. For example, some view organizational culture as the 'personality' of an organization, whereas for others it represents the things that make an organization unique. However, several assumptions about organizational culture are well accepted. These include:

1   Culture tends to be inflexible and resistant to easy or rapid change.

2   Culture is shaped by an organization's circumstances, its history, and its members.

3   Culture is learned and shared by members of an organization and is reflected in common understandings and beliefs.

4   Culture is often covert; the deep values and beliefs causing behaviour can be hidden from organizational members making them difficult to identify.

5   Culture is manifested in a variety of ways that affect the performance of an organization and its members.

Although elements of commonality exist in the way in which researchers conceive and define culture in organizations, much inconsistency and controversy can still be found. However, for the purposes of this chapter, we shall discuss organizational culture in a way consistent with the view of Schein (2016), who invokes a more psycho-dynamic view. This means that he believes culture is, in part, an unconscious phenomenon, driven by deep level assumptions and beliefs, and where conscious views are merely artefacts and symbolic representations. For example, most sport club members would report that on-field winning is important. Schein's interpretation of organizational culture would lead to questions about *why* winning is important. Does it have to do with a need to belong to a successful group, the pressure of peers, or some other more mysterious explanation? Although many people involved in sport would think this question easy to answer, it is less easy to specify the underpinning values that drive unusual ritual, ceremonies, myths, legends, stories, beliefs, memorabilia, and attitudes. For example, in current and former nations of the British Commonwealth, cricket is played with enormous enthusiasm, but can take up to five days to complete a single match, which often end in a draw. Similarly, to the uninitiated, American football seems quite strange with each team comprising separate players for offensive and defensive manoeuvres. Off the field can be just as odd. In Australia, many (Australian rules) football clubs have 'sausage-sizzles' (BBQs), 'pie-nights' (involving the traditional meal of a meat-pie), and a host of rituals associated with drinking beer. In addition, many sport organizations are packed with memorabilia and expect their employees to work during evening training sessions and weekend games. Sport organizations are rich with strong, meaningful cultural symbols, which on the surface seem easy to interpret, but sometimes are only superficial symptoms of deeper, more complex issues.

What we are searching for is not the superficial, but rather the unconsciously held, fundamental concepts of right or wrong; what an organization might perceive as correct or incorrect values. These values, which are the foundation of an organization's culture, do not simply exist or come into being by their own volition. Instead, members of the organization painstakingly build them up as they gradually learn to interact and achieve their collective and individual aims. An organization's founders, together with the more influential of the organization's past and present members, are usually the most influential in determining the culture. For this reason, we prefer to examine the long-held assumptions and beliefs in an organization.

For the purposes of this chapter, we shall define sport organizational culture as follows: *Sport organizational culture is a collection of fundamental values, beliefs, and attitudes that are common to members of a sport organization, and which subsequently set the behavioural standards or norms for all members*. This definition reflects the view that sport organizations have ways of approaching things that have evolved over time. In many ways, organizational culture answers questions about solving problems. Culture is how 'things are done around here' and how 'we think about things here'.

UNDERSTANDING SPORT ORGANIZATIONAL CULTURE

We can expect that different types of sport organizations will possess different kinds of cultures. For example, professional clubs and major national leagues are more likely to emphasize dispassionate business values, whereas smaller, not-for-profit associations are more likely to value participation and fun. Some sport organizations like Italian and Spanish football clubs are geared almost exclusively to winning and are prepared to go heavily into debt in order to do so. Others, like the company Formula One Holdings, manage the commercial rights to major events and have little other interest than to make money. Whereas the Fédération Internationale de l'Automobile seeks to regulate motor sport, others still, like the International Olympic Committee are interested in developing elite, Olympic sports around the world, and in so doing acquire vast sums of money and spend it liberally.

Sports organizations are increasingly compelled to join the commercial world and are under great pressure to adopt the operational and structural characteristics of business enterprises. The influence of modern communication has been profound, with sporting results available from any smart device connected to the Internet. Many sporting organizations have realized that in order to remain competitive they must provide high levels of entertainment value, just like any compelling leisure option from television to gaming consoles. Consequently, corporate boxes line major sporting venues, sport is blanketed across pay, cable, and free-to-air television, high profile athletes earn extraordinary sums, and politicians associate themselves with certain teams. The commercial and competitive pressures placed upon sport organizations from local football clubs, universities, and colleges, to professional leagues and teams, has encouraged sport managers to embrace business tools and concepts like organizational culture.

Perhaps the most powerful argument in favour of considering culture in sport organizations is that its understanding can help to bring about change. Because culture commands such an influence on the performance of an organization's members, it is critical that cultural traits remain both appropriate and strong. In the case of sport, it is common to have strong cultures that have been forged by tradition and a fierce sense of history. At the same time, some cultural characteristics like excessive drinking and on-field violence may no longer suit the more professional management approach that needs to be assumed in a media-savvy world where almost every individual carries a smartphone with a video camera.

Commentaries on organizational culture, although as disparate as the number of researchers pursuing its investigation, generally emphasize its most superficial manifestation. Moreover, sport culture is frequently seen as mono-cultural; perceived at one level, and as one entity. Here, a sport organization is distinguished as a giant cultural mass, constructed equivalently throughout, and with little or no internal variability. However, this way of thinking is difficult to sustain when analysing a sporting organization. Sporting club cultures possess numerous cultural themes and can be perceived readily at several levels or as several sub-cultures. For example, as an organizational or administrative unit comparable to other business organizations; as a supporter organization, whose aims, objectives, and traditions may be different (such as winning matches in preference to making a financial profit); and as a player unit, where motivation may vary from glory to money. Whereas a player may perform for a club because of loyalty or remuneration (or any number of other reasons), supporters are usually passionately attached to a club's colours and traditions, expecting only on-field success in return. At the same time, some sport organizations are driven by broader social and health agendas or values that relegate both winning and profit to background issues. Others still are held accountable to business returns by shareholders, owners, and sponsors.

In practice 9.1 Culture as strategy: aligning European football with Chinese values

Although the Chinese have had their own Super League since the former Chinese Football Association Jia-A League re-branded in 2004, football had never been genuinely dominant as a sport until the last few years. The catalyst was undoubtedly President Xi Jinping, a self-confessed devotee of the game, who in 2014, published a 50-point road map designed to turn China into a footballing supergiant. Following on President Xi's proposal, the Chinese government announced a 2020 plan that envisaged 50 million children and adults playing football, the formation of 20,000 soccer centres, and the construction of 70,000 football grounds. With a population of almost 1.4 billion, a recognized football following of over 100 million, and a political commitment to the sport by President Xi, football in China is booming – and European football clubs want part of it. One of those clubs is German heavyweight FC Bayern Munich.

Bayern's aim is clear. According to Jörg Wacker, Bayern Munich board member for internationalization and strategy, the club's aim is "to reinforce and promote FC Bayern's presence and values in China [and] to play an active part and make a contribution to the development of football in China". Seeing China as an "important component of [its] international strategy," the club has opened an office in Shanghai and is actively seeking additional local sponsorships. Although Bayern's cultural strategy is multi-fold, three critical success factors guide its path to aligning values between the club and its new target audience.

First, the club has established two football schools in China. One is the 'FC Bayern Football School' in Qingdao, a city of 9 million people in Eastern China, and one of the five cities named as 'football cities' by the government. The second is located in Shenzhen, a metropolis of 12 million. This school has been established in conjunction with the city-owned Shenzhen Investment Holdings Company and the China Sports Futurity Agency. Bayern will financially support the teaching and training of coaches and young players. As part of the process, the club will provide a succession of Bayern coaches in the two schools, along with an exchange program for youth players and local coaches to visit FC Bayern in Germany.

Second, Bayern have agreed to become a strategic partner of the Tsinghua University Centre for Development of Sports Industry, in Beijing. Tsinghua University is one of the elite sports related universities in China. The intent is for the university to use Bayern's economic and sporting knowledge to improve the country's sports industry. Bayern will provide guest lecturers and will promote the discussion of case studies and joint topics of interest. Bayern's Managing Director of its Shanghai offshoot has been appointed to the Supervisory Board of the university's sports faculty.

Third, and almost certainly most important, Bayern is investing a great deal of physical and financial capital into cementing its online presence in China, a country which boasts both the world's largest Internet user base and its most active environment for social media. The western social media outlets of Twitter, Facebook, and LinkedIn are either totally banned or heavily controlled in China. In their place, China has developed its own social media sites led by Weibo ('wei' meaning micro, and 'bo' meaning blog), Youku (similar to YouTube), WeChat (a message app), and many others. Of these sites, Weibo and WeChat are currently the most important social platforms for sport teams to grow their exposure and fan base. As of 2016, Bayern retained the highest presence on Weibo for the second consecutive year with over 70 million followers. On WeChat, the platform granting immediate access to merchandise, ticket sales, and sponsored content, Bayern scored 95 million reads during the year. Bayern accepts that this is well below the total monthly readership for clubs like Manchester United and Liverpool, but is putting effort, time, and money into expanding its fan base. To further deepen their cultural exchange while exploring commercial revenues, Bayern will likely open the first official WeChat store. In the meantime, following in the footsteps of several other major European football clubs, Bayern launched an e-commerce Chinese language online store.

FC Bayern Munich's strategy to influence its popularity in the Chinese market relies heavily on a cultural alignment revolving around values integration. Under such a cultural strategy, making a collaborative contribution and connecting via social networks seem to be the priorities.

SPORT AND SUB-CULTURES

In sport organizational cultures there is the additional hurdle of translating and adopting a culture directly from traditional business theory. It is dangerously simplistic to assume that a sporting organization should adopt the methods and practices of a traditional business without addressing the cultural variables. Although business methods can be transferred to accommodate the organizational strategies of a sporting club, a direct transfer fails to confront the issue of what it is that makes the culture of a sporting organization differ from that of a traditional business enterprise.

Ideal business culture tends to reflect a willingness by an organization's employees to embrace a standard of performance that promotes quality in the production of goods and services in the attempt to generate a financial profit. This cultural ideology, although cognizant of business necessities, is unable to cater for the more diverse structures that exist in a sporting organization. In any business, financial realities must be acknowledged, but in a sporting business, additional behavioural variables require recognition and respect. Different businesses have different cultures, but they are less variable than the cultural differences between individual sports. It cannot be assumed, for example, that a single unified culture exists for all sports. Sport managers must be aware of the cultural nuances of their respective sports and the influence they have upon players, employees, members, fans, and the general public.

Culture is not a simple matter within a single sport either. Professional players, for example, have a different cultural attitude from most amateurs and spectators. This variability of attitudes is symptomatic of a wider, more troublesome area: the clash of cultures within sports. This is illustrated best at an international level, where players from different countries have been brought up with profoundly different ideologies of the game, and how it should be played. Football – the 'world game' – is indicative of this culture clash, in addition to the immense cultural significance inherent in the game. Like all living cultures, sport is incessantly changing, dynamic in nature and subject to constant reinterpretation by its participants and viewers. The only apparent consistencies in sporting culture are the pursuit of competition, the love of winning, and the ability to summon strong emotional responses in both victory and defeat.

Undeniably there is a need to study organizational cultures, accounting for the effect of the sport itself. For example, in the same way that we might expect that accounting firms might share some cultural traits, so might we predict that bocce clubs do as well. Similarly, the tradition and discipline central to a bocce club might be expected to encourage cultural characteristics different to the youthful and eclectic philosophy found in a BMX club. Other sports, like ultimate fighting and mixed martial arts, laud different values again, reinforcing masculinity, toughness, and power. These cultural characteristics can even seep into the behaviours of executive officers and employees of the clubs, especially because many sport organizations like to hire past players. Given that so many sporting organizations covet tradition and the accomplishments of the past, they also tend to be resistant to change. However, before any change can occur, an organization's culture needs to be accurately diagnosed in the form of a coherent identity.

In practice 9.2 Innovation as identity change
with the Philadelphia 76ers

Founded in 1946, the Philadelphia 76ers are one of the U.S. National Basketball Association's (NBA) oldest teams. Usually the franchise inspires associations with its fierce defence of tradition, a rich history of success with three NBA titles, and a suite of past players now immortalized amongst the greatest the sport has produced, including Wilt Chamberlain, Hal Greer, Billy Cunningham, Julius Erving, Moses Malone, Charles Barkley, and Allen Iverson. However, the team has gained attention for reinventing the professional sport franchise business model. Pushed by an ambitious ownership group, the franchise recently appointed a CEO to conceive and develop an 'Innovation Lab', the first business incubator financed and operated by a NBA team. The aggressive push into the innovation space has also created a revitalized organizational identity where risk, energy, and agility have become permanent markers in the team's cultural standards. As a result, the 76ers are playing off the court with just as much emphasis on speed and innovation as they are on the court.

Although the 76ers are the first to establish an innovation playground within the franchise, several other professional sport franchises in the United States have made like-minded shifts in their business models over the last few years. For example, the Los Angeles Dodgers baseball team launched the 'Dodgers Accelerator' in 2015, and the Golden State Warriors NBA team created an investment subsidiary they named 'GSW Sports Ventures' in 2016. Although these new entities sought to capitalize on innovative new business opportunities – and in particular high risk, high return start-ups – both partition the activities from their parent franchises. As a result, unlike the 76ers' experience, the identity effects also stay contained within the new entities, and do not permeate into the NBA team's off court culture.

For the 76ers, cultural change was essential not just to bolster their chances of success, but also for their long-term survival with fluctuating financial returns, softening franchise value, and lengthy run of poor on-court performances including one record-breaking sequence of successive losses. With little sign of an upturn in fortune, the team fell into a mire, leading to a crisis culminating in the departure of General Manager Sam Hinkie in 2016. The farewell ushered in a new appetite for change. Gone was what Hinkie had described as a 'trust the process' slow burn in building up the franchise, instead replaced by a newfound sense of urgency and renewal.

Comfort with risk suddenly escalated as the owners and new management began to tinker with thoughts of growing beyond their core, on the court business. Thoughts coalesced into a sweeping new plan to drive innovation through the business. CEO Scott O'Neil reflected on the cultural direction that soon firmed up: "When we talk about the core values of who we are as an organization, innovation is always at the forefront. We like to do things differently. We get up every day and convince ourselves we have a lot to learn." As the scene revealed a newfound identification around innovation, a confluence of circumstances – including a vacant retail space and some radical suggestions about an innovation site – delivered the unique opportunity that aligned perfectly. So was born the Innovation Lab, designed to recruit and develop start-up companies, help them raise funds, and open hitherto dormant avenues for investment and high-yield returns. The incubator employs a 'loose' and flexible model ranging from simply providing space and support to taking an equity position. Although connecting with sport is seen as advantageous, the general focus remains far broader with priority given to consumer products. Manager of Operations Rhyan Truett observed:

> Sports teams are getting more innovative. I think they've gotten a little bit of a pass compared to other businesses in needing to get to 2017, and we're getting to see a lot of those business that can get them there. So we get to look at and hopefully eventually incubate something that could be the sports teams of the future, that change your game experience, that change the way you interact with your team. That would be the bullseye.

Since the incubator launched, the Dallas Cowboys National Football League (NFL) franchise and the NFL Players Association have each established business accelerators. Whether the Innovation Lab will deliver the leveraging effects that it promises might take years to determine. Nevertheless, the cultural impact has so far been substantial. Already the team has embraced an entrepreneurial start-up mentality where innovation and venture capitalist optimism have seeped through the cracks in tradition.

SPORT ORGANIZATIONAL IDENTITY

Like all social concepts, organizational identity allocates meaning to largely intangible but pivotal organizational behaviours. From a social perspective, identity describes how individuals perceive themselves, as well as how they are perceived by others. Because identity represents an individual's self-perception, it also tends to be durable, providing a long-term, stable, distinctive, and enduring image. Similarly, as social entities, sport organizations exhibit identities established by the adoption, reinforcement, and rejection of particular characteristics created by its members over time. The process operates as an extension of personal identity where individuals adopt or reinforce characteristics they perceive advantageous while discarding the negative. For example, an organization might adopt team-based work practices if its members expect collaboration to be advantageous. An organization establishes its identity through the collective self-perceptions of insiders, which in turn accompanies how it performs (culture), the way it expresses itself, and the way it is perceived by outsiders (image). However, a sport organization might perceive itself in a manner incompatible with outside perceptions. Change to bring the two into alignment is difficult because identity reflects long-term, stable perceptions about an organization's idiosyncratic characteristics. Such perceptions determine not only an organization's understanding of itself, but also how such statements are received and accepted (or rejected) by stakeholders.

Culture is about the way we do things and identity is about how we perceive or are perceived. Furthermore, things are done in a particular way due to culture, but also to reinforce or change perceptions. In this respect, organizational culture and identity work together in a reciprocal and dynamic manner. Culture is the more contextual, tacit and emergent side, whereas identity is the more textual, explicit, and instrumental side. Another way of looking at it expresses identity as a manifestation and artefact of culture. However, like culture, identity reveals an organizational contradiction. Change is necessary in order for an organization to survive a competitive environment, but at the same time, identity has to endure long enough to maintain a sense of continuity. Appropriate cultures change, whereas strong cultures endure. Understanding the role identity plays in organizations is also essential to culture's diagnosis.

DIAGNOSING AND MANAGING SPORT ORGANIZATIONAL CULTURE

In order to grasp the concept of culture and its relationship to the individual, the group, and the sport organization, an in-depth approach is required. Sport organizations create intentions and atmospheres that influence behaviour, routines, practices, and the thought systems of members. These systems and processes subsequently form patterns that are acquired primarily through socialization or learning over time from the reactions and behaviours of others. In essence, individuals within a sport organization are exposed to what researchers call 'culture revealing' situations, which might include the observable behaviour of other members, their organizational methods, 'artefacts' – the photos, honour boards and other memorabilia on show – and interactive communication, or the way in which individuals talk to each other. Some of these common, superficial, and observable representations of organizational culture are reproduced in Table 9.1. These are important to recognize because the driving values and belief systems behind them can never be seen as anything more than observable 'symptoms'.

Although the superficial aspects of culture can be observed, the difficulty comes in their interpretation because they are merely surface representations of deeper values. Thus, a useful cultural diagnosis will always seek to understand what drives the observable behaviour. For example, what does it mean if an employee makes a mistake and is severely reprimanded by his or her boss? What does common jargon imply? Why are certain rituals typical, like the moment when a new player is allocated a number or jersey?

TABLE 9.1 Observable symptoms of sport organizational culture

Symptom	Explanation
Environment	The general surroundings of an organization, like the building it is housed in and the geographical location, like the city or in a grandstand.
Artefacts	Physical objects located in the organization from its furnishings to its coffee machine.
Language	The common words and phrases used by most organizational members, including gestures and body language.
Documents	Any literature, including reports, statements, promotional material, memos and emails produced for the purpose of communication.
Logos	Any symbolic visual imagery, including colours and fonts, that convey meaning about the organization.
Heroes	Current or former organizational members who are considered exemplars.
Stories	Narratives shared by organizational members based at least partly on true events.
Legends	An event with some historical basis but has been embellished with fictional details.
Rituals	Standardized and repeated behaviours.
Rites	Elaborate, dramatic, planned set of activities.

The key question remains as to how overt observations relate to deeper values. Most researchers recommend some form of classification system that describes organizational culture in the form of 'dimensions', each one a deeper, core value. These dimensions reflect on particular organizational characteristics as an aid to categorizing cultures. The summation of these characteristics may be used to describe an organization's culture, which can then allow for comparisons to be undertaken between organizations. For example, observable evidence in the form of an end-of-season awards night in a sporting club might be suggestive of the nature of the organization's reward/motivation values. Enough observable evidence can lead a sport manager to make some tentative conclusions about each dimension. Table 9.2 lists some common dimensions used to describe organizational culture. They can be seen as continua, an organization's position somewhere between the two extremes.

Any analysis that captures the complexity of organizational culture may have great difficulty in separating the interwoven strands of organizational history and personal relationships. As a result, concrete conclusions may be difficult to establish. It is therefore important to take advantage of the symbolism created by sport's abundant myths, rituals, and ceremonies in order to gain a complete understanding of the full range of human behaviour within a complex organization. The traditions, folklore, mythologies, dramas,

TABLE 9.2 Cultural dimensions	
Dimension	Characteristics
Stability/changeability	Disposition toward change: Degree to which organization encourages alternative 'ways of doing things' or existing ways.
Cooperation/conflict	Disposition toward problem resolution: Degree to which organization encourages cooperation or conflict.
Goal focus/orientation	Clarity and nature of objectives and performance expectations.
Reward/motivation	Nature of reward orientation of organizational members: Degree to which organization encourages seniority or performance.
Control/authority	Nature and degree of responsibility, freedom, and independence of organizational members.
Time/planning	Disposition toward long-term planning: Degree to which organization encourages short-term or long-term thinking.

and successes and traumas of the past are the threads that weave together the fabric of organizational culture.

SPORT ORGANIZATIONAL CULTURE AND PSYCHOLOGY

A psychological approach is helpful in identifying and interpreting human behaviour in organizations as a cultural phenomenon. Psychologists, originally stimulated by the work of Carl Jung, suggest that there are different levels of behavioural awareness, from the conscious to unconscious. Organizational psychologists have appropriated this kind of thinking and transposed it to culture. The key analogy is that an organization is like a mind.

From the psychological viewpoint, the readily apparent and observable qualities of a sporting organization are the same as the conscious part of an individual mind. These include the physical environment, the public statements of officials, the way individuals interactively communicate, the form of language used, what clothes are worn, and the memorabilia that fills the rooms and offices. Another of the most important observable qualities involves the place of sporting heroes. They represent rich and highly visible indicators of the culture being sought. Heroes offer an insight into the culture of an organization, because the members as well as power brokers select them. In addition, heroes signpost those qualities in individuals respected and admired by a wider audience. The hero is a powerful figure in a sporting organization and may be simultaneously an employee and ex-player. The hero may also be charismatic, entrepreneurial, or just plain administrative, which often characterizes business enterprises. By understanding the orientation of hero figures, both past and present, it is possible to map trends in cultural change. Heroes can be both reactionary and progressive. For example, heroes that reinforce the dominant culture will not change the values and attitudes that the culture emphasizes. On the other hand, a hero that transcends and transforms the dominant culture will be a catalyst for change in the behaviours and values of a club. Often a hero is the most powerful medium for change to be successful.

Tradition is another window into the culture of an organization. Like heroes, traditions are readily observable through memorabilia. However, the underlying values and assumptions that give meaning to heroes and traditions reside in the deeper levels of a culture. Tradition may on one hand be preserved by the present cultural identity, whereas, on the other hand, the sporting organization may have developed a contemporary cultural personality. Thus, it is useful to acknowledge the importance of tradition and history to a sporting organization because it may be a cultural linchpin or a stepping stone from which their contemporary cultural character has been launched.

In order to bypass the obstacles (in the form of stereotypical views and superficial signs) that can block an assessment of culture, it is essential to analyse and explore natural, observable outcroppings of culture, places where the cultural understandings can be exposed. By analysing these sites, it is possible to gain a practical insight into the underlying culture of the organization. This level deals with organizational rites and rituals because their performance is readily apparent, and in performing these rites, employees generally use other cultural forms of expression, such as certain customary language or jargon, gestures, and artefacts. These rites, which are shared understandings, are additionally conveyed through myths, sagas, legends, or other stories associated with the occasion, and in practical terms may take the form of barbecues or presentations. In order to actively assess this level of culture, not only must observational techniques be employed, but meanings must be attached to them. This requires more than a superficial level of analysis.

There are also 'unconscious' parts of organizations as well. In effect, it is the unconscious that controls the individual. This incorporates the beliefs, habits, values, behaviours, and attitudes prevalent in a sporting organization. An accurate assessment of this level of culture is difficult and fraught with the danger of misrepresentation. For example, how employees say they behave and what they state they believe have to be compared to their actual behaviour.

As a cautionary note, sport managers should be aware that multiple interpretations can be made based on the same evidence. For example, one way of looking at culture is to focus attention on the consistency and congruence of policies and practices within a sport organization, as members are confronted with problems to solve. In contrast, it is also valid to consider ambiguities and inconsistencies in behaviour. These anomalies often represent the difference between espoused values and actual values. Cultural manifestations can be interpreted in multiple ways, and change over time and location. It is important to look for patterns, exceptions, and values targeted for change.

In practice 9.3 Embedding social responsibility into sport organizational cultures

A sport organization's social awareness impacts upon its stakeholders' perceptions and may be thought of in a range of ways from corporate responsibility to green issues. Its importance has also escalated in recent years, with calls for sport – and in particular professional sport and its associated manufacturers and commercial sponsors – to wield their social impact with greater thought. However, shifting to a position of more acute social sensitivity demands a commensurate transition in organizational culture. After all, winning or profit at all costs, is rarely aligned seamlessly with care for the broader, often deleterious social and environmental effects they can cause. Nevertheless, corporate sporting apparel manufacturers like Nike, Patagonia, and Asics have famously committed to a 'green' cultural identity in their documented strategies in order to attenuate stakeholder concerns about sport's environmental impacts, from the field of play to product manufacturing. At the same time, sport enterprises have embraced more socially aware cultural values to not only secure favourable brand and event associations, but also to attract corporate sponsors and benefactors. In some cases, sporting clubs and associations have adopted aspects of the United Nations General Assembly's Millennium Development Goals as a way of reinforcing their cultural recognition of sport's importance in protecting human rights.

Perhaps the most well-publicized case revolves around the social responsibility cultural change adopted by Nike, accused of exploitative labour practices in developing countries and vilified as using 'sweat-shop' suppliers. A comprehensive response by the company in transforming its outsourcing practices has slowly yielded a cultural swing, which has also had the effect of encouraging, and even forcing, other manufacturers to enact similar changes.

Other sport enterprises have incorporated social awareness into their activities, content to leave it an internal, cultural form rather than use it for marketing purposes where social commitments may be interpreted as cynical veneers. In the surf-fashion context, for example, brands like Quiksilver have developed equipment and clothing with a high level of environmental consciousness, but see the efforts as part of their stakeholders' basic expectations rather than as positioning or differentiation strategies.

Although cultural change can prove messy and nebulous, sport organizations successfully incorporating social values tend to begin by clearly declaring what they perceive their social responsibilities to entail. For example, relevant issues may include internal (e.g. policies on non-discrimination in the workplace), external (e.g. policy on labour standards of suppliers), accountability (e.g. commitment to reporting on social activities), and citizenship (e.g. educational programs for the promotion of social initiatives) elements guided by sources such as the UN Declaration of Human Rights, the UNESCO Project on Technical and Vocational Education, the UN Global Compact, the International Labour Standards Convention, the International Programme on the Elimination of Child Labour, as well as the more popularized issues of sustainability.

Sport enterprises have accepted a degree of accountability for their social and environmental footprints, and have therefore sought to find the intersection between social and economic (performance) dividends. But the commitment needs to come from cultural and identity commitments where new values, beliefs, and norms trump the win at all costs mentality that pervades most sport. For example, according to FIFA, the chief social effort used in concert with the 2010 World Cup held in South Africa was branded the 'Win in Africa, with Africa' program. But behind the marketing campaign was a real commitment by the continent to delivering a legacy well beyond the actual event.

MAPPING SPORT ORGANIZATIONAL CULTURE

Cultural understanding stems from successfully translating information into meaning. Every aspect of a sporting organization is symbolically representative in some way of its culture. All information is not equal, however, yet all possible data must be analysed in order to establish the most comprehensive image possible of the existing culture. In order for a culture to be created and bolstered, shared values and beliefs must in some way be reinforced and transferred to organizational members through tangible means.

A cultural map summarizes the predominant features of a sporting organization's culture, and provides a means through which raw data can be interpreted into measurable criteria. It works by providing sets of categories in which information can be collected and summarized with the intention of identifying the main themes that continually emerge. Some researchers believe that this approach can also be used in a more statistical form, with the numbers attached to responses from questions derived from the dimensions and answered by organizational members.

Although the range and diversity of information available for cultural analysis are profound, many cultural studies ignore all but the most apparent and accessible data. A holistic cultural analysis will utilize every available piece of information, with the more obvious elements becoming vehicles for the transmission of less tangible, more subjective facets of culture. However, the culture of any one sporting organization cannot be classified into one of just a few categories, even though many models offer a handful of neatly predetermined types. In reality, there are as many organizational cultures as there are sporting organizations, and they cannot be generically categorized into one of a fixed number of groups. Sporting clubs are immersed in tradition, history, values, and myths, and these should figure prominently in any diagnosis. From an accurate diagnosis, change becomes far easier.

The main lesson for cultural change is that it cannot be tackled without a clear, prior understanding of an organization's chief cultural traits and how they manifest. Once an accurate diagnosis has been undertaken, through some form of formal or informal cultural map, elements of culture can be managed. Because a sport manager cannot literally change peoples' minds, they instead have to change peoples' actions. To some extent this can be imposed or encouraged, but it is a slow process. For example, new rituals can be introduced to replace older, less desirable ones, like a club dinner instead of a drinking binge. Entrenched values and beliefs can be extremely difficult to change, and even with the right introduction of new symbols, language, heroes, stories, employees, and so on, genuine cultural change in an organization can take many years or even a new generation of organizational members before it takes hold.

SPORT AND CULTURAL COMPLEXITIES

Culture and identity cannot be avoided by any member of an organization. Although a slippery concept, hard to conflate to the simple or tangible, culture shapes the collective conduct of all organizational members. It does this by inculcating bundles of values and beliefs into members' minds. In turn, values and beliefs canalize and restrict ways of thinking. In short, culture shapes conduct and individual behaviour. For example, cultural values and beliefs might have to do with how men should relate to women, why profit should override environmental sensitivity, or why winning and success are more important than participation. As a result, some cultures create socially valued outcomes, whereas others create dysfunctional cultures. Culture can be changed for the better, but it requires astute and sophisticated management. Perhaps more than anything else, it demands a deep understanding of how culture works.

We emphasize the importance of building cultural understandings. Every aspect of a sporting organization is symbolically representative in some way of its culture. Cultivating a successful culture relies on shared values and beliefs that have been reinforced and transferred to organizational members through tangible means like rituals. Cultural change cannot be tackled without a clear, prior understanding of an organization's chief cultural traits and how they manifest. Once an accurate diagnosis has been undertaken, elements of culture can be managed. Of course, because sport managers cannot literally change peoples' minds, they can influence behaviour. For this reason, organizational rituals provide a mechanism through which entrenched values and beliefs can be influenced by new symbols, language, heroes, and stories. Keep in mind that cultivating a successful sport culture relies on translating information into meaning. And meaning is the path to a powerful cultural identity.

SUMMARY

In the world of sport management, organizational culture has gained prominence as a concept useful in assessing and managing performance. Sport organizational culture can be defined as the collection of fundamental values and attitudes that are common to members of a sport organization, and which subsequently set the behavioural standards or norms for all members. The difficultly remains, however, that the deep values common to organizational members are not easy to access. As a way of getting around this inaccessibility problem, sport managers can use cultural dimensions that suggest some of the possible values that are present. A step further, cultural maps show the variables and observable manifestations of culture that need to be investigated. These maps use the tip of the cultural iceberg (the accessible aspects of culture like symbols and artefacts) to estimate the iceberg's underwater composition (the deep values and beliefs of organizational members). Once a thorough diagnosis has been completed, sport managers can work toward adapting and replacing undesirable cultural characteristics.

REVIEW QUESTIONS

1   Why is organization culture important to sport managers?

2   Explain how organizational culture can be manifested at different levels.

3 Describe the difference between superficial elements of culture and deeper elements of culture. What is the difference between organizational culture and identity?

4 What is a cultural dimension?

5 How can organizational culture be measured in a sport organization?

6 How does measuring organizational culture help in changing it?

7 Select a sport organization you belong or have belonged to. Create a list of attributes or values that you believe embodies its organizational culture. What are the characteristics that distinguish it from other similar sport organizations?

8 Select a sport organization you belong or have belonged to. Describe 10 artefacts that are on show in its premises and explain how each illuminate organizational culture.

DISCUSSION QUESTIONS

1 Do all organizations affiliated with the same sport share cultural features?

2 Under what circumstances can culture actually change quickly? Discuss some examples.

3 Can someone who works within an organization diagnose its culture objectively? If so, how do you think they could go about it? If not, what should they do instead?

4 Discuss whether culture and identity can be affected through changes to strategy and structure. What about the other direction? Is one way preferable, or perhaps they all be pursued at once?

5 Identify some sport organizations that contain undesirable cultural elements. What are these elements and what can be done about them?

FURTHER READING

Bailey, B., Benson, A.J. and Bruner, M.W. (2017). Investigating the organisational culture of CrossFit. *International Journal of Sport and Exercise Psychology*, 1–15. http://dx.doi.org/10.1080/1612197X.2017.1329223

Davidovici-Nora, M. (2017). e-Sport as leverage for growth strategy: The example of League of Legends. *International Journal of Gaming and Computer-Mediated Simulations (IJGCMS)*, 9(2): 33–46.

Eskiler, E., Geri, S., Sertbas, K. and Calik, F. (2016). The effects of organizational culture on organizational creativity and innovativeness in the sport businesses. *Anthropologist*, 23(3): 590–597.

Manley, A., Roderick, M. and Parker, A. (2016). Disciplinary mechanisms and the discourse of identity: The creation of 'silence' in an elite sports academy. *Culture and Organization*, 22(3): 221–244.

Olson, E.M., Duray, R., Cooper, C. and Olson, K.M. (2016). Strategy, structure, and culture within the English Premier League: An examination of large clubs. *Sport, Business and Management: An International Journal*, 6(1): 55–75.

Schein, E. (2016). *Organizational Culture and Leadership*. 5th edn. San Francisco: Jossey-Bass.

Wagstaff, C.R., Martin, L.J. and Thelwell, R.C. (2017). Subgroups and cliques in sport: A longitudinal case study of a rugby union team. *Psychology of Sport and Exercise*, 30: 164–172.

RELEVANT WEBSITES

www.the-afc.com/member-association/chinese-football-association—Chinese Football Association http://bluestaraccelerator.com/—Dallas Cowboys Blue Star Accelerator
www.eslgaming.com/—Electronic Sports League
https://fcbayern.com/en—FC Bayern Munich
www.fifa.com/sustainability/index.html—Fifa Sustainability
www.nba.com/warriors/gswsportsllc/—GSW Sports
www.ie-sf.org/—International eSports Federation
www.dodgersaccelerator.com/—Los Angeles Dodgers Accelerator
www.oneteamcollective.com/—NFL Players Association One Team

Collective
http://about.nike.com/pages/sustainable-innovation—Nike Sustainable Innovation
www.unesco.org/new/en/social-and-human-sciences/themes/physical-education-and-sport/

UNESCO Sport
www.quiksilver.com.au/quiksilver-foundation—Quiksilver Foundation

CASE STUDY 9.1

From the home to the globe: eSports cultural challenges

In a surprise only to sporting traditionalists, eSports were recently conferred a place as an official medal 'demonstration' sport at the forthcoming 2022 Asian Games in Hangzhou, China. The move, championed by the Olympic Council of Asia (OCA) and bolstered by the commercial might of Chinese online retail powerhouse Alibaba, confirmed the emergence of eSports as fully fledged sports complete with both an immense participation base and a lucrative professional stratum. Its development also signals a major shift in culture for the nascent sport, having moved swiftly from the homes of most players to a global, online marketplace.

With eSports a component of the world's second largest multi-sport event – eclipsed only by the Olympic Games – the entry in the Asian Games foreshadows the maturation of a new and unique form of sporting culture. Although relentless improvements in technology have long played a role in sporting success, for the first time a generational leap has redefined what it means to be an athlete on the world stage. As a result, eSports have exploded in popularity across the developed world – faster than any sport in history. An inventory of eSports' current highlights underscores its startling growth: professional leagues, international contests, college and university scholarships, investments from mainstream professional sports team owners, exclusive broadcasting and digital rights deals, significant commercial sponsorships, generous prize money, and a burgeoning elite cadre of professional players earning up to seven figures. All of these developments have arisen because eSporting culture materialized in tandem with a new generation of participants and spectators inimitably attracted to the confluence of technology, gaming, and remote tribalism.

A curious eSports cultural feature is its fragmentation and diversity. Talking about eSports as a singular activity is not the same as talking about tennis or even a multi-event sport like gymnastics. The eSports audience is passionately heterogeneous. Each game within eSports commands its own distinctive following, usually on the basis of game title. In fact, eSports can be interpreted in two ways. First, it can be viewed as the competitive playing of an electronic game, irrespective of the game's specific content or nature. That is, the game might be associated with winning a war or with building a city; the central issue has to do with the competitive nature of the activity. Second, eSports can be viewed as the playing of electronic games directly associated with traditional sports such as football in its many codes, boxing, or baseball. From this vantage, eSports revolve around competitive performances in popular sporting simulations like Madden (NFL) and FIFA (Association Football). As a result, eSports are intractably connected to the specific modality of the games themselves. In some cases, like the ubiquitous war game simulations or first person 'shoot-em-ups', players and audiences have nothing to do with 'normal' sports. Other players of sport-related games may or may not hold an interest in the conventional versions of the sport they are duplicating. Both forms of eSports hold competition in common, so winning maintains its primacy as the sovereign purpose of participating, at least at the elite level.

With player cultural values – as well as eSport organizational cultures – intrinsically tied to specific game features, we should be cautious about typecasting eSport players and fans as just another set of sport consumers. For example, somewhat ironically, the vast majority of eSports participants do not focus on sporting games. Instead, what have become known as 'multiplayer online battle arena' (MOBA) games such as 'League of Legends' and 'Dota 2' dominate, with first person shooting games like 'Counterstrike' and 'Call of Duty' not far behind. At the moment, it appears unlikely that even the most popular sports-related games will break into the top tier of eSport followings. One explanation for the distance between the two versions of eSports proposes that audiences will prefer to watch or play 'real' sports over their electronic counterparts. Conversely, audiences do not have the option of participating in 'real' war, so its electronic facsimile represents a unique activity in its own right. Nevertheless, as game sales attest, millions of consumers choose both versions of eSports, unequivocally demonstrating their market appeal for at least a core segment.

The largest eSports organization is the Electronic Sports League (ESL). To the surprise of many, the league was founded more than 20 years ago and now boasts a registered membership exceeding five million with over one million teams. eSports was estimated by a Newzoo global eSports market report to generate around US$700m in revenue based on a global audience of nearly 400 million people. The trend estimates a 2020 revenue of US$1500m. So far, the largest prize pool in eSports was provided by the Dota 2 2016 International Championship Tournament, collectively worth US$20m. The winning team took home nearly US$10m and more than US$1.8m each.

With a formidable foundation of players located in Asia, it is unsurprising that the International eSports Federation (IESF) was founded and remains based in the world eSports capital, South Korea. A long campaigner for competitive gaming to be included in the Olympics, the IESF invested US$14.5m to produce the World Electronic Games in the Chinese Changzhou province. With 60,000 participants from 120 countries and regions, and a US$5.5m total prize purse, the major event raised enormous interest in eSports in the lead-up to the Asian Games announcement. Along with the IESF, the British International eGames Committee (IEGC) only recently submitted a request to the International Olympic Committee (IOC) for clarification on how to petition for the official Olympic program. Pertinent to this Olympic ambition, the Alibaba Sports Group – Alisports – which was established in 2015, announced in 2016 a US$150m sponsorship commitment to the IESF. The deal is particularly noteworthy because in 2017 Alibaba signed a US$1b 11-year deal with the IOC to be a prominent summer and winter Olympics sponsor. Other sponsors feature game developers such as Riot and Blizzard, tournament organizers like ESL Gaming Network, and companies with associated commercial products including Red Bull, LG, and Logitech Gaming. Sponsorship and advertising currently contribute around 75% of eSport revenue.

At the same time as eSports has proliferated in Asia, it has also enjoyed unprecedented growth in the United States. For example, in 2017, the University of Utah began promoting athletic scholarships to players who make the college's varsity eSports team, the first of its kind for competitive gaming associated with a National Collegiate Athletics Association (NCAA) participating university. In total, 15 U.S. colleges offer eSports scholarships, prestaging cultural acceptance as an authentic target of student interest.

Although the popularity of many sports divides along compatible geographical and ethno-cultural convergences, it is clear that eSports connects with a certain under 30, technologically savvy, well-educated, affluent, demographic segment, irrespective of their location. According to one study, for example, many elite eSport players are part-time or full-time undergraduate students, having been active in developing their skills since cultivating an interest in high school. After becoming recognized by professional gaming clubs through their high rankings and performances in online gaming forums, the developing elite players gained coaching and representative affiliations. Unlike most sports, however, the majority of serious players compete and practice from home, some of the best committing up to 10 hours a day at the screen. In this respect, eSports exemplifies some of the same cultural features as any other sport. Success demands a relentless schedule of practice and discipline. In addition, the sport's nascent sponsorship, inconstant prize money, and unrelenting change in the popularity of different games, means that the average players' competitive lifespan ranges only three to five years. Nevertheless, also like other sports, serious gamers report a suite of benefits accompanying professional gaming including comradeship, emotional gratification, personal growth, psychological resilience, and fun. Just as other elite athletes suggest, a commitment to eSports stimulates lifelong skills and development, including confidence and self-actualization.

One of the most interesting aspects of the eSports cultural transformation is its unusually hastened product lifecycle. Accelerated massively in comparison to traditional sports like tennis, wherein the premier event still demands compliance to a draconian dress code (eSports do not require the wearing of white underwear), eSports is evolving culturally as it strikes each new phase of development. For example, unexpectedly, despite its location independence, eSports seems to be heading towards a content distribution model largely predicated upon regional exclusively. That is, although some tournaments might be broadcast for free, the rise of pay per view platforms will likely ensure that a sizable proportion of content will fall behind a paywall. We may well expect that live sporting event brokers like Facebook and Amazon will make a play for exclusive distribution rights.

In addition, professional players are beginning to see signs that their restricted contracts will give way to standardized player agreements, enforced, or at least advocated as a result of newly forming player unions like the Professional eSports Association, which is premised upon revenue splitting between eSports organizations and players. How eSports' inexorable transition into professionalization will affect its founding culture of independence and freedom is unclear.

As a professional tier of competition emerges in eSports, so, too, do all the cultural problems that come with commercial dividends. First, the ESL recently announced plans to introduce an anti-doping program following the admission by one of its senior-most players to using the cognitive enhancer and pharmaceutical Adderall during a competition. With US$250,000 in prize money available for the competition, this singular admission may well be just the tip of the cognitive performance-enhancing drug iceberg. Second, gambling around eSports remains unregulated. It is anyone's guess to what extent the temptation for game fixing and other forms of corruption have permeated the sport's growing ranks. Third, like technology start-ups, and the infamous tech-boom and succeeding dot-com crash of the early 2000s, eSports is vulnerable to overreaching in attempts to capitalize on its seemingly exponential commercial inflation. The business models governing the monetization of the sport remain under-developed and to a large extent, experimental. Finally, eSports culture makes governance troublesome. Fragmentation abounds as new federations and competitions gain traction, typically clustered around specific games. No one really knows whether eSports will end up being represented by overarching governing bodies or by more stratified game, community, geography, or stakeholder affiliations. Some might even speculate that the most successful will ultimately associate directly with commercial providers or distributors in the case of MOBAs, or with existing clubs, leagues, and federations of conventional versions of sports that have electronic varieties.

Adding to the uncertainty is the powerful cultural norm within eSports to rebel against and subvert the mainstream. Many players joined eSports because they felt uncomfortable trying to fit into mainstream hobbies and sports – or could not access them – instead electing to join the ranks of the anonymous, distant, and fluid world of the electronic gamer. Nevertheless, eSports appear on a stellar trajectory, destined to take their place on the world sporting stage, complete with its own collision of cultural idiosyncrasies and commercial conundrums.

CASE STUDY QUESTIONS

1   Do you think that the basic competitive and sector structure for eSports has now been firmly established and that the future will look like a larger version of the current situation, or is eSports still too early in its development to reveal its likely composition?

2   What do you see as some of the cultural challenges associated with fandom for eSports?

3   Some commentators think that eSports will never be able to rival traditional spectator sports for popularity. Do some 'desktop' Google research to see what statistics and evidence you can find that supports or contradicts this prediction. What can you infer about the eSports culture based on these data?

CASE REFERENCE

Guo, Z. & Cahalane, M. (2017). The rise of the pro-player as Australia hosts its richest computer gaming event, *The Conversation*, May 5.

CASE STUDY 9.2

The changing culture of consumption: the case of sport broadcasting in the United States

Cultures in sport manifest at all levels. They influence beliefs and behaviours in organizations, mould values and norms in specific sport and events, canalize thinking in leagues, stimulate belonging and identification in fans, direct product opportunities for manufacturers and service providers, permeate strategy across governing federations, and define national sporting priorities and pride. However, culture is seldom given sufficient consideration as a variable affecting the way sport is consumed. Although sport managers might become attuned to the local cultures they work within – whether organizational, sporting code, or national – much less attention is given to the way cultural forces manipulate and transform the nature of the sporting experience. Sport's consumption may be vulnerable to a myriad of broader cultural pressures emanating from its social, political, economic, technological, demographic, and a host of further contexts. Some are soft nudges but others are violent shoves. Of the latter kind, sport is undergoing a revolution in its viewing culture. The disruption revolves around a suite of changes inexorably shifting the way sport is experienced by spectators and viewers. As a result, we are witnessing a collision of the digital and the analogue; of old ways and new opportunities for consuming sport. In fact, the sporting product itself is morphing rapidly, compressed between consumers' increasing desire for superior access, mobility, engagement, interaction, and choice. Nowhere is the changing culture of sporting consumption more apparent than in the world's most lucrative and mature national sporting market, the United States. Here, the transformation of sport broadcasting models has brought a significant cultural force to bear upon the way sport is, and no doubt, will be consumed in the future. Where watching sport on television was once the exclusive channel for consuming spectator sport outside of the venue itself, the viewing options have proliferated, encompassing a spectacular range of digital, pay-per-view, and bespoke compositions. In the messy consequence of all the ways an audience can engage with spectator products, the very heart of sporting culture appears to be beating hard to keep up. To understand how the culture of consumption is changing, a look at how sport broadcasting in the United States has exploded is instructive.

Unlike the European model where rights are more fragmented across subscription broadcasters, the U.S. approach – at least for the major leagues – remains largely in the hands of networks broadcasting free-to-air, in order to take advantage of other commercial benefits such as the sponsorships accompanying a diverse and vast audience reach. This is because initially the U.S. government issued local licenses for broadcasting, but media players naturally formed networks of exclusively affiliated local stations in order to secure national coverage and economies of scale, while complying with anti-competitive regulation. Up until the 1980s, the network affiliate market was cornered by CBS, NBC, and ABC, which also controlled the major U.S. sport broadcast market. Their dominance was solidified by the watershed 1961 Sports Broadcasting Act giving leagues the legal opportunity to sell their rights – effectively as supply-side cartels – but also in the process generating incrementally more competitive bidding only affordable by the major commercial networks. The bidding wars escalated with the arrival of a fourth network, Fox. At the same time, newer cable networks expanded their reach into sport, led by the dedicated sports network ESPN and Turner Broadcasting System (TBS), a subsidiary of Time Warner. Despite expectations that the shift from analogue to digital transmission in 2009 would encourage a wide-scale migration of rights towards subscription television, the networks have maintained their control over the major leagues, even though the total volume of sport available to consumers is far larger through the more fragmented cable and satellite pay services.

Since its emergence in the 1940s, commercial broadcast networks have dominated U.S. television broadcasting, with public broadcasting services (PBS) playing on a minor role (Evens et al, 2013). Outgunned in resources to spend on rights, PBS only vies for relatively small live sport coverage such as some high school and college sports like tennis and baseball. In contrast, broadcast networks represent the traditional (and current) powerhouses of U.S. sport broadcasting and rights ownership. The five major networks – CBS, NBC, ABC, Fox, and The CW (a subsidiary of CBS and Warner Bros) – command a national audience on a free-to-air basis. In terms of the business model, on-air advertising delivers the majority of revenue, which means that audience reach remains a critical variable and one to keep in mind as a driver of the way sport is delivered and therefore consumed.

At the same time, more than 100 cable networks operate in the United States directed to more targeted, niche audiences who must pay a subscription for access. ESPN is the dominant sport cable provider. Cable networks receive smaller advertising revenues due to their narrower audiences, relying instead on pay-for-service subscriptions sold to bundling platforms at wholesale prices who subsequently package and on sell to consumers. In the secondary market, premium networks constitute a subset of cable networks. However, where cable is sold as bundles of numerous networks, premium cable must be independently selected and purchased by a consumer. Given the specificity of premium networks, they tend to receive less censoring. Prominent examples include HBO and Showtime, which each provides sports content such as boxing. Premium networks receive less advertising revenue and focus on subscriptions like cable.

New technology companies are more recent entrants into the sports broadcasting arena and are attempting to take niche positions by offering digital and mobile viewing options. Google, Facebook, and Twitter have been testing the water with selected sports broadcasting rights deals. It is not yet completely clear where new technology companies will acquire the greatest revenues from their sport broadcasting efforts. Online advertising revenues are likely to be prominent, but subscriptions might also emerge as profitable options. For example, 'Twitter Amplify' has taken an early position as a powerful new channel to generate advertising revenue. The platform works by teaming with content providers like ESPN, which provide short video highlights very shortly after their live broadcast.

Sport properties as content providers such as leagues, competitions, clubs, teams, and franchises are increasingly experimenting with direct-to-consumer broadcasting. So far these subscription-based services have been modest and targeted for fan engagement around a selection of augmented products, rather than trying to compete with network and pay-TV broadcasters for live viewers. Content owners can sell advertising, attract more lucrative sponsorship contracts, and yield subscription fees.

Noteworthy is the effect of Internet penetration as consumers in the United States 'cut the cord', opting for digital platforms instead of conventional free, cable, or even satellite delivery. The number of digital application platforms has expanded radically as have their subscriptions. Such platforms provide 'over the top' (OTT) content because it requires no network and has been propelled by Internet penetration and fast online data streaming. Some like Apple TV require additional devices, whereas others such as Netflix only need an Internet connection or a smart TV.

Most broadcast and cable networks have entered the online space through indigenous platforms, add-on devices, or streaming web content. Many attempt to add value by repackaging recorded sport with commentaries, highlights, and new content in the form of regular episodes. Others – mainly cable due to the consistency of its business model based on subscription revenues – simply license the content to Netflix, Hulu, or other streaming services for a series of events, matches, or seasons. In contrast the broadcast networks have lost valuable advertising revenues as television spots have diminished in value commensurate with the rise of other sports-watching channels. More recently, networks have signed content deals with the likes of Netflix, which has solidified the former's revenues and the latter's content quality. At the same time, Netflix and others are venturing into content production in order to generate their own content; a move probably foreshadowing similar thinking from major sport content owners. At the least, it is reasonable to expect that sport owners will license parts of their content to digital platforms. Naturally, the rise of digital platforms has stimulated a commensurate rise in the value of digital advertising.

Another business model growing rapidly involves electronic sell-through or video on demand where consumers purchase or rent recorded shows, movies, or events. Amazon and Apple are the leaders in the area, but their model does not align favourably with live sport and the need to acquire event, match, or game rights. Advertising-based user-generated content providers like YouTube allow some sport recordings but also censor others, depending upon the vigilance of the content owners in identifying copyright infringements. For the moment, broadcasting live sport is not part of the model.

Finally, to add to the competitive clutter, telecom companies are entering the marketplace as well, with Internet service providers trying to duplicate services such as Google Voice, Skype, and FaceTime. These providers currently do not engage with sport content, but might well consider channel partnerships with content owners, particularly those with well-established niche audiences.

Content clutter and the absence of customized and flexible viewing options in network television have softened sports viewing, although it remains solid given that the large commercial networks own the rights to the lion's share of major sport programming. At the same time, bundled cable has suffered as consumers drop off, their specific sport viewing preferences forced into a gamut of other ostensibly worthless viewing options. Both free and pay television deliver curtailed, time-locked content. Although set-top box and DVR recording ameliorates the time issue to some extent, consumers' interests in on-demand, mobile, customized, and digital sport viewing is burgeoning as a way of cutting through the perceived irrelevance and clutter of unwanted broadcasts.

Despite projections about an imminent post-television consumer culture era, sport leagues continue to preference free-to-air broadcast network deals. At least part of the explanation is that the numbers simply do not add up for pay TV; subscriptions are dropping across the United States while free broadcast time slots remain resilient, although they have experienced some weakening in ratings. Audience reach drives sports broadcasting revenues, and will persist into the near future. At the same time, cable broadcasters are under pressure to bolster scrawnier revenues from declining subscriptions and inexorably escalating sports rights fees. New business models will therefore be essential in order to capitalize on multi-platform viewing expectations from a new generation of mobile audiences, catering for the fluid on-demand combinations associated with digital platforms. For example, it is likely that the longstanding exclusive licensing model will succumb to a fragmented suite of direct to consumer mechanisms. This revised business model will yield several attractive benefits, including superior access for consumers to a wide range of premium sports, as well as a far more expansive set of competitors eager to break into once exclusive network territory. Niche strategies for product composition, pricing and channels would emerge allowing consumers to select from a virtual smorgasbord of sports watching alternatives to shape their own customized packages.

In addition, broadcasting rights business models will inevitably have to accommodate the intervention of new technology giants such as Google, Apple, Amazon, Facebook, and Twitter, whose financial scale will undoubtedly ensure that sports leagues seriously consider the non-exclusive distribution channels that accompany a multiplicity of digital delivery platforms. For example, the NFL secured a deal with Twitter to provide live digital streams of Thursday Night Football to global audiences, beginning in the 2016 season. The deal is estimated to be valued at US$10m; a modest figure that presages the NFL's willingness to experiment in this new environment. Cable in particular seems vulnerable to the digital alternative.

Another variation, probably complementary to what was already noted, would see sporting leagues assume all broadcasting responsibilities and channels for their properties. Under this model, direct-to-fan content would be offered from sporting properties – and perhaps their digital channel partners – effectively converting the property owners into media companies in their own right. Of course, such a transformation has significant implications on sport enterprises and leagues. Moving from content creation in the form of a sporting competition to a full-service digital broadcasting business represents a non-trivial shift. There would also be fundamental changes to sponsorship transactions as well. Merely the possibility of contents owners vertically integrating into broadcasting would surely instantiate rapid change in the behaviours and offers of intermediary networks, cable stations, and technology channel companies, not to mention the imposition on consumers' consumption options.

Professional sports competitions, clubs, and franchise around the world have already ventured seriously into broadcasting their own content, although so far avoiding any risk of undermining the value of third-party rights contracts. As a result, most of the forays into self-broadcasting have focused on narrow, mostly peripheral content, directly to fans. U.S. examples include NBA.com and MLB TV, whereas Manchester United's MUTV, the Australian Football League's AFL Media, and a myriad of YouTube channels like Barcelona FC's barcatv, represent an international field of subscription services. By 2000, all the big-four U.S. leagues had developed 24-hour cable TV channels or Internet platforms for their surfeit and local content, with the pioneering station, NBA.com, having led the way in 1999.

One way or another, online streaming will eventually become the standard paid programming vehicle through a range of devices including Internet connected smart TVs, computers, and mobile smart devices. Such a future would place cable's sport broadcasting future in serious jeopardy as consumers, by implication, would prioritize customized, standalone services. Consumers will pay for precisely what they want and discard the rest; bundling will give way to an 'a la carte' model based on digital flexibility, or at least premium cable options. If correct, consumer demand will re-shape the industry, driving cable online and undermining the carriers, forever changing the consumption culture of sport.

CASE STUDY QUESTIONS

1   North American major leagues' preference for free-TV networks as recipients of their broadcasting rights contrast with European competitions, which tend to select pay-TV networks. Assuming that rights bids in the United States are typically handed to the largest offer, but that the maximum capacity to pay is not always held by a free network, what would explain the cultural and structural difference? Search the Internet to get an idea of who owns the largest broadcasting deals in the United States.

2   Traditional networks that have always relied on conventional television broadcasting are under heavy pressure to accommodate the new consumer culture of fast, on-demand, customized access. How can traditional networks remain competitive?

3   Speculate about the future of U.S. sport broadcasting consumer culture.

CHAPTER 10

Financial management in sport

OVERVIEW

This chapter introduces readers to the financial management function in sport organizations. Through the use of critical incidents and illustrative cases, a number of
core accounting principles will be discussed. Special attention will be given to the
budgeting process and the analysis of balance sheets, profit and loss statements,
and cash flow statements, together with the key principles of sound financial management. Throughout the chapter reference will made to a range of accounting terms
and financial management concepts. The overall aim is to have readers build a broad
accounting vocabulary that will give them a basic level of financial literacy, which can,

in turn, be used to better understand the administrative processes required to build a sport organization's financial viability.

After completing this chapter the reader should be able to:

- Explain how sport has changed over the last 50 years and what that means for the effective financial management of sport organizations;
- Understand the importance of professional financial management in sport;
- Identify the ways in which the financial operations of sport organization can be best reported;
- Explain how assets are organized and how they differ from liabilities;
- Explain how profits and/or surpluses are calculated for sport organizations and the difference between operating profit and net profit;
- Understand the importance of cash and the use of cash flow statements to ensure ongoing liquidity;
- Explain how budgets operate and explain why they are crucial to effective financial management of sport organizations; and
- Diagnose the financial health of a sport organization.

THE FINANCIAL EVOLUTION OF SPORT

As previous chapters have demonstrated, sport is now a sophisticated institution with an often complex legal and financial structure. It is, in many respects, a fusion of business and entertainment where the consumers are the fans and the players; the producers are the clubs, associations, and leagues; and the distribution channels are the sport arenas and sport stadia (Carter 2011; Foster, Greyser and Walsh 2006; Gomes, Kase and Urruria 2010; Quinn 2009; Shropshire and Davis 2008; Smit 2007. Like all forms of business, sport organizations require a strong system of financial management to ensure their long-term sustainability. However, this has not always been the case, and sport around the world has gone through four phases of commercial and financial development over the last 50 years.

This metamorphosis of sport into a form of business, with its associated financial systems, begins in Phase 1 with sport as a recreational and cultural practice where sport organizations are rudimentary, their revenue streams are small, sport is played mainly for fun, and activities are organized and managed by volunteer officials. This model is often described as a kitchen-table approach to sport management, because the game is administered by a few officials making key decisions from a member's home. It has some strengths because it not only ensures the involvement of grassroots players and members and provides a strong local community club focus, but it also nurtures a strong set of values that centre on playing the game for its own sake and the concomitant ideal of amateurism. At the same time, it perpetuates a simple system of management driven by an administrative committee made up of a few elected members and self-appointed officials.

There is the president who is the public face of the club or association and a secretary who keeps things ticking over by maintaining a member register and organizing others to manage teams, run events, and maintain the clubrooms and playing facilities. There is also a treasurer who looks after the financial affairs of the organization. The treasurer is more often than not unfamiliar with the theory and principles of accounting, but makes up for a lack of expertise with a mind for detail and a desire to ensure receipts run ahead of expenses.

The second phase is commercialization, where more revenue streams are utilized and both staff and players are paid for their services. Whereas the kitchen-table model depends on member subscriptions, player registration fees, and social activities for their financial viability, the commercialized sport model uses sport's commercial value to attract corporate and other sponsors. In this phase, sports that have the capacity to draw large crowds increasingly understand that these crowds can be used to attract businesses who want to increase product awareness, secure a special and exclusive sales channel, or obtain access to a market segment that will be receptive to their product. Sport is still a recreational and cultural practice, where the sport's overall development is the primary goal, but there is also an emerging or secondary strategy that focuses on elite development and the building of pathways by which players can move to the premier league or competition.

The third phase is bureaucratization, where the structures of sport organizations become more complex, administrative controls are established, and functional specialization increases. This phase is heavily dependent upon its antecedent phase, because an effective bureaucracy requires additional resources. In this phase, club, league, and association structures are transformed so as to include a board of directors whose prime responsibility is to set the strategic direction and ensure compliance with government regulation. This, then, establishes an organizational divide between the 'steerers' (the board) and the 'rowers' (the chief executive officer and operational staff) who are expected to implement the board's plans and policies. In addition, a business-like set of functions and processes are created, which are built around administrative support, marketing, finance, game development, coaching player development, and the like. In this phase less management space is given to the sport-as-recreation-and-cultural-practice model and more to the sport-as-business model.

The fourth and final phase is corporatization, where sport embraces the business model by valuing brand management as much as it does player and fan relations. Revenue streams are increasingly dominated by sponsorships and broadcast rights fees, merchandise sales are deepened, and managers adopt a more professional outlook where the need to secure a competitive edge overrules the desire to hold on to old traditions. This is the phase in which players become full-time employees, player associations are established to protect their interests, and the sport's governing bodies take on the role of employers. A formal industrial relations system is created that leads to detailed contractual arrangements, collective bargaining agreements, and codes of conduct. The marketing process also becomes increasingly sophisticated as the sport club, association, or league becomes a brand; members and fans become customers; sponsors become corporate partners; and the brand name and image are used to strengthen corporate partner arrangements and build up a merchandising arm.

This phase also features a move toward managerialism, whereby sport becomes more accountable to its stakeholders for its performance and use of resources. This is particularly evident in sport's relationship with government, where government funding becomes increasingly contingent upon sport meeting certain specific and agreed upon outcomes. This focus on managerialism also leads to greater transparency through an emphasis in performance measurement. Under this framework it is no longer appropriate to only measure player performance, but also things like internal processes and efficiency, financial performance, market performance, employer, and in particular player behaviour, and even social responsibility.

These forces make sport more complex to operate, and as a result sport organizations become generally more regulated. In some instances the regulations are initiated by government-framed legislation. Government controls include venue safety rules, anti-discrimination programs, and crowd-control policies. In other instances the regulations are internally imposed. Internal regulation is highly visible within professional sport leagues and competitions, where player recruitment is governed by drafting rules, player behaviour is constrained by a combination of collective agreements and codes of conduct, salaries are set within a total wage ceiling, revenues are redistributed from the most wealthy to the most needy clubs and associations, and games are scheduled to ensure the lowest cost and greatest revenue. Although this type of corporate regulation can be problematic because of its heavy emphasis on bureaucratic control and detailed performance measurement, it also ensures a disciplined system of management by creating a common purpose, setting a clear strategic direction, and securing strong leadership (Beech and Chadwick 2013; Stewart 2007a). A summary of each phase in the sport-as-business evolution is provided in Table 10.1.

TABLE 10.1 Sport as business: evolutionary phases and features

	Values	Revenue focus	Structural focus	Management focus
STAGE 1 Kitchen table	Amateurism Volunteerism	Member funds Social club income	Management Committee	Sustaining operations
STAGE 2 Commercial	Viability of sport Member service	Gate receipts Sponsorship	Management portfolios	Marketing the club
STAGE 3 Bureaucratic	Efficient use of sport resources Accountability	Corporate income Merchandising	Divisions and departments	Improving club efficiency
STAGE 4 Corporate	Delivering outputs Building the brand	Brand value Broadcast rights	Board policymaking Staff operations	Increasing club value Regulating constituents

FUNDING SOURCES FOR SPORT

It is clear that the new business-based, corporate model of sport involves a significant expansion of income. However, it is important to not throw the baby out with the bath water, and so traditional forms of revenue have been maintained, although in a slightly more sophisticated form. Member fees are still important, as are fundraising from social activities and gate receipts. However, as was touched upon previously, new and varied revenue streams have opened up over the last 30 years which have transformed sport and the way it operates (Foster Greyser and Walsh 2006; Szymanski and Kuypers 2000). The funding of sport organizations begs a number of questions, the main ones being listed here.

1   Where does the money come from?
2   Where is the money spent?
3   How are the movements of money monitored?

In answering these questions it is important to distinguish between funds that are used to create infrastructure and facilities, and funds for use in managing the day-to-day activities of a sport organization. So, there are two types of basic funding uses. The first is funds for investment in capital development, and the second is funds for recurrent and operating activities.

Capital funding

Capital funding, which is money to finance investment in assets, can come from a number of sources listed here.

1   Government grants which may be federal, state, or local. The point to note is that there are differences between sports which reflect not only their scale of operation but also their likelihood of generating international success. Funding may also be subject to certain conditions being met, such as adopting certain policy requirements or working within a legislative framework.
2   Loans and borrowing which could be short term (up to a year) or long term (up to 20 years). Loans and borrowings are known as debt finance. The points to note are that it provides ready cash for investment in facilities and income producing assets. On the other hand, it also incurs an interest burden and may not always generate an increase in income.
3   New share issue or a public float which is known as equity finance. The points to note are that, like borrowing, it provides ready access to cash, but, unlike borrowing, does not impose the burden of interest payment or repayment of the principle to lenders. However it does hand over control to shareholders, and there is expectation that a dividend will be delivered.
4   Retained earnings, which is money re-invested in the sport organization. The points to note are there is no interest payment and control is retained over funds used. For

nonprofit sport organizations, the retention of earnings is mandatory, because this is a legal requirement.

Recurrent funding

The recurrent funding of sport involves money to fund day-to-day operations, which comes from a variety of sources depending on the type of sport enterprise. The main revenue sources are briefly noted here, together with the strengths and weaknesses of each source:

1 Membership fees which may be full adult, associate, family, and similar categories. The points to note here are that they are usually upfront and relatively stable and therefore provide an immediate source of cash. Membership also serves a marketing function by establishing a core customer base.

2 Spectator admission charge which includes the categories of full adult, family, special groups, and premium. The points to note are that although there is a high degree of flexibility, it is subject to significant variation because of changing attendance patterns and differences in the scheduling of games.

3 Corporate facilities including boxes and hospitality. The points to note are that a large investment is required, but the strengths are that business connections are made and premium rental fees can be charged.

4 Player fees and charges include entry fees, facility charge, and equipment hire. The points to note here are that revenue is dependent on demand, and the user pays for the experience.

5 Special fundraising efforts are another source of recurrent funding and may include a dinner dance, rage-party, auction night, a trivia night, and so on. The points to note are that the burden is on staff and members to arrange and attend functions. However, these types of events can be profitable through large markups on food and drink.

6 Lotteries and gaming such as raffles, bingo, and gaming machines. The points to note are that permits are often required, margins are low, and there is solid competition from other venues.

7 Merchandising such as memorabilia, scarves, T-shirts, jackets, and autographed equipment. The point to note is that although it can produce is a significant short-run increase in revenue, it can also plateau out with a fall in on-field success.

8 Sponsorships and endorsement are another good source and may include naming rights, partnerships, signage, product endorsements, and contract deals. However, the points to note are that the organization can lose control and become dependent on sponsor income and defer to their partnership demands.

9 Catering may include take-away or sit-down food or drink. The point to note is that it is labor intensive, but because it is delivered in a non-competitive environment, higher profit margins can be sustained.

10 Broadcasting rights such as television and radio, and more recently Internet and mobile phone streaming rights. The points to note are that it focuses on elite sports with a large

audience base and may be irrelevant for most community-based sports associations and clubs. At the same time it provides the single largest revenue source for professional sport leagues.

11 Investment income such as interest earned and shared dividends. However the points to note are that share prices can vary at short notice, and losses can be made which increases the level of risk. In addition, interest rates may be low.

12 Government grants, which may be federal, state, or local. The points to note are that there are often marked differences between sports, they can vary from year to year, and like government capital funds, are subject to contain conditions being met.

The expenses incurred in running a sport enterprise are also varied. They include:

1 Wages and salaries such as permanent, contract, or casual administration staff and players. The points to note are that it is usually the largest expense item and is subject to inflation and competitive bidding as clubs aim to secure the best playing talent.

2 Staff on-costs, which include insurance, training, leave, and superannuation. The points to note here are that they are legally required, ongoing, and linked to the employment contract.

3 Marketing costs, which include advertising, sales promotion, site visits, trade displays, and give-aways. The point to note here is that it is easy to exceed budget estimates because there is always a tacit assumption that too much marketing and promotion is never enough.

4 Office maintenance includes power and light, phone and fax, postage and stationery, and printing. The points to note here are that it is ongoing and tight control is required.

5 Venue maintenance includes the playing area, the viewing area, and member facilities. The point to note here is that maintenance expenditure is ongoing and frequently absorbs a significant amount of revenue.

6 Player management includes equipment, clothing and footwear, medical services, fitness and conditioning, and travel. The points to note are that although they constitute an essential investment in improved performance, they also require tight budgeting.

7 Asset depreciation includes facilities, buildings, cars, and equipment. The point to note here is that assets lose value and must be replaced. Also, depreciation is a non-cash expense, and it is essential that assets be amortized as expenses over their lifetime.

KEY FINANCIAL MANAGEMENT QUESTIONS TO ASK

At the same time, it is important to note that although significant segments of sport are now big businesses, most sport organizations are relatively small and depend on the support of club members, volunteer officials, community businesses, and local government to sustain their operations. Whereas high-profile professional sport leagues turn over hundreds of millions of dollars a year, the majority of sport clubs and associations are lucky to secure any more than a million dollars to fund their operations

(Dolles and Soderman 2013; Quinn 2009). A majority of sport is really a form of small business. A suburban supermarket turns over more money than most sport clubs and associations.

However, no matter what the scale or size of sport organizations, they all need to be managed in a sound and responsible manner (Shibli and Wilson 2012). Many sport administrators do not feel comfortable handling money or planning the financial affairs of clubs and associations, which often arises out of poor background knowledge and a lack of experience in managing complex financial issues. In practice, there are many straightforward, but essential financial questions that sport managers need to answer. They include:

1 What do we own?
2 What do we owe?
3 What did we earn?
4 What did we spend?
5 Did we make a profit?
6 Do we have enough cash to pay debts when they fall due?
7 How big is our interest bill?
8 Are we borrowing too much?
9 Did we improve upon last year?
10 How do we compare with other similar sport organizations?

UNDERSTANDING FINANCIAL INFORMATION

There is also the problem of making sense of the vocabulary of accounting. The distinction between assets and liabilities is mostly clear, with assets amounting to all those things we own and liabilities being all those things we owe to others. However, the distinction between tangible and intangible assets and current and non-current liabilities may often be less clear. The concepts of owner's equity, shareholder's funds, and net worth can also cause confusion, and further difficulties can arise when contrasting operating profit with net profit.

Consequently the effective management of any sport organization requires not only a sound knowledge of the principles of financial management, but also the support of a financial recording and reporting system that allows a quick and easy reading of the club's or association's financial health (Hart 2006; McCarthy 2007). It is now taken for granted that a professionally managed sport organization will produce three integrated annual financial reports. The first document is a statement of performance, or profit and loss, which reports on the revenues earned for the period and the expenses incurred. The second document is a statement of position, or balance sheet, which reports on the current level of assets, liabilities, and equity. The third document is a statement of cash flows, which identifies the cash movements in and out of the organization. The cash flow statement is divided into activities related to day-to-day operations, activities that involve the sale and purchase of assets, and activities that involve the securing and borrowing of funds and their repayment. The balance sheet, profit and loss statement, and cash flow statement are discussed in more detail next.

THE BALANCE SHEET

The balance sheet measures the wealth of a sport organization. Assets are placed on the left-hand side of the balance sheet, and liabilities are placed on the right-hand side. Proprietorship (also termed owner's equity, net worth, or accumulated funds) is located on the right-hand side and represents the difference between assets and liabilities. The balance sheet gives a clear picture of a sport organization's wealth at a point in time by contrasting its assets (things it owns) with its liabilities (things it owes). The balance sheet also indicates how the assets of the organization have been funded. It can be through equity (i.e. the capital of the owner/s) or from borrowed funds from some other organization or individual.

It is important to note that not all assets are the same. They can be broken down into a number of categories (Hoggett, Edwards and Medlin 2006) as can liabilities. As a result a balanced sheet will be set up to provide a clear picture of the level of both current and non-current assets and current and non-current liabilities. The level of owner's equity or shareholders' capital (or accumulated funds as it is usually called in nonprofit organization statements) will also be identified in the balance sheet because it is effectively the difference between the two. This is because assets can be accumulated through either the owner's capital, reinvested profits, or borrowed funds.

Assets

As noted earlier, assets are all those things owned by an organization. To put it more technically, they constitute resources owned and controlled by an entity from which future benefits are expected to flow. The assets of a balance sheet are not only broken down into their various categories, but they are also listed according to their degree of liquidity, with the most liquid coming first and the less liquid coming later in the statement. The measure of an asset's liquidity is the ease with which it can be converted to cash, and all those assets which can easily converted are listed under the current assets heading. The most frequently cited currents assets are cash in bank, accounts payable or debtors (which include those short-term invoices or bills for payment has not yet been received), investments in the share market (which can be converted to cash through quick sale), and stocks of material and merchandise (which at a pinch can be sold for cash). Items like prepaid expenses (that is, bills paid in advance) can also be included here. The level of current assets is an important indicator of the financial health of a sport organization because it is the means by which bills are paid and creditors' demands for payment are met.

Assets are also listed as fixed or non-current. These assets include everything that cannot be easily and quickly converted to cash. Some stock and materials will be listed here when they do not have high turnover. The main items will be all those tangible or material

TABLE 10.2 Balance sheet: asset categories

Asset category	Degree of liquidity	Example
Cash in bank	High (current)	Trading account balance
Accounts receivable	Medium (current)	Monies owed by club members
Prepaid expense	Medium (non-current)	Payment of next year's insurance
Company shares	Medium (current)	Ownership of shares
Inventory	Medium (current)	Stock of sports equipment
Office equipment	Low (non-current)	Computer system
Other equipment	Low (non-current)	Office furniture
Motor vehicle	Low (non-current)	Ownership of vehicle
Property	Low (non-current)	Ownership of office building
Building improvements	Low (non-current)	Stadium renewal

assets that are essential for generating revenue, but are difficult to sell at an appropriate price in the short term. These items include office furniture and equipment (including all sorts of sports equipment), motor vehicles, buildings, and land. Building improvements (e.g. a stadium upgrade) are also examples of fixed assets. The main categories of assets are listed in Table 10.2.

The balance sheet of a sporting organization can be complicated by a number of other factors. For example, assets can either increase in value over time (i.e. appreciate) or decrease in value over time (i.e. depreciate). Property, stocks and shares, and various scarce artefacts and memorabilia are particularly prone to increase in value. On the other hand, there are other assets that can lose value quickly, and includes those things that incur constant use and wear and tear, or become obsolete, or both. Moreover, there are assets that, although not tangible, clearly add value to the organization and should be accounted for. Accountants have recognized these financial facts of life for many years and have consequently devised strategies for managing these phenomena (Atrill, McLaney, Harvey and Jenner 2006).

Depreciation

Depreciation is based on the principle that all non-current assets represent a store of service potential that the organization intends to use over the life of the asset. Assets therefore have a limited life as a result of their ongoing wear and tear and probable obsolescence. Accounting for depreciation is the process whereby the decline in the service potential of an asset, such as a motor vehicle, is progressively brought to account as a periodic charge against revenue. That is, the asset is devalued in response to its purchase price or market value and offset against income. In order to allocate the cost of the asset to the period in which it is used, an estimate must be made of the asset's useful life. This will usually be less than its physical life. For example, in the case of a motor vehicle, it may be decided that after three years it will not be operating as efficiently and therefore will be worth less after this period, even though it is still running. If an asset has a residual, or resale value, then this amount will be subtracted from the asset cost to establish the actual amount to be depreciated.

The simplest method for depreciating an asset is the straight line or prime cost method. This method allocates an equal amount of depreciation to each full accounting period in the asset's useful life. The amount of depreciation for each period is determined by dividing the cost of the asset minus its residual value by the number of periods in the asset's useful life. Take, for example, a computer system that was purchased for $11,000. It is anticipated that the system will have a resale value of $1,000 after five years. Using the straight line method of depreciation the annual depreciation will be $2,000. This figure is obtained by dividing the difference between the purchase price and the residual value ($10,000) by the five years of anticipated useful life. This annual depreciation will then be posted as an expense in the profit and loss statement for the following five years. This process of spreading the cost of an asset over a specific period of time is called amortization. The idea behind this process is that there needs to be a clear way of showing the relationship between spread of benefits from an asset's use and the costs involved in creating those benefits.

Asset valuation

Asset values can also change to reflect current conditions and prices. Unless otherwise stated, assets are valued at their purchase price, which is known as historical cost. However, many assets, particularly land and buildings, can increase in value over time. Unless this is periodically done, the true values of assets can be seriously understated. This problem can be overcome by a revaluation of the assets by a certified valuer, with a note to this effect accompanying the annual statement of financial operations and standing.

In practice 10.1 Sport stadia asset management: the case of the Melbourne Cricket Club

Around the world there are many sport stadia that have made a strategic decision to completely re-furbish and re-design their facilities. Of course, we all know that this type of 'grand plan' comes at a cost. We also understand that the stadia owners and managers will be most often required to secure funds from external sources to make it all happen.

Take, for example, the internationally famous and iconic Melbourne Cricket Ground (MCG) and its occupant, the Melbourne Cricket Club (MCC). In 2002 it decided to demolish its ageing stand and start again by putting up 'state of the art' facilities. But to make all this happen it had to borrow a significant amount of money. In fact, its borrowings totalled well over $300 million. In 2006, and just in time for the Commonwealth Games, it had spent all its borrowed money, but what it got in return was a scintillating bundle of world-class facilities. But, as we all know, when you borrow money, you not only have to pay back the full amount you borrowed – which is commonly called the 'principal', but you also have to pay an annual interest charge. If we assume the annual interest charge is around 8%, then in the first few years the total interest bill will be something in the order of $20 to 24 million. This represents a serious drain on one's cash deposits.

This heavy repayment burden immediately raises the question as to just what benefits are going to accrue from this very big investment and when it might be clear that the decision to borrow all this money was, in fact, a good one. And there is a risk that the repayment burden may be so severe that the ability to repay may be impossible.

But the MCC/MCG has a strong cushion against any cash flow problems. It is its 'membership'. It has many thousands of members and is able to maintain a 20-year waiting list with virtually no promotional or marketing effort whatsoever. Moreover, it is Australia's premier sport stadium and has no difficulty securing tenants, the main ones being the Australian Football League and the Cricket Australia. And, to top it off, it regularly attracts 50,000 to 80,000 spectators to games. These strong attendance figures consequently enable it to (1) negotiate big catering and hospitality contracts, (2) hire out expensive corporate suits with no difficulty, and, finally, (3) secure big-brand advertisers to place signage around the ground.

The financial 'moral' to this story is short and sharp. It is that investing in expensive assets is a sound thing to do, but only if you are sure the assets can deliver the best-quality services. If this occurs, then you can be confident that that these services will generate sufficient additional revenue so that not only will all loans and interest bills be paid off, but that there will be a handsome surplus with which to undertake even further investments. If, on the other hand, the newly created assets are unable to deliver these benefits, the future will look very uncertain indeed. In the case of the MCC/MCG, it took a calculated risk and reaped the rewards. Although in 2017, it still owed AUD$177 million to banks and other financial institutions, its revenue of AUD$149 million was more than enough to cover its interest and loan repayments, while also covering all its operational spending. And, its net worth – the difference between total assets and total liabilities – continued to grow, and at last count was AUD$298 million. There is now talk that the MCC will undertake a further infrastructure upgrade that will future-proof the stadium for the 2020s and beyond.

Liabilities

Simply put, liabilities are those things that an organization owes others. To be more exact, they are the present obligations of an entity which, when settled, involve the outflow of economic resources (Hoggett, Edwards and Medlin 2006). Like assets, liabilities can be categorized into current and non-current. Current liabilities included monies that are owed to people in the immediate future for services and goods they have supplied. For example, a club may have purchased some sporting equipment on credit for which payment is due in 30 to 60 days. This is called accounts payable or debtors. Other current liabilities include short-term borrowings, member income received in advance, and taxes payable in the short term. Income received in advance is an interesting case because it is often intuitively viewed as revenue or asset and not a liability. However, under the accrual accounting model it is clearly not relevant to the current flows of revenue and expenses. But as monies received it has to be accounted for. So, what happens is that it is debited to cash in bank and credited as something we owe to members in the future. That is, it is a liability which is listed as income received in advance. Non-current liabilities include long-term borrowings, mortgage loans, deferred tax liabilities, and long-term provisions for employees like superannuation entitlements.

The accumulation of liabilities is not of itself a problem, so long as the debt is used to build income earning assets. However, if increasing debt is associated with losses rather than profits, then the gap between assets and liabilities will increase. It is not uncommon in sport for clubs to have liabilities that exceed the value of their assets. Hundreds of football clubs in Europe make losses, and a sizeable proportion of these loss-making clubs have more liabilities than assets. This situation is replicated in Australia where the net worth of some clubs in rugby and Australian-rules football is negative (that is, they have more liabilities than assets). In the long run, these trends are unsustainable.

Balance sheets can say a lot about a sport organization's financial health. However, balance sheets do not tell us much about a sport club's earnings, profits, and losses over the course of a month, quarter, or year. For this information we must turn to the profit and loss statement, or as it is often called in the nonprofit sector of sport, the income statement.

PROFIT AND LOSS STATEMENTS

It is not just a matter of examining a sport organization's assets and liabilities at a point in time in order to diagnose its financial health, it is also crucial to shift one's attention to the financial operation of sport clubs and associations over time (Atrill, McLaney, Harvey and Jenner 2006). The first thing to be said about the profit and loss statement is that it can go under a number of names. It can also be called an income statement, which is the nonprofit sector terminology, and is also referred to as a financial statement of performance. The point to remember about most sport organizations is that they do not focus on profits and losses, but rather surpluses and deficits (Anthony and Young 2003). In any case, it does not alter the fact that these statements looks at the revenue earned during a period (say 3 or 12 months) and compare it with the expenses incurred in generating the revenue. Profit and loss statements are straightforward to compile and moderately easy to understand, but there are some tricky areas that need to be discussed.

The first point to make is that although profit and loss statements contain many cash movements, they do accurately represent the total cash movements in and out of the organization, because they are essentially about earned income and incurred expenses. As a result they will include many transactions that do not include the movement of cash. In other words, revenue can be earned, whereas the cash may come much later. But it is still a revenue item that needs to be identified in the profit and loss statement. For example, a sport consulting business may have completed a strategic planning exercise for a large national sport association and invoiced it for $50,000. If, at the end of the accounting period, the invoice has not been paid, it will still be included in the profit and loss statement as income. The adjustment or offset in the accounts will be an equivalent (i.e. $50,000) increase (or debit) in the accounts receivable asset account. If the invoice had been immediately paid, the adjustment would have been made as an increase (or debit) of $50,000 to the cash in bank asset account.

Revenue, or income as it is frequently called, is typically divided into operating and non-operating items. Operating items include all those revenues like member income and merchandise sales that provide the funds to support the day-to-day running of the club or association. Non-operating items include funds that are irregular, or even out of the ordinary. An asset sale, a special government grant or a large donation are examples of non-operating income. As noted in the early part of this chapter, sport organization revenues have expanded dramatically over recent years, but for the non-professional clubs the main sources are member fees, gate receipts, government grants, fundraising activities, and sponsors.

Expenses should also be treated cautiously. The profit and loss statement should include all incurred expenses rather than just paid expenses. Buying something on credit or by cash is an expense. On the other hand, paying for something that will not be used until next year, for example, should not be listed as an expense or the period under consideration. It is an asset (i.e. a prepaid expense). For example, rental or insurance paid in advance involves a movement of cash out of the club or association, but does not constitute an expense incurred for the current period.

Depreciation

Depreciation is another expense issue that has to be dealt with. And, to repeat, depreciation is an estimate of the wear and tear of working assets. In an office setting, computers are quickly depreciated for two reasons. First, they are heavily used, and second, they quickly become out of date and obsolete. Depreciation is therefore recognized as an expense and should be included in a profit and loss statement. Depreciation can be calculated in a number of ways, the most simple being the straight-line method. If, for example, a motor vehicle is purchased for $30,000 has an estimated life of five years and no residual value, then the depreciation expense for the following five years will be $6,000 per annum. Some sporting club finance mangers make the mistake of listing the full cost of the motor vehicle in year 1 as an expense, but this is clearly misleading. The correct way to treat this transaction is to list it as an asset and then depreciate (i.e. amortize) it over its estimated lifetime. Interest paid and interest earned also appear on profit and loss statements. Interest paid will be classified as an expense, whereas interest received will be classified as revenue.

Operating versus net profits

When analyzing profit and loss statements it is also important to distinguish between operating profit (or surplus) and net profit (or surplus). The differences between these two terms comprise abnormal revenue and expenses, and extraordinary revenue and expenses. A transaction will be classified as abnormal if it is a regular occurrence, but in a specific case is significantly higher than normal. In the case of a sporting club an abnormal item might be an accelerated depreciation of office equipment, or a supplementary government grant. A transaction will be classified as extraordinary if it is a significant transaction and

TABLE 10.3 Profit and loss statement template

Item	Amount ($)	Total ($)
Operating income		
Member fees	50,000	
Events	10,000	
Grants	30,000	
Total operating income		90,000
Operating expenses		
Administration	50,000	
Events	20,000	
Insurance	10,000	
Total operating expenses		80,000
Operating profit		10,000
Non-operating income		
Special government grant	10,000	
Non-operating expenses		
Depreciation	20,000	
Net profit		0

does not regularly occur. A sporting club example includes fines for breaching salary cap regulations (this happens frequently in the Australian Football League and the National Rugby League) or the sale of an asset (this occurs in the English Premier League where players can be traded under certain conditions).

Operating profit does not include the abnormal and extraordinary items, and is confined to those transactions that are directly related to day-to-day activities that regularly recur over the standard accounting cycle. So, operating profit is the difference between operating income and operating expenses. Net profit is something else again, and will take into account all abnormal and extraordinary items. If the sport club happens to be part of profit making entity, then it may be required to pay tax on its profits. This item will be subtracted from operating profit to get to a net profit figure.

Depreciation is also frequently listed as a non-operating item and can also make a significant difference to the level of profit. An operating profit can be transformed into a net loss by the inclusion of depreciation as a non-operating expense. Sometimes claims are made that depreciation can distort the real profit of a sport organization, but in fact the opposite is the case. Depreciation is a legitimate expense since it takes into account that amount of assets used up to generate revenue. In the context of this discussion, a typical profit and loss or income statement is illustrated in Table 10.3.

In practice 10.2 Australian National Football/Soccer League

A re-vamped Australian National Football/Soccer League, otherwise known as the A-league, was established in 2005 under the auspices of the national governing body, Football Federation Australia (FFA). It was built on the foundation of a national league fraught with financial mismanagement and deep ethnic rivalries. The aim of the A-league was to deliver a high-level professional competition that represented all the major urban areas of the nation, while discarding all ethnic influences on club identities. With this principle in mind, the following eight teams were founded: Adelaide United, Central Coast Mariners, Melbourne Victory, Newcastle Jets, New Zealand Knights, Perth Glory, Queensland Roar, and Sydney FC. Each club was given a five-year exclusivity deal in its own market as part of the league's 'one-city, one-team' policy. This was intended to allow clubs to develop an identity in their respective region without the impediment of local competition. However, despite this protection, some clubs floundered, and over the following 10-year period, Wellington Phoenix replaced New Zealand Knights, Gold Coast United and North Queensland Fury both joined the league and departed from it, Melbourne Hearts (which became Melbourne City) joined up, as did the Western Sydney Wanderers. All of these clubs were privately owned, which suggested that they were, in the long haul, keen to deliver a small profit at least, for the owners.

At one level, the A-League was very successful. Crowds increased, the league secured a lot of media attention – most of it positive – and the standard of play increased exponentially. Even Red Bull, the international energy drink business, was thinking of investing in a team. But the league was still unable to collectively balance its books, so to speak. Some clubs folded, and others – and in particular, Central Coast Mariners (situated about 50 kilometres north of Sydney) – were regularly running operating losses. In one instance the Mariners did not have enough ready cash to pay their players. It was estimated that, overall, the clubs' private owners lost more than $200 million combined – an astronomical amount. And all of the club losses occurred despite the support of the giant media conglomerate, News Corp. News Corp, which owns the monopoly pay-TV business Fox Sports, recently signed a broadcast rights agreement with FFA that delivered the game $58 million a year for six years.

So, how can a sports league like the A-league perform poorly from a financial perspective when it appears to be so popular and so well organized? It can only be explained by the failure of clubs to properly manage their spending and not have it exceed their revenue earning capability. The problems of the A-league were the result of not adhering to a basic financial management principle: do not spend beyond your income.

CASH FLOW

We can now move on to the cash flow statement. It should be apparent that profit and loss statements do not give a clear picture of the movement of cash in and out of a sporting club or association. Cash flow statements aim to fill this gap by listing all movements of cash under three main headings. These headings are operating activities, investing activities, and financing activities. The aim here is to get a picture of the net inflow and outflow of cash and the extent to which a club or association is able to meet its cash payment obligations. This is an important issue, because without sufficient cash to pay bills when they fall due, there is the lingering possibility that creditors will take legal action to ensure payment. This may result in insolvency and bankruptcy.

The transactions that are included in the operating activity section include all those day-to day activities that are required to keep the organization running. They include wages and salaries (cash out) and payment for supplies (cash out), on the one hand, and membership income (cash in) and government grants (cash in), on the other. Good financial management will aim to ensure that the cash coming from operating activities will exceed the cash going out, although a short-term net cash outflow may not be all that serious.

Investing activity transactions include all those things that involve the purchase and sale of assets. The sale of assets will be associated with cash inflow, whereas the purchase of assets will produce an outflow of cash. The purchase and sale of office equipment and property of various sorts will fall under the investing heading, and so too will the purchase and sale of stocks, shares, and debentures. Although the sale of assets can generate a quick supply of cash, it will also deplete the organization of income earning resources, so a balance needs to be struck to ensure that crucial assets are not depleted. On the other hand, the purchase of assets immediately absorbs cash, and it is therefore important to monitor the amount of cash being used for this purpose.

Financing activities involve all those things that involve the procurement of equity and borrowing of funds, on one hand, and the withdrawal of funds and repayment of borrowings, on the other. An increase in cash holding can come from loans, bonds, mortgages, debentures, and other borrowings, whereas a fall in cash holding will come from the repayment of loans and the redemption of debentures.

A cash flow statement provides a clear and concise picture of how cash is used internally and where it goes externally. It also signals the level of liquidity and the ease with which cash payments are supported by cash reserves. A chronic net cash outflow on operating activities is cause for concern, because it is likely to lead to asset sales or borrowings being used to finance the cash deficit. And, as was noted previously, this can lead to a fall in club or association net worth, and threaten its long-term viability.

BUDGETING SYSTEMS

Budgeting is a crucial part of the financial management process (Hoggett, Edwards and Medlin, 2006; Wicker, Breuer and Pawlowski 2010). It is one thing to construct some simple accounts and diagnose the financial health of sport clubs, associations, and leagues. It is another thing to make sure resources are available for allocation to the various parts of their operations. No matter how wealthy a sport organization is, its resource base will always be limited, and decisions have to be made as not only where the resources are allocated (facility maintenance, player salaries, coaching staff, equipment upgrade), but also how much each operational activity will receive. Moreover budgets are finite, and the constraining factor will always be the amount of available funds.

Budgets are really financial plans that involve the allocation of funds to strategically important operations and activities. Budgets are essential for ensuring costs and expenses are contained and do not exceed the planned revenue. Good budgets act as a constraint on spending and also provide a clear picture of the anticipated sources of revenue. Budgets came in different shapes and forms, but they all share the desire to control spending patterns and make sure the spending is grounded in an appropriate level of funding and financial backing.

Benefits of budgeting

A good system of budgeting is crucially important for sport clubs and associations. As already noted, the sport world has become increasingly complex, and the need to manage money effectively is stronger than ever. In addition a well-planned budget is the basis for efficient management and ensuring viability over the long term. The benefits of budgeting are many. They can:

1   help anticipate the future and thereby assist the strategic planning process;
2   give a clear picture of resource needs and program priorities;
3   signal where there may be revenue shortfalls;
4   allow management to better manage and monitor spending;

5 communicate the club or association's financial plans to key stakeholders; and

6 enable precise measures of financial performance to be made.

Types of budgets

As already noted, budgets indicate the spending limits on different activities over particular periods. On one hand, there is the operational budget (which is sometimes called a recurrent budget), and on the other hand, there is the capital expenditure budget (which is sometimes called an investment budget). Whereas an operating budget refers to spending on the day-to-day operations of the sport club, association or league, a capital budget refers to spending on buildings, facilities and equipment, and other tangible assets.

Operating budgets

An operating budget is a statement of the anticipated levels of revenue for a period of time and how the revenue will be spent. The figures are estimates only, because there will always be unforeseen circumstances that will change the financial parameters in which a club or association conducts its affairs. As a result, the financial projections that underpinned the budget figures may not be realized due to changing economic and social conditions. For example, a sponsor may want to renegotiate its agreement, membership income may fall because of poor on-field performance, and coaching and support staff costs may blow out because of an increased demand for skilled specialists.

An operating budget aims to accurately estimate the likely level of revenue that a club or association will have to play with and the anticipated expenses associated with the earning of that income. For every sport clubs and association, it is crucial to ensure that revenue and expenses will balance, and at best, work toward the generation of a healthy surplus. The following example in Table 10.4 illustrates what an operating budget will look like and what items might be included.

The budget in Table 10.4 immediately reveals a number of important things. First it identifies the main items of revenue and spending. Clearly, in this fictitious case, the Sleepy Meadows Table Tennis Club (SMTTC) is heavily dependent on the local sponsor which just so happens to be the main hotel in town. It also shows that the day-to-day administration expenses are significant, although it would be good to have a breakdown of this item, because it might reveal specific activities like marketing or office rental that need to be monitored. Second it also show when the revenue is earned and the expenses are being incurred. Although this is a not a cash budget, it does indicate possible times of cash flow problems. However, this is unlikely to be problem here because most of the revenue is expected to arrive early in the year. The budget consequently allows the SMTTC to monitor the balance between expense commitments and revenue collections for different parts of the financial planning period.

Operating budgets can be organized in different ways as well. For example an operating budget may be structured as a line-item budget which is illustrated in Table 10.4. This involves breaking down spending and income into specific categories like administration,

TABLE 10.4 Sleepy Meadows Table Tennis Club: operating budget

	March quarter ($)	June quarter ($)	September quarter ($)	December quarter ($)	Year total ($)
Revenue					
Donations	500			1,000	1,500
Sponsor	6,000				6,000
Member fees	1,400	200	200	200	2,000
Gaming	1,400	1,300	1,100	700	4,500
Total	9,300	1,500	1,300	1,900	14,000
Expenses					
General admin-istration services	2,000	2,000	2,000	2,000	8,000
Coaching					0
Event adminis-tration		1,000	1,000		2,000
Travel		500	500	500	1,500
Table Tennis supplies	2,000				2,000
Total	4,000	3,500	3,500	2,500	13,500

travel, marketing, and entertainment, and applying overall spending limits to each item. All of the different activities or programs in the organization will work to these limits. The SMTTC budget uses the line-item method in setting its forecast figures. At the same time, operating budgets can be re-jigged as program budgets or performance budgets.

RE-SHAPING BUDGETS

A budget can also be organized as a program budget. This involves allocating a designated amount of funds to each activity or program. Each program area is then allowed to spend on what they want, up to, but not beyond, the designated limit. For example the SMTTC may allocate funds to each of its junior, regional, and veterans' league programs along the following lines of Table 10.5.

Each program manager can then decide how best to distribute the funds to each of its program activities. Program budgets can be converted into performance budgets without too much difficulty. The strength of a performance budget is that it links the budget to the

TABLE 10.5 Sleepy Meadows Table Tennis Club: program budget

	Junior league program ($)	Regional league program ($)	Veterans league program ($)
Budget	4,000	8,000	2,000

TABLE 10.6 Sleepy Meadows Table Tennis Club: performance budget

Junior league program	Regional league program	Veterans league program
Goal: to provide activities that attract young children to the club	*Goal:* to provide activities that attract quality players through access to elite competition	*Goal:* to provide activities that balance social and competition table tennis
Anticipated outcome: increase in registered juniors	*Anticipated outcome:* all teams finish in top half of league table	*Anticipated outcome:* viable competition
Budget ($)	**Budget ($)**	**Budget ($)**
4,000	8,000	2,000

club or association's strategic plan. It forces the program manager to not only work within the budget parameters, but also ensure that the funds are directed to the achievement of relevant outcomes. In the case of the SMTTC a performance budget could take the following shape as indicated in Table 10.6.

In practice 10.3 Budgeting for mega sport events: London 2012 Olympic Games, the 2010 Delhi Commonwealth Games, and the 2016 Rio de Janeiro Olympic Games

In 2005 London won the right to host the 2012 Olympic Games. The bid was impressive, and there is little doubt that the Games, as both a spectacle and as a major sporting event, were a raging success. By all accounts the massive urban renewal program that accompanied the London Games project provided for significant commercial and social benefits. However, it was never clear as to whether it was a financial success. Like all bids before it, the London Bid Committee created a budget that quickly escalated in size.

In the initial draft bid document of 2003, the costs of staging the London Games were estimated to be just under 2 billion pounds, which by previous Games' standards was significant, and certainly in excess of the Sydney Games. In 2006 the budget was re-set at around 3.5 billion pounds. However in 2007, the minister for the Olympics, Tessa Jowell, announced an up-dated budget of 9.3 billion pounds. This was a massive increase, and it raised the questions of (1) just what capital and operating activities the budget would cover, (2) what specific costs had been identified or not identified, and (3) why they had escalated so much in such a short space of time. Although the then-mayor of London, Ken Livingstone, optimistically confirmed that the Games Organising Committee would aim to make a profit, there was growing concern that the Games budget was spiralling out of control.

As it turned out the London Games came in just over the adjusted budget of 9.3 billion pounds, but it was still a massively expensive event to organize, facilitate, and run. To make the London Games happen, around 1 billion pounds was spent on security, be it civilian or military. Just under 2 billion pounds was spent on preparing the Olympic Park site, and another 1 billion was spent on creating a user-friendly park once the Games had been completed and the Games experience was a distant memory. And this doesn't even include the facility construction costs or the operating costs.

The escalating costs of running the Olympic Games were starkly revealed soon after Tokyo was awarded the right to host the 2020 Games. Hakubun Shimomura, the minister for Education, Sports and Finance, proudly announced that the showpiece of the Games would be an 80,000-seat stadium that would double as a major public artwork. But when it was stated that the stadium would cost 130 billion yen, or almost 1.3 billion USD, enormous criticism erupted, with local architects claiming the project was indefensible, even if the stadium became an international design masterpiece. Even when the Olympics are involved, there are financial limits to be observed.

The 24th Commonwealth Games, succinctly known as CWG 2010, were held in Delhi, India, in October 2010. It was the first time that the Commonwealth Games were held in India and the second time it was held in Asia, with Kuala Lumpur, Malaysia's capital city, having staged the festival in 1998. Just over 6,000 athletes from 71 nations competed in 21 sports and 272 events. It was big, and in fact was the largest international multi-sport event ever to be staged in India, eclipsing the Asian Games of 1951 and 1982.

Although the opening and closing ceremonies were successfully delivered at the Jawaharlal Nehru Stadium, it was generally agreed that there were many organizational teething-troubles during the early stages of the Games. Crowds were also very thin during the first week of the Games. Despite these problems the Games were enjoyed by not only most of the people who attended, but also by the athletes themselves. The television broadcasts were professionally produced, and the events themselves were often quite memorable, with many outstanding individual results.

As is always the case with these types of events, the initial total budget estimates by the Indian Olympic Association in 2003 for hosting the Games were highly optimistic at around $360 million USD. This was quite a conservative figure for such a big event – and for some critics, frighteningly low – but it was considered reasonable in view of

India's world-renowned capacity to deliver solid results with meagre resources. However, by 2006, the event budget had escalated and projections at the time reached $1.4 USD billion, nearly a four-fold increase. A report of the Standing Committee on Human Resource Development provided a revised budget breakdown, and the following figures were published:

- the conduct/operation of the games would now cost $200 USD million,
- the Games Village would now cost $220 USD million,
- venue infrastructure, but without furnishing, was now set at $380 USD million,
- civil infrastructure came in at $294 USD million, and
- the Indian contingent's training program would cost $70 USD million.

In early 2010 another review found that the Games budget was out of control and had increased exponentially. Many explanations were given for the blow-out and included things like (1) there was a bout of steep inflation, (2) all projects have been delayed, (3) waste and inefficiencies were the rule rather than the exception, and (4) some projects had been mismanaged. It was also hinted that some additional 'shadowy' practices – that is, bribery – had occurred, but they were largely anecdotal. In a climate of high anxiety the following points were noted:

- The Commonwealth Games Village, which had an initial 2003 budget estimate of $100 USD million, was now about $230 USD million. In addition capital losses had occurred because many apartments remained unsold, and the Indian government was forced to buy them off contractors.
- The budget for 11 stadia was $280 USD million in 2003, but in the space of seven years had risen to $1.2 USD billion. Construction was also way behind deadline, which was another concern that had to be monitored.
- Work on road flyovers were altered mid-way, and new unplanned additions had to be made. The budget for this item came in at $380 USD million.
- Street-scaping was another unplanned expenditure with a budget of $250 USD million.
- Security, too – and not surprisingly – had been allocated additional expenditure with a revised budget of $80 USD million.
- In the light of frequent delays, event planning also suffered. What was estimated to cost $240 USD million in 2003 now had a budget estimate figure of $550 USD million.

As the Games approached, the official total budget – which took into account both capital and operating items – accelerated to an estimated US$2.6 USD billion, a figure which had crucially excluded non-sports–related infrastructure development. The American publication *Business Today* reckoned this was hopelessly conservative and claimed that the Games actually cost $13.3 USD billion when all the related urban renewal projects had been included. Whatever the precise number was, it was agreed that the 2010 Delhi Commonwealth Games were probably the most expensive ever and reached a figure that was never envisaged. So why did things go so horribly wrong?

In the first place, the organization of CWG 2010 was beset by delays. In January 2010, the Indian Olympic Association Vice-Chairman Raja Randhir Singh expressed concern that Delhi was not up to speed in forming and organizing its Games Committee. And following a 2009 Indian government report showing two-thirds of venues were behind schedule, the Commonwealth Games Federation president Mike Fennell stated that the slow progress constituted a serious risk to the whole event. Singh also called for a revamp of the Games Organising Committees. A. K. Walia, the Indian Finance Minister, also noted that that so many things had come at the last moment and cited the "street-scaping project as a case in point'. He went on to say that although the Indian government was looking at international sporting events as a chance to increase their urban infrastructure, it had actually resulted in several projects being approved which had no direct relation to the Games, but which had in fact been included in the budget allocation. In addition, all of this was framed by allegations of long delays and chronic corruption amongst many of the event planners and organizers. It was a very bad 'gig' indeed!

But even more to the point, why is there a budget blow-out at nearly every modern-day mega sports festival? The 2016 Rio de Janeiro Olympic Games suffered from the same financial disease. When all the public works programs were added to the list, the total spent was just over USD 13 billion, a massive investment, and well above the budgeted figure. The original budget when Brazil won the hosting rights to the Games in 2009 was USD 9 billion. And to make matters worse, the Rio 2016 Organising Committee ended up owing USD 27 million in outstanding payments to suppliers and third parties. The Games legacy was also well below expectations, when, in 2017, it was discovered that the flagship Maracana Stadium has been empty since the Paralympics closing ceremony, the tennis centre and a velodrome were lying dormant, and the Deodoro Olympic Park precinct, home to the second-largest group of venues – including equestrian, rugby, and field hockey – had also closed their doors pending a possible sale to private investors. Apart from the event itself, the massive financial investment in the games delivered a very small tangible return.

It has to be conceded that running mega-sport events is a complex logistic exercise, but there is also evidence of serious financial mismanagement. So are the people drawing up the budget estimates incompetent, or are they so optimistic that they cannot face the reality of a high cost operation? Or, alternatively, do they decide that escalating costs is part of the essential nature or, indeed, the embedded character of the mega-sport-event 'beast' and that it just cannot be controlled, whatever is done?

SUMMARY

The discussion of sport finances demonstrates that sound financial management is essential for the ongoing viability of sport organizations. The importance of having a proper system of financial planning, record keeping, monitoring, and evaluation becomes increasingly crucial as sport becomes more commercialized and corporatized. A basic starting point is to identify the different ways in which funds and can be raised to underwrite the operation of a sport club, association, event, or league. It is also essential that sport managers be able to design detailed budgets that provide transparent information that makes it clear as to not only what an activity, program, or event will cost to mount and operate, but also where the money will be coming from. It is equally important for sport managers to be able to understand financial statements; use them to diagnose the financial health of a club association, event, or league; and subsequently manage costs and revenues to ensure a regular surplus or profit. It is particularly important to be able to distinguish between the different ways of measuring surpluses and profits, and in particular, the difference between operating and net profit.

REVIEW QUESTIONS

1 Identify the different commercial stages sport has gone through in the last 50 years and the implications it has for sport's financial operations.

2 Explain the essential features of corporate sport and what makes it increasingly challenging to manage from a structural and financial perspective.

3 Why are budgets so fundamental to the effective management of sport clubs, associations, events, and leagues?

4 Distinguish between a capital budget and an operating budget.

5 Balance sheets are an important tool for monitoring and measuring the financial health of a sport organization. What comprises a balance sheet, and what does it measure?

6 Identify the main asset categories of a professional sport club, and explain under what circumstances players can be treated as assets.

7 Identify the main liability categories of a professional sport club, and explain under what circumstances long-term borrowings can be seen as either a drain on resources or a crucial means of generating revenue and profits.

8 Surpluses and profits are important to the long-term development of sport organizations clubs because they indicate that not only were all costs covered for the period under consideration, but that there are funds available for re-investment in the club or association's future activities and programs. What is required for a profits and surpluses to be generated, and under what circumstances an operating profit can be end up leading to a net loss?

9 What is the easiest way of distinguishing a wealthy sport organization from a poor sport organization?

10 What must a sport organization do if it aims to increase its wealth and financial health over the long term?

DISCUSSION QUESTIONS

1   Why is sound financial management essential for the operational sustainability of sport?

2   What does the income and expenditure statement illustrate about a sport organization's financial operations?

3   What does a balance sheet reveal about a sport organization's financial operations?

4   What does a cash flow statement illustrate about a sport organization's financial operations?

5   What factors (both externally and internally) can lead financial mismanagement in sport organizations?

FURTHER READING

The four-phase model of sport's economic and financial development was first developed by Bob Stewart in Stewart, B (Ed.) (2007) *The Games are Not the Same: The Political Economy of Football In Australia*, Melbourne University Press, Carlton, pp. 3–22.

The application of this 4-phase model to sport finance is illustrated in Stewart, B. (2015) *Sport Funding and Finance second edition*. London: Routledge.

For an extensive discussion of the finances of North American professional sport leagues see Howard, D. and Crompton, J. (2004). *Financing Sport*. 2nd ed. Fitness Information Technology. This book provides a chapter-by-chapter breakdown of revenue sources, with special attention to ticket sales and broadcasting rights' fees. See also Foster, G., Greyser, P. and Walsh, B. (2006). *The Business of Sports: Texts and Cases on Strategy and Management*. Thomson.

One of the most detailed analyses of English Premier League finances is contained in Szymanski, S. and Kuypers, T. (2000). *Winners and Losers*. Penguin. See also Carter (2011) for a lot of interesting updates on the financial structure of big time commercialized sport.

For a simple introduction to the structure and function of balance sheets and profit and loss statements and cash flow statement see Hart, L. (2006). *Accounting Demystified: A Self Teaching Guide*. McGraw Hill. For a more detailed and technical review of financial statements and what they say, see Hoggett, J., Edwards, L. and Medlin, J. (2006). *Accounting*. 6th edn. Wiley. See also Atrill, P., McLaney, E., Harvey, D. and Jenner, M. (2006). *Accounting: An Introduction*. Pearson Education Australia. For a succinct discussion of financial statements of nonprofit organizations see Anthony, R. and Young, D. (2003). *Management Control in Non-profit Organizations*. 7th edn. McGraw-Hill.

For an extensive introduction to the budgeting process see Hoggett, J., Edwards, L. and Medlin, J. (2006). *Accounting*. 6th edn. Wiley. A detailed analysis of costing and budgeting processes is also contained in Anthony, R. and Young, D. (2003). *Management Control in Non-profit Organizations*. 7th edn. McGraw-Hill.

RELEVANT WEBSITES

For details of Manchester United FC financial position and the general financial operations of the English Premier League, see <www.footballeconomy.com/stats2/eng_manutd.htm>.

For more details on the financial operation of the International Cricket Council see < www.icc-cricket.com/about/111/publications/overview>.

Then click on "annual reports" to secure finance details.

To secure a detailed evaluation of the London Olympic Games budget see the National Audit Office (NAO) Report at < www.nao.org.uk/report/the-budget-for-the-london-2012-olympic-and-paralympic-games/>

For an alternative assessment of the London Olympic Games budget, with a breakdown of the costs of various venues, see www.thisislondon.co.uk/standard-mayor/article-23484734-details/Mayor+seeks+City+financial+expert+to+check+growing+cost+of+Olympics/article.do

The total spending on the Rio Olympics is listed in: www.bloomberg.com/news/articles/2017-06-14/the-olympics-cost-rio-at-least-13-1-billion-and-probably-more Additional detail on the Rio Olympics finances are discussed in: www.insidethegames.biz/articles/1051553/cost-of-rio-2016-olympics-rises-to-132-billion-35-billion-over-budget

An evaluation of the Rio 2016 legacy is contained in: www.independent.co.uk/sport/olympics/rio-olympic-venues-disrepair-2016-brazil-worst-recession-economy-ruin-a7572786.html

The financial problems facing Australia's national soccer competition, the A-league, are discussed in www.afr.com/business/sport/soccers-big-money-challenge-make-the-aleague-attractive-to-investors-20170301-guo7bs

CASE STUDY 10.1

Living beyond its means: financial mismanagement in an English football club

Although prudent financial management is a core underlying principle for the effective administration of sport enterprises, there are many instances where things go horribly wrong. A financial meltdown might not only lead to a loss of status and a fall in service quality, but also, in the most serious of cases, closure. Many factors contribute to financial mismanagement, but the common denominator is a lack of proper financial control and a lack of public disclosure. Take, for example, the recent traumas experiences by the Coventry City Football Club (CCFC).

CCFC is the club that represents the city of Coventry, which is located in the west Midlands region of England. Coventry began as a manufacturing center in the 18th century, focusing on clothing and textiles. It became a major bicycle producer in the late 19th century, and by the beginning of the 20th century the bicycle trade was booming, and Coventry had developed the largest bicycle industry in the world. It employed nearly 40,000 workers in more than 250 manufacturing locations. However by the 1930s motor vehicles took over as the main manufacturing industry, with Daimler, Rover, and the Rootes Group being the three dominant producers. Coventry suffered severe bombing during WW2 but recovered strongly. But it did not adjust well to the forces of globalization and free trade during the 1980s, which led to high unemployment. Over the last 25 years it undertook an urban regeneration program and now has a strong service sector. Its population is now just over 300,000.

Coventry City Football Cub (CCFC) also goes back a long way. The club was founded in 1883 by Willie Stanley, an employee of the Singers bicycle building company, which was one of the largest in the region. It was known as Singers FC until 1898, when the name was changed to Coventry City. A year later it relocated to its Highfield Road site, which became its home for the next 114 years. For the first 50 years of the 20th century its progress was solid but uneventful. Coventry was better known for is motor vehicle industry than its football team, but this all changed in 1961 with the arrival of Jimmy Hill as manager. This sparked a revolution at the club. A new sky blue uniform was unveiled, the nickname was changed to the Sky Blues, trains were scheduled for fans to travel to away games, and pre-match entertainment became commonplace. In 1963, after an impressive FA Cup run, CCFC lost in the quarter-finals to Manchester United, but in the following season CCFC were champions of Division 3, boasting a season average crowd of 26,000. The Highfield Road stadium was also rebuilt around this time, and the club was primed for more success.

In the 1966–67 season CCFC went unbeaten for 25 games, and the campaign reached an exhilarating finale when CCFC defeated its arch-rivals Wolverhampton Wanderers in front of a record home crowd of 51,000. CCFC thus clinched the Division 2 championship and secured a place in the First Division, which was the equivalent of today's Premier League. Coventry stayed in the top flight of English Football from 1967 to 2001 – which was 34 years – without being relegated. At the time of its 2001 relegation only Arsenal, Everton, and Liverpool could boast longer tenures in England's 'premier' competition.

CCFC's greatest achievement came in the 1987 FA Cup Final against Tottenham Hotspur, which it won. The euphoria was palpable, but thereafter things only got worse. There were moments of hope, but they were mainly false. Crowds of 30,000 were common, ground improvements were made, and a few star players were signed on. In 1999 CCFC pulled off a major coup by signing the talented Republic of Ireland international, Robbie Keane, for GBP 6 million – a club record fee. But, as it turned out, this was the beginning of a massive slide for CCFC. Keane's departure to Inter Milan, a powerful Italian team, left the club in disarray, and in 2001 it was re-relegated to the lower division. The club was also in dire financial straits, having accumulated a GBP 60 million debt, despite having got GBP 13 million for Keane's Inter Milan transfer. But the club was still prepared to pay GBP 5 million for Lee Hughes from West Bromwich Albion around the same time. Huge cost cutting was consequently required to prevent the club from going into administration, and this was subsequently achieved in part through the sale of many high-earning players. The debt was reduced, but it was still a horrific GBP 23 million in 2004. The club had been living beyond its means for a long time, and as it was later revealed, the club had been propped up by the reckless borrowing of funds.

A bright – if tiny – light shone on the Sky Blues in late 2003 when the City Council gave the green light for a new rejuvenation project that would house the club's new 32,000-seat stadium. It got a naming rights sponsor in the form of Ricoh, but the rental agreement proved to be another liability it just could not afford. It struggled to pay the GBP 1 million annual rent to Coventry City Council who co-owned the facility. By the end of the 2007 season it was clear that something was seriously wrong with the financial affairs of CCFC. Its turnover for the year was a serviceable GBP 7.7 million, but its wage bill was more than GBP 8 million. Its operations were completely unsustainable.

And, what is more, the crisis worsened in the off-season, when club was facing administration and potential liquidation. A London-based investment group, SISU, stepped in and took ownership of the club. With the club at this point losing over GBP 500,000 a month, Coventry supporters would have been forgiven for thinking that SISU would be the club's savior, but it proved to be the antithesis of this. It turned out that SISU was not an effective caretaker, and all it could do was sell off some of the club's key squad members for bargain basement fees. The pool of player talent dropped considerably, but it did little to improve the club's financial health. SISU was also reported to have injected GBP 40 million on the club since it took over in 2008, but it did nothing to stop the rush into ruin.

At the end of 2012 the off-the-field situation continued to be precarious. The club was forced to look for a temporary home to play their home games from 2013/14 following unsuccessful talks with the Ricoh Arena management. It culminated in an announcement that SISU – who still owned the club despite their failure to stop the hemorrhaging – would fund the construction of a new stadium which would hand the club access to all match-day revenue streams. This plan was a long way off, though, so it was decided to seek a ground share arrangement with the League Two side Northampton Town for three years while a new stadium was being built. The first of those fixtures saw the Sky Blues host Bristol City in their League One clash in August 2013.

So, by 2013 the club had been relegated to League One. It had a shoestring squad, it was riddled by crippling debt, it was a tenant in another club's stadium, and it had gone through 10 managers in the 11 years prior to 2013. Surely things could not get any worse. As it turned out, things did improve, relatively speaking. The club made an operating loss of GBP 8 million in 2015, which fell to GBP 2 million in 2016. However, the club still had GBP 44 million of debt to deal with.

From an outsider looking in, though, things would suggest that Coventry City FC, although clearly not up to EPL standard, should still be at least a top-level Championship side. This because it secured a 'state of the art' new stadium in 2005, it is a club with a very strong football tradition, and it is relatively well known across Europe. And most importantly it is the only major football club in a city of 300,000 people, which gives it a significant supporter base to work from. Things are in place for Coventry to be a success, and for a while they were. So what went wrong, and how did the club slide so quickly into a financial quicksand?

ADDITIONAL DATA

The following numbers, all in GBP, give a feel for the scale of the problem CCFC faced over the last few years. They do not provide a pretty picture, and it also puts successive administrations in a very poor light.

- Cash in bank fell from 592,000 to 103,000 in 2011.
- Current liabilities increased from 20 million in 2007 to 57 million in 2011.
- Current assets fell from 1.8 million in 2007 to 418,000 in 2011.
- Long-term liabilities fell from 13 million in 2007 zero in 2011.
- Total liabilities increased from 33 million in 2007 to 57 million in 2011.
- Total assets fell from 4 million in 2007 to 2 million in 2011.
- Total revenues increased from 8 million in 2007 to 10 million in 20011.
- For every year between 2007 and 2011 every dollar of revenue was swallowed up by wage and salary demands.
- Operating losses of 6 to 8 million were incurred for each year between 2007 and 2011.

CASE STUDY QUESTIONS

1 What does this case illustrate about the challenges that football managers face in English football?
2 What does it say about the financial management acumen of the CCFC management team?
3 What made CCFC continually overspend?
4 How successful was CCFC in trading players in improving its financial position?
5 How would you describe the over-riding driver of CCFC operations: profit maximization or performance maximization?
6 Does it make sense for a sports club like CCFC desire to be successful at any price?
7 Was there any evidence that CCFC had a financial safety net to lower the risk in the case of financial failure?
8 What would you have done had you been the CRO of CCFC?
9 Why was CCFC management so secretive when answering questions about its financial affairs?
10 If you were CEO of CCFC, what would you have done to be more honest and forthcoming when talking about the club's financial affairs?

FURTHER READING

www.birminghampost.co.uk/news/local-news/coventry-city-fc-finances-of-3920178
www.theguardian.com/football/blog/2016/oct/12/coventry-city-decline-despair-league-one
www.coventrytelegraph.net/news/coventry-news/coventry-city-make-600000-profit-12679244
www.theguardian.com/football/blog/2016/dec/23/coventry-city-broken-apart-sisu-otium

CASE STUDY 2

The quiet achiever: money management at the International Cricket Council

The international governing bodies for sport, otherwise known as international sporting organizations (ISOs), are responsible for ensuring the global development of their respective sporting codes. Specific roles include managing and monitoring the rules of the game, organizing competitions, dealing with disputes, raising and distributing finance, promoting their sport, enhancing coaching capabilities, and offering technical advice to national governing bodies, clubs. ISOs also depend for their financial viability not only on the contributions from the national governing bodies, but also the on the revenues they can secure from major sport events. One of the most highly credentialed and well-resourced ISOs is the International Cricket Council (ICC).

The ICC governs the organization of cricket around the world. It has 96 member countries, although the game is dominated by seven nations: Australia, England, India, New Zealand, Pakistan, Sri Lanka, and South Africa. The ICC conducts three international competitions: the World Cup, the Champions Trophy, and the Twenty20 international tournament. The Twenty20 Championship was conducted in 2016 and the World Cup was conducted in 2015. As Table 10.7 indicates, the ICC is heavily dependent on its international tournaments to build its profit and assets. At the same time, the ICC is financially very strong and has enough surplus to support the development of cricket around the world.

Over the last few years it has continued to grow from a very healthy base. For example, in 2011, revenue from ICC events, which included the World Cup, was USD 321 million. With the event running, costs came in at 122 million. This delivered an operational profit for the year of 199 million. After all of its additional

TABLE 10.7 Financial indicators for International Cricket Council

	2016 (USD million)	2015 (USD million)
Operating income	299	451
Event income	290	440
Event costs	56	139
Member subscriptions	10	11
Operating surplus	92	263
Dividend to members*	NA	NA
Total assets	428	238
Cash assets	45	89
Total liabilities	279	180
Current liabilities	179	81

*Data not provided

activities had been accounted for, its net surplus for the year was just under 204 million. It had also accumulated 160 million in assets and incurred liabilities of 126 million, 77 million of which were monies owed to its member nations. By any measure, this was a very sound result. And, things got even better over next few years. In 2015 the World Cup generated 440 million, a substantial increase over 2011. In 2016, the Twenty20 series generated 290 in revenue, another impressive outcome.

The ICC is, whatever way you look at, in a very healthy financial position. Total assets jumped by 190 million in a single year, although cash holdings fell by 44 million. However, the ICC's a strong financial position did not come about through chance. There was a confluence of factors that enabled the ICC to massively increase its annual revenue, while also containing its operating expenses and not increasing its long-term debt, especially loans and borrowings.

The ICCs financial successes have also benefited its member nations, and they will continue to do so. In 2017 the ICCs member distribution formula was adjusted, and based on the latest forecasts for revenues and costs across an eight-year cycle, the Indian Cricket board would receive USD 293 million, the England and Wales Cricket Board would be the second-best earners with USD 143 million, Cricket Australia and the remaining six full members would get USD 132 million, and Zimbabwe would receive USD 94 million. As a result everyone benefits from having profitable international events. The financial future of cricket at the international level looks very bright indeed.

CASE STUDY QUESTIONS

1 What is the role of the ICC?

2 What is the dominant revenue generator for the ICC?

3 What are the other main sources of revenue?

4 What are the strengths and weaknesses of relying so much on a single income source for nearly 90% of annual revenue?

5 What soaks up most of the ICC's revenues?

6 It is sometimes said that you need to spend money to make money. How does this motto apply to the IOC's operations?

7 Where do most of the ICC profits go?

8 Which ICC members secure most of the ICC's profits, and, in your mind, is distribution fair and reasonable?

9 If you were the CEO of the ICC, how would you distribute profits to ensure the growth and sustainability of the game?

10 How wealthy is the IOC, and what figures did you use to calculate it?

11 How transparent is the ICC when it comes to giving the public access to its financial operations?

12 Is there space for a test match style world cup in the future, and would it be financially viable?

ADDITIONAL READING

For details on the financial operations of the ICC, go to. . .

www.icc-cricket.com/about/the-icc/publications/annual-report

www.news.com.au/sport/cricket/australia-india-and-england-hit-by-new-icc-move/
news-story/5af2c2cd584ff1bd280e694b7080d3e1

A discussion of a proposal to introduce a 9-team test-match world cup is contained in:

www.theguardian.com/sport/2017/feb/03/icc-agree-plan-nine-team-test-championship

CHAPTER 11

Sport marketing

OVERVIEW

The principles and tools of sport marketing are essential knowledge for sport managers to be able to position their sport club, player, code, or event in the highly competitive sport market. This chapter examines the marketing of sporting organizations, sport leagues and codes, players and athletes, sporting equipment and merchandise, and sporting events. The purpose of this chapter is to overview the key concepts of sport marketing, with special emphasis on the process of sport marketing as outlined in the Sport Marketing Framework provided.

After completing this chapter, the reader should be able to:

- Explain the key concepts of sport marketing;

- Describe the process of sport marketing using the steps of the Sport Marketing Framework;
- Define the role of strategy, positioning, and branding in sport marketing; and
- Understand how to deploy the sport marketing mix.

UNDERSTANDING SPORT MARKETING

Marketing generally refers to the process of planning and implementing activities that are designed to meet the needs or wants of customers with particular attention on the development of a product, its pricing, promotion, and distribution. Marketing seeks to create an exchange, where a customer or consumer relinquishes money for a product or service that they believe is of equal or greater value. Sport marketing is focused on satisfying the needs of sport consumers, or those people who use sport-related goods or services through playing sport, watching or listening to sport, buying merchandise, collecting memorabilia, or using sporting goods. There are two dimensions to sport marketing: the marketing *of* sports and marketing *through* sports. The first dimension is the marketing *of* sport products and services directly to consumers such as sporting equipment, professional competitions, sport events and facilities, and recreational clubs. The second dimension involves the marketing of other, non-sport products and services *through* sport. Some examples include a professional athlete endorsing a food or fashion brand, a corporation sponsoring a sport event, or even a drinks manufacturer arranging to have exclusive rights to provide their products at a sport event.

In order for a sport organization to be successful, it must mean something to sport consumers. In practice, this demands that a consumer is aware of the sport organization, its brand, and the products or services it offers, and has responded to them in a positive way. The process of cultivating such a response is known as branding, and when a sport brand has carved out a firm place in the market and in consumers' minds, then it is said that it is positioned. The consequence of successful branding and the acquisition of strong market positioning is an ongoing relationship between a sport brand and its users.

Sport marketing is therefore best understood as the process of planning how a sport brand is positioned and how the delivery of its products or services are to be implemented in order to establish a relationship between a sport brand and its consumers. This may be achieved by the marketing *of* a sport brand or marketing *through* a sport brand.

THE SPORT MARKETING FRAMEWORK

The Sport Marketing Framework puts the sport marketing definition into practice by providing an approach to meeting sport consumers' needs. The Framework outlines a step-by-step process for planning and implementing the key principles of sport marketing. The Sport Marketing Framework involves four stages: 1) Identify sport marketing opportunities; 2) Develop a sport marketing strategy; 3) Plan the marketing mix; and 4) Implement and control the strategy.

Stage one of the Sport Marketing Framework, Identify sport marketing opportunities, involves analysing the conditions of the external marketplace, considering the conditions within the sport industry specifically, and examining the activities of competitors. This stage also involves studying the internal capabilities of a sport organization by identifying its goals and limitations. Finally, in order to identify marketing opportunities, it is necessary

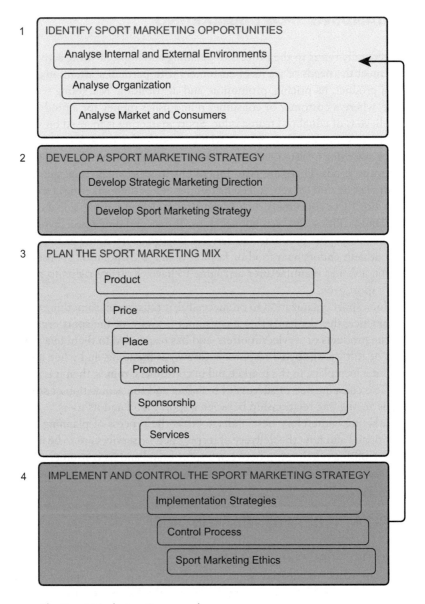

FIGURE 11.1 The Sport Marketing Framework

to collect information about market circumstances with a particular emphasis on existing customers and other potential consumers. After all of this information has been collected and analysed, stage two of the Framework, Develop a sport marketing strategy, may be undertaken. Stage two involves determining the direction of the sport marketing program, taking into account what was learned during stage one. It is important at this stage to document the strategy with both objectives and performance measures in order to keep it on track, and ultimately to evaluate whether the strategy was successful. Once the direction is set, the specific tactics of the strategy can be specified revolving around how to distinguish or 'differentiate' the sport organization's brand and products in the market, deciding on to whom the strategy is targeted towards to (segmentation), and what marketing mix (the product offering, pricing strategies, promotional strategies, and distribution systems) will be employed. Stage three of the Framework involves the precise determination of the sport marketing mix and how they will combine to achieve the strategy set out. Finally, stage four, Implement and control the strategy, involves measuring outcomes and taking remedial action so that the plan stays on target. Figure 11.1 provides an illustration of the Sport Marketing Framework.

STAGE 1: IDENTIFY SPORT MARKETING OPPORTUNITIES

This step shows that it is important to collect information and conduct research before introducing sport marketing activities. It is essential to know what opportunities exist in the marketplace, what competitors are doing, what can be delivered, and what consumers actually want. Identifying sport marketing opportunities involves three elements: 1) analysing the internal and external environment, 2) analysing the organization, and 3) analysing the market and consumers.

Analyse the internal and external environment

The first element in identifying sport marketing opportunities involves assessing the internal and external environments of the sport organization. The internal environment refers to the conditions in which a sport organization undertaking the marketing process is placed. The external environment refers to the market in which the sport organization is operating, including the broad national/global environment, the sport industry, and the sport organization's competitors. There are five main tools for conducting an internal and external analysis: 1) SWOT analysis, 2) competitor analysis, 3) five forces competitor analysis, 4) organizational analysis, and 5) market and consumer research. Given that these aspects of internal and external analysis overlap with those conducted for any strategic planning and are covered in more detail in Chapter 5, they will only be mentioned briefly here.

The term SWOT is an acronym for the words strengths, weaknesses, opportunities, threats. The SWOT analysis can be divided into two parts. The first part represents an internal analysis of an organization, which can be summarized by its strengths and weaknesses. Strengths are those things an organization does well, and weaknesses are the things an organization finds difficult to do well. The second part of the SWOT technique is concerned with external factors, or opportunities and threats. Opportunities could include environmental situations used to the organizations' advantage. The SWOT analysis influences what a sport organization is capable of achieving in their marketing plan and highlights potential areas in which there might be an opportunity.

A competitor analysis focuses on the external environment by revealing opportunities or threats associated with other organizations in the same marketplace. A competitor analysis should examine several kinds of competitors: *direct* competitors who produce a similar product or service; *secondary* competitors who sell *substitute* products that meet similar customer needs but in a different way; and *indirect* competitors who sell different products and services altogether that might satisfy consumers' needs. A competitor analysis should consider a wide range of variables, including their strategies, strengths, vulnerabilities, and resources, as well as their next likely actions.

In addition to conducting a competitor analysis, it is possible to conduct a five forces analysis that focuses on five forces driving competition in the sport industry. It is used to help work out whether the industry is an attractive one to conduct business in and whether there is scope for existing or new products to be developed. The five forces are described in detail in Chapter 5.

Analyse the organization

The second component of stage one involves understanding the purpose, aims, and goals of the sport organization developing the plan, as well as understanding the needs of its stakeholders. The first three of these elements can be determined by locating (or if necessary developing) the mission statement, vision statement, and objectives of the sport organization. More about these can be found in Chapter 5.

Stakeholders are all the people and groups that have an interest in a sport organization, including, for example, its employees, players, members, the league, association or governing body, government, community, facility-owners, sponsors, broadcasters, and fans. A marketing strategy can be strongly influenced by the beliefs, values, and expectations of the most powerful stakeholders. As a result, careful analysis of the goals and objectives of each stakeholder must be completed before a strategic direction can be set.

Conduct and examine market and consumer research

The final step in the first stage is to conduct and examine market research. Market research means gathering information about the market and the consumers it contains. It is the process of learning about the marketplace and what consumers want, listening to their desires and expectations, and determining how to satisfy them. It is also used to determine whether consumers have reacted to a marketing plan as expected.

In general, there are two broad types of market research: quantitative and qualitative. Quantitative research gathers statistical information that is superficial but diverse. The most common method of gathering quantitative information is to conduct a survey or questionnaire. Qualitative research gathers non-numerical information (such as words from an interview of a person). Qualitative information is in depth, and usually gathered from a narrow and relatively small sample of people. Common types of qualitative research in sport include focus groups, suggestion boxes, and complaint analysis. This information is pivotal in deciding what kinds of products and services should be offered to sport consumers.

STAGE 2: DEVELOP A SPORT MARKETING STRATEGY

The second stage of the Sport Marketing Framework involves two components: 1) develop strategic market direction; and 2) develop a sport marketing strategy. With the information-gathering stage completed, the direction of the sport marketing strategy can be determined and documented in the form of objectives and performance measures. These act as a guide through all the coming stages of the Sport Marketing Framework. Next, the actual sport marketing strategy can be decided in the form of a positioning approach that differentiates the sport organization's brand and product offerings from competitors and segments the market into target groups.

Develop strategic marketing direction

A marketing objective is a goal that can realistically be achieved as the result of the marketing strategy. It can be expressed as a sentence expressing what will occur as a result of marketing activities. There are basically four different types of marketing objectives that sport organizations might wish to pursue: higher levels of participation or involvement, on-field performance, promotion of messages about the sport or its benefits, and profit.

For each objective set it is important to add a performance measure. In this case, the term means a way of objectively estimating, calculating, or assessing whether the objective has been achieved. It usually involves finding a way to quantify or put a number to the objective.

Develop a sport marketing strategy

Assuming that sport marketing objectives and performance measures have been set, the second part of stage two can be undertaken by developing the actual sport marketing strategy. The process of developing a sport marketing strategy requires four steps. Step one and two are associated with market segmentation, step three is the choice of market positioning strategy, and step four involves determining the marketing mix.

Market segmentation is a term that describes the process of categorizing groups of consumers together, based on their similar needs or wants. A market is the total group of potential consumers for a product and includes retailers, businesses, government, media, and individuals. Market segmentation is a process of breaking this total group down into smaller groups based on a characteristic that the consumers have in common like age, gender, sporting interests, or attendance levels. Once a particular segment or segments of the market have been targeted, it is possible to customize the product and marketing strategies to meet their specific needs.

The process of market segmentation involves two steps. First, the market must be divided into sub-groups based on a common feature or features. This can be done with the help of market research. Six common factors are often used to divide a market into sub-groups: demographic, socio-economic, lifestyle (psychographic), geographic, product behaviour, and product benefits. After the market is divided into sub-groups, the segments to be targeted must be specified. The segment or segments chosen must be big enough and different enough from the others to justify the effort.

There are three approaches to segmentation: focused segmentation, multiple segmentation, and undifferentiated segmentation. Focused segmentation occurs when one segment only is chosen and one marketing mix is customized for it. Multiple segmentation involves choosing more than one segment and then developing one marketing mix for each segment. Finally, undifferentiated segmentation involves no choice at all where the entire market is considered a legitimate and worthwhile target.

Once decisions have been made about market segmentation, the next step is to choose a market positioning strategy for each segment identified. Market positioning refers to how a sport organization would like consumers to think and feel about their brand and its product offering when compared to competitors. For example, does a sport organization want to be thought of as offering luxury, high quality, or basic, value-for-money products? Do they see it as conservative and reliable or exciting and changeable? There are many different positioning strategies that can be selected that may suit the segment that is being targeted. It is important that the positioning strategy reflects a form of differentiation. That is, the positioning strategy must communicate to each target segment that the sport organization's brand and product offerings are special or different in some way from others available. It may be on the basis of the components of the product offerings, the quality of the products or services delivered, the price at which they are offered, or even the method that they are delivered. If stage one has been completed carefully, there should be many possibilities for capitalizing on market opportunities that align strongly with the internal capabilities of the sport organization. Like all strategic decisions, market positioning and differentiation should reflect a match between external opportunities and internal competitive advantages.

The idea of branding is closely linked with positioning. A brand is like an identifying badge (often a name or a logo) that helps consumers recognize a product or an organization. A brand becomes linked with the consumers' opinions and views of the sport organization. Because branding and positioning are linked, it is important to keep branding, segmentation and positioning strategies closely related.

STAGE 3: PLAN THE SPORT MARKETING MIX

The marketing mix is a set of strategies covering product, price, promotions, and place (distribution) and is commonly referred to as the 'four Ps'. They are collectively identified as a 'mix' because they should be combined and coordinated together in order to deploy the market positioning strategy. To the traditional four Ps it is necessary to add two more elements of the marketing mix: sponsorship and services. Both are already part of the marketing mix; sponsorship is part of 'promotions' and services are considered through 'product'. However, both are of central importance to sport marketing and are therefore given elevated status here.

Product

A product can include 1) a good (physical item being sold); 2) a service being delivered; 3) an idea; and/or 4) a combination of any of these. A sport product can be defined as the complete package of benefits that a sport organization presents to sport consumers through offering goods, services, and/or ideas. Sport goods are physical items that can be touched. Sport shoes, tennis rackets, memorabilia, golf balls, and skateboards are examples. These goods are all tangible, meaning that they exist as physical objects. Sporting goods usually have a high degree of reliability, meaning that their quality does not change much from one product to the next. They can also be stored after they are made because they are not perishable. Sport services will be considered independently in a forthcoming section.

A sporting product can be made up on a mixture of both goods and services. One important principle in sport marketing is to try to design products to have a mixture of tangible and intangible elements in order to help it stand out from competitors. To do this sport marketers think of the sport product as having three important variables: 1) the core benefit, 2) the actual product and 3) the augmented product. Figure 11.2 shows that the core benefit represents the main advantage that consumers receive from buying the product. The actual product refers to the features of the product itself. As long as consumers

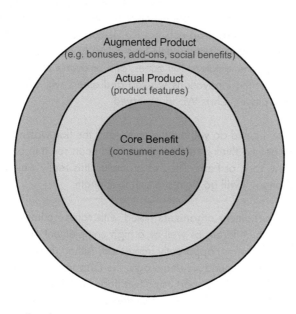

FIGURE 11.2 Sport product features

want the core benefit of the product, then developing the right features can help to make it fit their needs perfectly. The augmented product refers to any extras or extensions that are added to the features of the product. These may be additional benefits, bonus extras, or even the image of a product and how people see it.

In practice 11.1 Product innovation and speedy GolfSixes

Perhaps no sport grasps so firmly its history and tradition as golf. Yet even this most venerable sporting institution has capitulated to the fickle nature of shifting fandom and a cramped competitive environment by introducing its first permanent, alternative format version. In marketing terms, golf – in this case the European Tour – has unwrapped a product innovation as an augmented offering to attract new followers.

Driven by fears of being left behind by a sports-viewing landscape shifting inexorably towards faster, shorter, bespoke, mobile packages of 'product', golf's European Tour custodians created what they see as an innovative new format that will appeal to a new slice of the sport entertainment marketplace. 'GolfSixes' made its debut in 2017 through a tournament-style, 16-country, two-player team structure. Competing for a robust prize fund of 1 million euros, the six-round series worked by elimination, whittling the 16 teams down to a final over two days. Live spectators were treated to what the organizers called 'amphitheatre' viewing platforms around the tees and greens, complete with music and pyrotechnics at certain holes. With the players 'miked up' as well, the format worked hard to create a pacey, millennial-friendly atmosphere, somewhere roughly equidistant between professional wrestling and St Andrews. By golfing standards this was radical, but more of an old-school English revolution than a Silicon Valley insurgency. For example, there were 'nearest-the-pin' measurements to award third place, longest drive holes, and even 'whiskey huts'. Warm-up acts got the demure crowds bemused, if not quite riotous, while 'loudest cheer contests' delivered prizes to galleries. Add to all of these shot clocks, celebrity commentators, fan zones, and on-course player interviews.

Naturally, some of the innovations worked and others will still need some refinement. English team player, Chris Wood observed,

> To be honest, I could do without the music and the flag-waving and all that . . . But I totally get it. I think it really worked, and I can see it in big cities like Manchester, New York, or Paris. They've promoted this really well and I think, with the odd change, it will go from strength to strength.

Nevertheless, tournament organizers noted with some optimism that the crowds included families with children, as well as a high complement of continental Europeans to whom the novel format apparently impressed. Although promising, GolfSixes is not yet out of the sand. Around six years ago, the European Tour trialled 'PowerPlay Golf', a nine-hole version of the sport using two flags on the greens, one easy and the other difficult, with the latter with extra shots offered against par. It didn't catch on, but the appetite for product innovation in golf may well have shifted since.

SPORT PRODUCT INNOVATION

Sport marketers may consider the possibility of new product development through a process of innovation. Developing a new product can be expensive and risky. Every year a proliferation of new sport products is introduced to the market, but only a small fraction of these are successful. If a new product is a failure, the sport organization has lost time and money, and perhaps even some of their reputation. But what does it mean to develop a new product? A new product does not have to mean a brand new product. In sport marketing, a new product can take many forms, such as the improved performance of an existing product, new functions added to an existing product, a new way to use an existing product, combining existing products, or a new look or design for a product. Whatever form the new or revised product takes, it arises through a successful process of innovation.

Innovation has come to mean a multiplicity of things from simple creativity to complex manufacturing. For us, from a sport product perspective, innovation refers to the translation of a new idea into a tangible deliverable via a technology, physical product, or process-based service. Unlike an invention or a discovery, an innovation actually takes a place on the real-world stage, whether as a novel solution to an existing consumer problem, an improvement to a consumer experience, or even a completely new offering for a consumer to try that they had never contemplated before. Because innovation tends to be synonymous with inspiration, considerable mystery surrounds it cultivation.

In sport, product innovations can be found in several forms. First, mobile technology is changing the way consumers and participants connect with sport. For example, smart devices allow consumers to watch and experience sport from anywhere and at any time. Participants, and especially elite athletes, can collect, store and analyse a vast amount of training and performance data that offer vital clues for subsequent improvement. Second, sport product innovations have made a serious impact on the support systems for sport performance, such as sports medicine, rehabilitation, pharmaceuticals, nutrition, and supplements. Also, of course, sport managers and marketers can benefit from new innovations that augment audience size, consumer viewing experiences, broadcasting coverage and quality, media channels, regulation, rule enforcement and officiating, and general spectator safety and comfort.

As a result of these major opportunities arising from the application of innovations, sport marketers would be well advised to become conversant with the processes surrounding innovation. But this does not mean that sport marketers must await the development of new technologies. Instead they can aggressively pursue new product innovations through the application of available ideas and tools in new ways. Many sports, for example, have founded modified versions of their games in order to attract new audiences, including formats specifically designed for children and those exclusively conceived for maximum entertainment. For our purposes, innovation relates to product outcomes that are more attractive to a targeted audience. An innovation can be incremental in that it shifts the existing product in modest but important ways, or radical, where a product can be completely re-designed or even replaced by something consumers never expected.

This first step of product innovation involves creating and collecting new product possibilities and ideas. Although the product innovation process can occur either spontaneously or evolve almost unnoticed over a long period of incremental improvements, sport marketers can benefit from noting a series on steps typically present in any innovation outcome. Although beginning with a problem to be solved is a conventional and quite obviously sensible approach, innovation does not necessarily need something wrong to get it going. Most product developers and marketers imagine new products and services impelled by thoughts on new opportunities. Opportunities are the engine of innovation. For this reason, product innovation begins with the desire for new value. Step one in the sport product innovation process therefore seeks to cultivate an abundant, diverse, and rich platform of potential concepts from which to conceive new value. It is important that the ideas are remain unconstrained from the usual practicalities associated with convention, resources, and preconceived assumptions about what sport consumers want.

The second step in new product innovation involves sifting through all the ideas that have been collected and only keeping the ones that fit with the marketing objectives of the sport organization. It is also helpful to consider how well the new product ideas fit with existing products and how they relate to current trends. This is not the stage to be concerned about financial realism. However, by the end of this step, new product opportunities should be ranked according to priorities determined by marketing objectives. In short, the lengthy set of ideas from step one need to be reduced to a workable handful. A range of methods can be employed, including voting and weighting systems, predetermined priority areas, expert advice, panels and workshops, and the capability product champions have to quickly develop their ideas into testable prototypes. Subsequently, new product and service innovations should be tested as quickly and inexpensively as possible, in step three, rapid prototyping and testing of new products.

Step three of the process involves a more careful assessment of the ideas that were retained following step two. In fact, the highest-ranking options should be identified and piloted to determine their potential in the market. This is the time to check feasibility by undertaking cost and financial estimates and to conduct additional market research, or concept testing. Concept testing involves giving potential customers a description of the new product and asking them if they would be likely to buy it. It may also mean providing a prototype of the new product for customers to try. One powerful option at this stage involves creating a 'rapid prototype'.

Recently popularized and infused into marketing and business circles, rapid prototyping is a method of quickly testing an idea to see whether it could work before significant resources are expended in creating it for the market. Because rapid prototyping has been appropriated from designers, the process reflects the fluid and iterative methods they use in testing their nascent ideas. A prototype can range from a basic sketch or flowchart to a mock-up product or an unrefined but fully functional technology. The key is not in the finish but rather in the start. Most innovations never make it to the market because they take too long to develop or require too much investment without really knowing whether it will pay off or not. Rapid prototyping attempts to sidestep the development lag that most product innovations face. By quickly converting an idea into something tangible that can be tested – preferably by the same kinds of sport users and consumers who might buy it in the end – and subsequently refined and re-tested, the innovation process can be radically shortened. Often, the result is the choice to abandon the new innovation. This is sometimes referred to as 'fast failure' or 'cheap failure', but reflects a positive outcome where resources have been protected from wastage in the light of early trials. In rapid prototyping, experimentation remains central, which leads to better design, faster.

It is important to understand that the rapid prototyping method does not seek to create fully functional products or services. But they do need to evoke an experience in users that will provide them with a first-hand insight into what it is like to try the new product. For example, a marketer might conceive a new process for sport consumers to purchase tickets to events though a mobile application. Instead of spending months and thousands of dollars on development, the marketer might simply construct some cards or off-line screens reflecting the steps through which a consumer would use the application. By working with users to test the idea, the marketer can quickly ascertain whether their consumers have an appetite for the actual product. A prototype could range from the low fidelity, like a series of sketches on paper, to high fidelity, like a working application with limited functionality. The important issue is that users can be exposed to the kind of experience that the ultimate product seeks to elicit. Better prototypes duplicate the final product experience with greater precision than lesser prototypes. But even a poor prototype can be enough to provide sufficient feedback for a successive, refined version.

Most consumers find it difficult to imagine their responses to new product innovations in the absence of any tangible experience in which to base their expectations. Prototypes vastly amplify the productivity of market testing, and have therefore become a pivotal tool in the sport product development arsenal.

With the results of the new product's feasibility and market testing available, it is time to make a final decision about how to proceed. It is possible that the best decision is not to proceed and to choose the next highest ranked new product opportunity to investigate. If the feasibility and testing results are promising, the final product composition should be determined. This involves specifying the core product benefits, actual product features and augmented product composition. The other elements of the marketing mix will also need to be determined to provide the appropriate positioning strategy.

Finally, if a sport product has successfully made it through all these stages, it is ready to be released onto the market. With this decision, an implementation plan will need to be created to support the deployment of all the variables in the marketing mix.

Branding

Branding is one of the key strategies that sport marketers use to augment their products by associating them with certain ideas. The added value that a product has because of its brand name is called brand equity. Branding is much more than choosing a good name, or having a good logo designed; it revolves around building the brand. Once potential consumers are aware of a sport brand, it is important to help them connect certain ideas about what it stands for that reflect an intended positioning strategy. Sport marketers achieve this by manipulating the brand image, which encompasses all of the symbols and ideas that influence the image of a brand such as its name, logo, product features, product quality/performance, packaging, price, advertising, promotion, customer service and distribution channels. The ultimate goal of branding is consumer loyalty. Brand loyalty is improved through high levels of product quality, convenience of distribution, keeping up regular contact with customers, and customer loyalty programs.

Related to the idea of branding is licensing. Licensing occurs when a sport organization allows another organization to use their brand name or logo for a fee. The company who buys the right to use the brand (called the licensee) will then produce a good, service, or promotion and will give a percentage of the money they make back to the real owner of the brand (called the licensor). Licensing is a common product strategy in sport, and each year it generates billions of dollars in sales internationally. It is particularly popular with merchandising (toys, collectible cards, games, school supplies, videos, DVDs, and magazines) and apparel. Sport clubs and leagues do not have the resources to make all of these products by themselves. Instead, they may make an agreement with another company to make the merchandise for them and agree to share a percentage of profits.

Price

The way that a sport product is priced not only influences it financial impact, but also has a powerful effect on the way that consumers perceive it. The price of a sport product represents what a consumer gives up in exchange for using or owning it. Price is usually thought of in financial terms, but may include other things that a customer has to give up in order to obtain the product, such as time (e.g. waiting in a queue), or social costs (e.g. being in an aerobics class with others instead of a one-on-one instruction). A useful way to think about pricing decisions is to consider them in terms of value. In sport marketing, the value of a product is a factor of how its price relates to the benefits that consumers believe they will receive in exchange. The value of a sport product is the relationship between its price and the benefits a consumer believes they will receive from it.

There are six main steps involved in setting the right price for a sport product: 1) setting a pricing goal, 2) determining price sensitivity, 3) conducting a break-even analysis, 4) assessing pricing variables, 5) selecting price tactics, and 6) setting a price point. First, because different pricing strategies will achieve different things, it is important to determine what outcome is being sought and should be specified in the form of pricing goals. These may range from those focused on maximizing profit to those designed to provide the product or service to as many different sport consumers as possible. Second, it is necessary to determine how sensitive consumers are to price changes. Consumers are sensitive to price if they do not buy a product when the price is high, or if they buy more of it when the price is lowered. The more sensitive they are, the more they will change their buying habits when the price changes. Third, a break-even analysis should be conducted to ascertain how many sales are needed in order to recover the costs of producing the product. Fourth, other variables that might affect price should be considered including the pricing strategies of competitors, legal or regulatory limitations that may be relevant, and the impact of the other marketing mix variables. Fifth, a pricing strategy should be selected that underscores the overall market positioning strategy. There are many different types of pricing strategies that sport organizations might use, including those designed to maximize profit, following competitors, setting a low introductory price, adding a flat margin to costs, using market demand as a guide, and pricing according to the segment of consumers being targeted. Sixth, and finally, a price point is selected. It is important to realize that price needs to be re-considered constantly and should always remain consistent with a market positioning strategy.

Promotion

Promotion is concerned with communicating with consumers, providing them with information about product offerings and trying to persuade them to buy. Ultimately, promotion is pivotal in shaping and cultivating brand image. Sport promotion can be defined as the way that sport marketers communicate with potential consumers to inform, persuade and remind them about their product offerings.

There are four main promotional activities known together as the promotions mix because they are typically used in concert to create an integrated promotional strategy. The promotion mix elements are 1) advertising, 2) personal selling, 3) sales promotion, and 4) public relations. Advertising is a form of one-way communication where a sport marketer pays someone else to have their product or company identified. Common examples include television commercials, magazine and newspaper advertisements, radio spots, Internet pop-ups, posters, billboards, and advertisements on public transport. Personal selling involves one-to-one communication between a consumer and a salesperson such as talking to a customer on the phone, talking face to face, or even telemarketing. Endorsements and sponsorships are two forms of personal selling that are common in the sport industry. Sales promotions are short-term programs that aim to stimulate an increase in sales. They give consumers an incentive (or a bonus) to use the sport product. Common examples include 'two-for-one' offers, prize give-aways, competitions, and free trials or samples. Public relations programs try to build a favourable image for a sport organization, its brand, and product offerings in the community. It is not paid for by the sport organization and usually involves publicity in the media in the form of a news item.

Place

Place refers to the location where a sport product or service is delivered or the method of distributing a product. As a result, the terms 'place' and 'distribution' are interchangeable. Both describe how a sport product or service gets from the producer to the final consumer. The process of distribution can be explained through the concept of a sport distribution channel, which comprises a series of organizations or individuals through which a sport product must pass. There are both direct and indirect distribution channels. A direct distribution channel is short where the producer sells the product directly to the consumer. Examples include Internet sales of sporting merchandise and sport services like live matches and coaching lessons. An indirect distribution channel is longer where there are a number of organizations or people (called intermediaries) involved along the way. Examples include sporting goods products like athletic shoes and equipment.

Ticket sales are one of the most important sources of revenue for sport organizations that run competitions or events. Ticket distribution is therefore an extremely important issue for sport marketers that relates to the 'place' element of the sport marketing mix. When consumers contact a ticket distributor to buy a ticket for a sport event, they are often looking for more than just a ticket. They want convenience, fast and friendly service, questions answered, and a reasonable price. If a consumer becomes unhappy with the service or price they receive from a ticket distributor, they can feel dissatisfied about the sport event or club as well. It is essential that sport organizations carefully control their contracts with ticket distributors.

The sport facility is perhaps the most important distribution channel in the sport industry. There are numerous features of sport facilities that affect their success as a distribution vehicle for sport products. The important features of a sport facility can be summarized into four main areas: 1) location and accessibility, 2) design and layout, 3) facilities, and 4) customer service. Table 11.1 summarizes the variables influencing distribution in sport facilities.

TABLE 11.1 Distribution variables of sport facilities

Location and Accessibility	Attractive location
	Convenient to get to
	Good signage and directions
	Enough parking
	Accessible by public transport
	Accessible by different forms of public transport
	Easy to enter and exit facility
	Disabled access (ramps, lifts, washroom facilities)
Design and Layout	Fits in with local area
	Attractive design (size, colour, shape, and light)
	Ambience and atmosphere
	Easy to get from one area to another
	Good direction signs
	Seating arrangements with good viewing
	Weather protection
	Control of noise levels
	Areas for non-smokers and non-drinkers
	Lighting of playing area
	Protection from heat and cold
	Air circulation
	Adequate storage

Location and Accessibility	Attractive location
	Safety issues (emergency procedures, fire detection, stand-by power, emergency communication, exits)
	Security (surveillance, control room, entrance security)
	Spectator control (zones, safe barriers, security, police)
Facility Infrastructure	Variety of food and drink outlets
	Overall seating quality
	Premium seating available
	Corporate boxes and special services
	Toilets – number and location for convenient access
	Child-care facilities
	Scoreboards and screens
	Message centres and sound systems
	Emergency medical services
	Merchandise areas
	Broadcasting and media requirements
Customer Service	Queuing and waiting times
	Prominent information stands/booths
	Efficient, friendly, and helpful staff
	Sufficient security and emergency staff
	Entrance staff, ushers
	Services for elderly, disabled, and children
	Telephone enquiry service

Sport marketers do not always have control over the features of sporting facilities and may be able to do little to enact change without substantial resources. For this reason it is important that sport marketers attempt to bolster the distribution of sport by managing a number of other aspects of the venue. First, seating selection influences sport consumers' experiences and can be used to enhance their viewing comfort as well as the marketing messages they are exposed to. Second, scoreboards and signage are an essential method of communicating marketing messages, irrespective of the size of a venue, and can enhance sport consumers' experience of the event. Third, lighting and sound systems can be used to attract sport consumers at attractive times and can also improve the atmosphere of a venue and event. Fourth, transport can be used to assist sport consumers in accessing a facility and can be marketed as a special customer service. Fifth, media facilities can encourage broadcasting and general media interest in events that occur in a sport facility. Sixth, the provision of childcare facilities can be important in attracting sport consumers during non-peak periods or to special events. Seventh, selling merchandise in sport facilities is a powerful marketing tool because it provides sport consumers with a convenient way of spending more money on items that emphasize the sport product's brand image. Finally, the supply of food and beverages is amongst the most lucrative of all services that can be offered at a sport facility.

In practice 11.2 Data-driven marketing with ski manufacturer Rossignol

Outdoor apparel and ski, alpine, and Nordic equipment manufacturer, Rossignol, recently abandoned the notion of being a ski company in favour of becoming an 'experience company'. The decision relied upon the company's newfound confidence in both the importance and their ability to wield and mobilize digital data. As a result, the company has focussed on developing a market-leading suite of social engagements with their customers, and in the process, has acquired a vast goldmine of data and a hitherto untapped network of loyal customers. By using the data received from its nearly 400,000 Facebook fans, along with dedicated engagement strategies via Twitter and Instagram, Rossignol has attracted more than 300,000 users of the world's first mobile ski 'app'.

In addition to the social media platforms the company seeds, data from more than 3 million annual visitors to the official website have helped develop a smorgasbord of customer relationship programs and offerings, including an immensely successful loyalty program as well as new business-to-customer, business-to-business, and trade marketing channels. Rossignol's marketing strategy revolves around engagement, which has grown into a five-stage program. First, Rossignol seeks 'awareness' in order to attract a consumer to test out a product in the second stage, 'evaluation'. Given a positive test, the third stage, 'conversion' attempts to capture the new customer, who will receive further attention, customized products, and attractive offers via a fourth stage, or 'loyalty' program, to help them get over the line. In the final stage, repeat Rossignol customers are encouraged to practice 'advocacy' where they attract product discounts and other benefits from peer-to-peer promotion of the brand.

Underpinning the five-stage engagement process, the marketing team at Rossignol employ a toolbox of digital and social media platforms as sites to enact consumer-to-customer conversion. Of course, a website lies at the core. Although it provides a stalwart brand identity for the company, the main purpose of the site is to facilitate e-commerce. Thus, the website principally operates as a webstore and as the culminating location for a consumer's journey. That is, Rossignol presumes that they must drive consumers to the webstore through other, more engaging mechanisms like social media, rather than just assume that consumers will automatically head to the site to make a purchase. In concert, the company's marketing team remains sensitive to the possibility of undermining its traditional retail partners. To combat any cannibalization of critical retail sales from long-standing distributors, the webstore delivers orders directly to these outlets with customers motivated through discounts. In the end, the retailers also get a bonus through a coupon provided at Rossignol's expense. A relatively trivial investment in discounts and rewards for customer and retailer, respectively, leads to 40% of the brand's total sales originating from the webstore. Furthermore, customers can sign up for a loyalty program and collect points for both purchases and promotions that can be redeemed for more discounts, and in some cases, other benefits like event tickets or the chance to meet high-profile, Rossignol-sponsored athletes.

At the same time, five social media platforms jointly attract around 600,000 followers. Each platform emphasizes a different brand dimension and employs a unique engagement strategy. Twitter delivers the real-time 'brand newsfeed' of sporting results, images, and athlete news. Facebook represents the 'brand magazine', focussing on more polished imagery and stories designed to shape brand attributes and perceptions. Instagram offers the brand 'look-book', in the form of a slick content-rich inventory of professional photography, short clips, and sponsored athlete's performance photos. Finally, YouTube is used to deliver the television-styled 'official' brand channel through which videos introduce or promote products, technologies, and sponsored athlete performances. Rossignol's entire marketing strategy relies on the sophisticated application of data in order to build brand identity, engage with consumers towards converting them into loyal, advocating customers, and leveraging web sales through customized social media networks.

Sponsorship

Although sponsorships and endorsements are part of the promotional mix, they are so important to sport that they deserve special treatment. Sport sponsorship is a business agreement where an organization or individual provides financial or in-kind assistance to a sport property (the sport organization or person being sponsored such as an athlete, team, event, association, or competition) in exchange for the right to associate itself with the sport property. Sponsorship is an example of marketing through sport. The objectives of sponsorship can vary greatly, depending on the size of the partners, the type of sponsorship, and the type of sport property being supported. Some common objectives for the sponsor are to promote the public image of their organization, to increase customer awareness, to manage their brand image, and to build business relationships. In general, sponsorship helps to generate goodwill amongst consumers. The amount of goodwill generated can vary depending on the kind of sport property being sponsored, the degree of involvement that consumers have in the sport property, the time at which the sponsor becomes involved, and when/how the sponsor ceases the sponsorship.

Sponsorship works through an image transfer from the sport property to the sponsor. This image transfer works best when there is a strong sponsorship affinity, or a good fit or match between the sponsor and the sport property. Two things are particularly important for ensuring a good match: 1) an overlap of target markets and 2) an overlap of brand positioning strategies. As a result, sponsorship works best when the two partners are linked to the same group of consumers and have a similar kind of message. Most sponsors support their sport sponsorship programs by leveraging them with additional marketing activities. For a sponsor to make the most of a sponsorship they usually need to undertake other promotional activities drawing attention to it. Sometimes sponsorship leveraging can cost several times the amount that is spent on the sponsorship itself. Sponsors also have to be careful about ambush marketing, where another company (other than an official sponsor, and often a competitor to the official sponsor) creates marketing communications that give the impression that they are associated with the sport property. Whilst evaluating sponsorships can be difficult, it is important that a careful evaluation strategy is implemented. Being able to demonstrate that sponsorship has a positive outcome for corporations is the best way to legitimize it as a marketing technique and to attract and retain sponsors.

Services

Sport services cannot be seen, felt, or tasted; they are intangible because they exist only as an experience, inconsistent in terms of quality, and perishable in that they can only be offered and experienced once at any point in time. Sport services are inseparable because they are consumed at the same time as they are produced. Sport organizations offer services where their staff, team, or athletes provide an experience to consumers. For example, services are offered through fitness centres, local participation-based competitions, professional sport matches, and support services like sport physiotherapists.

It is a common view that when it comes to marketing a service, there are three additional Ps that should be added to the standard four. These are participants, physical evidence, and process. Participants are those individuals who are involved in delivering and receiving a service. Physical evidence refers to the tangible or visual elements of a service such as a sporting facility. Process is concerned with the steps involved in delivering a service. All three of these new Ps revolve around service quality and customer satisfaction. Sport consumers are more likely to be loyal users of a service if they perceive it to be of high quality with consistent levels of delivery, leading to satisfaction.

Service quality may be seen as the degree to which a service meets the needs and expectations of customers. For example, if a customer expects a level of service that is higher than what they feel they actually receive, they are likely to believe that the service is lower quality, and will tend to be dissatisfied. One key method of focusing on service quality is to work hard on ensuring that five aspects of its delivery are present. These five areas are reliability, assurance, empathy, responsiveness, and tangibles. Reliability refers to the ability to offer a service in a consistent and dependable way. Responsiveness refers to a willingness to help customers and to provide them with the service on time. Assurance refers to the level of confidence and trust that a customer has in the service. Empathy refers to the ability to get to know customers and their needs and to deliver a personalized service. Tangibles refer to the physical features of the service such as information booklets, equipment, appearance of staff, facilities, and characteristics of a sport venue. If these aspects of service quality are emphasized, then customer satisfaction is likely to be maximized.

DIGITAL SPORT MARKETING

It is easy enough to understand digital sport marketing as any form of marketing that utilizes technology, which of course means a focus on the Internet and all the devices, channels and media that it implicates. At the same time, this broad definition no longer helps distinguish digital marketing from other forms in an era when just about every marketing activity involves a digital aspect. Even conventional printed flyers rely on print-on-demand technologies, and even modest sporting events utilize digital ticketing in order to save money. The simple act of watching sport live cannot escape the digital era either. Most surveys suggest that around half of sport fans refer to their smart phones for extra content during events. At the same time as the technologies and tools of the digital era have become entrenched in our marketing expectations, sport marketers must come to terms with a new way of looking at their offerings. In short, sport digital marketing and social media demands a new kind of mind-set where the conventional distance between sport properties, their marketing representatives, and fans is completely blurred and where success means constant adaptation. No longer are digital and social media tools just 'add-ons' to the standard marketing methods. Today, a digital world needs a digital message.

Digital marketing is often described as electronic marketing and is usually associated with the Internet, computers, and forms of mobile communications. To phrase this more generally, digital marketing refers to communications that are generated by electronic means or through recent (non-analogue) technological platforms. Digital marketing refers to technologically sophisticated platforms or vehicles for transmitting and communicating information. In this chapter, we describe how all of these digital platforms are revolutionizing sport marketing and have justifiably become essential tools in the toolkit. By implication of the escalation of digital channels, as a secondary goal of this chapter, we also explain how social media must become a central element in a sport organization's digital profile. The term 'social media', like the term 'marketing', can mean different things depending on the context. We take a broad view in referring to social media as any instrument or means of communicating information that relies on the interactions between networked groups of individuals. It is important to take a broad view like this because technology has provided the sport marketer with so many innovative ways of communicating with the general public that they no longer have to rely only on traditional 'media' organizations.

Today, digital content is delivered through many devices such as smart phones, PDAs, tablets, and MP3 music players. The information can even be transferred seamlessly from one digital technology to another and from one digital format to another (for example, from a mobile phone to a computer). Another feature of digital media is that data, or information, is accessible in real time. Digital media is especially important in sport marketing because it permeates all aspects of consumers' lives.

Not long ago, digital media, and especially social media, were seen as the latest technological trends, but it has now become indisputable that they have significant and permanent implications for sport marketing. Digital media is more than technology and tools; it requires a different style of marketing where sport marketers can communicate in novel ways with sport consumers. It is also important because it creates additional opportunities in sport, such as new assets and revenues (like website and mobile digital rights, as well as new sales channels) and new possibilities in licensing and merchandising (such as computer games). Although the types of technologies that are available continue to change and develop, the principle remains the same: sport marketers can use advanced technology to communicate with their customers and sell them extra products and services that are associated with sport. Perhaps more importantly, the social media dimension of the digital revolution allows marketers and sport organizations an unprecedented connectivity with their customer and fan base.

The popularity and prevalence of digital and social media technology mean that it provides sport marketers with innovative ways of communicating with consumers. Many of these communication approaches are far more rapid, responsive, and interactive than other marketing strategies. For example, compare the one-way content of television with the opportunity to customize a replay directly to a consumer's smart phone. Not only are digital media platforms fast and direct, they are also inexpensive compared with traditional techniques of sport marketing. Even more importantly, digital media enables sport organizations to develop messages that are personalized to key target audiences.

SPORT MARKETING AND SOCIAL MEDIA

You want to know how your team performed. Forget about the TV or the newspaper, and even the online news is a bit slow and cumbersome. Go directly to Twitter for your live sports ticker, and for more information, and perhaps a conversation about the results; go directly to the sport fans' hub, Facebook. And hyperlinks to YouTube can offer the footage within moments of the big play. All of this on the run; on your smart phone, iPad, or any other Wi-Fi or mobile device. In fact, most surveys in North America, Western Europe, and the Asia Pacific report that about three-quarters of fans use social media during games, whereas up to half check scores or watch highlights after the event using smart phones. By the time you read this text, the figures are likely to have climbed even higher. However, as we shall discuss in this section, savvy digital sport marketers know that although data and updates are compelling services for fans, the real power of social media lies in its unprecedented ability to create close, personal engagements between sport properties and their followers. In the end, like all marketing, we aim for better relationships, experiences, feedback, and advocacy. One conclusion is absolutely undisputed: the use of social media has become an essential investment rather than an interesting experiment at the periphery of sport marketing.

Few could argue that the contemporary sport consumer has changed radically in just a few short years. We want sport content at our convenience, which typically means on the run, and often comes with the expectation of updates from our favourite and most trusted sources of social networking insight. In short, we want to know what is going on, and we want to be able to find out 24/7. In a world rapidly heading towards 2 billion smart phone owners, the implications for digital sport marketing are prodigious. To start with, sport consumers want instant access. Next, that access must be customized, or at least 'customizable', in order to meet the fickle preferences of each fan. Access must also arrive seamlessly. That means a smooth download, as well as an integrated platform where the sport fan needs only engage with a single or a few locations for their updates. Integration plays a central role in effective digital marketing because consumers are using their smart phones and mobile devices for Internet browsing almost as much as through computers. In addition, they check email and social networking messages and sites, post photos and comments, listen to voice messages, consult their calendars, check the weather forecast, use apps, and play music and games. Although it varies depending on the region, some studies suggest that consumers within certain demographics pick up their phones more than 100 times a day. No wonder hardware manufacturers and app developers are so focused on providing an interface that captures the user's demand for intuitive functionality. Because sport consumers are so well educated about sport and technology, they expect more than the garden-variety results. Rather, content must be accompanied by novelty, entertainment, and insight. Finally, attending sporting events can be prohibitively expensive, leading sport consumers to find alternative ways of engaging with game content as well as looking for new ways of generating the excitement and buzz of the contest. Enter social media.

In practice 11.3 Facing the dark side of social media with the National Basketball Association

Case studies exemplifying the exponential scale of social media impact in sport frequently invoke terms such as 'viral' and 'followers'. Indeed, the unique nature of the platforms offers prodigious opportunities to get messages out fast and to secure remarkable fan interest in the process. Despite the self-evident need for sporting organizations and personalities to engage with followers via social media, few cautionary guidelines tend to accompany the hyperbole urging immediate and frequent fan contact. Yet many sport organizations have had challenging experiences with social media too. In some cases, like with the U.S. National Basketball Association (NBA), numerous social media events have prompted the rapid invention of rules to avoid, or at least mitigate, the potential damaging brand effects when social media goes wrong.

Of course, successful social media relies on the immediacy and intimacy between brands and fans, especially when posts come from players offering unsolicited, 'behind the scenes' insights about their personal thoughts, feelings, experiences, or opinions. Naturally, as with any close interpersonal communications, frank exchanges can sometimes get hairy, from the insensitive and inopportune, to the provocative and insulting.

If the NBA's experience is anything to go by, three aspects of social media's dark side merit comment. First, fans and other commentators – including troublemaking 'trolls' – can voice their dissatisfaction, inappropriate opinion, or even outright anger towards just about anyone, often with anonymity, which also means without consequence. Social media's instant distribution ensures that such messages can become swept up in an escalating chain of dissemination, leaping over lines of good taste and ethics in the process. For example, the NBA and its constituent teams face the on-going challenge of responding constructively to the negative publicity, insulting remarks, and even bigotry and racism towards certain teams and individuals. Given that social media contributors to franchise team accounts remain independent of the NBA's influence or can hide behind a pseudonymous account profile, the NBA has no control over posts and cannot moderate any of the ensuing fallout to attenuate the brand or personal damage.

Second, the NBA has little governance over the immediate responses team representatives post in reaction to highly emotive and other inflammatory events, the worst of which tend to be posted without the intention of inciting an equally vigorous retort. A governing association like the NBA cannot control the proliferation of feeds individual players, coaches, or staff from within a team can post, irrespective of whether they go out in poor taste or bad judgement. For example, in 2013, former New York Knicks player J.R. Smith directed an aggressive rant towards an opposition player via Twitter, for which the NBA ultimately fined him US$25,000. Because Twitter delivers instant communication and subsequent feedback, by the time the team and the NBA had realized the damage done, it was too late.

Third, problems can also arise when a corporate sponsor or shareholder creates negative publicity, again completely outside of the NBA's sphere of direct influence. An infamous example occurred in 2014 when the (then) owner of the Los Angeles Clippers, Donald Sterling, was filmed and recorded making controversial comments that were subsequently uploaded into social media. The story 'went viral' via social media and remains a source of contention, having incurred Sterling a lifetime ban from the NBA, not to mention the substantial brand damage to the Clippers.

In response to these vulnerabilities accompanying social media use, some prominent professional sport competitions like the NBA (and their member teams) have devised risk-mitigating policies. The NBA policy outlines the nature of acceptable content that can be posted by players, coaches, officials, and support staff working for the league or for a participating team. Some examples include rules governing when and where players can communicate with fans, imposing bans on tweets during games and 45 minutes on either side. With social media now the preferred means of communications by fans, and often to fans as well, these governance policies overseeing appropriate content have become a mainstay of today's sport marketing.

STAGE 4: IMPLEMENT AND CONTROL THE SPORT MARKETING STRATEGY

The final stage of the Sport Marketing Framework is to implement and control the sport marketing strategy. Implementing a sport marketing strategy means putting the plans into action. Many sport organizations discover that it is harder to implement a marketing strategy than it sounds. There are, however, two important actions that sport marketers can perform in order to help them to implement a marketing strategy more effectively. These are to use implementation strategies and to use a control process.

A sport marketing plan is more likely to be successful if there is a clear leader or group of leaders who take responsibility for its implementation. In addition, it is important that all members of the sport marketing team have a good understanding of the marketing plan and, where possible, have all made a contribution according to their unique skills and knowledge. This demands a team comprising a combination of staff and volunteers who have the right mix of skills, experience, and attitudes in the first place. Whether the implementation of marketing strategy will be successful depends on the individual and team efforts of staff and volunteers. The final part of implementing a marketing strategy is to review and evaluate its outcomes on a regular basis. It is vital to keep track of how well the plan is going and to make changes if things are not going as intended. A control process provides the structure to this feedback.

The sport marketing control process has five main steps. The first step involves setting performance measures. These should already be in place in accordance with stage two of the Sport Marketing Framework. The second step is to put the performance measure into action by evaluating performance before and after the marketing strategy has been implemented, leading to the third step, a comparison of results to determine gaps, shortfall, and performance successes. With these variations in the fore, the fourth step is to determine whether the variance is favourable or not and whether intervention needs to occur. The final step is to make remedial changes to the marketing strategy and mix in order to bring it back in line with marketing objectives.

Although the implementation of a sport marketing plan should align with a sport organization's objectives, it should also fit within the broader boundaries of ethical behaviour. Ethics in sport marketing typically refers to whether the traditional four Ps of the marketing mix are deployed within a moral and professional code. Mostly these include issues associated with unsafe or poor quality products, deceptive or predatory pricing, misleading or dishonest promotions, and exploitative or collusive distribution. In the sporting world, other major marketing issues are concerned with publicizing the private lives of athletes, exploiting passionate fans and children who idolize sport stars through athlete endorsements of commercial products, the use of venues with unsafe facilities, unrealistic promises associated with health, fitness and weight loss products, the use of performance-enhancing drugs, and the over-pricing of high-profile matches and special sport events. In short, informed, autonomous consumer decisions based on the faithful representation of the product features and its price lie at the core of responsible and ethical sport marketing.

SUMMARY

This chapter was structured around the Sport Marketing Framework. Stage one is to identify sport marketing opportunities which involves undertaking several kinds of assessments: a SWOT analysis, a competitor analysis, a five forces competitor analysis, an organizational analysis, and market and consumer research. All of these analyses allow sport marketers to better understand market circumstances, consumer preferences, the sport industry, competitors' activities, and the internal organization context.

Stage two of the Sport Marketing Framework is to develop a sport marketing strategy. This stage begins with decisions about the direction of the marketing program, which is subsequently documented using marketing objectives and performance measures. Stage two also involves deciding on the basic theme of the marketing strategy. To that end, it requires the identification of the target market/s (segmentation), the positioning strategy (differentiation), and the composition of the marketing mix to deploy the strategy.

Stage three of the Sport Marketing Framework requires planning the sport marketing mix in detail. Here, decisions about the four P's of marketing, the product, price, promotions, and distribution (place) are determined, along with specific approaches to sponsorship and the management of sport services.

Finally, stage four is to implement and control the plan. Plans are put into action, facilitated by implementation strategies. It is also essential to keep the plan on track by using a control process that emphasizes the comparison of the results from marketing activities with the performance indicators and objectives set in stage two. Remedial action is then taken to correct the plan where it has been unsuccessful, has strayed off course, or needs supplementation in order to capitalize on some unexpected opportunity.

Sport marketing revolves around the premise of satisfying the needs of sport consumers, in so doing cultivating a relationship with them that leads to a strong brand loyalty. Sport marketing lies at the intersection of strategy, where sport organizations focus on what they are good at, and market opportunities, where sport consumers are offered what they want. The best way of finding this intersection is to use a systematic approach like that outlined in the Sport Marketing Framework.

Most of modern life is spent within close proximity to several screens, including the television, computer, pad, and smart phone. In fact, most of us take at least one device with us everywhere we go, and sport viewing is no exception irrespective of whether it is live or through a broadcast. Sport marketers have grasped the opportunities that go with constant connectivity to draw fans more deeply into the game, its players, and all the intrigue, excitement and hype that occurs via the seemingly personalized communications that smart phones deliver. A sporting experience no longer means just viewing a game or event. Sport fans have at their fingertips a smorgasbord of information, statistics, live feeds, replays, messages, and insider observations with which to engage. Twitter feeds and Facebook posts can integrate with broadcasts. Venues and media channels can provide customized apps with real-time updates to enhance the viewing experience. It has now also become common for major sporting venues to provide enhanced Wi-Fi in stadia to encourage fan use of social media and content highlights. Numerous stakeholders have an interest including the social media platform, sport properties, advertisers, sponsors, and broadcast content-owners.

REVIEW QUESTIONS

1   Explain the difference between the marketing of sport and marketing through sport.

2   What are the steps in the Sport Marketing Framework?

3 What is the relationship between sport marketing objectives and performance measures? How are these relevant to controlling the marketing plan?

4 What is the purpose of market positioning?

5 What is the difference between a sport product and a sport service?

6 What effect does pricing have on positioning? Provide an example of how price can influence a consumer's perception of a product.

7 What are the four tools of the promotions mix? Provide an example of each.

8 Provide a good example of a sponsor and sport property relationship that enjoys a high level of affinity.

9 What is the relationship between service quality and customer satisfaction?

DISCUSSION QUESTIONS

1 Do you think that marketing sport is really different from marketing any other type of product or service?

2 Assuming that sport fans are generally loyal to their teams (and clubs), what do you think that team marketers should focus on?

3 Which sports have successfully introduced product innovations in the form of new game versions? Which sports tried but failed? Discuss why some worked while others did not.

4 Some commentators suggest that technology, mobile social media, and instant communications constitute sport marketing 'game changers'. Discuss whether this is an exaggeration or an accurate statement.

5 Has the nature of sport sponsorship changed much over the last decade? What trends seem to be foreshadowing change in the future? Provide examples of 'new' or 'novel' sponsorship arrangements and discuss their importance to cutting edge sport marketing.

FURTHER READING

Funk, D.C., Alexandris, K. and McDonald, H. (2016). *Sport Consumer Behaviour: Marketing Strategies*. London: Routledge.

Greenhalgh, G., Dwyer, B. and LeCrom, C. (2017). A case of multiple (brand) personalities: Expanding the methods of brand personality measurement in sport team contexts. *Sport Marketing Quarterly*, 26(1): 20–30.

Jensen, J.A., Wakefield, L., Cobbs, J.B. and Turner, B.A. (2016). Forecasting sponsorship costs: Marketing intelligence in the athletic apparel industry. *Marketing Intelligence & Planning*, 34(2): 281–298.

Jular, J. and Kasnakoglu, B.T. (2017). Why do we make sport: The importance of psychosocial motivations in adult sports participation. *International Journal of Marketing Studies*, 9(3): 39–49.

Kelly, S.J., Ireland, M., Mangan, J. and Williamson, H. (2016). It works two ways: Impacts of sponsorship alliance upon sport and sponsor image. *Sport Marketing Quarterly*, 25(4): 242–259.

Kunkel, T., Doyle, J.P. and Berlin, A. (2017). Consumers' perceived value of sport team games – a multidimensional approach. *Journal of Sport Management*, 31(1): 80–95.

Pedersen, P.M., Laucella, P., Kian, E. and Geurin, A. (2016). *Strategic Sport Communication*. 2nd edn. Champaign, IL: Human Kinetics.

Smith, A., Stavros, C. and Westberg, K. (2017). *Brand Fans: Lessons from the World's Greatest Sport Organisations*. London: Palgrave Macmillan.

Tokuyama, S., Greenwell, T.C. and Miller, J. (2016). Examining links between participant sport and spectator sport: A case with tennis consumers. *Journal of Contemporary Athletics*, 10(1): 51–66.

Yuksel, M., McDonald, M.A. and Joo, S. (2016). Cause-related sport marketing: An organizing framework and knowledge development opportunities. *European Sport Management Quarterly*, 16(1): 58–85.

RELEVANT WEBSITES

www.europeantour.com/en/europeantour/—European Tour (Golf)
https://NBA.com—National Basketball Association
www.rossignol.com/—Rossignol
www.afl.com.au/womens—Women's Australian Football League

CASE STUDY 11.1

Marketing the Chinese sports industry

Sport has long been an established part of Chinese culture and society, with the majority of funding historically provided through a centrally planned economic and social system under state control. In the past, this system has proven reasonably reliable, clearly evident in Olympic success culminating in China's 51 gold medals at the Beijing Summer Olympics.

The Chinese model demands that any individual control of sport should be subsumed by the greater good of the state. However, the model has so far left the marketing of sport largely confined to minor sponsorships and limited brand exposure.

Over the last 30 years while Chinese industry aggressively globalized, sport was slow to embrace marketization or become more financially self-sufficient. Slowly, however, the Chinese government has developed the economic and educational value of the sports sector. Although a more open-door policy was established in the 1980s, the first serious shift in government intention came in 2010 when China's

State Council issued a 'Guiding Opinion' encouraging China's sports industry to seek greater market exploration. Although a start, the Guiding Opinion lacked sufficient detail or strength to tackle China's complex sports administrative approval procedures.

In 2014, two announcements gave the Guiding Opinion teeth. In March, President Xi Jinping, a fervent football fan, issued a 50-point roadmap for developing China into a global football power, and in October the State Council under Premier Li Keqiang, issued a document entitled 'Several Opinions of the State Council of the People's Republic of China on Accelerating the Development of the Sports Industry and Promoting Sports Consumption'. Sport had finally become national strategy and sport development an official policy with the aim of incorporating sport into China's economic growth.

In May 2016, China's 13th five-year plan directed that the sports industry should comprise 1% of GDP by 2020, an increase from its then estimated 0.63%. The eventual goal was for the sports industry to increase from around US$50 billion to a US$750 to 800 billion industry by 2026, to have 500 million sports participants, and to establish sports facilities in all Chinese neighbourhoods. Considering that in 2014, the size of the entire global sports industry was estimated to be only US$1 trillion, a Chinese target of US$750 billion within 10 years was an enormous task.

It is worth considering what gave China the confidence to believe that it could overturn years of government regulation and ambitiously increase the size of the sports industry to such an enormous extent all within a period of 10 years.

Underlying the confidence was the political imperative. If the state believed in the sports industry, then so must the Chinese population. Politics and society have always been intertwined, and with the central government focused on expanding the sports service sector, generous funding was forthcoming. The government reduced the corporate income tax for high-tech sports companies and reduced tax on other selected companies associated with sport.

Other, more solid foundations underpinned the confidence as well. In 2008, the average GDP per capita was a little over US$3,000. By 2016, that figure was well over US$7,000. The Chinese population, enormous at 1.4 billion, with a middle class growing at a rate of 2% to 3% per year, has the money to spend generously on sports and entertainment. In addition, China has almost 600 billionaires, many of whom are willing and able to tie in to the presidential and state dream.

At first China's plan had its detractors. Many argued that government regulations still existed, that the sports market was not sufficiently mature, that the fan base was too small, and that sports agents and sports marketing professionals were too few in number and too inexperienced. Also, problems with television coverage existed with only state channels and provincial satellite TVs accessible across the whole of China. In fact, there was only one state TV channel dedicated to sport content. In addition, Twitter, Facebook, Instagram, and YouTube were all unavailable. Nonetheless, Chinese social media was extensive, using sites such as Sina Weibo, WeChat, and MiaoHi.

Despite some misgivings, in the last couple of years, the sports industry has powered ahead at a conservative rate of 16% a year, driven by the marketing of sport and sporting goods. Indeed, China has become the world's largest supplier of sporting goods equipment, the majority of which is manufactured by small-scale enterprises. In addition, founded on the success of former NBA star Yao Ming and retired Chinese tennis star Li Na, sponsorship deals have grown exponentially. Prior to Li Na's Grand Slam victory in Melbourne, Chinese sports sponsorship was worth an estimated US$2 billion a year. By the beginning of 2017, that figure had grown to about US$18 billion. The overwhelming success of Nike's sponsorship of Li Na and the NBA's sponsorship of Yao Ming proved the value of home grown stars.

By 2015, the sports media rights and sponsorship markets had exploded. Ti'ao Dongli, a major Chinese sports broadcasting company, acquired the five-year broadcasting rights for the Chinese Super League (CSL) at a cost of around US$1.3 billion, a huge increase from the US$50 million the CSL had received only two years earlier. Multimedia rights were on-sold to China's leading Internet-based company, Le Sports, for US$420 million, and Chinese Insurer Ping An became a prime sponsor. In February 2015, the Wanda Group became the majority owner of sports marketing company, Infront Sports and Media, integrating it later that year into Wanda Sports Holding. This included the iconic endurance brand IRONMAN, making Wanda Sports one of the world's leading sports business entities.

By May 2016, China Everbright, a leading financial services company, together with Beijing Baofeng, an Internet entertainment and technology company specializing in virtual reality and digital entertainment, had acquired a majority interest in MP & Silva, one of the world's largest media rights companies. Further, in 2016, the Hisense Group secured a sponsorship with the UEFA European Championship. Hisense subsequently claimed that the sponsorship increased sales in China by almost 9%, and sales elsewhere by close on 6%. Hisense did not simply put their name before the public; they actively sought to connect their brand with consumers.

Of all sports, football proved the key driver due to three major factors. First, it was essential, politically, economically, culturally, and patriotically, to be involved in sports – China's 13th five-year plan had made that plain. Second, football was (and remains) the stated passion of President Xi Jinping, and many Chinese billionaires saw the political advantages that an association with football might provide. Third, football is the most-watched game in the world and contributes in some way to more than 40% of the entire industry's profit. To ignore football was to ignore a large part of the sporting world.

Involvement started gradually but increased at an exponential rate. The giant Alibaba Group purchased a minority holding in Guangzhou Evergrande, a five-time CSL champion and the first Chinese club to participate in the FIFA Club World Cup. Building on this, between 2015 and 2017, Chinese investors poured almost US$2.5 billion into world football, purchasing stakes in, among many others, Italy's Inter Milan and AC Milan, England's Manchester City, West Bromwich Albion, Aston Villa, Birmingham City, and Wolverhampton Wanderers, Spanish clubs Espanyol, Granada CF, and Atletico Madrid, French club Sochaux, Dutch club ADO Den Haag, and Czech club Slavia Prague. Even clubs in the United States and Australia have been brought into the Chinese sphere.

Most Chinese investors have not simply sought to involve themselves in football because of their love of the game. Rather they are using their position to vigorously market their own products. Suning Holdings Group, one of the largest non-government retailers in China, recently purchased a controlling interest in Italian club Inter Milan. Zhang Jindong, the billionaire chairman of Suning Holdings and a man with noted connections to President Xi Jinping, noted that the aim was to integrate Suning into the local area and then into Italy. "Ours is an international business", he stated, "and our brand will soon be big in Europe too."

Football is not the only sport that has interested China's billionaires. Soon after buying control of Spanish football club Granada CF, Lizhang Jiang, general manager of Shanghai Double-Edged Sports, together with real estate investor Meyer Orbach, bought a minority share in the NBA's Minnesota Timberwolves.

Also gaining rapid growth is China's sport equipment manufacturing sector, which has capitalized on the benefits of marketing home-branded sports equipment to the vastly growing Chinese sports market. Anta Sportswear revenue, for example, reached US$1.72 billion by the beginning of 2016, giving it a net recorded profit of US$417 million.

At this time, the Chinese sport investment model's marketing success remains unclear, if promising. After all, government support into other industries has not always guaranteed success. It also remains uncertain how, or if, China's destabilizing mountain of debt may affect the sport industry and its marketing yield. For some individuals and companies, the cost of long-term personal and financial commitment will become a burden. There are plenty of challenges ahead. But, for some, like Wanda Group's Wang Jianlin, one of China's richest individuals, there are few fears. As he put it, "The Wanda Group is not solely about making purchases in the sports industry." Rather, its aim is "to enlarge and strengthen its business in related industries like tourism through involvement in the sports industry." He emphasized that "The longer you build your brand, the better you'll benefit. That's the merit of the sports industry."

CASE STUDY QUESTIONS

1 In order to better understand the current status and potential for the sports industry in China, discuss what you perceive as its key opportunities and challenges.

2 To what extent have the political, social, and cultural aspects of China influenced its sports industry?

3 How successful do you think Chinese companies will be in marketing European football teams to the Chinese public? What problems might you envisage?

CASE STUDY 11.2

Marketing women's AFL in Australia

If you are a resident of Australia or you have visited the country, then you would be intimately familiar with Australians' love of 'Aussie Rules', or to give it the correct name, Australian Rules Football. First started under the auspices of the Victorian Football League in 1897 and then the Australian Football League in 1990, Aussie Rules has grown to be arguably the foremost sport in Australia. There are now 18 teams in the AFL competition spread across five states. Each week during the season, over 33,000 fans on average gather to watch each of the games, giving the AFL the fourth-highest attendance figures of any professional sport in the world. Since its first formal game, Aussie Rules' speed, aerial leaping, kicking, and combative nature have made the sport a favourite in most of the country's regions. Despite the sport's popularity and professionalism, it has remained almost exclusively a male-dominated sport. That is, until recently.

The idea to have a professional women's Aussie Rules League (AFLW) was born several years ago. Interestingly, the initial thrust for the development of the game came from women players, rather than from the men's sport or from any marketer who might have considered the marketing implications of introducing what was at that time considered a novelty sport. In 2010, an AFL-sponsored report recommended that the AFL Commission – its independent board of management – begin working toward the establishment of a national women's league. This was followed in 2013 by an exhibition match. Two years later a further exhibition game was shown on free-to-air television, which perhaps surprisingly, attracted extremely strong ratings with over 1 million viewers tuning in.

The marketing problems inherent in forming the AFLW were, however, quite formidable. Three in particular were of obvious concern. First and foremost was the question of how the league, and thus the players, were to be funded. Second, was the simple fact that there existed only a small coterie of female players already playing the sport at anything like a senior level. And third, was the vexatious question of how to sell a women's game to an audience already fixated on the male sport.

Despite a certain amount of initial controversy concerning whether or not the men's sport should subsidies that of the women's, the AFL, together with a major sponsor, the National Australia Bank, ultimately came to an interim agreement to financially support an AFLW. The pay deal struck for the founding 2017 seven-match and finals season gave marquee players a financial package of AUS$27,000, which included allowances for marketing and ambassadorial roles, priority players AUS$12,000, and other players AUS$8,500. For 2018, pay was increased by between 3% and 16%. Some ancillary costs for travel, insurance, out-of-pocket expenses, and carer's allowance were also included. By comparison, the average salary of female Australian cricketers will raise to AUS$52,000 by 2021, whereas the pay for elite female players will reach AUS$210,000 by that year. The average pay of around AUS$12,000 for women's players compares to an average of around AUS$300,000 for their male counterparts, albeit for a much longer season.

The issue of finding sufficient players for the proposed eight-team AFLW posed a separate puzzle. Almost without exception, the marquee players were self-selected. All were playing or had played in recognized women's amateur leagues. Most had played the game since early youth. A few priority players had some experience of the game, but for the most part all the remaining players were junior or elite athletes from other sports. Of course, the idea of transferring skills from one sport to another is not new, but has rarely been undertaken on such a vast scale. Women from numerous different sports together with Olympic-level athletes tried out for the AFLW, and in the main, were given strong support from their established sports.

Marketing the sport to a sceptical audience was another matter. Under the auspices of the AFL, the league was branded the 'AFL Women's League' with a stylized rendition of an Australian Rules football goal square and goal posts drawn from a perspective which shows a 'W' as the official logo. The National Australia Bank was named as the league's naming rights sponsor with a number of smaller sponsors backing individual clubs.

Rather cleverly, the AFLW marketing team revamped an old advertisement taken from a 1994 campaign for the men's game. This saw some of the world's foremost athletes viewing scenes showcasing the skills of AFL players with the tag line, 'I'd like to see that'. The advertisement drawing on the historical legacy of the game portrayed black-and-white footage of the AFLW and ended with Moana Hope, probably the foremost female exponent of the sport, commenting, "Women making a name for themselves in Aussie Rules Football? We'll show you that."

Jemma Wong, AFL campaign lead and marketing manager, argued that the promotional campaign would be "bold, empowering and inclusive" and would "rally a generation of young girls". Although aimed directly at a younger female population, the vague, pseudo-sexual overtones of lithe, attractive females in a combative mode were also considered advantageous. This, of course, simply reflected the way in which the male sport was marketed. The advertisements were pivotal to the marketing of the game and were largely successful.

In the inaugural AFLW season a deal was struck which saw one selected Saturday night game per week being shown on free-to-air Channel 7 television, the AFL website, the league's 'app', while all the games were shown on pay TV network Fox. Costs were borne by the television channels and no licensing fee was paid to the league. Ensuring total professionalism, Channel 7 engaged a previous best and fairest Brownlow medallist, Patrick Dangerfield, as an on-air commentator. He was supported by other recognized superstars. With the exception of some double-headed matches, nearly all normal league games had free entry. Now, after proving the viability of the concept, fans appear far more likely to be prepared to pay for entry.

How successful has the AFL Women's League been? The initial week saw over 50,000 attend the four matches with one stadium locking out over 1,000 fans because of the at-capacity crowd, and the Grand Final was watched by a gate of 16,000 exuberant fans.

Although undoubtedly successful, the question remains whether the initial success can be followed up during future seasons. Much depends upon the attitude of the AFL. Certainly, the interest in the AFLW together with its influential media coverage has offered the men's sport the opportunity to market itself into a different social demographic. If success is to continue, the AFL must make the venues more attractive to the public. Deliberately choosing small or inadequate grounds on which to play the women's game denotes a lack of genuine concern for the nascent league. Similarly, the women's game requires much greater coverage on the AFL website and social media platforms.

In addition, for the sport to prosper, far greater financial assistance is needed. Club payments in 2017 for the women totalled only AUS$2.275 million. Further support from the AFL took this amount to over AUS$4 million. Around AUS$3 to 4 million flowed into the sport from sponsorship. However, as a general rule, sponsors are unwilling to finance individuals and teams that fail to get good exposure. In the case of the AFLW, adroit marketing developed immense hype, and many minor sponsors jumped on board seeking to reach a new audience. Having a new sport marked a clean slate for sponsors.

It is worthwhile speculating what made the initial season of the AFLW league connect so profoundly with the Australian public. Certainly, it was the novelty of the sport at the elite level, the potential for seeing women in combative games, and the opportunity for women fans of men's AFL to support their own gender. But, it was probably much more than these factors as well. Although not an elite sport, there are some 350,000 girls and women playing the game at a grassroots level. These numbers provide a compelling explanation for why the sport attracted so much attention. Add to the number of players all the parents, families, partners, and friends of the participants, and the market becomes significant. Indeed, one wonders why women's football never progressed beyond the amateur level before.

One should not be too critical of the AFL. Despite many lost opportunities for promoting the game, their support for the successful marketing strategy proved instrumental. Their ability to get free-to-air television as well as pay TV coverage without cost was close to genius. With games on TV every week a ready-made audience was assured. Additionally, having the women's teams bear the same names and wear the same outfits as the men's teams provided ready identification and a supporter base. In addition, many of the traditional AFL audience were fed up with the off-field behaviour of male players in all codes and probably thought that there was far less chance of such behaviour in the women's league. Many of the female players were already well known in their own sports and brought with them an established fan base interested to see how their skills would translate to a new environment. And one should never discount Australian's love of sport. Now the AFL must persist in ensuring that TV provides higher-quality coverage and higher-quality commentary that includes female presenters.

Nonetheless, before getting too excited about women's AFL, the game needs to find a way to overcome the traditionally limited concept that views female sports as less interesting to watch than male sports. Quoted in the U.S. *The Nation* magazine, Dr Marie Hardin, dean of Penn State University's College of Communications and a long-time student of sport marketing, suggests that simply providing greater access to female sports or promoting women to more sports journalist or editorial positions will not suffice. "If that were true" she observed, "media outlets would be doing it. Nobody does more audience research and understands consumers of women's sports better than ESPN. If they thought they could make massive amounts of money from coverage of women's sports, they would be doing it."

Will Australians' love affair with women's Aussie Rules continue? Realistically, there is little expectation that the league will be self-funding for a number of years. Making any sort of commercially viable female sports competition has always been a challenge. However, the women's league may be expected to bring in thousands of additional fans with around 27% of the AFL participation base now being female. The junior AFL Auskick program also now has thousands of young girls taking up the sport. For the first time they will have inspirational role models to look up to in the women's league and potentially a pathway to a professional career. Regardless of any other reason, the inauguration of the AFLW league is a significant step in the progress of women's sport marketing.

CASE STUDY QUESTIONS

1   Women in sport are often seen as second class in comparison to men's sport despite the fact that almost 40% of all participants are female and provide about a third of the fan base. This is generally given as a reason that TV coverage of women's sport rates far below that of men's sport. Do you consider this a true statement and, if so, why?

2   What do you perceive to be the strengths and weaknesses of the AFLW marketing campaign? Can you suggest any improvements?

3   Traditionally, sponsorship for female sport receives less than 15% of that given to male sport. Is this a failure of the corporate world or are there more valid reasons? Should sponsorship be provided based on the gender of the participants?

CHAPTER 12

Media

OVERVIEW

This chapter examines the key features of the relationship between sport and the media with reference to its management. It provides an examination of the ways in which sport and the media interact depending on the three-sector model of sport, the commercial foundations of the sport media relationship, in particular the sale of broadcast rights, and the ways in which governments regulate the sport media relationship. It concludes with a brief acknowledgement of the role of the sport media manager in the professional sport industry.

After completing this chapter the reader should be able to:

• Identify the ways in which the sport media relationship is dependent on the three-sector model of sport;

- Understand and explain the various dimensions of the commercial foundations of the sport media relationship;
- Understand and explain the rationale for government to intervene in the sport media relationship via regulation;
- Comment on the development of the role of the sport media manager.

WHAT IS THE MEDIA?

The media is often considered to provide three broad functions in a society: information, education, and entertainment. However, in terms of the sport media relationship, it has become increasingly clear that media organizations and consumers are interested in professional sport in particular because of its entertainment value. The exploits of leagues, teams, and athletes are reported throughout the world, across a wide range of print (e.g. newspapers and magazines) and broadcast (e.g. radio, television and the Internet) media. Some of this media coverage is provided as 'news', which essentially means that media organizations report on what is happening in sport in much the same way they report on politics or world events. However, a significant component of broadcast coverage is provided through exclusive arrangements in which media organizations purchase the rights to broadcast an event or season(s).

In understanding the management of the sport media relationship, it is important to keep in mind that the word 'media' has a diverse set of meanings. The word 'media' can represent the entire media industry, particularly when we refer to the sport media relationship, or the way in which the media reports on a particular sport or athlete. The word can also be used to refer to a form, channel, platform, company, network, or station, depending on the context. Television, radio, print, and Internet can all be considered media forms or distribution channels. These media forms and channels also have individual outlets: television networks or stations such as ESPN (a network) or FUEL TV (a station on the Fox Sports network), specific newspapers (such as *La Gazzetta dello Sport*, the Italian sport newspaper published since 1896), radio stations (such as SEN, a sport radio station in Melbourne, Australia), or Internet websites (such as www.si.com, the website of *Sports Illustrated*, owned by company Time, Inc.). These outlets are typically privately owned and employ journalists, writers, and commentators to generate content in order to attract an audience, in the hope of returning a profit. A television network is typically a collection of individual stations that people tune into to watch their favourite sport or catch up on daily news, which is owned by a media company. More recently, the term platform has been used to describe media such as Facebook or Twitter, where the interactivity and user-driven content is such that they cannot be considered a media outlet in the same way as a single newspaper or television station.

THE SPORT MEDIA RELATIONSHIP

In the first chapter of this book you were introduced to the three-sector model of sport: public, nonprofit, and private. In Chapters 2 and 3 the public and nonprofit sectors were examined, and in Chapter 4 the professional sport industry was explored. In order to understand the relationship between sport and the media, it is important to acknowledge that all three sectors of sport need the media in order to survive and prosper in contemporary society. However, it is also important to acknowledge that each sector seeks to establish a relationship with the media for different purposes. In order to provide context for the rest of the chapter, and for other chapters within the book, it is important to explore each sector in turn.

In Chapter 2 the role of the state and the reasons for state intervention were explored. When the state seeks to regulate or control sporting activities, for example, it also typically seeks to explain the rationale for its decisions and any subsequent actions it might take. The state might wish to make its citizens aware that it has regulated a particular sporting activity in order to make it safer for children, to reduce the injury toll, or to ensure that corruption is eliminated. It is very difficult for the state to communicate effectively with its citizens directly – this is most problematic for national governments and least problematic although still difficult for local governments. Instead, the state relies on the media to act as an intermediary between it and its citizens. Governments and government departments also use the media to seek social, political, and economic legitimacy, as well as promote their activities and gain status. National sporting institutes are often funded almost entirely by national governments and operate as de-facto government departments. Taxes collected from citizens are spent on the selection, training, coaching, accommodation and welfare of elite athletes in order to secure international sporting success at events such as the Olympic Games and world championships. As such, the success or failure of a nation's elite athletes is invariably a public issue – the Games or events are broadcast on television and widely reported throughout the media. If a nation's athletes perform well then the state and its agencies are likely to claim that they had an important role and that this demonstrates their strategic and managerial abilities. These claims are made through the media and in doing so the approval of a nation's citizens is sought. If a nation's athletes perform poorly and below expectations, then the media is likely to actively question the performance of the elite institute and by association the government and its agencies. In these cases the state is somewhat unwillingly drawn into discussion about its performance that is conducted by and through the media.

In Chapter 3 the role of nonprofit sport organizations was examined and it was noted that nonprofit sport organizations exist at all levels of the sport industry and landscape, which influences the ways in which they interact with the media. For example, the following organizations are all nonprofit: the International Olympic Committee (IOC), which runs the Olympic Games; New Zealand Rugby, the national governing body for rugby union in New Zealand, which is responsible for the development of community rugby as well as the performance of the national team the All Blacks; Netball Queensland, the governing body for the sport of netball in the State of Queensland, Australia; and Hills Ultimate Frisbee, an ultimate Frisbee league in the Western suburbs of Sydney, Australia. The relationship with the media is vastly different across each of these nonprofit organizations. The IOC receives approximately US$3 billion every four years from media organizations for the right to broadcast the summer and winter Olympics. The media interact with New Zealand Rugby on a number of levels, but perhaps most of all in covering the All Blacks, the most popular and prominent national team in New Zealand and in paying broadcast rights fees for international and Super Rugby matches. Netball Victoria seeks the support of regional media outlets in encouraging more people to play the sport of netball, as well as in promoting the Queensland Firebirds, a semi-professional team in Suncorp Super Netball (the Australian netball league). Hills Ultimate Frisbee predominantly seeks the support of local media in promoting the sport of ultimate Frisbee in order to attract more people to the sport, which in turn ensures the viability of its leagues and clubs. These examples all illustrate that the nonprofit sector is the most varied of all the sport sectors in terms of the types of organizations, in addition to the sport-media relationships that are developed and fostered.

In Chapter 4 the role and activities of professional sport organizations were examined. Professional organizations, such as the teams that play in the National Football League (NFL) in the United States, compete in Formula 1 across the world or play in the English Premier League, are considered to be at the apex of the sport industry because of the scope of their operations and because the athletes and staff associated with these organizations are full-time professionals. These organizations have an intimate relationship with the media to the point that the financial viability of large media organizations and professional sport leagues and teams are inextricably linked. Professional sport organizations receive broadcast rights fees directly from media organizations, leverage the media coverage they receive through these agreements to secure lucrative sponsorship deals, as well as seek to secure as much media coverage as possible through media outlets not governed by exclusive rights agreements. At the same time, media organizations are seeking to cover professional sport organizations in order to increase their audience, which has necessitated sport organizations to employ staff in a variety of media, public relations, and communication management roles. The proliferation of media channels, particularly online and social, has made these roles more complex and specialized.

In order to understand the management implications of a relationship between sport and media organizations, it is essential that you are aware of the type of media organization and the type of sport organization that is involved. As illustrated by the earlier discussion of the three sectors of sport, the type of sport organization can significantly alter the type of sport media relationship that is negotiated or entered into. For a sport organization the relationship could be predicated on securing a financial return on investment, generating political legitimacy or credibility in the marketplace, or promoting activities and events in order to attract more members or increase participation. These goals and outcomes will also be influenced by the type of media organizations that are engaged in the relationship. It is important to keep in mind that not all sport media relationships are the same, and each must be examined in detail in order to reveal the expectations, agreements, and benefits.

In practice 12.1 The NBC Olympics

NBCUniversal (NBCU) is an America multimedia company majority owned by Comcast, of which the most important divisions are NBC, one of the three major free-to-air television networks in the United States, and Universal Studios, one of the world's leading film studios. NBC has been home to some of the world's most popular and iconic television programs, such as *Seinfeld* and *Friends*, as well as sports such as the National Football League (NFL), NASCAR, and the National Hockey League (NHL).

NBC has also been a long-time broadcaster of the Olympic Games, televising its first Games in 1964 (Tokyo), with unbroken coverage beginning in 1988 (Seoul) for the summer Games and 2002 (Salt Lake City) for the winter Games.

NBCU reportedly paid US$3.5 billion for the rights to broadcast the Games from 1996 to 2008, then paid US$2.2 billion for the rights to the 2010 winter and 2012 summer Games. In 2011, NBCU acquired the rights to broadcast the Olympic Games until 2020, which at the time included the 2016 and 2020 summer Games and the 2018 winter Games. In 2014 NBCU and the International Olympic Committee (IOC) announced a landmark agreement that IOC President Thomas referred to as helping to ensure the Olympic Movement's "financial security in the long term", such is the importance of the U.S. broadcasting rights to the overall financial health of the Games. NBCU acquired the rights to broadcast all Games up until 2032 across "all media platforms, including free-to-air television, subscription television, internet and mobile" for US$7.65 billion. NBCU also provided the IOC with a US$100 million signing bonus, to be used to promote Olympism and Olympic values between 2015 and 2020.

Brian Roberts, chairman and CEO of Comcast, noted as part of the announcement that the

> Olympics are the world's greatest cultural and athletic event, and presenting them to the American audience is an honour and privilege for our entire company. Our long-term commitment to and investment in the Olympic Movement are a reflection of our belief in the future of broadcast television.

Following the 2016 Games, however, some media commentators were questioning whether NBCU's investment was worth it, as it appeared that ratings dropped among 18- to 49-year-olds, compared to the 2012 Games, with speculation that younger people were turning away from broadcast television and accessing content via other channels and outlets, especially social and digital media.

Sources: NBCUniversal website at <www.nbcuniversal.com>; IOC website at <www.olympic.org>; Bloomberg website at <www.bloomberg.com>

COMMERCIAL DIMENSIONS OF THE SPORT MEDIA RELATIONSHIP

The way in which the commercial dimensions of the sport media relationship operate can be divided into five interrelated components, which are represented in Figure 12.1. First, media organizations pay for the right to broadcast a sport event, season, or series of games. These broadcast rights are typically limited to free-to-air television, pay television, radio, the Internet and digital mobile, and of these five the two television forms are by far the biggest players. In Figure 12.1 this is demonstrated by the sport organization providing the official broadcaster with content and in return the broadcaster pays a rights fee. In

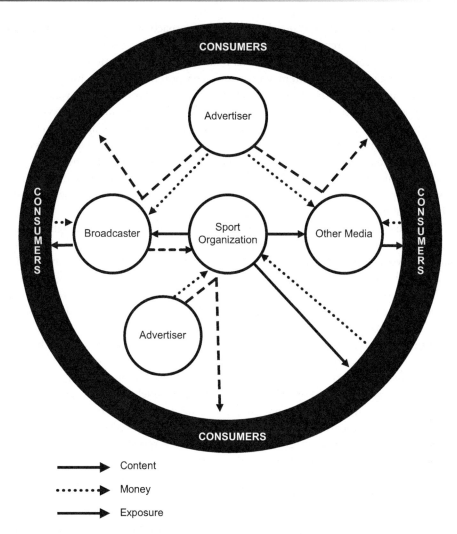

FIGURE 12.1 Sport and media relationships

Source: adapted from Nicholson (2007)

contrast to most forms of electronic media, however, the print media typically reports on sport in a heavily competitive environment in a news or public-interest capacity, rather than a promotional capacity via an exclusive contract or arrangement, and as such are not charged a fee by sport organizations.

Second, media organizations that purchase the rights to broadcast a sport event, season, or series of games seek to secure a return on investment. On free-to-air television this is primarily achieved through the sale of advertising space and time, which in Figure 12.1 is represented by the advertiser acquiring exposure to consumers via the broadcaster. The number of people, as well as the type of people, watching the sport is directly proportional to advertising revenue and to broadcast rights fees. On pay television, a return on investment is achieved by the sale of advertising space and by attracting subscribers who, in general terms, are prepared to pay for a generic service, dedicated sport channels, or pay-per-view events. In Figure 12.1 this relationship is represented by the consumer paying the broadcaster for content which has been purchased by the broadcaster from the sport organization. In the case of pay television, the number of people watching sport and, more specifically those who are prepared to pay, is directly proportional to the broadcast rights fees. The popularity and appeal of sport also mean that acquiring the rights to broadcast sport events and games can increase the broadcaster's brand awareness, which in turn might increase the demand for other non-sport related content (Hoehn and Lancefield 2003). This phenomenon is likely to be greater if a broadcaster has held the rights for an extended period of time and consumer loyalty to both the sport and media products has been established.

Third, media organizations that do not have the exclusive broadcast rights will also seek to attract advertising revenue through coverage of sport. For example, a sport magazine or newspaper will invest in the coverage of sport in a non-exclusive and typically a non-official capacity, which will in turn attract consumers. This is represented in Figure 12.1 where consumers pay other media providers for sport-related content. Based on the size and demographics of the readership, advertisers will pay the magazine or newspaper to access consumers.

Fourth, sport organizations seek to attract sponsorship revenue based on the sport's popularity, which in turn is proportional to the amount of media coverage achieved. In this way, sport organizations secure additional revenue via the broadcaster, as well as via the media coverage provided by other media outside the exclusive rights agreement. The consumer might pay for the content by purchasing a newspaper or magazine, or may receive the content for free through an Internet or radio news program. These relationships are represented in Figure 12.1, whereby the sponsor receives exposure to consumers via the broadcaster and other media, and the sport organization receives a direct financial benefit. Thus, sport organizations must not only maximize media coverage that results from exclusive broadcast rights agreements, but must also seek to maximize general media coverage, thereby increasing exposure, awareness, interest, and audience share.

Finally, sport organizations are able to provide mediated sport content directly to consumers. In Figure 12.1 this is represented by consumers paying the sport organization for the product or content. With the rapid advancement of technology, over the last 10 years in particular, organizations have been able to provide content direct to fans and consumers. Large sporting teams in popular national leagues now have their own 'television' channels, which are typically broadcast through the Internet, either free or as a special addition to subscription and membership packages. Whether the product or content is free or has been purchased, the popularity of sport organization created content is such that companies beyond the traditional suite of sponsors are now prepared to pay to get access to the consumers of this media. In Figure 12.1 this is represented by advertisers paying sport organizations directly in order to get access to the consumers and fans of the sport organization. The amount that advertisers are prepared to pay is directly proportional to the size and type of the audience. Prior to the development of technologies that have enabled sport teams, leagues, and federations to become their own broadcasters, these type of advertising relationships were rare and commercial relationships were limited to key sponsors. Although it is still true that sponsors are the dominant advertisers within this setting, the value of being able to access a distinct and measurable consumer market is now also becoming evident to non-sponsor advertisers.

The example of the Australian Football League illustrates the importance of the media to the commercial success of contemporary sport organizations. The Australian Football League is the governing body for Australian football and manages the national competition, the AFL, as well as being responsible for game development throughout the nation. The AFL competition consists of 18 teams and is the most popular sport in Australia in terms of live attendance, television ratings, and the size of its television broadcast rights. The AFL is also one of the world's most popular sports using the criteria of average game/match attendance. In 2016 the AFL's revenue was AUS$517 million, of which 'broadcasting and AFL media' accounted for AUS$264 million. In addition, commercial operations accounted for AUS$186 million, a significant proportion of which was received from sponsors. These sponsors, as demonstrated by the earlier discussion of the commercial foundations of the sport media relationship, are prepared to invest in the sport on the basis of increased exposure, awareness, and sales, which are generated most significantly through the sport's media coverage. It is clear that the financial stability of the AFL, like almost all national sporting leagues throughout the world, is dependent on the media.

In practice 12.2 Ronaldo – Twitter MVP

Twitter is a microblogging service launched in July 2006 that has grown to be one of the world's largest social networking sites. It allows users to send messages of up to 140 characters. Users follow other users to create a personalized newsfeed and interact by tagging others using their handle (e.g. @Twitter) or hashtags. According to Twitter Counter, as of July 2017, the top 10 individuals followed on Twitter were 1. Katy Perry, 2. Justin Bieber, 3. Barack Obama, 4. Taylor Swift, 5. Rihanna, 6. Ellen DeGeneres, 7. Lady Gaga, 8. Justin Timberlake, 9. Christiano Ronaldo, and 10. Britney Spears. The top 10 lacks diversity, dominated by North American musicians, with Obama, DeGeneres, and Ronaldo the exceptions.

Christiano Ronaldo is a professional footballer who plays for the Portuguese national team and Real Madrid, a Spanish club in La Liga. In 2017, Ronaldo was ranked by *Forbes* as the world's highest-paid athlete, with total earnings of US$93 million, comprising US$58 million in salary and US$35 million in endorsements, and Real Madrid was ranked as the fifth most valuable sport team in the world at US$3.58 billion, behind the Dallas Cowboys, New York Yankees, Manchester United, and Barcelona. In July 2017, Ronaldo had 55.4 million Twitter followers, and Real Madrid had 24.6 million. According to Twitter Counter, on average, Ronaldo is followed on Twitter by another 49,360 followers per day, meaning that he will achieve 73 million followers in 2018 and, if the trend continues, 235 million followers by 2027.

Ronaldo's social media popularity is one of the main reasons that he is able to generate endorsement revenue of US$35 million per year. An analysis of his Twitter feed reveals posts that promote a wide range of Ronaldo's sponsors, such as major sponsor Nike, particularly the range of CP7 clothes and footwear, Herbalife Nutrition, Nubia smart phones, Egyptian Steel, EA Sports, Altice, Tag Heuer, and Poker Stars, among others. Ronaldo also uses Twitter to promote social causes, such as World Refugee Day and World Blood Donor Day, as well as appeals regarding the Syrian crisis. In 2016 it was reported that a single tweet from NBA basketball player LeBron James to his 27.9 million followers (at the time) was worth $165,000, which means that a single Ronaldo tweet is worth more than US$200,000. Twitter, along with other social media platforms such as Facebook and Instagram, has given athletes like Ronaldo the ability to communicate directly with fans in ways that were not available even at the end of the 20th century, as well as to commercialize their popularity. The social media revolution has forever changed the ways in which fans, athletes, teams, and leagues interact.

BROADCAST RIGHTS

The importance of sport is such that major national and international broadcasters almost always bid for the rights to high-profile sports (Hoehn and Lancefield 2003). In fact, the rights to 'premium' sports have become such an important commercial property that not having them can adversely affect a company's financial bottom line or in extreme cases lead to the demise of media organizations (which in some jurisdictions has led to the regulation of exclusive rights agreements with a single broadcaster). Sport and sport broadcasting rights have special features that are not exhibited by other media products, making them extremely valuable national and global commodities. Sport events and games are an ephemeral product or perishable good, which means that they endure or last for a very brief period of time (Tonazzi 2003; Sandy, Sloane and Rosentraub 2004). Consider the difference between sport programs and drama programs broadcast on television. Sport programs almost always exist for the duration that they are live – the unpredictability of sport attracts people to a spectacle that appears to unfold or develop as the audience is experiencing it. Great sporting events and contests contain enough stories, intrigue, and emotion that they prompt commentators and fans alike to wonder whether a script writer could have written it any better. This is particularly true when games are won in the last seconds; when heroic deeds are performed at personal expense; and when sport transcends political, racial, and geographic barriers and stereotypes. Drama programs, by contrast, have a significant 'shelf life'. Popular television drama programs are watched again and again by fans, often in large quantities as part of 'binge consumption'. Even though consumers know the plot, characters, and ending after a first viewing, second and third viewings are still pleasurable. Except for the diehard fan, this is almost never the case with sport, perhaps in part because there are new games and matches being played continuously around the world. Individual instances of sporting consumption are fleeting, but the institution itself is enduring, which makes it extremely attractive to broadcasters.

The value of sport broadcast rights is also increased by the fact that it is also very difficult for consumers of sport to satisfactorily substitute one product for another (Tonazzi 2003). In other words, a viewer who wants to watch televised games of a football league has little option but to consume the product offered by the broadcaster who has secured the rights. It is unlikely that the viewer will consider watching tennis or golf on another network a viable substitute. By contrast, a viewer interested in watching a criminal or legal drama is likely to be able to substitute a variety of products on a variety of networks and stations. In essence, each sport is a relatively unique product, which means that it is of more value than a product with multiple variants or imitations. Finally, unlike the multitude of news and drama that is available to television networks in particular, the amount of professional sport is finite (Tonazzi 2003). Moreover, premium sport leagues and events are even more limited, which means that competition to acquire the rights is greater.

The limit of substitutable products and the desire of consumers to view matches or events 'as they happen' make sport a highly valued and sought-after commodity for media organizations. Media organizations that bid for the rights to sport often view these rights as an opportunity to capture a specific demographic or new market. Premium sport content can in the best cases draw consumers to a television network, increase advertising revenue, and make non-sport network programming more popular and viable through association and cross promotion. The fact that sport is viewed as a key driver of direct and indirect revenues for media organizations has a significant impact on the size of broadcast rights, the competition to secure them, the ability of sport organizations to maximize their revenue through sponsorship, and the service that media organizations demand from their sport partners.

In practice 12.3 The National Football League – the biggest show in town

The National Football League (NFL) is the premier professional football league in North America and one of the most prominent sporting leagues in the world. In 2017, *Forbes* identified that 29 of the 32 teams in the NFL were in the top 50 most valuable sporting teams in the world, all of which had a value in excess of US$1 billion. The financial success of the teams and the League is underpinned by massive broadcast rights deals with FOX, NBC, CBS, ESPN, and DirecTV. In late 2011 the NFL signed record television rights deals worth US$28 billion, a landmark figure in the history of sport and the media. The 10-year deal announced extensions to its broadcast rights agreements with FOX, NBC, and CBS, in which the networks paid 60% more than they did under the previous agreement. These new agreements run through to the 2022 season, having been activated in 2014. They provide unprecedented financial security for the NFL and its teams, but are often questioned by media and business analysts in terms of the profitability for the media networks that fight to secure them.

Under the agreements signed in 2011, each network (FOX, NBC, and CBS) gets the rights to three Super Bowls. In 2017, the first overtime game in Super Bowl history, between the New England Patriots and the Atlanta Falcons, was watched by

111.3 million television viewers in an average of 53.6 million homes. According to Nielsen, since 2010 the Super Bowl has been watched by more than 100 million viewers, with television networks recouping their rights investment by charging as much as US$5 million for a 30-second advertising spot. NBC has the broadcast rights to Sunday night games, and from week five of the season onwards (there are 16 games per team conducted over a 17-week season) these Sunday games operate on a flexible schedule, which allows particularly attractive match-ups to be moved to primetime, which benefits the broadcaster. NBC also has the rights to the primetime Thanksgiving game (the other two games on Thanksgiving are broadcast by CBS and Fox), as well as the single games that kick off each season. ESPN has the broadcast rights to the iconic *Monday Night Football*, one of the most popular programs on American television. Both CBS and Fox broadcast Sunday games.

With the rise of time-switching (where people record programs to watch later) and streaming services such as Netflix, television networks realize that there is a dwindling amount of must-see live programming, which is why the NFL can command almost US$3 billion per year for its rights. The NFL is still the 'king' when it comes to delivering audiences to advertisers; in-season games account for 23 of the 25 most-watched TV programs during the fall period in the United States, and overall, they attract twice as many viewers as primetime shows. In addition, the NFL produces its own programming through the NFL network, which broadcasts Thursday night football games, allowing the NFL the flexibility of managing its own content while maximizing its revenue through broadcast rights agreements.

Sources: NFL website at <www.nfl.com>; Forbes website at <www.forbes.com>; Nielsen website at <www.nielsen.com>;

REGULATING THE SPORT MEDIA RELATIONSHIP

The interdependence of the sport and media industries, and in particular the overtly commercial relationship between sport and television, has presented a series of challenges for governments all over the world. These challenges have included ensuring that its citizens have reasonable access to sport broadcasting on television and that media and sport organizations do not engage in practices or behaviour that is anti-competitive. The regulation of sport broadcasting by government (the state) attempts to ameliorate the problems that result from often divergent interests of audiences, broadcasters, sport organizations, and governing bodies. Hoehn and Lancefield (2003) noted that the

> pre-eminent position of sports programming in a channel's offering and as a key driver of a TV delivery/distribution platform has forced governments to intervene in media merger proposals, sports-rights contract negotiations, and disputes among TV distribution systems over access to content.

(p. 566)

This government intervention has had a significant impact on the way in which sport is broadcast, the amount of sport that audiences have access to via free-to-air (network) television, the ways in which sport organizations are able to sell broadcast rights and in some celebrated cases the ownership of sport teams.

The media industry's ever-changing complexity and diversity is such that governments often find it difficult to apply regulatory frameworks that adequately meet their policy objectives and allow the market to function as efficiently as possible. The sport media landscape is also often regarded as a separate component of the much broader media landscape because of its special features: significant audience appeal, vigorous competition between broadcasters, relatively cheap production costs, and a mutually reinforcing web of promotion between different types of media (modes and relationship to the sport). The importance of sport to both the modern media industry and consumers has resulted in government seeking to regulate the relationship between sport and broadcast media in four major areas. First, government regulation attempts to prevent the broadcast rights to sport events migrating exclusively from free-to-air television to pay or subscription television. Second, governments have developed regulatory policy aimed at ensuring that sport and media organizations do not engage in anti-competitive behaviour in the buying and selling of these broadcast rights. Such behaviour can lead to monopolies being created that will necessarily restrict supply, which in turn will raises price to a level that will exploit consumers (New and LeGrand 1999). Third, governments regulate to prohibit certain types of advertising being associated with sports broadcasting, such as tobacco advertising. Finally, government regulation attempts to limit or prevent any negative consequences of the vertical integration of the sport and media industries, such as the purchase of a sport team or league by a media organization.

Preventing the migration of premium sport content from free-to-air (network) television to pay (cable) television has been the area of most significant government regulation. Prior to the introduction of subscription and pay-per-view television, the general public were able to access sport via commercial free-to-air broadcasters and in some instances via public broadcasters funded by the state. Advocates for the continuation of this system, in which consumers have free access to major sporting competitions and events, have argued that sport has cultural and social significance that needs to be protected and that the migration of sports to pay or cable television will result in less people having access to the product because the cost imposed on the consumer will be too great. The responses by governments have varied depending on national and regional contexts. In the United States, relatively little government regulation has been required for major sports such as NFL, because no single company or network can afford the exclusive rights and segmenting the rights across free-to-air, pay, and satellite providers is financially beneficial for the league. The European Commission has argued that events such as the FIFA World Cup, the European Football Championship, and the Olympic Games are of major importance to society and as such has regulated to prevent instances where these events are broadcast exclusively on pay television. In smaller nations such as Australia, where the number of commercial free-to-air television networks was small and the perceived threat from pay television providers was considered high, the national government regulated in favour of the commercial free-to-air networks. Ensuring that free-to-air broadcasters essentially had first access to the rights to major sports and events, the government placed pay television operators at a commercial disadvantage in order to protect the interest of its citizens. This was particularly problematic for pay television providers as sport is one of the major drivers of pay television's market penetration.

A ROLE OF GROWING IMPORTANCE: THE SPORT MEDIA MANAGER

In 1919 Notre Dame Football Coach Knute Rockne forever altered the relationship between sport and the media. Dissatisfied with the way in which his college football program was being reported in the local newspaper, Rockne appointed sportswriter Archie Ward as a 'press agent', whose role was to be an 'official correspondent' for Rockne's football program. Ward was able to set the agenda for what was reported in the press, which in the contemporary sport and media landscape seems entirely reasonable but in the early part of the 20th century was a revolutionary response to managing the media. As such, Ward is considered to be the first public relations practitioner in sport (Stoldt 2013). Professional leagues in the United States soon adopted the Rockne model of media management and control by employing staff in 'press offices'. The role of the sport organization based sport media manager developed slowly during the middle part of the 20th century, but by the latter part of the century, once sport had commercialized in the 1970s and 1980s, media relations and media management were entrenched divisions within the largest sporting leagues and teams throughout the world. By the start of the 21st century staff within sport organizations in media management, media relations, or sport communications were being employed to make it as easy as possible for the media to cover their sport, essentially by facilitating access to athletes, coaches, and administrators via interviews and press conferences and by supplying media releases, media guides, and assorted information to help sport journalists and commentators do their job.

The advent of the Internet, the rise of social media, and the desire of sport organizations to take a more strategic approach to setting and shaping the sport media news agenda has changed the role of media and communications managers within sport organizations. This change has been particularly evident in large professional sport leagues and clubs. These organizations were previously concerned with facilitating as much media coverage as possible, in as many and varied media outlets as were prepared to cover them. The rise of social media platforms like Facebook and Twitter has meant that 'citizen journalism' is much more prevalent, where a person only needs access to a smart phone and the Internet and they can become an individual 'broadcaster'. This has meant that sport organizations no longer have as much control as they once did, for 'official' media outlets now comprise a small proportion of the total overall coverage. This is compounded by the fact that athletes are using social media to enhance their profile and sponsorship potential. As a result, the role of the sport media manager is becoming increasingly complex and important as sport organizations seek to protect their image, brand, and status.

SUMMARY

This chapter has provided an outline of the relationship between sport and the media. It has explored the media and the various sport media relationships prevalent within the three-sector model of sport. Importantly, this chapter examined the commercial foundations, particularly with professional sport, that underpin the sport media relationship. The chapter also examined broadcast rights, the most significant way in which sport and the media interact in the contemporary professional sport landscape. The chapter explored the reasons why governments seek to intervene in the sport media relationship through regulation, particularly in order to protect the interests of consumers via preventing the migration of premium sport content to pay or cable television. The chapter concluded with a brief introduction to the role of the sport media manager.

REVIEW QUESTIONS

1 Examine some of the largest media companies in your nation. Do many of these large media companies have an interest in sport and sport organizations via broadcast rights or the ownership of sport teams? Are sport broadcast rights held by one or two media companies or by most of the companies?

2 Explore the operations of a sport within the public sector from a media perspective. What is the relationship of this organization to the media, and how does it use the media to further its interests?

3 Explore the operations of a sport within the nonprofit sector from a media perspective. What is the relationship of this organization to the media, and how does it use the media to further its interests?

4 Explore the operations of a sport within the private sector from a media perspective. What is the relationship of this organization to the media, and how does it use the media to further its interests?

5 Using the three examples noted earlier, which organization interacts with the most diverse media? Why do you think this is so? Which organization do you think is most dependent on the media and why? What does this tell you about the interaction between sport and the media across the various sectors of sport?

6 What are the media regulations governing the broadcasting of sport in your nation or region? Are there regulations that ensure free-to-air access of particular sports? Do you think there is a political advantage in governments instituting regulation of this type? Why?

7 Examine a prominent sporting league in your nation or region, perhaps by reading their annual report or accessing publicly available documents related to the finances of the organization. What proportion of revenue is derived directly or indirectly from the media?

8 Examine a prominent sporting team in your nation or region, perhaps by reading their annual report or accessing publicly available documents related to the finances of the organization. What proportion of revenue is derived directly or indirectly from the media? Does the proportion differ from the league that you previously examined? Why might this be the case?

9 Which media form or platform is most dependent on sport and why?

10 What are the major reasons the role of a sport media manager within a professional sport organization is more complex now than it was prior to 1990, prior to 2000, and prior to now?

DISCUSSION QUESTIONS

1 Digital and social media provide sport organizations with increasing opportunities to sell their 'products' directly to fans and consumers. What are these products, and what implications does this direct selling have for traditional sport broadcasters and retailers?

2 As sport broadcasting rights have grown, some commentators have speculated that the fees that sport broadcasters, such as television networks, are paying mean that achieving a return on investment is difficult, if not impossible, from the sale of advertising or subscriptions. What other ways does sport content assist broadcasters such as television networks, and is this enough to sustain a return on investment into the future?

3 How does the ability of smaller sport organizations to sell their content directly to fans and consumers improve their ability to secure advertising and sponsorship revenue? What information or data is required to assist them to maximize the revenue gained through these sources?

4 Sport is often viewed as a product that is unable to be substituted. Does the move away from traditional broadcasting channels and towards a multitude of sport offerings mean that this is no longer the case and sport is now similar to other broadcast products such as news, drama and reality television? Why?

5 The rise of digital and social media, in addition to the rapid rate of change in media and consumption technologies, is making it difficult for governments to regulate the sport media industry. Should governments bother to regulate this diverse industry, given how many different ways and through how many channels we can now access sport, or do consumers still need governments to intervene to protect their interests?

FURTHER READING

Billings, A. and Hardin, M. (eds) (2014). *Routledge Handbook of Sport and New Media*. London: Routledge.

Boyle, R. and Haynes, R. (2009). *Power Play: Sport, the Media and Popular Culture*. Edinburgh: Edinburgh University Press.

Hutchins, B. and Rowe, D. (2012). *Sport Beyond Television: The Internet, Digital Media and the Rise of Networked Media Sport*. London: Routledge.

Nicholson, M., Kerr, A. and Sherwood, M. (2015). *Sport and the Media: Managing the Nexus*. 2nd edn. London: Elsevier Butterworth-Heinemann.

Pederson, P. (2013). *Routledge Handbook of Sport Communication*. London: Routledge.

Raney, A. and Bryant, J. (eds) (2006). *Handbook of Sports and Media*. London: Lawrence Erlbaum Associates.

RELEVANT WEBSITES

ESPN – http://espn.go.com
Fox Sports – www.foxsports.com
Sports Illustrated – www.si.com
Twitter – https://twitter.com

CASE STUDY 12.1

Telephone broadcasters and the rights to the English Premier League

This case study examines one of the most popular and visible sporting leagues in the world, the English Premier League, and the ways in which the rights to broadcast its matches are distributed worldwide. Formed in 1992, the English Premier League (EPL) is arguably the highest-profile national sporting league in the world. Although the National Football League in the United States has 29 of the top 50 most valuable sporting teams in the world (according to *Forbes*), the EPL has greater global reach as a result of its high-profile teams and players. Manchester United tops the *Forbes* 2017 list of the world's most valuable football teams, with Manchester City, Arsenal, Chelsea, Liverpool, and Tottenham Hotspur also in the top 10. Of these six teams, five have participated in every season of the EPL (Manchester City is the exception, and Everton is the only other club to have done so).

Manchester United is an example of why the EPL can claim to be the highest-profile sporting league in the world. Since the formation of the EPL in 1992, Manchester United has won a record 13 EPL titles (as of 2017), as well as two Champions League titles in 1999 and 2008. Using data gathered by market research agency Kantar, the club claims to have 659 million followers worldwide, an increase on the 139 million core fans, and 333 million followers it claimed as part of its 2010 bond prospectus and research conducted by TNS Sport. The figure of 659 million followers is staggering, particularly when it is acknowledged that this equates to approximately 1 in every 10 people on the planet. Kantar surveyed 54,000 respondents across 39 countries and then extrapolated this data, suggesting that Manchester United has 325 million followers in Asia, 173 million in Africa and the Middle East, 90 million in Europe, and 71 million in the Americas. A follower of the club included 'a respondent who either watched live Manchester United matches, followed highlights coverage or read or talked about Manchester United regularly'. Even when a stricter definition of 'favourite football team' is applied, Manchester United can apparently claim 277 million of the 659 followers as their own, which is still impressive, despite potential methodological questions relating to the data and broader population assumptions.

The popularity of EPL clubs like Manchester United and its global fan base has driven a staggering increase in the value of the league's broadcasts rights. In 2017 *Forbes* reported that the broadcast rights for the top five football leagues in the world were as follows:

- EPL (US$4,550 million: US$2,340 million domestic and US$2,210 million international)
- Bundesliga (US$1,568 million: US$1,299 million domestic and US$269 million international)
- Serie A (US$1,264 million: US$1,056 million domestic and US$208 million international)
- La Liga (US$1,260 million: US$989 million domestic and US$271 million international)
- Ligue 1 (US$903 million: US$813 million domestic and US$90 million international)

These figures illustrate the dominance of the EPL, with the league earning almost US$3 billion more in broadcast rights than its European competitor leagues, but also provide an insight into the global appeal of the EPL. International broadcast rights represent 49% of the EPL's total broadcast rights, compared to 17% for the Bundesliga, 16% for the Serie A, 22% for La Liga, and 10% for Ligue 1. The higher percentage for La Liga is driven in large part by the popularity of Real Madrid and Barcelona, but is nowhere near the figure commanded by the EPL, which secures more income via its international rights than the total rights of the other four leagues.

The broadcast rights for the EPL have grown exponentially since 1992. The first five-year deal, signed with broadcaster Sky Sports for 60 matches per year, was worth £191 million. Sky Sports remained the sole broadcast partner from 1992 to 2007, a period in which the number of matches per season increased from 60 per season to 138. The 2004–2007 broadcast rights deal was worth in excess of £1 billion, which meant the fee per year increased almost 10-fold from 1992 to 2004. Concerned about the implications of joint selling of broadcast rights, in which leagues package together all media rights and sell them to a single broadcaster in each territory, the European Commission investigated the practices of the EPL and found that individual clubs were prevented from selling rights, that only a small proportion of matches were broadcast live, and that these matches were limited to a single broadcaster. As a result of discussions between the European Commission and the EPL, amendments were made to the sale of the rights from 2007 onwards. As part of the deal, the EPL agreed to offer six balanced packages of rights (which has since increased to seven), with the additional clause that no single bidder would be allowed to buy all six. This broadcasting rights amendment agreed to by the European Commission and the EPL ended the Sky Sports monopoly of live rights to the EPL. It also introduced other players into the rights market.

In the 2007–2009 broadcast rights period, Sky Sports purchased four of the six packages and rival broadcaster Setanta purchased the remaining two. In the next round of rights, Setanta was replaced by ESPN and then in 2012, in a surprise development, the rights were shared between Sky Sports and British Telecom. The deal was worth £3 billion for three years and included Sky purchasing five of the seven available packages and BT outbidding ESPN for remaining two packages, equivalent to one quarter of the available live matches, for which it paid £246 million per season. The 2016–2019 season rights were also shared between Sky Sports and British Telecom, with £5.1 billion paid to the EPL for the rights over the three-year period, with Sky Sports paying £4.1 billion for five of the seven packages, or 126 matches per season, and British Telecom paying £1 billion for the rights to 42 matches per season.

Unlike many sporting leagues around the world, the EPL runs a blind auction for its broadcast rights. This means that media organizations do not have the opportunity to negotiate a deal to secure the rights, but rather must submit their best offer, as their competitors do the same. This blind auction process, and the massive international popularity of the league, resulted in an unusual outcome in Australia, whereby telecommunications company Optus was able to secure a three-year deal from 2016, outbidding the incumbent, pay television broadcaster Foxtel. This scenario was similar to what had occurred in 2012 in the UK, when BT Telecom was able to secure EPL matches previously broadcast by ESPN; however, in Australia the EPL rights cover all matches, whereas in the UK where there are multiple EPL rights packages, as discussed earlier. The international rights to the EPL have no collective selling clauses, which led to an unusual situation that maximized the broadcast right revenue for the EPL, but may have disadvantaged Australian EPL fans.

In Australia there are three main telecommunications companies. Using mobile phone consumers as an example of their market share, Telstra has 39.1%, Optus 24.4%, and Vodafone 19.4%, with all other providers less than 5% of the market. Bidding for and securing the broadcasting rights for the EPL was a strategic decision designed to drive additional business for Optus. Prior to 2016, Australian EPL fans had been able to watch live matches via pay television provider Foxtel, but in 2016 telecommunications company Optus won the broadcast rights, paying a reported

US$150 million for three years, compared to the previous agreement in which Foxtel reportedly paid US$45 million for three years.

In order to watch EPL matches from the 2016 season onwards, Australian consumers had to become Optus customers (such as mobile, broadband, or mobile broadband), with existing Optus customers getting free access as long as their plans were of a certain value. Optus pre-paid mobile customers needed to switch to a long-term contract (post-paid) in order to be eligible. In an open letter following the announcement of Optus securing the EPL rights, Foxtel's CEO Peter Tonagh told Australian EPL fans that Foxtel were disappointed at not being able to retain the rights and that they had competed strongly. Furthermore, he noted that after Foxtel missed out, they had sought to reach an agreement with Optus, but had failed to do so. In response to Optus' rights deal, Foxtel brokered agreements with Manchester United, Liverpool, and Chelsea to carry their 24-hour club channels, as well as programming from Arsenal, Manchester City, and Tottenham. As part of these arrangements, Foxtel subscribers would get delayed coverage of matches involving these clubs only. In 2016 and 2017 there were mixed reports about the impact of Optus' purchase of the EPL rights, with suggestions that the media coverage and audience for the EPL in Australia had dropped as a result, while at the same time Optus' sales of post-paid mobile phones in the first six months of the EPL deal were its best since 2010 and more than double its main rival.

CASE STUDY QUESTIONS

1   Given the situation that occurred in Australia as a result of the broadcast rights offered by the EPL, should the EPL consider amendments to its international collective selling practices? Why?

2   What factors explain the total broadcast rights, as well as the percentage of international broadcast rights of the EPL, compared to European competitor leagues?

3   Examine the broadcast rights for the EPL in your country. How much are the rights worth, who holds the rights, and how does the amount paid for the rights compare to the rights fees paid to broadcast national leagues (of football or other sports)?

4   Examine the distribution of the EPL rights to its constituent clubs and compare the amount received by EPL clubs from the rights to the total revenues of clubs in European competitor leagues. What does this tell you about the EPL teams and their ability to compete on the international player market?

Sources: English Premier League website at <www.premierleague.com>; Manchester United website at <www.manutd.com>; Roy Morgan website at <www.roymorgan.com>; Optus website at <www.optus.com.au>; Sydney Morning Herald website at <www.smh.com.au>; Business Insider Australia website at <www.businessinsider.com.au>

CASE STUDY 12.2

The live stream: sport in America via Facebook and Twitter

This case examines the 'broadcasting' of sport via social media platforms such as Facebook and Twitter as a way of illustrating the rapid changes occurring to the sport and media industries. The 'in practice' in the chapter that referred to the massive broadcast rights in the NFL and the previous case that referred to the broadcast rights secured by the EPL appear to suggest that television is still the dominant player in terms of sport broadcasting. But the rise of social media platforms and their increasing popularity, particularly among young people, is beginning to lay the foundations for a challenge to the traditional players in the sport media industry.

Facebook was the first social media network to be adopted by the mainstream after being founded by Harvard student Mark Zuckerberg in 2004 (it went global in September 2006). Originally designed as a network for university students to share experiences (posts), photos, and 'like' the posts of others, Facebook soon became a powerful tool for organizations and brands to connect with users. Some of the world's most popular Facebook sites are associated with sport. Cristiano Ronaldo's Facebook site has 122 million likes, Real Madrid's site has 104 million, and Barcelona has 103 million.

Micro-blogging service Twitter was launched at around the same time as Facebook, in July 2006, and has grown to become one of the world's largest networking sites. Sport has been one of the most popular forms of content on Twitter, as it is well suited to live events. Like Facebook, Twitter is also heavily associated with sport, with many of the world's sporting teams and athletes using it as a promotional platform. As noted in the 'in practice' in the chapter, as of July 2017, Cristiano Ronaldo had 55.4 million Twitter followers and was ranked in the top 10 most popular Twitter users on the planet.

Large social media players like Facebook and Twitter have spent money, time, and resources in exploring how they can occupy the territory occupied by traditional sport broadcasters. This development has not only created competition for sporting audiences, but also changed the landscape of sport broadcasting. Sport is now surrounded by a plethora of media outlets, with each outlet attempting to exploit sport's unrivalled capacity to assemble a broad audience base that can be targeted with an array of news, commentary, opinion, and product promotion. The historically 'symbiotic' relationship between sport organizations, sports fans, and media outlets has been strengthened by the entry of social media, and the result is a sport media nexus that is more varied and powerful than ever before.

In the United States, social media and sport have become heavily intertwined. This is not surprising, because a large part of sport fandom is communicating to others about the game they love. Social media gives fans a platform for discussion 24 hours a day, 7 days a week, with people from around the world electronically connected by a shared interest. This allows professional sporting teams and athletes to develop an international following, and in doing so communicate directly with fans in a way that was not possible at the end of the 20th century. Social media also allows people to voice their opinion, and in this sense it is highly democratic, because everyone has the right to speak candidly and promote their views, no matter how bizarre or strange they may appear to be. Importantly, social media also plays a significant commercial role within the sport industry, from live streaming to digital marketing. Leagues, teams, and athletes are only beginning to explore the possibilities that new social media platforms and channels provide in allowing them to connect with fans and commercialize products and services that were previously only available to a select few.

In 2016 Twitter began to expand its live streaming and has targeted sport as content that can attract both audiences and advertisers. As a centrepiece of its strategy, it purchased the rights to stream 10 Thursday night NFL games in 2016. The NFL announced that it has chosen Twitter to provide a live and free digital stream, which would be part of a 'Tri-Cast' model, in which NBC and CBS will broadcast the games, in addition to the NFL network and Twitter. In doing so, the NFL highlighted that this live streaming video would be available without authentication to over 800 million registered and non-registered users worldwide on mobile phones, tablets, PCs, and connected televisions via Twitter. NFL Commissioner Roger Goodell was quoted as saying that "Twitter is where live events unfold and is the right partner for the NFL as we take the latest step in serving fans around the world live football". It is clear that in partnering with Twitter the NFL hoped to expose its product to the widest possible market, while Twitter was seeking to attract audiences to its live streaming, and in turn attract advertisers. Twitter CEO Jack Dorsey was quoted as saying that "this is about transforming the fan experience with football", moving fans from commenting on the football via Twitter, to consuming the game through the platform.

Twitter has followed its foray into NFL live streaming with agreements with Major League Baseball (MLB), NFL Network, the PGA Tour, and the WNBA. In 2016 it was announced that Twitter had partnered with MLB to live stream one game per week, and via MLB Advanced Media's purchase of the digital media rights to the National Hockey League (NHL), would also stream one game per week of the NHL. In 2017 Twitter live streamed an MLB game each Tuesday, and in a bonus for MLB fans, this was complemented by a live stream of an MLB game via Facebook Live on Fridays. In 2017 the PGA Tour announced that as a result of a successful live streaming collaboration during the 2016 FedExCup Playoffs, Twitter would be the "exclusive global platform to distribute, on a free basis, more than 70 hours of live competition coverage across 31 tournaments through the remainder of the 2016–2017 season".

Twitter also signed an agreement in 2016 to produce exclusive live programming in conjunction with the National Basketball Association (NBA). The NBA announced that the partnership would result in the live streaming of a weekly pregame show "with first-of-its-kind elements created specifically for integration with Twitter conversation". NBA Commissioner Adam Silver was quoted as saying that "we've seen technology bring fans closer to our game, teams and players in ways we could have only imagined a decade ago. This expanded partnership will help feed our fans' growing demand for the NBA". Tellingly, Silver was also quoted as saying that Twitter has proven to be an "ideal destination for real-time sports conversations", which the NBA is acutely aware of, to the point that it has used Twitter use as a significant marketing and engagement tool.

The social media business model that NBA teams are following has become something of a benchmark. In 2011, Twitter followers of all 30 NBA teams grew by a combined 5,000%, and combined 'Likes' on NBA team's Facebook pages grew by an astounding 195,000%. This was mainly due to the willingness of NBA teams to creatively engage with their social media market. In other sports, however, the potential has only been partly explored, which is often due to restrictive rules imposed by the governing bodies. For example, Formula One racing driver, Lewis Hamilton, believes the sport should relax its restrictions on social media and instead use it to both strengthen the F1 brand among young adults and establish more intimate connections with its fans.

CASE STUDY QUESTIONS

1   Does the model of 'Tri-Casting', as highlighted in the example of NFL Thursday night games, benefit the social media platform or the sport organization more? Why?

2   Twitter broadcasting of games and sport content has largely been limited to a single game, often also broadcast on another platform, content that is not available on television, or specially created content. Is this reflective of Twitter's strategy, the greater resources of the television networks or the fan's desire for non-traditional programming?

3   Explore Twitter and Facebook broadcasting of sport content. Which is more successful? Why?

Sources: NFL website at <www.nfl.com>; PGA Tour website at <www.pgatour.com>; MLB website at <www.mlb.com>; Sports Illustrated website at <www.si.com>; NBA website at <www.nba.com>

CHAPTER 13

Sport governance

OVERVIEW

This chapter reviews the core concepts of organizational governance, explores the unique features of how sport organizations are governed, and summarizes the key research findings on the governance of sport organizations. The chapter also provides a summary of principles for governance within community, state, national, and professional sport organizations, including a section on the ethical conduct of directors.

After completing this chapter the reader should be able to:

- Identify the unique characteristics of organizational governance for corporate and nonprofit sport organizations;
- Differentiate the various theories of governance relevant to sport organizations;
- Understand and explain the role of boards, staff, volunteers, members, and stakeholder groups in governing sport organizations;
- Understand some of the challenges facing managers and volunteers involved in the governance of sport organizations;
- Have an appreciation of the importance of ethics in relation to sport governance; and
- Identify and understand the drivers of change in governance systems within sport organizations.

WHAT IS GOVERNANCE?

Organizational governance is concerned with the exercise of power within organizations and provides the system by which the elements of organizations are controlled and directed. Governance is necessary for all groups – nation-states, corporate entities, societies, associations, and sport organizations – to function properly and effectively. An organizational governance system not only provides a framework within which the business of organizations are directed and controlled but also "helps to provide a degree of confidence that is necessary for the proper functioning of a market economy" (OECD 2004, p. 11). Governance deals with issues of policy and direction for the enhancement of organizational performance rather than day-to-day operational management decision making.

The importance of governance and its implied influence on organizational performance was highlighted by Tricker (1984, p. 7) when he noted "if management is about running business, governance is about seeing that it is run properly". The Australian Sports Commission (ASC) defines governance as "the structures and processes used by an organization to develop its strategic goals and direction, monitor its performance against these goals and ensure that its board acts in the best interests of the members" (ASC 2004). Good organizational governance should ensure that the board and management seek to deliver outcomes for the benefit of the organization and its members and that the means used to attain these outcomes are effectively monitored.

A 1997 report to the Australian Standing Committee on Recreation and Sport (SCORS) identified a major concern amongst the sporting community, which was the "perceived lack of effectiveness at board and council level in national and state sporting organizations" (SCORS Working Party on Management Improvement 1997, p. 10). Over the past two decades, major sport agencies in the UK, New Zealand, and Canada have also identified improving governance of sport organizations as a strategic priority and continue to invest in governance guidelines, reviews, and assistance to improve governance practices in sport. Failures in the governance of national sport organizations, together with reviews of professional sport governance such as those conducted by the Football Governance Research Centre at the University of London, continue to highlight the importance of developing, implementing, and regulating sound governance practices in both amateur and professional sport organizations.

CORPORATE AND NONPROFIT GOVERNANCE

The literature on organizational governance can be divided into two broad areas: (1) corporate governance that deals with the governance of profit-seeking companies and corporations that focus on protecting and enhancing shareholder value and (2) nonprofit governance that is concerned with the governance of voluntary-based organizations that seek to provide a community service or facilitate the involvement of individuals in social, artistic, or sporting activities.

Studies of corporate governance have covered "concepts, theories and practices of boards and their directors, and the relationships between boards and shareholders, top management, regulators and auditors, and other stakeholders" (Tricker 1993, p. 2). The literature in this field focuses on the two primary roles of the board in first, ensuring conformance by management, and second, enhancing organizational performance. Conformance deals with the processes of supervision and monitoring of the work of managers by the board and ensuring that adequate accountability measures are in place to protect the interests of shareholders. Enhancing organizational performance focuses on the development of strategy and policy to create the direction and context within which managers will work.

The unique characteristics of nonprofit organizations demand a governance framework different to that of the corporate firm. Nonprofit organizations exist for different reasons than do profit seeking entities and generally involve a greater number of stakeholders in their decision-making structures and processes. The relationships between decision makers – the governance framework – will therefore be different from that found in the corporate world. The management processes employed to carry out the tasks of the organizations might well be similar, but a fundamental difference between nonprofit and corporate organizations is found in their governance frameworks.

Although many sports organizations such as major sporting goods manufacturers, athlete management companies, retail companies, and venues can be classed as profit seeking, the majority of sport organizations that provide participation and competition opportunities are nonprofit. These organizations include large clubs, regional associations or leagues, state or provincial governing bodies, and national sport organizations.

IS THERE A THEORY OF SPORT GOVERNANCE?

Clarke (2004) provides a unique overview of the development of theories of corporate governance. Some of the important theories applied to the study of organizational governance include agency theory, stewardship theory, institutional theory, resource dependence theory, network theory, and stakeholder theory. In this section we shall examine each of them in turn and assess how relevant they are to understanding the governance of sport organizations.

Agency theory proposes that shareholders' interests should prevail in decisions concerning the operation of an organization. Managers (agents) who have been appointed to run the organization should be subject to extensive checks and balances to reduce the potential for mismanagement or misconduct that threatens shareholders' interests. This has been the predominant theoretical approach to the study of corporate governance and has focussed on exploring the best ways to maximize corporate control of managerial actions, information for shareholders, and labour in order to provide some assurance that managers will seek outcomes that maximize shareholder wealth and reduce risk. In relation to corporations operating in the sport industry that have individual, institutional, and government shareholders, this theory helps explain how governance systems work. For the majority of nonprofit sport organizations, which have diverse stakeholders who do not have a financial share in the organization (aside from annual membership fees), agency theory has limited application.

Stewardship theory takes the opposite view to agency theory and proposes that rather than assume managers seek to act as individual agents to maximize their own interests over those of shareholders, managers are motivated by other concepts such as a need for achievement, responsibility, recognition, and respect for authority. Thus, stewardship theory argues that managers' and shareholders' interests are actually aligned and that managers (agents) will act in the best interests of shareholders. This theoretical view can also be applied to sport corporations such as Nike, Fox Sports, or a listed professional football club franchise. The application of either agency or stewardship theory is dependent on the actions of the managers (who choose to act as agents or stewards) and the view of shareholders (who create either an agent or stewardship relationship through their conscious choice of governance framework). Stewardship theory is arguably more applicable than agency theory to the study of nonprofit sport organizations where managers may have a connection to the sport as an ex-player, coach, or club official and therefore have a deeper sense of commitment to the organization and are more likely to act as stewards.

Agency and stewardship theories focus on the internal monitoring issues of governance. Three theories that seek to explain how organizations relate to external organizations and acquire scarce resources are institutional theory, resource dependence theory, and network theory. Institutional theory argues that the governance frameworks adopted by organizations are the result of adhering to external pressures of what is deemed acceptable business practice, including legal requirements for incorporation. Such pressures reflect wider societal concerns for proper governance systems to be employed. Further, if all organizations of a similar type and size seek to conform to these pressures, they are likely to adopt very similar governance frameworks, a situation known as institutional isomorphism. Evidence of this is apparent throughout club-based sporting systems such as in Canada, Australia, New Zealand, and the UK where most national and state or provincial sporting organizations operate under remarkably similar governance frameworks.

Resource dependence theory proposes that in order to understand the behaviour of organizations, we must understand how organizations relate to their environment.

Organizations paradoxically seek stability and certainty in their resource exchanges by entering into interorganizational arrangements which require some loss of flexibility and autonomy in exchange for gaining control over other organizations. These interorganizational arrangements take the form of mergers, joint ventures, cooptation (the inclusion of outsiders in the leadership and decision-making processes of an organization), growth, political involvement, or restricting the distribution of information (Pfeffer and Salancik 1978). Such arrangements have an impact on the governance structure adopted, the degree to which stakeholders are involved in decision making, and the transparency of decision making.

A final theory that attempts to explain elements of governance based on how organizations relate to external organizations is network theory. Network theory posits that organizations enter into socially binding contracts to deliver services in addition to purely legal contracts. Such arrangements create a degree of interdependency between organizations and facilitate the development of informal communication and the flow of resources between organizations. This is particularly true of sport organizations that, for example, rely on personal contacts to facilitate the success of major events by securing support from high-profile athletes, using volunteers in large numbers from other sports organizations, and depending on government support for stadia development of event bidding. Network theory can help explain how governance structures and processes, particularly concerning the board of sports organizations, evolve to facilitate such informal arrangements.

These three theories emphasize the need to examine governance in terms of the external pressures that organizations face and the strategies, structures, and processes they put in place to manage them. Such an approach offers a more realistic view of how and why organizations have a particular governance framework than agency and stewardship theories.

Stakeholder theory provides another perspective for examining the relationship between organizations and their stakeholders. It argues for conceptualizing a corporation as a series of relationships and responsibilities which the governance framework must account for. This has important implications for corporations acting as good corporate citizens and particularly for sport organizations that need to manage a myriad of relationships with sponsors, funding agencies, members, affiliated organizations, staff, board members, venues, government agencies, and suppliers.

Much of the writing and research on organizational governance has been based on corporations rather than nonprofit entities. Applying a particular theory to the study of sport organizations must be done with regard to the type and industry context of the sport organization being studied. Sport organizations and their governance frameworks have diverse elements that prevent the development of an overarching theory of sport governance. The value of the theories presented here is that each of them can be used to illuminate the governance assumptions, processes, structures, and outcomes for sport organizations.

GOVERNANCE STRUCTURAL ELEMENTS

The governance elements of a corporate or profit-seeking sport organization are the same for any general business operation. These elements can include paid staff, including a CEO who may or may not have voting rights on a board, a board of directors representing the interests of many shareholders (in the case of publicly listed company), or directors who are direct partners in the business. The real differences in governance elements can be found in volunteer sport organizations.

A simple governance structure of VSOs is depicted in Figure 13.1 and comprises five elements: members, volunteers, salaried staff, a council, and a board. Normally, members meet as a council (usually once per year at an annual general meeting) to elect or appoint individuals to a board. If the organization is large enough, the board may choose to employ an executive and other paid staff to carry out the tasks of the organization. Together with a pool of volunteers, these employees deliver services to organizational members. The board acts as the main decision-making body for the organization, and therefore the quality of its activities is vital to the success of the organization.

Members of a VSO can be individual players or athletes, or in some cases, members are classified as other affiliated organizations such as a club that competes in a league provided by a regional sports association. Members can also be commercial facility providers such as basketball, squash, or indoor soccer stadiums. The membership council comprises those people or organizations that are registered members and may be allocated voting rights according to membership status. The board comprises individuals who have been elected, appointed, or invited to represent the interests of various membership categories, geographic regions, or sporting disciplines in decision making. The senior paid staff member, often designated the CEO, is employed by and reports directly to the board. Other paid staff are appointed by the CEO to assist in performing various organizational tasks. These staff must work with a variety of volunteers in sport to deliver essential services such as coaching, player and official development, marketing, sport development, and event delivery. Finally, a wide range of stakeholders such as sponsors, funding agencies, members, affiliated organizations, staff, board members, venues, government agencies, and suppliers must be consulted and managed in order for the organization to operate optimally.

The majority of national and state or provincial sport organizations that provide participation and competition opportunities in club-based sporting systems are governed

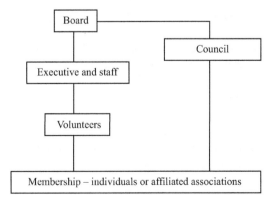

FIGURE 13.1 Typical governance structure of a VSO

voluntarily by elected office bearers, who fill positions on either committees or boards. Most of these VSOs operate under a federated delegate system with club representatives forming regional boards, regional representatives forming state or provincial boards, and state or provincial representatives forming national boards.

This traditional governance structure has been criticized for being unwieldy and cumbersome, slow to react to changes in market conditions, subject to potentially damaging politics or power plays between delegates, and imposing significant constraints on organizations wishing to change. On the other hand, the majority of sports organizations still use this model today and value its ability to ensure members have a say in decision making, the transparency of decisions, and the autonomy granted to organizations at every level of the system. In practice 13.1 explains a typical governance structure of a large national sport governing organization and their range of responsibilities.

In practice 13.1 Archery Australia

The sport of archery was introduced to Australia by European settlers in the 18th and 19th centuries and is known to have been a flourishing social and competition activity during the mid-1800s. The Archery Australia website claims that based on records held at the Australian National Library, officers of the First Fleet practised archery at Sydney Cove in 1789, making archery the oldest organized sport practised in Australia. Archery became a codified sport in Australia at a conference of state delegates held in Sydney on 17–18 January 1948. The first Annual General Meeting of the association was held in Sydney in October 1948, and in 1993, the Archery Association of Australia changed its name to Archery Australia, Inc.

Like so many other national governing bodies for sport, at that time the association was governed by a board comprising eight societies (Archery Society of NSW, Archery ACT, Archery Victoria, Archery Society of Tasmania, Archery South Australia, Archery Society of Western Australia, North Queensland Archery Association, and the South Queensland Archery Society) and the day-to-day affairs of the association were managed by an executive committee. In 2001, the constitution was amended, allowing for a more streamlined modern structure following best practice governance principles. The Archery Board now comprises four elected and up to three appointed board members. The day-to-day affairs of the association are managed by a full-time chief executive officer and national office.

Archery Australia is a not-for-profit community and membership-based organization recognized by government at all levels as the national controlling body for the sport of archery in Australia. Archery Australia operates at three levels: the Archery Australia office and board, state-based recognized governing bodies (RGBs), and local clubs. The national level of the sport provides standardized rules and regulations, policies and procedures, awards, and classifications while delivering open and fair events and equity, as well as participation at all levels of the sport. The national level also represents the interests of its members to government, other sporting organizations, and the international archery federation (World Archery). Each year, Archery Australia conducts national championships (target, field, and clout), youth national championships (target, field, matchplay, and clout), Australian Open Championships (matchplay and field), and indoor national championships. The sport also caters for a wide variety of disciplines and equipment styles during national championships.

The responsibilities of Archery Australia, like other NSOs, are comprehensive, as they:

- Are the recognized governing body for the sport in Australia
- Are an integrated sport federation with state associations and an extensive club network in all facets of the sport
- Maintain a status as the national governing body of the sport by federal, state, and local government
- Maintain a status as the recognized governing body of the sport of archery with the Australian Sports Commission and AIS
- Are a member of World Archery, the Oceania Archery Federation, and the Asian Archery Federation
- Are the governing body for archery with the World Masters Games Association and Australian Masters Games
- Are a founding and active member of the Archery Alliance of Australia
- Are a member of the Australian Olympic Committee, Australian Paralympic Committee, Australian Commonwealth Games Association, Australian University Sports, Outdoor Recreation Industry Council
- Maintain a full-time national office providing a visible presence for the sport
- Act as an effective communications channel with international federations
- Act as an effective communications channel with federal, state, and local governments
- Provide administrative support for RGBs and clubs, including when they are applying for grants
- Are responsible for selection and support of national teams to World Archery Championships, World Games, Para Championships, Olympic Games, Paralympic Games, and Commonwealth Games
- Are the voice of archery at the national level in the media
- Maintain a national member database to provide improved member management and communications at all levels
- Maintain policies and procedures, which provide consistency and transparency to all; and
- Provide clear and consistent rules and regulations by and under which the sport operates in Australia.

Source: Archery Australia website at www.archery.org.au

STRATEGIC ROLE OF THE BOARD

Ferkins and Shilbury (2012) articulated the meaning of a strategically capable nonprofit sport board, identifying four key elements based on a study of New Zealand NSOs. First, the need to have capable people who can think longer term or 'big picture', who can make decisions impartially, and collectively have a mix of complementary skills and knowledge of the sport. Second, a frame of reference or being able to set a very clear vision and mission for the organization and the requisite skills to monitor progress toward a strategic direction or set of goals. Third, facilitative board processes such as a board agenda focussed on strategy, genuine shared leadership between CEO and board members and an annual work plan for the board. Finally, the existence of facilitative regional relationships, where regional affiliate organizations worked cooperatively with the NSO, with genuine board-to-board relationships.

Ferkins and Shilbury (2015) later articulated six factors and their relationships in influencing the strategic capability of sport boards: meaningful contributions of volunteer board members; the extent of a board's operational knowledge; boards integrating affiliated bodies into the governance of an overall sport organization; boards maintaining the monitoring and control function; and boards co-leading in strategy development and integration of that strategy into its processes. They argued that these six factors all need to be present for boards to be strategic and that these factors were interdependent. Although untested to date, this emerging theory provides a useful framework in which to examine governance practices, relationships, and impacts on sport organization outcomes.

BOARD STAFF RELATIONSHIPS

The gradual introduction of professional staff into VSOs over the last 20 years has created the need for volunteers and paid staff to work together at all levels, including the board table. This has led to some degree of uncertainty about what roles should be performed by each group and the extent to which staff and volunteers should be involved in strategic planning, policy development, performance evaluation, and resource acquisition. The potential for tension between these groups as they negotiate their respective roles has been well established, as has the ongoing desire of volunteers to maintain a degree of involvement in decision making while at the same time utilizing the expertise of paid staff to assist them in running their organizations. This then is the crux of board staff relationships: What areas do volunteers maintain control over and which do paid staff control?

Hoye and Cuskelly (2003) found that VSO boards perform better if a degree of trust exists between the board and staff and that board leadership was shared amongst a dominant coalition of the board chair, executive and a small group of senior board members. As mentioned earlier, the executive controls the flow of information to board members and so the quality, frequency, and accuracy of this information are vital to their ability to make decisions. Ensuring the board and executive work together effectively enhances this information flow and therefore the performance of the board.

More recently, research has focused on one of the major criticisms often directed toward the boards of nonprofit sport organizations – their inability to be strategic (Shilbury and Ferkins 2011; Ferkins and Shilbury 2012, 2015). Using three case studies of New Zealand NSOs, Shilbury and Ferkins (2011, p. 110) illustrated the ongoing challenges of largely volunteer-led boards dealing with the increasingly complex commercialization of the operations of NSOs, specifically the "delicate balance between volunteer involvement and professional management by paid staff". This first paper reaffirmed the increasing centrality of the paid CEO and staff in shaping the strategic direction of NSOs but importantly, "demonstrated that the traditional expectations of volunteers might be at risk" (Shilbury and Ferkins 2011, p. 124). The increasing requirements for nonprofit boards to be strategic increases the time commitment and competency required of volunteer board members, an issue that Shilbury and Ferkins (2011, p. 124) suggests "that the traditional volunteer sport board director might be at risk, which may serve to undermine the role that sport has traditionally played in the community for the community".

PRINCIPLES OF GOOD ORGANIZATIONAL GOVERNANCE

The notion of good organizational governance extends beyond ideas of monitoring to ensure conformance and developing to improve performance discussed earlier in this chapter. Henry and Lee (2004) provide a list of seven key principles for good organizational governance in sport organizations:

1   Transparency – ensuring the organization has clear procedures for resource allocation, reporting, and decision making;
2   Accountability – sports organizations need to be accountable to all their stakeholders;
3   Democracy – all stakeholder groups should be able to be represented in the governance structure;
4   Responsibility – the board has to be responsible for the organization and demonstrate ethical stewardship in carrying out that responsibility;
5   Equity – all stakeholder groups should be treated equitably;
6   Efficiency – process improvements should be undertaken to ensure the organization is making the best use of its resources; and
7   Effectiveness – the board should establish and monitor measures of performance in a strategic manner.

This list of principles is not exhaustive, but it does give us a clear indication of the philosophical approach organizations should adopt in designing and implementing an appropriate governance framework. It may be somewhat surprising to find that even some of the more high-profile sport organizations in the world struggle to implement good governance standards.

Corporate governance of English Premier League football clubs has come under increasing scrutiny in recent years, due in part to the annual reviews of corporate governance undertaken by the former Football Governance Research Centre (FGRC) based at Birkbeck in the University of London. The Premier League (PL) is the flagship of the game's governing body in England, the Football Association (FA). The FA is in turn under the control of a European governing body, the Union of European Football Associations (UEFA), which in turn is a member of the world's governing body, the Federation of International Football Associations (FIFA).

The regulatory system for Premier League clubs comprises four elements: (1) regulation by the football authorities; (2) regulation through the legal system in terms of company law, consumer law, labour law, and competition law; (3) regulation by a code of corporate governance developed by the Premier League; and (4) shareholder activism and stakeholder participation. The football authorities (namely FA and UEFA) have developed criteria such as a 'fit and proper person' test aimed at improving the quality of individuals appointed or elected to govern Premier League clubs, and the development of a code of corporate governance that provides guidelines for good governance. These actions are largely designed to ameliorate the effects of poor financial management within the Premier League clubs (since 1992 50% of PL clubs have been in hands of administrators or insolvent) and to improve the sustainability of cubs that are promoted or relegated between the FA leagues. The FGRC noted that the PL clubs that regularly compete in the UEFA Champions' League hold a distinct financial advantage over other PL clubs. As a consequence the governing body of the PL must be cognizant of the more powerful clubs and their potential to influence decision-making at the board table.

The English legal system requires PL clubs to fulfil a number of obligations for communicating with shareholders, consultation with fans, the use of customer charters, and dialogue with supporters' trusts. The FGRC noted that although the majority of PL clubs do an adequate job in this area, there was room for improvement. In addition, PL clubs that are listed public companies must follow a combined code that sets out principles for the activities of directors, director's remuneration, accountability and audit requirements, relations with shareholders, and institutional shareholders. The FGRC found that although PL clubs are moving towards having more independent directors, they fall short compared to other listed companies.

There are now more than 70 supporters' trusts for clubs in the FA, and about 60% of PL clubs have a supporters' trust. The trusts fulfil an important governance role, with 25% of PL clubs having a trust representative on their board. This representation means that committed fans have the chance to participate in decision making at the highest level in regard to the future of their club, and in return support the club in sport development, marketing, and fundraising activities.

Although there are signs that PL clubs have generally accepted good governance practices and abide with the majority of codes of conduct and principles for good governance, they do fall down in certain areas of governance practice. These include the lack of performance evaluation of individual directors or the overall board in a small number of clubs, and a significant portion of clubs failing to adopt standard strategic planning practices. The English PL enjoys an enormous global profile as a leading football competition, but the governance of the member clubs does not reach such exalted heights.

These failures in football governance are also evident in other countries; Hamil et al (2010) documented the failings in governance that have plagued Italian football in recent years, noting

> there is a clear and transparent system of regulatory oversight for the Italian football industry. . . [and a licensing system that] . . . suggests a high standard of club governance should exist.[but].there is a very serious gap between theory and practice, a gap which has had significant consequences for the health of the Italian football industry.
>
> (Hamil et al 2010, p. 379)

They argue that inappropriate ownership and governance structures among football clubs have led to a series of problems that have dogged Italian soccer over the last three decades including betting scandals, doping, false passports, bribery and match fixing, and violence. They cite the problems of clubs being controlled by familial networks with little separation of ownership and control (one of the central tenets of effective governance) as being a central cause of these problems. Hamil et al (2010, p. 388) also noted that "what emerges in football are networks consisting of powerful individuals connected with clubs, governing bodies, political parties and the media, which are in prominent positions to influence decision making within football and the business of football". The legacy of a lack of competitive balance in the Italian league and the growing disparity of resources that exists between mid-tier clubs and those few large clubs that play in the lucrative UEFA Champions League also compound the problem. They concluded that Italian football should adopt "modern regulation – including sanctions for misdemeanours – and clear guidelines for strong governance" (Hamil et al 2010, p. 404). The importance of good governance for a sport is highlighted via In practice 13.2.

In practice 13.2 Swim England: a nation swimming

The Amateur Swimming Association (ASA) was the first governing body of swimming to be established in the world (1869) and has evolved to become Swim England, the English national governing body for swimming, diving, water polo, open water, and synchronized swimming. Their vision is "A Nation Swimming" and their mission is to create a happier, healthier, and more successful nation through swimming.

Swim England supports over 1,100 affiliated swimming clubs through a national/regional/and sub-regional structure. It endeavours to ensure every athlete – whatever their age or level of experience – belongs to a club that provides the best possible support and environment. It organizes competitions throughout England, from the grassroots to elite level, including the highly successful age group and youth championships that attract more than 1,600 young swimmers aged 11 to 17 and the ASA Nationals.

The Swim England website (www.swimming.org/swimengland) states that the English talent program is a world-leading, seamless pathway that puts in place performance opportunities for swimmers to develop their skills and potential. The ASA operates a Learn to Swim award scheme based on the National Plan for Teaching Swimming. Over 2 million certificates and badges are issued to children all over the world under this scheme. Swimming is the number one participation sport in England, with over 20 million people swimming every year, and Swim England is dedicated to giving more people more opportunities to swim for health and for fun.

It should be noted that Swim England is not a provider of swimming facilities; therefore it acts as a catalyst and facilitator to ensure suitable facilities, with appropriate access and programs, are provided to meet the needs of the community and aquatic clubs. Swim England operates comprehensive certification and education programs for teachers, coaches, and officials. It has pioneered work on the UK Coaching Framework and is developing e-learning programs, all of which are helping to drive up quality and 'raise the bar' to ensure Swim England has an appropriately skilled workforce for the whole swimming industry.

Swim England's Strategy for 2017–2021 sets out six strategic objectives:

1 Provide strong leadership and be the recognized authority for swimming
2 Substantially increase the number of people able to swim
3 Significantly grow the number and diversity of people enjoying and benefitting from regular swimming
4 Create a world-leading talent system for all our disciplines
5 Deliver a high quality, diverse, and motivated workforce within swimming
6 Strengthen our organizational sustainability for future generations

Swim England's success is dependent on many people across the organization, both staff and volunteers, working together to deliver services at the right standard. Good governance is essential in monitoring and supporting the performance of individuals and member clubs and associations in that endeavour.

Source: The Swim England website at www.swimming.org/swimengland

BOARD PERFORMANCE

Board performance has been found to be related to the use of appropriate structures, processes and strategic planning, the role of the paid executive, whether the board undertakes training or development work, personal motivations of board members and the influence of a cyclical pattern in the life cycle of boards. How to measure board performance, however, is a subject of ongoing debate. Herman and Renz (1997, 1998, 2000) support the use of a social constructionist approach to measure board performance based on the work of Berger and Luckmann (1967). Their view is that the collective judgements of those individuals directly involved with the board can provide the best idea of its performance. A widely used scale, the Self Assessment for Nonprofit Governing

Boards Scale (Slesinger 1991), uses this approach and provides sporting and other non-profit organizations with an effective way to gauge board performance.

Aspects of board activity that are evaluated using a scale of this type include the working relationship between board and CEO, working relationships between board and staff, CEO selection and review processes, financial management, conduct of board and committee meetings, board mission statement and review of the mission, strategic planning, matching operational programs to the mission and monitoring program performance, risk management, new board member selection and training, and marketing and public relations. The performance of the board in undertaking these activities is then rated by board members, executives, and the chair of the board. Although this approach is open to criticisms of self-reporting bias, the fact that the whole group makes judgements on performance and then compares perceptions is an aide to board development and improvement.

The evaluation of individual board member performance is more problematic. Research into the human resource management practices related to board members shows that smaller sports organizations may struggle to find board members, whereas larger sports have an element of prestige attached to them so the problem is the opposite – how to engage in succession planning within a democratic electoral process. Very few board members are inducted, trained, provided with professional development opportunities, and evaluated at all in regard to their role and the role of the board, a potentially serious problem for nonprofit sport organizations given the significant responsibilities with which board members and board chairs are charged.

DRIVERS OF CHANGE IN GOVERNANCE

VSOs are increasingly under pressure from funding agencies to improve the delivery of their core programs and services. Funding agencies recognize that sports' capacity for this delivery depends to a large extent on sport organizations being appropriately governed and as a result have implemented a range of measures to improve the governance of VSOs. For example, the Australian Sports Commission has a dedicated program of management improvement for NSOs that provides advice on governance issues, funding to undertake reviews of governance structures, and provides information on governance principles and processes. Sport England has negotiated detailed strategic plans with NSOs to improve the delivery and coordination between regional sport organizations.

The threat of litigation against sport organizations, their members, or board members has forced sport organizations to address issues such as risk management, fiduciary compliance, incorporation, directors' liability insurance, and board training and evaluation. The heightened awareness of the implications of governance failure due to several much publicized corporate cases of impropriety worldwide has also forced sport organizations to improve their governance systems. Legislative changes to address issues of equity and diversity are additional pressures sports organizations must face, and their governance systems, particularly membership criteria, voting rights, and provision of information must change accordingly.

The threat of competition in the marketplace also has forced sports organizations to become more commercial and business focussed, primarily through employing paid staff. Large clubs and regional sports associations that in the mid-1990s were exclusively run by volunteers are increasingly investing in paid staff to manage the increased compliance demands from government and their members and customers. As discussed earlier, the employment of paid staff changes the governance structures, the decision-making processes, and the level of control exerted by volunteers. Maintaining governance structures devised decades ago creates many problems for sports organizations.

Arguably the most influential change agent in the governance of NSOs is countries such as Australia, New Zealand, and the UK have been their respective national governments seeking to overtly influence the governance of sport organizations via the imposition of performance targets as part of funding agreements between elite sport agencies and national governing bodies, direct interventions to reshape and professionalize governance systems in sport, and indirectly influencing strategy and governance priorities through funding support. Olympic and Commonwealth Games sports largely dependent on government funding for their high-performance programs in each of these countries seemed to have responded to these influences, whereas the professional sport codes (i.e. cricket, football codes, golf, and tennis) have not. To date, very little research has focussed on the effectiveness of these interventions and how national sport agencies might best be able to influence future improvements in the governance of sport organizations.

In practice 13.3 Governance reform in sport

The Australian Sports Commission has attempted to improve governance standards amongst Australian NSOs for more than two decades. During the period 2013 to 2015, the ASC released updated governance guidelines for NSOs and worked directly with some of them to facilitate change. These reform efforts focused on issues such as:

- Board chair elected by the board not the members;
- Performance evaluation processes for boards;
- Corporate rather than association structures;
- Establishment of key board committees, including nominations, audit and risk; and
- Board diversity and skill mix.

They point to four key drivers that are shaping why they are becoming increasingly interventionist with the governance of NSOs (ASC 2016, p. 2):

- the growing importance of integrity, safety, and duty of care responsibilities;
- increasingly lucrative commercial broadcast and media deals for the larger professional sports, which are placing smaller sports at a growing competitive disadvantage in the sports marketplace;

- a challenging and highly competitive sports sponsorship market, causing sponsors to focus increasingly those sports with large broadcast audiences; and
- national economic pressures which mean that sports cannot rely on increased government funding to bridge the revenue gap to remain competitive.

Their most recent attempt to influence governance practices came in mid-2105 when they released a white paper for discussion throughout the Australian sport industry. The white paper focused on three themes:

- Voting structures and appropriately delineated roles of members, boards, and management;
- How the collection of member registration fees is best managed; and
- The need for sports to continuously evolve their governance for improved performance.

By focusing on these themes, the ASC was attempting to improve alignment within NSOs with federated structures, improve the revenue streams of NSOs, focus boards on more strategic matters, and clean up inconsistent voting rights within NSOs. In response to the feedback they received from sport organizations through a detailed consultation process, the ASC focused on the lack of trust evident within sport, stating (ASC 2016, p. 3) that:

It is also clear to the ASC that many Australian sports are held back today from realising their full potential by a lack of trust between key stakeholders. Sometimes this manifests itself in a lack of trust between the national Board and state Boards, sometimes it is between state Boards themselves. Trust cannot be mandated by an external party in documentary governance principles, it has to be built and earned over time by behaviours between stakeholders in a sport; particularly by the demonstration, and receipt in return, of respect. It is true, however, that organisational structures and governance processes can enhance or diminish trust.

The outcome of the consultation process was that rather than develop additional guidelines, the ASC proposed all sports work toward a unified whole-of-sport approach.

The Commission is proposing therefore that all sports now work towards adopting "unified whole-of-sport" aligned behaviours. A unified approach does not require change in organisational structure. However, it does require leaders within sports to demonstrate cohesive behaviours for the common good of the sport nationally, that are likely to enhance outcomes in the overall interest of the sport. A key aim of a unified approach within each sport is to increase the trust and confidence across all levels of the sport from the NSO and SSO to associations and clubs. This can only be achieved if there are communication protocols established by each sport to ensure there is transparency and respect for all groups involved in the sport.

Key aligned behaviours of a unified approach include:

- *Strategy: Whole-of-sport strategic plans with a common set of goals that are endorsed by all members and which provide for the sport to work towards the achievement of these goals in an effective, efficient, and coordinated way. These plans should cover all areas from community participation to high performance, and provide flexibility for state member plans to address relevant local issues. The plans will ensure there are clear roles and responsibilities across the management of the whole sport, and will be responsive to both national and local needs;*

- *Commercial: Consistency in branding and commercial offerings within each sport, which will support commercial agreements allowing sports to negotiate and manage strategic assets more effectively. This will provide for certain protected sponsorship categories to be managed and offered for sale nationally, with transparency of benefits and service costs clear to all stakeholders and safeguards that state organisations will not be worse off as a result of this nationally aligned approach;*
- *Financial management: Nationally aligned financial systems whereby sports produce consolidated annual financial reports and which allow simpler and more transparent assessments of the performance and sustainability of the whole of the sport;*
- *Digital and IT: Digital alignment and data sharing to create aligned collection, management and analysis of data on a common database; and*
- *Staff: A consistent approach to workforce management leading to well-resourced people management systems providing greater opportunity to attract, retain and develop excellent staff for the sports.*

The ASC position was summarized as:

Sports adopt unified whole – of-sport, aligned behaviours, irrespective of their governance structure, which include aligned strategic plans that contain the key objectives of the national plan and flexibility for state plans to address local issues, whole-of-sport financial reporting, development of integrated national databases, a consistent approach to workforce management and coordinated sponsorship offerings that maximise benefits for the sport including providing opportunities for key categories to be leveraged on a national basis.

Source: Australian Sports Commission website at www.ausport.gov.au and ASC. (2016). *Governance Reform in Sport*. Canberra: Australian Sports Commission.

ETHICS

The ethical conduct of directors on sport organizations has come under increased scrutiny in recent years as sport is beset with challenges around high-profile cases of drug use in sport, scandals about the bidding process for awarding hosting rights for sport events to host cities, and failures in oversight of management teams. One of the more damning pieces of research was completed by Hamil et al (2010, p. 379) who documented the many failings in governance that have plagued Italian football through the 2000s, noting that although "there is a clear and transparent system of regulatory oversight for the Italian football industry. . . [and a licensing system that] . . . suggests a high standard of club governance should exist . . . there is a very serious gap between theory and practice". Their paper identified an exhaustive list of problems that have plagued Italian soccer between 1980 and 2010, including betting scandals, doping, falsification of passports, bribery and match fixing, and violence – all of which they concluded is largely a result of inappropriate ownership and governance structures among football clubs.

More recently Geeraert, Alm, and Groll (2014) provided a telling analysis of the quality of governance within the 35 Olympic sport governing bodies and highlighted a number of problems, including a lack of accountability arrangements and transparency in the distribution of funding to members, a lack of independent ethics committees overseeing the conduct of these organizations, a lack of athlete participation in governance, inequitable gender representation on governing boards, and a lack of term limits for board members that concentrates power with incumbents.

Government agencies such as the ASC have acted by imposing tighter restrictions on term limits for directors, auditing standards for sport organizations, use of nominations committees for appointment of directors, and good practice around declarations of interest for directors who may benefit from sitting on a board by having a register of such conflicts. One of the more meaningful requirements is to ensure all directors are independent. The ASC principles require directors not be elected to represent any group, are not employed by the organization, do not hold any other material office within the organizational structure, and have no material interests in being a director. The ASC also requires NSOs, and their directors, to sign up to all ASC integrity measures on anti-doping, protocols for sport science, and match fixing as well as publish annual reports consistent with the Corporations Act requirements.

SUMMARY

Organizational governance has been described as the exercise of power within organizations and provides the system by which the elements of organizations are controlled and directed. Good organizational governance should ensure that the board and management seek to deliver outcomes for the benefit of the organization and its members and that the means used to attain these outcomes are effectively monitored.

A distinction is made between corporate governance that deals with the governance of profit-seeking companies and corporations that focus on protecting and enhancing shareholder value, and nonprofit governance that is concerned with the governance of voluntary based organizations that seek to provide a community service or facilitate the involvement of individuals in social, artistic, or sporting activities.

Sport organizations and their governance frameworks have diverse elements that prevent the development of an overarching theory of sport governance. A number of theoretical perspectives, namely agency theory, stewardship theory, institutional theory, resource dependence theory, network theory, and stakeholder theory can be used to illuminate parts of the governance assumptions, processes, structures, and outcomes for sport organizations.

The traditional governance structure for VSOs outlined earlier has been criticized for being unwieldy and cumbersome, slow to react to changes in market conditions, subject to potentially damaging politics or power plays between delegates, and imposing significant constraints on organizations wishing to change. On the other hand, the majority of sports organizations still use this model today and value its ability to ensure members have a say in decision making, the transparency of decisions, and the autonomy granted to organizations at every level of the system.

VSO boards perform better if a degree of trust exists between the board and staff and that board leadership is shared amongst a dominant coalition of the board chair, executive, and a small group of senior board members. Although evaluation systems for board performance are still relatively simplistic, they do cover a wide range of board activities. Evaluation of individual board member performance is more problematic and is the subject of ongoing research.

Finally, VSOs are increasingly under pressure from funding agencies to improve the delivery of their core programs and services. The threat of litigation against sport organizations, their members, or board members has forced sport organizations to address issues such as risk management, fiduciary compliance, incorporation, directors' liability insurance, and board training and evaluation. The heightened awareness of the implications of governance failure due to high-profile corporate cases worldwide has also forced sport organizations to improve their governance systems.

REVIEW QUESTIONS

1 Explain the difference between corporate and nonprofit governance.

2 What theory would you apply to the study of negligence on the part of a board of directors of a sport organization?

3 Explain the role played by boards, staff, volunteers, members, and stakeholder groups in governing sport organizations.

4 What criteria would you apply to gauge the performance of a nonprofit VSO? How would these criteria differ for a professional sport club?

5 What are the important elements in developing good relationships between boards and paid staff in VSOs?

6 Compare the governance structures of a multi-disciplinary sport (e.g. gymnastics, canoeing, athletics) with a single discipline sport (e.g. field hockey, netball, rugby league). How do they differ? What impact does this have on volunteers involved in governance roles?

7 Review the governance performance of a VSO of your choice using Henry and Lee's (2004) seven principles of governance presented in this chapter.

8 What issues does a potential amalgamation present for a VSO?

9 How are board performance and organizational performance linked?

10 Interview the CEO and the board chair of small VSO. Who do they perceive to be the leader of the organization?

DISCUSSION QUESTIONS

1 Why is sport governance such an important topic in sport?

2 What are some of the reasons sport seems to struggle to be governed well?

3 Why is it important to have boards with a mixture of elected and appointed directors?

4 Why do national sport agencies seek to intervene so regularly in the governance of national sport organizations?

5 Can a sport organization perform well if the board is dysfunctional?

FURTHER READING

Clarke, T. (ed.) (2004). *Theories of Corporate Governance*. Oxon, UK: Routledge.

Ferkins, L. and Shilbury, D. (2015). Board strategic balance: An emerging sport governance theory. *Sport Management Review*, 18: 489–500.

Garcia, B. and Welford, J. (2015). Supporters and football governance, from customers to stakeholders: A literature review and agenda for research. *Sport Management Review*, 18: 517–528.

Geeraert, A., Alm, J. and Groll, M. (2014). Good governance in international sport organizations: An analysis of the 35 Olympic governing bodies. *International Journal of Sport Policy and Politics*, 6(3): 281–306.

Grix, J. (2009). The impact of UK sport policy on the governance of athletics. *International Journal of Sport Policy*, 1: 31–49.

Hamil, S., Morrow, S., Idle, C., Rossi, G. and Faccendini, S. (2010). The governance and regulation of Italian football. *Soccer & Society*, 11: 373–413.

Henry, I. and Lee, P.C. (2004). Governance and ethics in sport, in J. Beech and S. Chadwick (eds), *The Business of Sport Management*. England: Prentice Hall.

Hoye, R. (2017). Sport governance, in R. Hoye and M.M. Parent (eds). *Handbook of Sport Management*. London: Sage, pp. 9–23.

Hoye, R. and Cuskelly, G. (2007). *Sport Governance*. Oxford: Elsevier Butterworth-Heinemann.

Hoye, R. and Doherty, A. (2011). Non-profit sport board performance: A review and directions for future research. *Journal of Sport Management*, 25(3): 272–285.

Sport New Zealand. (2015). *Governance Benchmarking Review 2014*. Wellington, New Zealand: Sport New Zealand.

RELEVANT WEBSITES

The following websites are useful starting points for further information on the governance of sport organizations:

Australian Sports Commission at www.ausport.gov.au

Sport Canada at www.pch.gc.ca/progs/sc/index_e.cfm

Sport England at www.sportengland.org
Sport Scotland at www.sportscotland.org.uk

CASE STUDY 13.1

Kicking on: governance reform in British judo

In response to the UK government publishing a Charter for Sports Governance in the UK in May 2016 that set out key governance principles that they expect all sports in the UK to follow, the British Judo Association (BJA) recognized the need to review its governance. The BJA had also recently been stripped of its licence to host the European Judo Championships in Glasgow a year earlier, an unusual action taken by the European Judo Union and based on two key issues. First, a failure of the BJA to pay its licence fee on time, and second, the BJA had entered into a sponsorship arrangement with the Ultimate Fighting Championship (UFC) that did not conform to the EJU values.

The BJA appointed Jonathon Hall, previously Director of Football Services and Director of Governance at the Football Association, to undertake the review. The terms of the review focused on the memorandum and articles of association, particularly the structure of the board. Hall was asked to review the composition; size; responsibilities; representation; diversity and skills of the board; term length of directors and chair, selection processes for all directors and the role; and purpose of council, panels, and commissions. He was also asked to provide recommendations on the ongoing operation of the board such as skill-based appointments, board evaluations, conflicts of interest, confidentiality, transparency, and other good governance practices. Hall conducted many interviews, facilitated group meetings, and used an online survey as well as a desktop review of all available documentation during his review.

His 110-page report makes for interesting reading. The key themes from the review were a need for the BJA to improve its engagement with its members, not just by providing better information via their website but by face-to-face meetings with key stakeholders and a need to clarify the roles and responsibilities of the different parts of the BJA, in particular the decision making role of the board. Hall made 40 separate recommendations, some of which were to update guidelines or bylaws to reflect current practice, but some were about fundamental governance change. Some of the more important recommendations were:

- Consider moving from a club-based membership model to one where individuals are the members of BJA;
- Clarify the role of the council in relation to the board;
- Impose term limits on council and board members, as well as limits to how many consecutive terms members may serve;

- Reduce the number of board members;
- Create the opportunity for the board to appoint individuals in addition to elected members;
- Improve the diversity of the board by imposing a minimum gender ratio for board members;
- Utilize a nominations committee to recommend direct appointments to the board;
- Clarify that the board should appoint its chair from amongst the board rather than by direct election;
- Simplify the number of technical panels and commissions reporting to the board;
- Undertake an annual board evaluation exercise;
- Undertake a board skills assessment to identify skill gaps in the board;
- Introduce a confidentiality policy for the board; and
- Improve its engagement with the membership by publishing board minutes and other important outcomes from the board.

The BJA has subsequently published a summary of this review, along with the full report and adopted all 40 of the recommendations. The process for the review also highlights the challenges in achieving useful governance reform. In their summary report, the BJA outlines an eight-step process that was used to secure governance reform:

1   Report by Jonathon Hall commissioned by the BJA;
2   Audit of existing practices, investigations, research, and regional roadshows for consultation;
3   Presentation of report and recommendations to the BJA;
4   Distribution of the report to all members including a bespoke website for all related materials;
5   Member consultation period;
6   Distribution of Extraordinary General Meeting (EGM) papers;
7   Extraordinary General Meeting; and
8   Integration of recommendations as agreed at the EGM.

An extract from the summary report from Hall points to the need to look at these recommendations as a group, rather than as isolated suggestions:

> Many of the recommendations deal with the need to clarify the roles and responsibilities of different parts of the BJA, so that there is a clear understanding on how the Board runs the organisation on behalf of the members and is accountable to them like any member or shareholder organisation. Much of this focus is on how the BJA, through its Board, makes its decisions and looks at ways in which it can improve these processes for the benefit of the sport. The recommendations are drawn from

best practice in both the corporate and sports worlds and are aimed at providing an efficient and effective decision making process and structure for the BJA. The report states that if implemented, the recommendations should put the BJA in a good position in relation to the principles set out in the Charter for Sports Governance. It remains to be seen if they will meet all the requirements of the new Sports Code which is due out in the autumn, but the recommendations should put the BJA in a much stronger position to do so. Please note the advice from Jonathan Hall is that whilst it is of course possible to view some of the recommendations as isolated points, many of them interlink, and so the suggestion is for the reader to review all the recommendations in the full report before forming a view on any or all of them.

The BJA has also published an implementation plan for how it will adopt all of the recommendations at www.britishjudo.org.uk/wp-content/uploads/2017/07/EGM-Implementation-Plan.pdf that also highlights the length of time required to secure governance reform in a national sport.

CASE STUDY QUESTIONS

1   Why did the BJA initiate a review into their own governance?

2   What were some of the more important or significant recommendations from the report by Jonathon Hall of the BJA? Why do you consider them important?

3   Why is it important to have an independent review of governance in sport? Why can't boards undertake their own reviews?

4   Why do governing bodies of sport seem to be in a perpetual state of review, in particular in the areas of governance and structure?

5   Access the BJA website and see if there are any further updates to this governance review. Are you confident that all the planned changes will be put in place? Is the BJA now compliant with the UK Sport governance guidelines?

Sources: Hall, J. (2016). *Governance Review for the British Judo Association*. Loughborough: British Judo Association and the British Judo Association website at www.britishjudo.org.uk

CASE STUDY 13.2

Shooting Australia: on target?

A case that illustrates the difficulty in achieving governance reform is that of Shooting Australia, the NSO for a range of competition shooting disciplines in

Australia. Shooting Australia is the peak national sporting organization for competition shooting in Australia, recognized by the Australian Sports Commission (ASC), Australian Olympic Committee, Australian Paralympic Committee, Australian Commonwealth Games Association, and the International Shooting Sport Federation. There are approximately 42,000 club members in Australia who participate in the sport of shooting and they belong to the member bodies of Shooting Australia:

- Australian Clay Target Association;
- Field and Game Federation of Australia;
- National Rifle Association of Australia;
- Pistol Australia; and
- Target Rifle Australia.
- The NSW Shooting Association is an associate member.

Shooting Australia had moved significantly to adopt and operate under the ASC's Mandatory Sports Governance Principles but in 2015, Shooting Australia and the Australian Sports Commission engaged a consultant to undertake a review of the governance of shooting in Australia with the aim, in part, to develop a new contemporary and appropriate governance structure.

Selected passages of the executive summary of the report produced in April 2016 highlights the challenges for this sport:

> Shooting Australia has a particularly complex governance structure given its five Member Bodies are National Sporting Associations in their own right and with their own varying membership structures. SA also has a (non-voting) Associate Member in NSW Shooting. At the national and state level, the sport has 42,000 shooters governed by 43 separate legal entities, 365 directors, and 125 committees. There are no centralised participation programs, coach and official education is ad hoc, around 330 events are staged each year, and high performance programs are split between SA and Member Bodies. All of this is managed by only 25 full time paid staff across the entire sport creating a significant reliance on a volunteer workforce. There is limited centralised knowledge around participation data and complex communication channels make meaningful engagement with the clubs and shooters difficult. Not surprisingly, the single biggest issue facing Shooting in Australia is fragmentation. This is exacerbated by increased financial pressure from a stagnant registered participant base combined with an older demographic and overreliance on volunteers. The sport urgently needs to embrace and take advantage of technology and social media.
>
> There are many obvious and evident benefits of adopting a more whole of sport approach, including strategic alignment of priorities, improved expertise, economies of scale, and resource sharing. There is power in numbers and the sport needs to

advocate as one to respond to threats created by anti-social activities involving firearms, competitor sports shooting bodies, and the closure of shooting ranges.

This Report makes a number of recommendations culminating in the development of an Optimal Governance Framework focussed on constructing strategic alignment and operating efficiencies to ensure best use of limited resources. All recommendations are cognisant of the specificities created by the different shooting disciplines. A sound financial base is important for the long-term sustainability and success of Shooting and recommendations are mindful of available resources.

Not all recommendations can be implemented immediately and need to be introduced in a phased and prioritised approach over the next four years. An implementation strategy has been designed to assist SA and Member Bodies to transition from current structures to best practice governance and administration.

In summary, Shooting Australia needs to operate with unity of purpose to deliver better services and resources to clubs, achieve operating efficiencies and focus on diversifying revenue streams. This will ensure the long-term survival and sustainability of Shooting. Strong leadership is required from SA to promote an inclusive culture and to drive change at both the governance and operational levels in a transparent, consultative and accountable manner.

Although this summary provides a useful overview of the challenges and opportunities for the sport, the report did highlight a number of specific governance challenges. First, SA does not comply with some of the ASC's mandatory sport governance principles in terms of having the ability to work with their member organizations as a single national entity, and they are not able to report consolidated national financial accounts.

The report also points out that:

The sport of Shooting is governed by 43 different legal entities, all of which have differing structures, brands, and names adding to the complexity and confusion. The current governance structure is overly complex and unwieldy and does not enable leadership, focussed direction, or growth, all of which underpin sustainability and success. This multi-layered governance structure also necessitates a significant number of people to administer the sport, almost all of which are volunteers. This compounds their effectiveness as it is a relatively small pool of volunteers who tend to be overworked and are not necessarily experts in their designated area. At the national level, there are currently 65 national directors between SA and its Member Bodies with an additional 300 directors for the State Associations. All of these are volunteer positions. This raises a number of issues: (a) conflicts of interest, (b) independence of decision making, (c) dependence on key individuals, (d) expertise and skill set, and (e) overreliance on committees

The complexity in governance structure affects the ability of a limited number of paid staff to manage the operations of these many disparate organizations. The report emphasizes this challenge:

> *Shooting's complex governance structure necessitates a significant number of people to administer the sport. The additional problem is that the vast majority are volunteers, and hence time poor and not necessarily experts in required skill areas. Nationally across the sport there are 19 full time and 4 part time paid staff. Excluding SA, this reduces to only 10 full time and 2 part time paid staff. Indeed, both SCA and TRA have no paid staff at all. The paid staff in bodies like NRAA, are also focussed on the sale of ammunition rather than administration of their sport. At the State level, there are only 6 full time paid staff. Whilst people working in the sport are very good at the shooting aspects of the sport, there is more limited expertise on the business and management of the sport.*

The 52-page report also lists a range of critical management challenges for the sport, including limited data analysis capability, lack of understanding of member needs, inefficient coach and officiating development pathways, a crowded event calendar, poor communication channels, limited marketing expertise or capacity, and variable financial capability across member bodies. In that context, achieving meaningful governance reform within a reasonable time frame is an enormous challenge.

The report recommended a three-stage approach over four years to implement a number of governance reforms:

1 Improve collaboration by improving trust and transparency;
2 Identify the value proposition of undertaking reforms; and
3 Transition planning to roll out the constitutional changes required.

At the time of writing this case, the report had been accepted and SA had begun the process of adopting the many recommendations required to improve its governance.

CASE STUDY QUESTIONS

1 Why is it important for organizations such as SA to engage an independent reviewer for any governance reform process? What are the possible negatives and positives of such a process?

2 Why is it so difficult for national boards within federated structures to vote for changes to board composition or voting procedures?

3 Why might state-level organizations be critical of national-level organizations within such federated models?

4   A major focus of similar reform processes is to align the strategic plans of state- and national-level organizations. What are the challenges of getting this done within this sport, and why is governance reform important in aiding this outcome?

5   Access the SA website and see if there are any further updates to this governance review. Are you confident that all the planned changes will be put in place? Is SA now compliant with the ASC mandatory sport governance principles?

Sources: Shooting Australia website at www.shootingaustralia.org and the report titled *Whole of Sport Governance Review Report* (2016) produced by Suiko Consulting, an external consulting firm, also available on the Shooting Australia website.

CHAPTER 14

Performance management

OVERVIEW

This chapter examines the ways in which sport organizations monitor their operations and evaluate their performance. Particular attention is given to the special features of sport organizations and how these features create the need for sport-specific models of performance management. The imperative of using a multi-dimensional model of performance management is highlighted, together with the need to not only accommodate the conflicting demands of multiple stakeholders, but also manage the risk. Key cases and critical incidents are used to illustrate the concepts and principles that underpin effective performance in sport organizations.

After completing this chapter the reader should be able to:

- Explain the concept of performance management in sport organizations;
- Describe how the special features of sport necessitate the formulation of a

sport-specific model of performance management;

- Identify stakeholders that that need to be taken into account when building a performance management model for sport organizations;
- Explain why risk management is essential to ensuring high-level performance in sport organizations;
- Conceptualize the universal importance of financial sustainability as a measure of performance;
- Understand the importance of social responsibility as a performance indicator;
- Construct multi-dimensional models of performance management that uses sport's special features, stakeholder analysis, risk assessment, financial factors, and social responsibility; and
- Apply the model to a variety of sport situations and contexts.

SPORT AND PERFORMANCE

From a management perspective sport is a very interesting institution to study since it is both similar to and different from traditional business organizations (Smith and Stewart 1999; Smith and Stewart 2010). Its similarities have arisen out of its relentless drive over the last 30 years to become more professionally structured and managed. Large segments of sport have consequently copied the values and practices of the business world, and as a result players and administrators are paid employees, and strategic plans are designed. In addition, games and activities become branded sport products, fans become customers to be satisfied and surveyed, and alliances with corporate supporters are developed (Carter 2011; Slack 1997).

At the same time, sport is also different from business (Smith and Stewart 2013). First, it has a symbolic significance and emotional intensity that is rarely found in an insurance company, bank, or even a betting shop. Although businesses seek employee compliance and attachment, their primary concern is efficiency, productivity, and responding to changing market conditions. Sport, on the other hand, is consumed by strong emotional attachments that are linked to the past through nostalgia and tradition. Romantic visions, emotion, and passion can override commercial logic and economic rationality (Foster, Greyser and Walsh 2006; Quinn 2009). Second, predictability and certainty, which are goals to be aimed for in the commercial world, particularly with respect to product quality, are not always valued in the sporting world. Sport fans are attracted to games where the outcome is uncertain and chaos is just around the corner (Fort 2011; Sandy, Sloane and Rosentraub 2004; Szymanksi 2009; Zimbalist 2006). Third, sport is not driven by the need to optimize profit in the ways that large commercial businesses are. In practice, sport organizations face two conflicting models of organizational behaviour when deciding upon their underlying mission and goals. The first is the profit maximization model, which assumes that a club is simply a firm in a perfectly competitive product market where profit is the single driving motivational force. The second is the utility maximization model, which emphasizes the rivalry between clubs and their desire to win as many matches as possible (Downward and Dawson 2000; Fort 2011). The utility view assumes that sporting organizations are by nature highly competitive and that the single most important performance yardstick is competitive success. These differences therefore beg the question of where to begin when setting up a performance management system for sport organizations.

WHERE TO BEGIN?

In many respects sport is always subject to intense scrutiny. For example, in elite competitive sport, players and teams are rated and ranked continuously. In cricket, for example, an ever-expanding array of statistics is used to calculate not only batter-scoring rates and bowling-strike rates, but also patterns of scoring and fielding efficiency. Moreover, everyone has an opinion on the performance of coaches in various professional sport leagues which range from win-loss ratios to how the game strategies affect scoring efficiency and player movements.

At the same time, many sporting clubs do not take the time to undertake a comprehensive evaluation of their off-field performance. This is surprising in view of the fact that, like other organizations that aim to be around for a while, sport clubs and associations must also make sure they can deliver growing memberships and balanced budgets. As a result, it is always better to use a performance evaluation model that covers a range of performance dimensions and embraces a variety of measures.

A systematic approach to performance management is thus an essential tool for identifying strengths and weaknesses and revealing the ways in which overall organizational performance can be improved. It is also important for deciding where scarce resources should be allocated in order to achieve the best possible outcome. It can also give a picture of how one organization, club, or league is doing in relation to other organizations, clubs, or leagues. This performance snapshot can be used to identify weaknesses and design strategies than improve critical result areas in the next season or annual sporting cycle. In short, the use of some sort of performance management model is crucial to the long-term success of sport organizations. However, the question remains as to how best to go about implementing an appropriate model of performance management and where to begin.

A good starting point is to look at performance management from a strategic perspective. That is, we should initially focus our attention on what the organization wants to achieve. In other words, a performance management system should be linked to an organization's vision, goals, and objectives (Hums and Maclean 2009; Robbins and Barnwell 2002). These objectives can be used to identify what it needs to do well to improve its performance. It is at this point that the primary goals of sport organizations become quite different from those of business organizations. Whereas commercial leisure centres and most American professional sport teams seem to be focused on maximizing profits, most other sports clubs, even with a large revenue base, are more concerned with priorities like winning more games than their rivals and servicing the needs of members. However, it is not always clear just what the primary goal of a sport organization is or what is the best measure for deciding how well the organization has performed. In commercial terms the most successful association football (or soccer) club is Manchester United, closely followed by Real Madrid and Barcelona, whose capacity to secure revenue is unrivalled in European football. However, Manchester United did not even make it into Champions League final 32 in 2016; it was won by Real Madrid. Overall, though, the wealthiest teams generally dominate the Champions League, which suggests that commercial size and on-field success are in fact related. On balance it has to be said that there is a close correlation between revenue and success in most professional sport leagues. In other words, clubs that have a large resource base and the capacity to secure the best facilities, the best coaches, and the best players, will, on balance, have the best win-loss ratio.

But this also begs the question as to whether there may be other ways of measuring performance and estimating the success and failures of a sport organization. In some instances it may be important to consider what are called process factors, which includes items like staff retention, player development, and overall level of morale and job satisfaction. However, despite these additional complexities and anomalies, it is clear that any performance management system must take into account, and indeed, should reflect, the primary goals of the relevant club, team, facility, event, or league.

BUILDING A PERFORMANCE MANAGEMENT MODEL FROM A STAKEHOLDER PERSPECTIVE

Performance management should also be linked to an organization's key stakeholders (Atkinson, Waterhouse and Wells 1997; Bryson 2004; Carter 2011). If stakeholders are satisfied with the organization's performance, then clearly it is doing well. In a publicly owned sport retail business, for example, a large profit and dividend will be good for management and shareholders alike. However in a member-based sport club, success will be more about on-field performance and member services than massive profits. On the other hand, for a sport's governing body the interests of its registered players may take the highest priority. In other words, different types of sport organizations will have their own unique goals and priorities, which will in turn reflect the ways in which they rank their stakeholders (Friedman, Parent and Mason 2004).

Stakeholders may also have conflicting needs. Sponsors may want maximum media exposure and access to players, but the clubs have a primary interest in improving player performance, which may mean less, not more, player involvement in sponsor activities. In the case of a national sporting body, the national government may want international success to justify its investment in elite training and coaching programs, whereas the rank-and-file players who make up the bulk of the membership may want more local facilities. Sport organizations are therefore required to balance the often-conflicting needs and "contradictory interests" of the various stakeholders (Chappelet and Bayle 2005, p. 43). The major sport organization stakeholders and their expectations are summarized in Table 14.1.

The key point to note here is that a sport organization will have multiple stakeholders, and their interests need to be integrated into its evaluation processes.

TABLE 14.1 Stakeholder expectations of sport organizations

Stakeholder type	Expectations of sport organization
Players	• On-field success • Appropriate pay and benefits • Low injury rates
Employees	• Appropriate pay and benefits • Job security • Professional development
Equipment suppliers	• Reliability of demand • Player endorsement • Brand awareness
Members	• Services and benefits • Overall satisfaction
Owners/Shareholders	• Return on investment • Public recognition of club or association
Sponsors	• Positive reputation of club or association • Brand awareness and recognition
Player agents	• High player morale • Payment of market rates
Fans	• Game quality and excitement • High win-loss ratio
Community/Society	• Civic pride • Provides role models for young adults
Media	• Mass market • High level of public interest

AN INPUT–OUTPUT APPROACH TO PERFORMANCE MANAGEMENT

In developing a model for evaluating a sport organization's performance, a number of additional principles should be utilized. A second approach is to focus on inputs and outputs. This involves looking at things like quality, quantity, efficiency, cost–benefit ratios, and employee productivity (Anthony and Young 2003; Bouckaert 1995). This approach provides a checklist of essential performance dimensions that need to be addressed. It ensures that no one measure is dominant and also provides for measures that not only focus on internal processes, but also look at the organization's relationships with key suppliers and customers. A summary of the ways in which input-output analysis can be applied to sport organizations is illustrated in Table 14.2.

TABLE 14.2 An input–output approach to performance management in sport

Dimension	Measure
Output: Quantity	• premierships • attendance • membership • participation
Output: Quality	• standard of play • features of venue/facility • standard of service • overall customer experience
Output: Cost/benefit	• operating profit • costs of operation • net economic benefit • social benefit
Input: Efficiency	• cost of providing service • administrative support cost • waiting time
Input: Staff performance	• customer/member/fan satisfaction ratings • staff skills and experience • staff achievements

A BALANCED SCORECARD APPROACH TO PERFORMANCE MANAGEMENT

A third approach is to avoid the often obsessive emphasis that shareholders place on financial measures by balancing it against the benefits that might accrue to customers, suppliers, and employees (Harvard Business Review 1998). This approach is exemplified in the Balanced Scorecard (BSC) model designed by Kaplan and Norton (Kaplan and Norton 1992; Kaplan and Norton 1996). The BSC has four dimensions which are reviewed next.

One of the first things Kaplan et al note is that a good performance measurement tool should not be a "controlling system" obsessed with keeping "individuals, and organizational units in compliance with a pre-established plan" (p. 25). Rather it should be primarily a "learning system" concerned with "communication and informing" (p. 25). To this end Kaplan et al aimed to design a performance measurement system that balanced external and easily quantifiable measures like market share and return on investment against internal and more ephemeral factors like administrative processes and staff development.

Kaplan et al's first dimension is "Financial Perspective". Although they argue that too much emphasis has traditionally been given to the so called bottom-line result, financial measures are nevertheless a fundamental starting point for evaluating the economic sustainability of an organization. They can range from total sales, operating income, and net cash flow to return on assets, debt-to-equity ratio, and net profit. This dimension answers the question "how do we look to shareholders"?

The second dimension is "Customer Perspective". In this instance the emphasis is on identifying the "customer and market segments in which the business will compete" and to develop measures that will indicate how well the organization competes in these segments (p. 26). These measures will include total sales in each segment, market share, customer acquisition, customer retention, and customer satisfaction. Kaplan et al also suggest that for this performance dimension attention should be given to the factors like short lead times and on-time delivery that actually underpin the levels of customer satisfaction and retention. This dimension addresses the question "how do customers see us"?

The third dimension is the "Internal-Business-Process Perspective". This perspective requires management to identify the "critical internal processes in which the organization must excel" in order to secure a competitive advantage (p. 26). Kaplan et al note that it is not just a matter of ensuring that current value-adding processes are efficient and streamlined, but that there are also systems in place to improve and re-engineer existing processes and products. This dimension addresses the question "what must we excel at"?

The fourth dimension is the "Learning and Growth Perspective". Kaplan et al see this perspective as crucial to the long-term success of organizations. In a turbulent business environment there is an ever-increasing likelihood that the technologies and processes required to sustain a market advantage and competitive edge may race ahead of the technical and managerial skills of the staff who are responsible for managing those technologies and processes. In order to close this gap organizations will "have to invest in re-skilling employees, enhancing information technology and systems, and aligning organizational procedures and routines" (p. 27). This dimension addresses the question "can we continue to improve and create value"?

Finally, Kaplan et al suggest that each of these perspectives should be linked to a common over-arching objective that ensures consistency and mutually reinforcing conduct. In other words, the BSC is more than a "dashboard" of "critical indicators or key success factors" (p. 29). In order to be effective it must reflect the organization's mission and goals.

Although the BSC has been around for nearly 20 years, it has stood the test of time and still provides a solid framework for undertaking an analysis of a sports enterprise, sport event, or sports league. Moreover, it is just as applicable to a small community club as it is to a major professional sports team. This is because it allows the analyst to immediately take four different perspectives: (1) financial (2) customer (3) internal-processes, and (4) learning and growth.

COSTS AND BENEFITS OF A PERFORMANCE MANAGEMENT SYSTEM

Planning and implementing a performance management system can be costly, because it involves much time-intensive analysis of an organization's processes and activities. It can also become a bureaucratic nightmare because it can produce hundreds of microscopic statements about the ways thing should be done and how they must be measured. It should be remembered that the concept of performance management arose out of the mechanistic time-and-motion studies of Frederick Winslow Taylor in the early part of the 20th century. According to Taylor the key to increasing productivity was to systematically analyse work practices in order to identify the most efficient process, which could then become a best-practice template (Anthony and Young 2003; Stewart 1989). Taylorism also underpinned the development of Management by Objectives (MBO) and Total Quality Management (TQM) which were later refined into a broader model of performance management (Bouckaert and van Doren 2003). As a result, a rigidly structured performance management system can stifle initiative and creativity by setting narrowly defined work standards and strict standards of workplace behaviour.

At the same time, a well-thought-out performance management system can provide a number of long-term benefits (Anthony and Young 2004; Williams 1998). First, it makes sure that the core activities of an organization are directly linked to its primary aims and goals. Second, it can motivate employees by setting targets which are rewarded when they are attained. Third, it ensures greater accountability by clearly identifying not only what is to be achieved, but also who is responsible for making it happen. Fourth, it completes the management cycle by making sure processes are monitored and outcomes are measured against some sort of minimum performance standard. Finally it forces management to come up with a quantifiable measure of its key outputs and eliminate ambiguous aims and nebulous objectives (Anthony et al 2004). In short, a process of performance management is essential component of any evaluation program. But in order to ensure an appropriately focussed process, it must be tailored to fit the structural and operational parameters of the particular sport under review. Take, for example, the case of a football league.

In practice 14.1 Football leagues: an Australian perspective

The rapid commercialization of sport during the 1980s and 1990s produced many additional sport leagues around the world. This was especially true in Australia, where four football codes had vied for supremacy for most of the 20th century with varying degrees of success. These codes were Australian Rules football, rugby league, rugby union, and soccer.

Things came to a head in 2006 when a revitalized national soccer competition was established comprising eight new professionally run teams, was set up. It was completely re-badged, clubs were stripped of their ethnic origins, and the A-League was launched. By 2014 it had become a highly successful spectator sport, and some matches claimed a 40,000 attendance figure. However, most teams found it difficult to scratch out a balanced operating budget.

The National Rugby League competition (NRL) is equally robust, with all players on a full-time professional roster. Although the competition was fractured with the establishment of a rival Super League in 1995, it is solidly entrenched in New South Wales and Queensland, and to a lesser extent Victoria. However, the competition no longer has teams in either South Australian or Western Australia, although this structural problem is slightly compensated for by having a team playing out of Auckland in New Zealand.

Rugby League is an equally interesting, but more brittle case. Like League, it has only moderate support in Australia's southern states, but is a major code in New South Wales and Queensland. Union's Super-12 competition initially comprised five New Zealand teams, three Australian teams, and four South African teams. However, in 2007 another two teams were added to the competition, namely Perth in Western Australia, and a fifth South African team, thereby making it a Super-14 competition. A Melbourne and Perth team was admitted for the 2011 season, and now there are 16 teams in the competition which has been divided into a New Zealand division, an Australian division and a South African division.

Finally, there is the Australian Football League (AFL), which is Australia's most popular indigenous sport and the nation's most popular sporting competition. Having been a 16-team competition in 1986, in 2011 it became a 17-team competition, having admitted a team from the Queensland Gold Coast. A second New South Wales team was admitted in 2012, making it an 18-team competition with a minimum of two teams in every mainland state. The AFL has thus made significant inroads in the so-called 'hostile' rugby territory of New South Wales and Queensland.

Each of these football codes has their own unique history and culture, but it is also the case that they are serious rivals in a highly competitive sporting marketplace. There are many arguments about the relative strengths of each code and which national competition is the most successful (Stewart 2007a). In performance management terms, this is an interesting issue to address, but it is not immediately clear as to how one should best go about doing a comparative evaluation of the performance of the leagues. This is because there are many different ways of undertaking the performance management task.

The first point to note is that the management of each national competition is sensitive to developments in the rival leagues. They are also eager to trumpet and promote their successes, particularly if it means they have secured some of strategic advantage over their competitors. At the same time, there are a number of critical success factors that are commonly used to rank the performance of the national leagues. These factors are first, total season attendance, second, total club membership, third, aggregate league revenue, fourth, income from television broadcast rights, and finally weekly television audiences.

These five somewhat crude measures give a very good indication of just how well each league performs. However, over recent times some additional measures have been incorporated into their performance management models. First there is the issue of the viability of teams and the ability to balance their budgets. Second, there is the competitive balance of the league and the extent to which it can guarantee fans a close and exciting contest. Third, there is the reputation of the league and the extent to which it is seen as a responsible sporting citizen. To this end the leagues are eager to promote equal opportunity for players and administrators, put in place anti-harassment rules, and have a strong anti-doping policy. In general the leagues are sensitive to criticism about player misconduct, particularly when it involves illicit drug use, racist abuse, homophobia, or some sort of sexual assault. A sample of key indicators for measuring the performance of Australian national football leagues is listed in Table 14.3.

TABLE 14.3 Performance measures for Australian national football leagues

Item	Descriptor/measure	Examples
Financial stability	• League turnover • Net assets	Australian Football League (AFL) turnover is more than $450 million. National Rugby League (NRL) turnover is around $250 million.
Corporate support	• Sponsorship income • Stadium suites	AFL supported by more national brands (e.g. Vodafone, Air Emirates, Toyota) than NRL.
Broadcasting rights fees	• Fees from TV stations • Fees from radio stations	AFL TV rights fee currently $180 million pa; NRL TV rights fee currently around $120 million pa.
Media exposure	• Television rating • Print media coverage	AFL grand final draws 2.9 million TV audience; NRL grand final draws 2.3 million TV audience.
Public interest	• Brand awareness • Match attendance	AFL average match attendance 38,000; NRL average match attendance 18,000.
Spread/ coverage	• Media coverage • Spread of teams and venues	AFL teams spread around five of six states; NRL teams spread around three of six states plus New Zealand.
Competitive balance	• Win-loss ratios for each team • Premierships won by each team	NRL teams have slightly more closely aligned win-loss ratios (i.e. smaller standard deviation).
Game development	• Junior development programs • Regional development programs	AFL spends $50 million a year on community development; NRL spends $22 million on community development.

Source: AFL. (2016). *Annual Report 2015*. Melbourne: Season AFL; Stewart, B. (ed.) (2007). *The Games Are Not the Same: The Political Economy of Football in Australia*. Melbourne University Press (chapter 8).

A MULTI-DIMENSIONAL PERFORMANCE MANAGEMENT MODEL FOR SPORT

The BSC has many strengths, but it also requires significant adjustment to make it better fit the special requirements of sport organizations. One approach is to maintain the four basic dimensions that underpin the BSC and use it to design a customized performance model that reflects the special features of sport organizations. To this end the following 'nine-point' model of performance management has been designed.

The first performance dimension focuses on ***wins, awards, and successes***. This dimension recognizes the fact that most sport associations and clubs want be seen to be doing well and producing winning players and teams. In other words, faced with the choice of winning a championship or increasing profits, most clubs would prefer the winner's pennant or medal.

However, like all organizations, sport leagues, associations, and clubs need ongoing funding to ensure their long-term viability, to pay their debts when they fall due, and to cover their operating costs from year to year. Therefore, the second dimension is concerned with ***financial sustainability***. In this respect, measures of revenue growth will not be enough, and more specific measures of profit, liquidity, long-term indebtedness, return on investment, and net asset growth are all useful indicators.

The third dimension is ***market distribution***, or the extent to which a sport league, association, or club is able to facilitate the consumption of its particular sporting practice. If its major concern is with participation, then it needs to be aware of how many facilities it provides, their location and spread, and the experiential quality they offer. If the major concern is the potential audience that can be attracted, then it needs to aware of the number of spectator seats it can provide, the radio exposure it will receive, and the scale and breadth of any television broadcast.

The fourth dimension is ***market size and share***. It is one thing to have a broad range and spread of facilities and venues and a large number of television-broadcast hours, but it is another thing to attract a consistently large number of participants, spectators, and viewers. It is also important to compare the numbers for these indicators with the numbers for other related sports that are seen to be competitors.

The fifth dimension is ***customer satisfaction***, which is really a measure how strongly participants, fans, and members approve of the performance of the league, association, or club. Sport organizations usually engender very passionate connections with their customer and member base, but there are also many instances when they attend games or activities less frequently or more seriously downgrade their involvement. Surveys of participants, members, and fans can reveal early signs of dissatisfaction, or alternatively indicate what is sustaining the relationship.

The sixth dimension is ***internal procedures and processes***. Like Kaplan and Norton's similarly labelled dimension, it aims to highlight the key links in the value chain and how each stage is performing relative to the others. For sporting organizations it often begins with how well players are recruited, their numbers, and overall quality. The recruitment and retention of members is also an important consideration, and the question often arises as to the capacity of members to contribute time, expertise, and money to the association and club's activities. The ability of players to improve their skill and overall performance is also a function of the support system, and in particular the skill and abilities of the coaching staff. This leads to the capacity of the organization to ensure a safe environment where the management of risk is taken seriously and the incidence of litigation is slight. All these processes are, of course, linked to **administrative functions** that can either enhance the player and member experience as poor training or sloppy systems can make the experience both unpleasant and costly. Many of these factors can be difficult to quantify, but they nevertheless need serious consideration.

The seventh dimension is ***product improvement***. In this respect sport is no different from business in that it operates in a very competitive marketplace, and constant innovation and product improvement are essential to attract new customers and retain the old. Some sports have been very successful in modifying their games to suit the needs of special groups, whereas others have been unable to move beyond their traditional practices. In some spectator sports there have been very slow improvements in venue quality, whereas in others there has been a virtual revolution in terms of stadium design and spectator comfort. Progressive changes in the design of sporting equipment have also improved product quality. In tennis, for example, the use of carbon fibre racket frames and the creation of larger 'sweet spots' have enabled average club-players to improve their standard of play and overall skill levels.

The eighth dimension is ***staff development and learning***. Sport is a very person-centred, time-absorbing activity, and therefore requires staff who have highly refined people management skills and the capacity to create an organizational culture that retains players and members. The growing technical sophistication of sport also means that traditional administrative, officiating, and coaching skills are no longer adequate, and therefore large-scale re-training and education are necessary to ensure a proper fit between the staff competencies and the new technologies and infrastructure that underpin contemporary sport.

The ninth dimension covers the ***economic, social, and environmental impact*** that a sport league, association, or club has on its surrounding community. Increasingly the level of support a government will provide a sport organization is contingent upon the organization's ability to produce a positive economic, social, or environmental impact. This trend has been exaggerated by the growing popularity of the triple-bottom-line accounting concept, which highlights the importance of going beyond profitability and wealth creation as the sole measure of an organization's contribution to society to include environmental and social impacts (Hums and Maclean 2009; Norman and MacDonald 2004). In this case sport organizations also have a responsibility to carefully manage and sustain its environment and establish an organizational culture that values things like diversity, equal opportunity, and the fair treatment of gays, lesbians, and religious minorities.

This performance management model has the advantage of being broad and inclusive and geared to the needs of sport in general. But it needs to be customized to fit different sporting organizations. As we indicated before, an organization's strategic intent and stakeholder interests will shape the design of a performance evaluation model (Anthony and Young 2004; Atkinson, Waterhouse and Wells 1997; Robbins and Barnwell 2002; Williams 1998). For example, the evaluation model for a national sporting body should be different from the model used to evaluate a professional sport club. The national sporting body will be more interested in participation rates, club development, and the provision of quality local facilities. On the other hand, a professional sport club will be more concerned with its win-loss ratio, sponsor income, television ratings, and membership levels. Motor sports is also an interesting case study because it has to balance the spectator need for noisy, spectacular action, and the occasional collision against the demand for safety, risk management, and environmental sensitivity. The Formula 1 Grand Prix is worth investigating in this respect.

In practice 14.2 Formula 1 Grand Prix

Ever since the first motor cars rolled of the assembly plants in the United States in the early part of the 20th century, people around the world had had an often obsessive fascination with them. The idea that cars could be used to create a new form of sport was quickly converted into practice, and by the 1930s many types of race meetings were established, where stock-standard touring cars were competing with customized race cars for the hearts and minds of car-racing enthusiasts.

An international governing body for motor sports was also established at this time, and having been headquartered in Paris, was given the name of The Fédération Internationale de l'Automobile, or FIA for short (Hums and Maclean 2009). It was, and still is, a nonprofit association that now brings together more than 200 national motoring and sporting organizations from just over 130 countries on five continents.

FIA has a multi-faceted role. First, it represents the rights of motoring organizations and motor car users throughout the world. It has campaigned on such things as such as safety, mobility, the environment, and consumer law. FIA also promotes the interests of motorists at the United Nations, within the European Union, and through other international bodies. FIA is also the governing body for motor sport worldwide. It administers the rules and regulations for all international four-wheel motor sport, including the FIA Formula One World Championship, FIA World Rally Championship, and FIA World Touring Car Championship (www.fia.com).

However, plans for an elite level, high performance 'Formula One' drivers' championship were not formulated until the late 1930s. The plans were shelved with the onset of World War II, but in 1946 the idea was rekindled, races were held, and the following year a decision was made to launch a drivers' championship (Hums and Maclean 2009). The first FIA endorsed world championship race was held at the Silverstone in England, in 1950, and although only 7 of the 20 Formula One races that season counted towards the title, the championship was nevertheless up and running (Hums and Maclean 2009).

There was no shortage of so called 'privateers', who were drivers who operated on their own and bought and raced their own cars. Nevertheless, the Formula One was very quickly dominated by major pre-war manufactures such as Alfa Romeo, Ferrari, Maserati, and Mercedes Benz. Although Giuseppe ("Nino") Farina won the inaugural title in 1950, the dominant driver over the decade was Juan Manuel Fangio from Argentina, who won five drivers' championships. The 1960s was a also a period of growth, with Stirling Moss, an Englishman, and Jack Brabham, an Australian, being the best-known racers.

In the early 1970s Bernie Ecclestone, the English motor-sports entrepreneur, rearranged the management of Formula One's commercial rights and turned the sport into a billion-dollar global business. In 1971 he bought the Brabham team and subsequently gained a seat on the council of the Formula One Constructors' Association (FOCA). In 1978 he became its president. Before the Ecclestone era, FIA and circuit owners controlled many aspects of the sport, but Ecclestone changed all this when he convinced the teams that their net worth would be enhanced by by-passing FIA and negotiating directly with manufacturers and circuit managers as a coordinated unit. In 1979 FIA not surprisingly clashed with FOCA over revenues and regulations, and matters deteriorated to such an extent that FOCA threatened to boycott races and even form a breakaway global circuit. But, in the end it was understood that FOCA and FIA had to work together to achieve the best outcome for the sport, with Ecclestone front and centre.

Further tensions arose in the early 2000s when manufacturer-owned teams – which included Renault, BMW, Toyota, Honda, and Ferrari – dominated the championship. They also used the commercial muscle of their Grand Prix Manufacturers Association (GPMA) to negotiate not only a larger share of Formula One's rapidly increasing revenues, but also to have a greater say in the sport's planning and management processes.

Under the ever-opportunistic eye of Ecclestone, the global expansion of Formula One continued, with new races located in lucrative markets in East Asia and the Middle East. Whereas the inaugural 1950 world championship season comprised only seven races, the schedule expanded rapidly over the following 60 years. The number of races plateaued between 16 and 17 during the 1980s and 1990s, but has recently risen to 20.

The current global circuit arrangements for Formula One are impressive and take in every continent except Africa. But Formula One has also been surrounded by controversies and allegations of greedy, anti-social, and sometime even corrupt behaviour, which, according to the sport's critics, have taken the following forms:

- It assaults the environment by occupying public space and making an enormous amount of noise.
- It has an embedded dependence on fossil fuel products which makes it at odds with current global government policies aimed at controlling greenhouse gasses by reducing carbon emissions and consequently softening so-called carbon footprints.
- There are regular governance and management battles between FOCA, FIA, and GPMA.
- Teams often seem to be on the verge of breaking away from F1 and creating rival circuits.
- There are frequent accusations of race result manipulation. These allegations were confirmed in 2009 when it was revealed that Nelson Piquet Jr had been ordered

to crash his car at the 2008 Singapore Grand Prix for the benefit of his team mate. Renault boss Flavio Briatore was subsequently banned from the sport.

- In some cities, and in Melbourne in particular, there is growing concern that the costs of mounting the race are increasing at such a rate that the costs of conducting an event will eventually outweigh the benefits. The Melbourne event, for example, is suffering from a fall in live attendance and has had extreme difficulty securing sufficient heavyweight sponsors. There is also resentment over the management fee that has to be paid to Ecclestone to retain the event. At last count it was more than $25 million, an amount which led some critics to suggest that there was no longer any point in conducting the race in Melbourne, because it was nothing more than a burden on local taxpayers.

Controversies aside, Formula One motor racing is a highly profitable enterprise, and it has enormous global reach through its international circuit, its high-profile global sponsors, and its lucrative television broadcast contact arrangements. Its total viewing figure is now in excess of 350 million, and it regularly attracts 100,000 to 150,000 fans to its race meets (Hums and Maclean 2009). It is the archetypal hyper-commercial, hyper-modern sporting enterprise. According to an analysis undertaken by Deloitte International, one of the world's largest accounting firms, Formula One now boasts the world's highest revenue-generating annual sporting events. Each of its top eight Grand Prix events in 2008 had an average revenue of just under $220 million. This compared favourably with the per-game/event values of $25 million in the American National Football league (NFL), $8 million in the English FA Premier League, and $2 million in the American Major League Baseball (MLB) (Carter 2011; Zimbalist 2006).

The Formula One's 2008 global revenues of just over $4 billion made it the third most commercialized sport competition in the world. Only the NFL ($7 billion) and MLB ($6 billion) earn more revenue, but they did it by running substantially more so-called events. The Premier League clubs' combined revenue was just under $4 billion for the same period. The $4 billion is comprised of (1) central revenues, which come from broadcasting rights fees, race sponsorship, and corporate hospitality; (2) team revenues which include sponsorship and contributions from commercial partners and owners; and (3) and circuit revenues which comes from ticketing and additional sponsorships (Carter 2011; Hums and Maclean 2009; Zimbalist 2006).

However, when compared with many other major sports, Formula 1 attracted a much lower proportion of its revenues from event-day attendees. Ticket receipts and other attendee secondary spending currently represent only around 10% of total revenue, and this is a weakness that organizers are hoping to address in the near future.

So, how should we go about measuring the performance of the Formula One Grand Prix Circuit? Well, the short answer is 'with great difficulty'. The fundamental problem is to actually sort out what it is we aim to measure. In a global enterprise of this type there are not just the financial performance issues to consider, but also its economic, socio-cultural, and environmental impacts. One approach is to build a model of performance evaluation that takes into account all of these factors to some extent or other. A multi-factorial approach is gaining more credence as governments around the world are trying to secure the best outcomes from these mega-sport events. The fact of the matter is that commercial businesses are often criticized for thinking only of the profits they make and ignoring the social consequences of their strategic decisions and the outputs they deliver. This dilemma is particularly striking in the case of tobacco companies, which have always had close commercial links to motor racing. On one hand there are profits to be made, but on the other hand there is evidence that links smoking cigarettes to lung cancer and heart disease. Sport, and motor racing in particular, has for many years had a close relationship with tobacco producers, who have provided millions of dollars of sponsor funds to both community and professional sport (www.thelancet.com).

There is now growing pressure from both government and the public in general for businesses to move beyond the bottom line and take into account the effect their decisions have on the wider community. This idea has given rise to the concept of triple bottom-line accounting, which gets business to consider their contribution to not just economic prosperity, but also social justice and environmental quality. Although the measurement of social justice and environmental quality is fraught with danger, the overall aim is to see that profits and net worth are just one measure of the performance of an organization. Triple bottom-line accounting consequently provides for three measures of how a business contributes to society, with each measure being geared around the value-added concept. These measures – which are summarized in Table 14.4 – are economic value-added, social value-added, and environmental value-added.

A broad-based, multi-dimensional approach to performance management in sport is time absorbing and presents many challenges for sport organizations. At the same time, it has already been shown that sport organizations are motivated by more than money. For a national sporting body the growth of the sport may be equally important, and for a professional sports club the dominant goal may be on-field success.

And, further complications arise when, despite the primacy of these generally positive goals, sport organizations make decisions and produce outputs that have negative consequences for society in general. The heavy use of tobacco companies as sponsors may have secured a valuable source of funds, but the subsequent association of tobacco products with glamorous sport stars was instrumental in convincing young people that smoking was socially desirable, even if it might kill them in the long run. In some sports heavy drinking of alcohol products is part of the club culture, and in these cases no success is seen as complete without a long binge-drinking session. Similarly, in professional sport leagues, where neo-tribalism is strong, groups of rival supporters will often resolve their antagonism with a wild brawl. Football hooliganism in Britain is the archetypal model in this respect. All of these outputs have negative social consequences, and it therefore makes senses to encourage sport clubs, associations, and leagues to measure their overall performance in terms of their social

TABLE 14.4 GRI performance indicators

Performance category	Performance measures
Direct economic impacts	Sales to satisfied customers Purchases from suppliers Employees hired Taxes paid Dividend and interest paid
Product responsibility	Safety and durability Truth in advertising and product labeling
Work practices	Health, safety, and security Training, education, and consultation Appropriate wages and conditions
Social practices	No bribery and corruption Transparent lobbying Free from collusion and coercion
Human rights	Non-discriminatory hiring practices Free from forced labor
Environmental impacts	Efficient energy use Appropriate water recycling Controlled carbon and other emissions Waste management Maintenance of biodiversity

and environmental impact, as well as their participation impact, win-loss impact, or revenue-raising impact.

Recently a number of global businesses with the support of the United Nations developed a CSR program called the Global Reporting Initiative (GRI). The mission of GRI is to design and promulgate sustainability reporting guidelines for each of the economic, social, and environmental outputs identified earlier. Organizations that sign up for GRI are expected to enact reporting systems that are transparent and accessible, provide quality and reliable information, and include information that is relevant and complete. GRI has also compiled a list of factors under each of the economic, social, and environmental headings that indicate specific issues that require addressing.

Although the GRI model of performance management is complex, it will encourage sport organizations to be more systematic in the way they build their stakeholder relations. It will also enable them to go beyond revenue growth and on-field success and evaluate the contribution they are making to the wider society and monitor their impact on the physical environment. This can only be a 'good thing'. But when applied to the Formula One Grand Prix, it is also a 'hard thing'. But it is not impossible, and there is great advantage in taking a more holistic approach to measuring its performance.

Overall, this in-practice example confirms that performance measurement covers many and varied issues. It is thus important to be careful about what will be measured and what will be not. It is important to be clear about first, the mission of the sport enterprise; second, what it aims to achieve; and third, what it values in the broader social sense.

RISK, UNCERTAINTY, AND PERFORMANCE

The multi-dimensional performance management models referred to earlier have breadth, which is a strength. However, sometimes breadth can come at the expense of connectivity, and this can be problematic. One way of securing a stronger sense of integration is to view the model through the operational lens of risk and uncertainty. Risk and uncertainty are pivotal components of any performance management model because they can seriously undermine performance levels if left unattended.

But what exactly is risk? At its most succinct, risk is the likelihood that a chosen action, initiative, or activity – or alternatively, a choice to not act, take no initiative, or remain inactive – will deliver some type of harm, lead to a loss, or produce a sub-optimal, or wholly undesirable outcome. This, of course, implies that the chosen action, initiative, or activity will, in fact, have some influence over the anticipated performance outcome

For the technically minded and those readers who like to think in short 'grabs', risk can be defined in terms of the following equation:

Risk = Probability * Consequences

That is, risk is the probability of a 'bad' or 'harmful' thing happening multiplied by the consequences that will occur if the 'bad' or 'harmful' things do, in fact, happen. Take, for example, the curator of a sports field, who finds that he has not been able to create the expected smooth and well-grassed playing surface, and indeed, has failed to fill some serious potholes, and forgot to remove large bits of broken glass from an expanse of the playing surface. In this case risk is exceedingly high, because the probability of something nasty happening to players will be high, and if something unpleasant does happen, the consequences – including overall levels of performance – will be very serious indeed.

So, we can go on to say that risk management is all about being aware of what may happen as you go about your business and taking steps to limit the chances of something going wrong, or deciding that you accept that something may occur and that you are prepared for the consequences. Risk management therefore aims to be proactive rather than reactive, and thus provide the conditions for creating safer physical environments, safer operational procedures, safer playing spaces, and finally, higher levels of performance.

When examining the delivery of a sporting experience, risks can be viewed from a number of perspectives, with each perspective carrying its own mix of clarity and fuzziness. The first perspective is **_strategic_**. In this case the risks are associated with the high-level longer-term goals, objectives, or strategies of the organization, club, association, or league. The second perspective is **operational**. In this case the risks are associated with the daily functions of the organization such as finance, decision making, marketing and promotion, and the administrative areas of clubs, associations, and leagues. The third perspective is related to a **project or event**. In this case the risks are linked to specific stages of the operational outcome. They include the (1) initiation and concept phase, (2) planning phase, (3) execution and implementation phase, and (4) the performance evaluation phase. It is one thing to note the influence risk can have on conduct and performance, but it is another thing to assess the scale and scope of the risk for different phases of an activity, program, or event.

Risk assessment involves analyzing the likelihood and consequences of each identified risk using whatever measures might be provided. When multiplied out, the overall level of risk can be calculated. The purpose here is to separate high risks from low risks and to prioritize those areas where resources should be allocated to ensure continuity, predictability, and safety.

At this point the two key terms to address are 'likelihood' and 'consequence'. Likelihood is a qualitative description of probability and frequency. For anything even slightly unpredictable or uncertain it is always useful to ask: What is the likelihood of the risk occurring? Consequence is the outcome of an event or situation expressed qualitatively or quantitatively, being a loss, injury, disadvantage, harm, benefit, or gain. In this instance it is always useful to ask: What is the consequence if the risk does indeed occur?

In summary, high levels of risk may, in a few lucky instances, lead to a miraculous performance, but in most cases will deliver obstacles, excessive anxiety, and a high probability that things will go wrong. From a performance management perspective, this is the worst possible environment to create. And, unfortunately, this is exactly what happened in an ultra-marathon event conducted in the Australian outback in 2011.

In practice 14.3 The 2011 Kimberley Ultra-marathon

In early September 2011, a 100-km ultra-marathon event was conducted in the remote, but picturesque, Kimberley region of Western Australia, which is in the northwest part of the state. It involved a predominantly off-road course starting from the Emma Gorge airstrip at El Questro and finishing in the town of Kununurra.

The event was titled the 2011 Kimberley Ultra-marathon and was organized by a Hong Kong–based events management business called Racing The Planet Events Limited, or RacingThePlanet, its abbreviated title. It had attracted a sponsorship commitment from EVENTSCORP, the Western Australian Government's events agency and an operating division within Tourism WA, for around $105,000 with an option for a further two years. It was a significant event. It had captured a lot of media interest, and it attracted competitors from around the world.

The RacingThePlanet business was also very experienced in conducting these sorts of events and had staged more than 33 footraces in eight countries over the preceding 10 years. This was the second event that RacingThePlanet had staged in the Kimberley region. In April 2010 RacingThePlanet had successfully organized a 250-km seven-day event in the same area.

The 2011 event secured massive publicity, but for all the wrong reasons. During the event, at least 13 competitors were directly confronted by a large bushfire. Five competitors – Turia Pitt, Kate Sanderson, Martin Van Der Merwe, Michael Hull, and Mary Gadams – were unable to escape the flames and suffered burns of varying degrees of severity. The injuries suffered by Ms Pitt and Ms Sanderson were life threatening, and left them with permanent scarring, disfigurement, and disability. Overall, the event turned out to be a catastrophe.

In response to a public outcry over what appeared to be management incompetence, the WA Legislative Assembly directed its Economics and Industry Standing Committee to investigate the incident. The committee was asked to examine the actions of the organizer and the roles and actions of a range of government agencies in respect of the event. The committee was also asked to consider whether RacingThePlanet had taken all reasonable steps to identify and reduce risks and maintain the safety of competitors, employees, contractors, spectators, and volunteers in (1) planning for the event, (2) running the event, and (3) responding to the fire and the injuries, including access to medical support and evacuations.

Having taken thousands of pages of written submissions and oral evidence, the committee found that RacingThePlanet did not take all reasonable steps to identify risks associated with the 2011 Kimberley Ultra-marathon. Nor did the committee believe that RacingThePlanet had taken all reasonable steps to reduce risks to the safety of competitors, employees, contractors, spectators, and volunteers.

The committee also identified a series of factors which demonstrated that RacingThePlanet did not take all reasonable steps to maintain the safety of these parties. In the first place, the committee concluded that RacingThePlanet, in its planning processes leading up to the 2011 Kimberley Ultra-marathon, did not involve people who had an appropriate knowledge in identifying risk. Second, the level of communication and consultation with relevant agencies and individuals regarding the event's Management and Risk Assessment Plan was seen to be inadequate, both in terms of its timeliness and its approach. Third, and as a result of the previous two failings, RacingThePlanet deprived itself of the opportunity to identify risks that it may not have contemplated and to establish relationships with key agencies that may have been able to provide ongoing assistance with risk identification and mitigation.

The committee found that most crucially, RacingThePlanet did not communicate properly before the event pre-race with the local fire authority. It did not link into their fire monitoring expertise and advice prior the race. This would have been highly valuable to RacingThePlanet in terms of whether the race needed to be re-routed – with fires in the vicinity of the course – or possibly cancelled. Similarly, the committee found that during the race, when a message of fire approaching a checkpoint was relayed to RacingThePlanet staff, proper counsel with the local fire authority regarding the appropriate response could have improved the decision-making capacity of the organizer. The committee also believed that RacingThePlanet was aware of fires on and in the vicinity of the course prior to and on the day of the event. It also found that it was advised to contact the fire authority, but did not do so. In short, RacingThePlanet did not have a plan to monitor fire on the course other than by direct observation.

According to the committee, another critical shortcoming in the pre-event consultation process was the planning for an emergency helicopter. Despite knowing for some time that a helicopter was the only means of evacuation from the Tier Gorge section of the course, RacingThePlanet only sought to make arrangements for the use of a helicopter in the event of an emergency the day before the race. RacingThePlanet decided not to put a helicopter on stand-by, and instead made informal and inadequate arrangements for the use of the helicopter hired separately by a media company filming the event. The committee also noted that this helicopter was not appropriately equipped for a range of emergency and evacuation scenarios. Moreover, as the event unfolded on the day, RacingThePlanet's plan for using this helicopter in the event of an emergency was not enacted correctly, was not well understood, and suffered from only having been determined the day before the event.

Given the trauma the event created for its participants, and despite the publicity it gained and profit it extracted, the event can only be measured as a massive failure. The organizer's risk-management strategy was not up to the task, and the social costs produced by the event completely negated any positive contribution it made to the broader community. This is a classic case of an event that could only be rated as less than zero. In short, the event would have, perversely, received a higher rating had it not been held.

PERFORMANCE MEASURES: LONGITUDINAL OR COMPARATIVE?

Once a performance management model is in place, it is then crucial to design performance measures. These measures should be able to precisely identify and quantify specific indicators of success or failure. Sometimes it is difficult to 'put a number' on a measure. Customer and fan 'satisfaction' readily comes to mind in this respect, but there are often ways of converting a subjective opinion into a measurable indicator.

It is one thing to identify some key performance indicators and to collect some data under each heading. However, it is another thing to make sense of the data. It is therefore important to develop some sort of benchmark or standard by which to measure the performance of a sport organization. There are two ways of doing this.

The first is to undertake a *longitudinal study* that examines the progress of a sport organization over time. Take for example the performance of Athletics Australia (AA), the national governing body for athletics in Australia. A 10-year analysis of its financial performance would show it was often unable to balance its books. In 2003 it had accumulated a seriously worrying level of debt which brought on an organizational crisis. The crisis was addressed, and over the following eight years it expanded its revenue base substantially, and in preparing for the London 2012 Olympics, was relatively resource rich. At the same time it was still reliant on government funds to balance its books. By any financial measure,

AA's performance had improved dramatically over this period, although it was starting off from a low base. The same sort of longitudinal analysis could be applied to its participation levels and elite international performance. In each case the data indicated small but significant improvement.

Another way of looking at AA's performance would be to **compare** it with other national sport bodies to see how it ranks. That is, it will also be important to undertake a comparative study by which the performance of AA is stacked up against a number of other national sport organizations. There are two ways of doing this. The first way would be compare it with similarly funded Australian national sport bodies like Swimming Australia or Rowing Australia. In this case, AA has not performed well, because both swimming and rowing have achieved regular gold medal winning performances at both World Championships and Olympic Games over the last 10 years. The second way is to compare AA's performance with an equivalent national athletic association from another country. An appropriate point of comparison here might be the Canadian Athletics Federation because both countries have similar populations, and the national athletic associations have a similar resource base. In this case the comparison would yield an elite performance outcome inferior to Swimming Australia, which by international standards performs just below the level of the USA national swim governing body, which makes it number two in the world.

PERFORMANCE MEASUREMENT: FROM GLOBAL TO LOCAL

As noted earlier, performance measurement has many variants, especially when applied to sport. It could be directed to the impact a mega-event has on a local economy or the operating profit of an international field hockey tournament. It can focus on player achievements in a professional basketball club, it can also revolve around changes in a club's levels of debts, or it can be concerned with the growth in the number of registered players in a local tennis association. It can be global, but it can also be local. It can involve a profit-making gym of a nonprofit fitness centre. This is the focus of the following case.

In practice 14.4 Facility evaluation and staff appraisal

As we indicated in the early part of this chapter, performance management systems have infiltrated their way into every nook and cranny of the business environment and public sector (Robbins and Barnwell 2002; Bouckaert and van Doren 2003). Moreover, they are not only applied to corporate performance, but also to many of the so-called micro-activities that comprise the day-to-day operations of business enterprises. Community leisure centres in particular lend themselves to micro-measurement. In the first place, they provide an array of person-centred activities that are subject to strong user responses and perceptions. Second, their services are not only rated on the scale, range, and quality of its tangible facilities, but also on the quality of the service provided by the staff. Third, many community leisure centres are funded and subsidized through local government rates and taxes and therefore need to ensure that scarce community resources are utilized as efficiently as possible (Graaff 1996).

It is useful to examine the performance of community leisure centres from two perspectives. The first perspective focuses on the efficient use of funds, staff, and space. To get some idea of how funds are being used, it is always good to start with some idea of the relationship between operating costs and income. This will generate an operating profit indicator and an expense recovery rate. And where more detail is needed, something like fees (admission charges) per visit or fees per unit of space can be calculated. It is also very important to identify not only the gross subsidy that may apply, but also the subsidy per visit. There are also a number of sales- and marketing-related measures that can be used to indicate how well funds are being used in attracting visitors. They include things like total visits per space used and promotion cost per visitor. It is also important to measure facility usage. In this instance measures include visit per metre of space, maintenance cost per unit of centre expenditure, and energy cost per metre of space. Finally, there are a number of measures that provide an indication of how well staff are being utilized. They include staff cost as a percentage of total income, staff costs as percentage of total centre expenditure, and the ratio of desk staff to programming staff. A sample of performance indicators for community leisure centres is listed in Table 14.5.

TABLE 14.5 Sample of efficiency indicators for a community leisure centre

Indicator	Description	Examples
Expense recovery rate	Ratio of total centre income to total centre expenses	Income of $5 million, expenses of 4.5 million, expense recovery rate is 111.
Admission fees per visit	Total fees divided by number of visits	1,000 visits per week, $6,000 in fees, admission fee per visit is $6.
Visits per space available	Visits divided by amount of space	1,000 visits per week, 50 square metres of space, visit per metre-space is 200.
Promotion costs per visitor	Promotion costs divided by number of visitors	1,000 visits per week, $1,000 of promotion per week, promotion cost per visit is $1.
Maintenance costs rate	Ratio of total centre maintenance costs to total centre income to	Maintenance costs are 1.5 million, centre income is $5 million, maintenance cost rate is .30 or 30%.
Staff costs per unit of space	Staff costs divided by space	Staff costs are $3 million, space is 50 square metres, staff cost per unit of space is $6,000.

The second perspective focuses on the level of service quality. In this instance it is a matter of finding out what visitors think of their experiences in the centre (Beech and Chadwick 2004). Their experiences are usually divided into five categories. They are, first, the quality of the tangible product or service itself; second, the reliability and dependability of the service; third, the responsiveness of staff and their willingness to assist; fourth, an assurance that staff will be trustworthy and courteous; and finally, the degree to which staff are empathetic and provide individual attention. There are many models to choose from and many rating tools. Some of the more sophisticated tools aim to calculate a service delivery gap, which is nothing more than the difference between what customers expected and what they experienced (Graaff 1996). In the end, all they are doing is providing a customer rating of the facilities and personal service provided. Typically this will be done by a survey or questionnaire that asks visitors to score the specific services on a rating scale of 1 to 5. Ratings of 1 usually indicate low levels of satisfaction, whereas ratings of 5 will indicate high levels of satisfaction.

RATING SPORT COACH PERFORMANCE

Another example of a localized performance management activity might involve the assessment of a coach's job over the course of season. At first glance, the problem of working out how to best to judge the performance of a sport coach appears quite simple. The intuitive response to any question about coaching performance is to examine the sport team's performance by referring to its win-loss ratio. It would follow, then, that a team with a win-loss ratio of 0.80 or 80% has outperformed a team whose win-loss ratio was 0.60 or 60%. Alternatively, a current season win-loss ratio of 0.70 or 70%, when contrasted with a previous season win-loss ratio of 0.50 or 50%, would also suggest an improved level of performance. Not only would the coach be happy with this sort of result, but so too would the club officials and the fans.

It is fair to say that coaches are responsible for securing the best outcomes from their team. However, it is also reasonable to propose that coaches can only work within the limits set by the resources and playing talent at their disposal. There is a theory of strategic management called the resource-based view (RBV), which says that the key to getting a competitive edge is all to do with the quality of resources at your disposal. This competitive edge can be best secured by assembling resources that are (1) valuable and can consequently generate greater efficiencies; (2) scarce, which means they are difficult to secure; and (3) inimitable and therefore not easy to replicate. In short, superior performance will result from a strong endowment of resources that cannot be matched by competitors.

This model brings into question the idea that a coach's performance can be measured solely against a series of win-loss ratios. Under the assumptions of the RBV model, team performance has as much to do with playing talent and support service quality as it has to do with the leadership style and technical capacities of the coach. In other words, any rating of coaching performance should take into account the quality and scale of resources that the coaches have at their disposal.

SUMMARY

This discussion suggests that although the introduction of performance management systems into sport organizations may seem costly and possibly create an administrative straitjacket for its staff, officials, volunteers, and members, it can also bring substantial benefits (Anthony et al 2004). In fact, a sport organization that does not provide a systematic evaluation of its performance would be derelict in its duty to stakeholders. The question is really one of what form and shape the performance management system should take. At this point it is important to say that there is no one best performance management system. It all depends on the particular sport organization being studied, its primary strategic goals, and the environment in which it operates. A good starting point is to use Kaplan and Norton's BSC as the foundation and customize it to the fit the sport organization's specific needs. The nine-point model described earlier gives a number of possibilities, but at all times the measures should be quantifiable, linked to the sport organization's primary goals, and consistent with stakeholder expectations.

REVIEW QUESTIONS

1   What does a performance management system aim to do?

2   What are the origins of performance management, and what do these origins tell us about its possible strengths and weaknesses?

3   What might prevent a sport organization from implementing a system of performance management?

4   What are the benefits that will follow from the implementation of a performance management system?

5   What are the key components of Kaplan and Norton's BSC?

6   How might you go about modifying the BSC to make it better fit the special features of sport organizations?

7   What specific measures can best reveal the financial performance of a sport organization?

8   How can the intrinsically vague concept of customer satisfaction be 'hardened up' to provide a quantitative, concrete measure of the service quality in a community leisure centre?

9   What would you advise a sport club or association to do in order to ensure it was delivering its sport services in a fair, equitable, and environmentally friendly way?

DISCUSSION QUESTIONS

1   What is meant by the term performance management?

2   What are some performance indicators a manager might use for measuring the operations of a sport organization?

3   What are some specific tools a manager might use to measure organizational performance in a sport setting?

4   Explain why risk management processes are essential for sustained levels of performance in sport organizations.

5   What is meant by the term social responsibility, and how can it be used to indicate either low or high levels of performance?

FURTHER READING

To get a more detailed picture of the fundamentals of performance management and how it has been used in both private and public sectors, see Anthony and Young 2003; Bryson, 2004; and Bouckaert et al (2003). In order to obtain a fuller appreciation of the theoretical foundations of performance management, its relation to organizational effectiveness, and problems of implementation, refer to chapter 3 of Robbins et al (2002), and Bouckaert (1995).

To secure more details on what makes sport both similar to and different from the world of business go to Smith, A. and Stewart, B. (2010).

For a detailed account of how to set up performance management systems for Olympic sport organizations see Chappelet, J. and Bayle, E. (2005). *Strategic and Performance Management of Olympic Sport Organisations*. Champaign, IL: Human Kinetics, pp. 39–110.

A comprehensive comparative evaluation of the four professional football leagues operating in Australia can be found in chapter 8 of Stewart, B. (ed.) (2007). *The Games Are Not the Same: The Political Economy of Football in Australia*. Melbourne University Press.

RELEVANT WEBSITES

For an update on the Balanced Scorecard approach to performance management, go to <www.balancedscorecard.org>

Japan's professional soccer (ie association football) league, the J. League is one of Japan's most popular sport competitions. To obtain a general picture of its overall level of performance, go to < www.j-league.or.jp/eng/ >.

In Australia, the Australian Football League is highly profitable, but paradoxically some of its member clubs have had to fight severe financial turbulence over many years. The Institute of Chartered Accountants undertakes an annual survey of club finances. For further details search for the *Enhancing Not-for-Profit Annual and Financial Reporting* report on the www.icaa.org.au site.

The Western Australian Government inquiry into the 2011 Ultra marathon disaster is available at: www.parliament.wa.gov.au/parliament/. . . /Report+No.+13+-+Final+-+20120816.pdf

For a detailed discussion of the Global Reporting Initiative (GRI) and related indicators go to www.globalreporting.org

Nike has developed a strong corporate social responsibility program in recent years, For a detailed discussion of their sustainable business program go to www.nikeresponsibility.com/report/

CASE STUDY 14.1

Making performance management a multi-dimensional experience: the case of Nike

Nike is known around the world for its catchy slogan, Just Do It. Its vision exemplifies this motto. According to one of its 2013 promotional messages, Nike, Inc., is the "world's leading innovator in athletic footwear, apparel, equipment and accessories". In some ways this has always been the case, because even in its early days it was in the forefront of running shoe design. This is not surprising given the talents and imagination of its founders Phil Knight and Bill Bowerman. Knight was a middle-distance runner from Portland, Oregon, who, having attended the University of Oregon in the 1950s, went on to complete a master's degree in Administration at California's Stanford University. Bowerman was a track and field coach at the University of Oregon, coached Knight for a short time, and became internationally known for his constant innovation in both training schedules and equipment design. They established Blue Ribbon Sports (BRS) in 1964 and secured an agreement with Japan's Onitsuka Co. to be a distributer for the Tiger running shoe brand. The rest, as they, was history. Nike is now one of the most recognizable brands on the planet.

This was the beginning of Nike, because it soon led to BRS creating the Nike vision that has become one of the world's best-known and profitable sports businesses. The Nike enterprise was established as an independent legal entity in in 1970, and in the following year it opened a mail-order system, established its first retail store – in Santa Monica, California – and created the "Swoosh" brand mark. The new Nike line of footwear debuted in 1972, and through the use of a lightweight 'waffle' sole immediately captured a solid market, especially amongst serious runners. The big sales breakthrough occurred in 1979 with the launch of the Tailwind running shoe. It not only sold well amongst track runners, but also made a massive mark on the running and jogging movement that was sweeping America at the time. It all took off after that and for the next five years Nike had entered a golden age of escalating commercial growth.

However, things changed in the early 1980s. Nike had slipped from its position as the industry leader, in part because the company had badly miscalculated on the aerobics boom. Reebok had captured this market, and Nike's stocks fell both materially and figuratively.

As the 1980s progressed, Nike regressed, and there were concerns that the branding bubble had burst and Nike was to become just another bland running shoe. But this changed dramatically with signing Michael Jordan in 1985. This single decision rejuvenated the brand, and Jordan went on to become the world's best basketballer, the world's best known athlete, and the symbol of Nike's product line. In 1987, using Jordan as its premier salesperson, Nike launched a massive product and marketing campaign designed to regain the industry lead and differentiate Nike from its competitors. The focal point was the Air Max, the first Nike footwear to feature Nike Air bags that were visible. In 1989, Nike's cross-training business exploded, thanks in part to the incredibly popular 'Bo Knows' ad campaign. By the end of the decade, Nike had regained its position as the industry leader.

In 1995 Nike undertook another bold initiative when it signed up the entire World Cup–winning Brazilian National Team. It went on to sign up the U.S. men's and women's national soccer teams, as well as dozens of national teams around the world. In 1996, Nike struck another pot of product-endorsement gold when it signed up the vastly talented but as-yet-unproven amateur golfer named Eldrick 'Tiger' Woods for a reported $5 million per year. Competitors laughed and critics howled at Nike's 'folly,' until Tiger won the 1997 Masters by a record 12 strokes. Nike continued its relentless sales drive in the new millennium by introducing a new footwear cushioning system called Nike Shox, which debuted during the Sydney Olympic Games in 2000. The development of Nike Shox culminated in more than 15 years of perseverance and dedication, as Nike designers stuck with their idea until technology could catch up. The result was a cushioning and stability system which Nike modestly claimed was worthy of joining Nike Air as the industry's gold standard.

By 2012 Nike had achieved its goal of beings the world's leading supplier of sports footwear and sports apparel despite intense competition from Adidas. This was reflected in its financial statements. Its total global revenue was USD 24,000 million which delivered an operating profit of USD 2,200 million. That is, for every USD 1 earned there was a profit margin of USD 0.09. Or, to put it another way, every dollar of spending generated USD 1.05 in of revenue. Nike had accumulated USD 15,500 million of assets, 11,500 million of which were identified as current. But in increasing its stocks of assets it had also built up USD 11,500 million of debt, 3,900 million of which were current. Overall, its net worth was posted as USD 10,400 million. As at 2017, it is still the industry leader, and although Adidas has had many product line successes, it is very much the follower.

But this is only part of the Nike story. Along the way it has been accused of

- Exploiting its labour force by taking production offshore and locating it in low-wage countries in Southeast Asia.
- Creating obscenely large mark ups on the footwear and apparel and getting away with it by building a brand around quality and status.
- Using its market power to eliminate competition and maximize profits
- Destroying the economic, social, and physical environments in which they operate.

Most of these accusations were true, and as a result Nike has, in recent times, promulgated the idea that it is, in reality, a socially responsible business that not only cares about its suppliers, employees, customers, and the environment in which it operates, but also does something about it. It has, for example, taken the following initiatives recently:

It implemented an advanced "Manufacturing Index," a single evaluation system, covering all products and brands that the company uses to assess and improve performance of its off-shore contract factories, in line with international standards. In addition to traditional metrics of quality, delivery, and cost, the metrics of environmental sustainability and ethical labor practices have been incorporated into the index. The index creates one score for each factory and ranks them as Gold, Silver, Bronze, Yellow, or Red; all factories are expected to achieve a minimum Bronze rating.

As part of its environmental sustainability program and desire to limit the use of natural resources, it deployed 'eco-friendly' materials, products, and practices in its production processes. For example, its Flyknit technology used a single thread to knit a shoe upper, which helped in the preparation of more custom-fitted and lighter shoes, while also generating less waste during the upper production process.

It also implemented programs to address a range of social problems, the main one being childhood obesity and related diseases and their association with physical inactivity. Having understood the scale of the problem – in the United States, only one out of three children is physically active – it committed $50 million to support Michelle Obama's Lets Move! Initiative. It worked with the U.S. Departments of Health and Human Services and Education to educate and inspire children to pursue outdoor activities and have them make physical activity a core part of their daily lives.

CASE STUDY QUESTIONS

1   Where does Nike fit on the scale of international sport footwear and clothing businesses? Does it have any rivals and, if so, who are they?

2   During the 1980s and 1990s, Nike suffered from a number of commercial meltdowns. First, Adidas took away a lot of its market share. Second, its international image was tarnished by its use of low-wage workers in developing countries and premium prices in developed countries. What does this tell you about the corporate social responsibility (CSR) of Nike?

3   What did Nike do to turn around its highly unfavourable image?

4   To what extent did this turnaround involve producing better footwear, on the one hand, or being more socially responsible and less exploitative, on the other?

5   How would you rate the overall performance of Nike at the moment, giving examples.

6   What are Nike's prospects for the next decade?

7   Is it possible for Nike to both run at a profit and meet its social responsibility obligations?

8   What should Nike do to ensure a high level of corporate performance in the future?

FURTHER READING

More details about Nike's social responsibility programs can be secured from recent annual reports for Nike. See, for example:

http://about.nike.com/pages/sustainable-innovation

See also:

http://panmore.com/nike-inc-stakeholders-csr-analysis

The 2016 Annual Report for Nike is available at:

https://materials.proxyvote.com/Approved/654106/20160722/SHLTR_293228/HTML1/default.htm

CASE STUDY 14.2

Going beyond raw numbers: performance management in the American National Women's Basketball Association

The Women's National Basketball Association, or WNBA, as it is more colloquially known is a national competition for women and is situated in the home of professional sport leagues, the United States. The United States is the cultural home of women's basketball, and the national team regularly wins the world and Olympics titles. During the latter part of the 20th century there was constant chatter amongst the American basketball fraternity that a national women's league should be introduced. There were good reasons for this initiative. Not only was women's basketball played across the nation, but it was also especially popular amongst college students. There were many national advertisers and sponsors waiting in the wings, so to speak, and there was an optimistic belief that a professional women's basketball competition would attract both viable attendances and a solid television audience.

So, in early 1996, after a lot of deliberation and careful planning, the National Basketball Association (NBA) Board of Governors approved the concept of a women's professional basketball league, the WNBA. There had been some earlier abortive attempts to get a women's league off the ground, but they had failed due to poor organization and a lack of a strong cash flow. This initiative was different because it had the support of the NBA and its huge resource base, and it therefore followed that the WNBA had a good chance of paying its way to a successful future.

Things got off to a flying start when, even before any players had signed a playing contract, the league established its broadcast partnerships with three major television networks: NBC, ESPN, and Lifetime. This not only meant a guaranteed stream of revenue, but it also meant that games could be televised live. The league was also given an interesting twist when it was decided that the WNBA season would be played during the summer. Additionally, it secured the Spalding sport equipment supplier as national advertiser, who designed the orange-and-oatmeal coloured WNBA signature ball. The league also heavily marketed its catchy slogan, 'We Got Next', prior to the season commencing.

Eight teams were announced for the inaugural season and were organized into two conferences or divisions. The Eastern Conference consisted of the Charlotte Sting, Cleveland Rockers, Houston Comets, and New York Liberty, and the Western Conference was composed of the Los Angeles Sparks, Phoenix Mercury, Sacramento Monarchs, and Utah Starzz. Teams were allocated players, and a so-called 'elite draft' was used to recruit foreign players.

The season commenced in the summer of 1997. In the early part of the league's development there were few problems and many successes. As noted earlier, the league was backed, both symbolically and financially, by the NBA. It also had a unique organizational and legal structure, because every team was effectively owned by the league. In this 'single-entity' competition, clubs were not franchises, but rather operating divisions of the league. This meant the central body had control over wage levels recruitment, and therefore substantial control over costs, which in the first instance seemed a very good thing.

The league also captured the imagination of television viewers in the first instance. During a successful inaugural season, more than 50 million viewers watched WNBA games on the three networks. The WNBA also delivered a unique audience profile for an elite sporting competition. In the case of at-arena attendance, the gender breakdown was about 70% female and 30% male. The TV audience was around 50% female and 50% male, with a stronger percentage of non-adult viewers than is normally the case. In short, a lot of young, mostly middle-class women supported the league.

Following on from the successful inaugural season, the WNBA expanded from eight teams to 16. The Detroit Shock and Washington Mystics joined the league in 1998, the Minnesota Lynx and Orlando Miracle in 1999, and the Indiana Fever, Miami Sol, Portland Fire, and Seattle Storm in 2000. The 2002 season was highly successful and signalled to the sports-going public that professional sport leagues for women were not only viable, but also destined to become an integral part of the North American sporting landscape. There were 176 women playing professional basketball in 256 regular-season WNBA games. In the inaugural 1997 season only 28 games were played. The future of the league looked assured.

However, the gloss faded, and the optimism was blunted over the following 10 years. The WNBA went through difficult times, and by 2013 – the 17th year of the competition – there were only 12 teams in the league. So what went wrong, both strategically and financially? Strategically, it appears that the league may have expanded too rapidly and exposed itself to a build-up of costs. Financially, the evidence now indicates that despite its initial progress, and despite the committed support from millions of women who desperately wanted the competition to succeed, it was never going to be financially viable. Looking back it becomes clear that operating revenues rarely covered operating costs, and most clubs were running losses.

As one commentator claimed, the WNBA had, over the course of its first 17 years "never made a dime", which in accounting parlance means it could never deliver an operating profit for its owners, the NBA. In other words, the WNBA has survived – from a financial perspective – only because of the subsidies provided by the NBA. This may be a harsh and even an unfair thing to say and additionally play into the hands of sporting traditionalists who see real professional sports as a 'men's-only' affair. But it may be also the only reasonable conclusion to be drawn from the facts. But what are the so-called facts, and who do we believe anyway? To assist in the analysis of this case, the following points are considered:

- The WNBA started out with 8 teams and grew to 16 before several franchises folded. It now fields 12 teams. Six teams – Indiana, New York, Minnesota, Phoenix, San Antonio, and Washington – are owned by NBA franchises. The WNBA teams share training facilities and arenas.
- Just how bad, then, are the WNBA's finances? Apparently the league's first-ever 'cash flow–positive' team was the Connecticut Sun in 2010. NBA Commissioner David Stern regularly conceded that the NBA has subsidized the WNBA in recent years by up to $4 million a season.
- Sponsorships have been an important revenue stream for the league, boosted by the league's successful marketing campaign geared towards branding the league showcase for healthy values. Team sponsorship revenue has increased by around 10% from 2005–2010. The WNBA also secured a strong commercial relationship with Boost Mobile (BM), and the BM logo was placed on 11 of the league's 12 shirts. The league recently added Anheuser-Busch as a major sponsor.
- Average attendance over recent years has fallen by more than 4%. Average game attendance for the league is now around 7,700.
- In 2011 the WNBA signed new partnerships with Jamba Juice, Coca-Cola, and Pirate's Booty snack food.
- The WNBA often averages a 0.2 cable rating (around 263,000) on ESPN2. By any measure this is a minuscule audience for a nationally telecast American television program.

This information provides some insight into the structural and financial problems facing the WNBA, but does not provide any significant financial data that can illuminate the overall problem, or identify or even expose the key cost burdens and revenue shortfalls. We can only imagine what is going on, but it is clear that the problem is not a cost one. To put it more precisely, the problem is not one of an inflated player salaries. According to the league's collective bargaining agreement (CBA), the 2012 team salary cap was just under USD 900,000. When allocated over the player roster it comes in at around US$70,000 per player per season. This, by any professional sports league measure, is meagre. In contrast, the salary cap for the men's league is US$25 million. Most male basketball players claim an annual salary of 3 to 4 million. The gap is obscene from a gender equality perspective, but this is the reality of professional sport. It is all about capacity to pay, which suggests that the revenue base of the WNBA has been frighteningly low for the entirety of its existence.

This case has many facets to it. It is about women's sport, it is about the role played by subsidies, and it is also about the lack of transparency that operates in many sports around the world. In this instance we just do not know what is going on from a financial perspective, and this is not a good thing. The other interesting about this case is that it has been played out in a setting that, at first glance, lends itself to accommodating a women's professional sports league. The United States has a population of more than 330 million people, it is one of the world's wealthiest nations, women are for the most part liberated from the oppression of hyper-masculine men with hyper-masculine belief systems, and, additionally, sport is a national obsession. It should, by any account, be the perfect setting for a sports league of this type to flourish, both culturally and financially. But something has gone horribly wrong somewhere. There were high expectations for this sports league, and it was underpinned by a lot of goodwill and strong stakeholder support. And, what is more, the WNBA is a vocal proponent of women's rights, with a special interest in the human rights of black Americans.

But despite all these positive developments, it appears that unless there are dramatic changes ahead, the league may not be around, at least in its present form, in 2020. If commercial sustainability is the ultimate performance measure, then the WNBA has a very low rating indeed. On the other hand, if fan engagement, inclusiveness, learning, and equity are prioritized as the key performance indicators, then the WNBA has made a very positive community impact. At the moment, the WNBA has an uncertain future. The problems it faced in 2012 are still present in 2017.

CASE STUDY QUESTIONS

1 When did the WNBA league begin? And how was it initially organized?

2 How did the WNBA league perform in its first few years of operation?

3 What were its strengths and limitations over this period?

4 To what extent was the WNBA league self-sustaining financially?

5 How would you rate the strength of its relationship with television?

6 How would you rate the quality of its partnerships and sponsorships?

7 How would you rate the average venue attendance?

8 How would you rate the pay rates for women basketballers compared to men basketballers? Is there a problem here, and how might it be addressed?

9 From a manager's perspective, does it make sense to continue to conduct a women's sport league if it had difficulty balancing its budget?

10 How might you justify the continuation of a women's sport league despite its lack of financial viability?

11 Which stakeholders would have been comfortable, and indeed happy, with the overall performance of WNBA, and which stakeholders would have been disappointed with its performance.

FURTHER READING

The WNBA game attendance problem is discussed at:

www.nytimes.com/2016/05/28/sports/basketball/after-two-decades-wnba-still-struggling-for-relevance.html

The WNBA player salary problem is discussed at:

www.myajc.com/sports/basketball/salaries-issue-for-wnba-players/3altjAlKWhILYX-eOlg0TDK/

The WNBA's image problem is discussed at:

www.huffingtonpost.com/lyndsey-darcangelo/the-wnbas-biggest-problem_b_9437480.html

Details of the social responsibility projects supported by the WNBA are listed at:

www.slate.com/blogs/xx_factor/2016/07/25/the_wnba_s_black_lives_matter_protest_has_set_new_standard_for_sports_activism.html

An update of the WNBA is available at:

www.wnba.com/

Bibliography

Adamson, J. and Spong, S. (2014). *Sport Makers Evaluation*. London: CFE Research.

Allison, M. (2002). *Sports Clubs in Scotland Summary: Research Digest No. 59*. Edinburgh, Scotland: Sports Scotland.

Amar, A.D., Hentrich, C. and Hlupic, V. (2009). To be a better leader, give up authority. *Harvard Business Review*, 87(12): 22–24.

American Marketing Association. (2004). *Code of Ethics*. Revised edn. Chicago, IL: American Marketing Association.

Amis, J. and Cornwell, T.B. (2005). *Global Sport Sponsorship*. Oxford: Berg.

Amis, J. and Slack, T. (1996). The size-structure relationship in voluntary sport organizations. *Journal of Sport Management*, 10: 76–86.

Anthony, R. and Young, D. (2003). *Management Control in Non-profit Organizations*. 7th ed. New York: McGraw-Hill.

Atkinson, A., Waterhouse, J.H. and Wells, R. (1997). A stakeholder approach to strategic performance measurement. *Sloan Management Review*, Spring, 25–37.

Atrill, P., McLaney, E., Harvey, D. and Jenner, M. (2006). *Accounting: An Introduction*. Frenchs Forest, NSW: Pearson Education Australia.

Australian Bureau of Statistics. (2005). *Involvement in Organised Sport and Physical Activity, Australia, Cat. No. 6285.0*. Canberra, Australia: Australian Bureau of Statistics.

Australian Sports Commission. (2000). *Committee Management, Active Australia Club/Association Management Program*. Canberra: Australian Sports Commission.

Australian Sports Commission. (2003). *Independent Soccer Review: Report of the Independent Soccer Review Committee into the Structure, Governance and Management of Soccer in Australia*. Canberra: Australian Sports Commission.

Australian Sports Commission. (2004). *Sport Innovation and Best Practice – Governance.*. Canberra: Australian Sports Commission. Retrieved from www.ausport.gov.au/ibp/governance.asp

Australian Sports Commission. (2007). *Report of the Steering Committee into the Structure and Governance Review of Basketball in Australia*, November. Canberra: Australian Sports Commission.

Australian Sports Commission. (2008). *Review of High Performance Pathways in Australian Basketball*, January. Canberra: Australian Sports Commission.

Australian Sports Commission. (2016). *Mandatory sports governance principles*. Canberra, Australia: Australian Sports Commission.

Baldwin, R. and Cave, M. (1999). *Understanding Regulation: Theory, Strategy and Practice*. Oxford: Oxford University Press.

Baldwin, R., Cave, M. and Lodge, M. (2012). *Understanding Regulation: Theory, Strategy and Practice*, 2nd edn. Oxford: Oxford University Press.

Bass, B.M. (1985). *Leadership and Performance Beyond Expectations*. New York: Free Press.

Bass, B.M. (1990). *Bass & Stogdill's Handbook of Leadership: Theory, Research, and Managerial Applications*. 3rd edn. New York: Free Press.

Bass, B.M. and Avolio, B.J. (1994). *Improving Organisational Effectiveness Through Transformational Leadership*. London: Sage.

Beech, J. and Chadwick, S. (eds) (2004). *The Business of Sport Management*. Harlow, UK: Prentice Hall.

Beech, J. and Chadwick, S. (2013). The commercialization of sport, in J. Beech and S. Chadwick (eds). *The Business of Sport Management*. 2nd edn. London: Pearson, pp. 3–23.

Bellamy, R. (1998). The evolving television sports marketplace, in L. Wenner (ed). *MediaSport*. London: Routledge, pp. 73–87.

Berger, P. and Luckmann, T. (1967). *The Social Construction of Reality: A Treatise on the Sociology of Knowledge*. London: Penguin.

Bettinger, C. (1989). Use corporate culture to trigger high performance. *Journal of Business Strategy*, 10(2): 38–42.

Blake, R.R., & Mouton, J.S. (1964). *The managerial grid: key orientations for achieving production through people*. Houston, Tex: Gulf Pub. Co.

Block, S.R. (1998). *Perfect Non-profit Boards: Myths, Paradoxes and Paradigms*. Needham Heights, MA: Simon & Schuster.

Bloomfield, J. (2003). *Australia's Sporting Success: The Inside Story*. Sydney: University of New South Wales Press.

Bouckaert, G. (1995). Improving performance management, in A. Halachmi and G. Bouckaert (eds). *The Enduring Challenges in Public Management*. San Francisco: Jossey-Bass.

Bouckaert, G. and van Doren, W. (2003). Performance measurement and management in public sector organisations, in T. Bovaird and E. Lofler (eds). *Public Management and Governance*. London: Routledge.

Boyle, R. and Haynes, R. (2000). *Power Play: Sport, the Media and Popular Culture*. Sydney: Longman.

Braithwaite, J. (2008). *Regulatory Capitalism: How It Works, Ideas for Making It Work Better*. Cheltenham, UK: Edward Elgar.

Braithwaite, J. and Drahos, P. (2000). *Global Business Regulation*. Cambridge, UK: Cambridge University Press.

Brohm, J. (1978). *Sport: A Prison of Measured Time*. London: Ink Links.

Brown, A. and Walsh, A. (1999). *Not for Sale: Manchester United, Murdoch and the Defeat of BSkyB*. London: Mainstream.

Bryson, J. (2004). *Strategic Planning for Public and Non-profit Organisations: A Guide to Strengthening and Sustaining Organizational Achievement*. San Francisco: Jossey-Bass/Wiley.

Carter, D. (2011). *Money Games: Profiting from the Convergence of Sport and Entertainment*. Princeton, NJ: Princeton University Press.

Cashman, R. (1995). *Paradise of Sport*. Melbourne: Oxford University Press.

Chalip, L., Johnson, A. and Stachura, L. (eds) (1996). *National Sports Policies: An International Handbook*. Westport: Greenwood Press.

Chappelet, J. and Bayle, E. (2005). *Strategic and Performance Management of Olympic Sport Organisations*. Champaign, IL: Human Kinetics.

Chelladurai, P. (2006). *Human Resource Management in Sport and Recreation*. Champaign, IL: Human Kinetics.

Clarke, T. (ed.) (2004). *Theories of Corporate Governance*. Oxon, UK: Routledge.

Colyer, S. (2000). Organizational culture in selected Western Australian sport organizations. *Journal of Sport Management*, 14: 321–341.

Cook, R.A. and Szumal, J.L. (1993). Measuring normative beliefs and shared behavioral expectations in organizations: The reliability and validity of the organizational culture inventory. *Psychological Reports*, 72: 1290–1330.

Cousens, L. and Slack, T. (2005). Field-level change: The case of North American major league professional sport. *Journal of Sport Management*, 19(1): 13–42.

Coakley, J., et al. (2009). *Sport in Society*. Sydney: McGraw Hill.

Cuskelly, G. (2004). Volunteer retention in community sport organisations. *European Sport Management Quarterly*, 4: 59–76.

Cuskelly, G., Hoye, R. and Auld, C. (2006). *Working with Volunteers in Sport: Theory and Practice*. London: Routledge.

DaCosta, L. and Miragaya, A. (2002). Sport for all worldwide: A cross national and comparative research, in L. DaCosta and A. Miragaya (eds). *Worldwide Experiences and Trends in Sport for All*. Oxford: Meyer and Meyer.

Dejonghe, T. (2001). *Sport in de wereld: Ontstaan, evolutie en verspreiding*. Gent: Academia Press, p. 117.

Deming, W. (1993). *The New Economics for Industry, Government, Education*. Cambridge, MA: MIT Press.

Denison, D. and Mishra, A. (1995). Toward a theory of organizational culture and effectiveness. *Organizational Science*, 6: 204–224.

Dess, G. and Lumpkin, G. (2003). *Strategic Management: Creating Competitive Advantages*. Boston: McGraw-Hill Irwin.

Dheensaw. C. (1994). *The Commonwealth Games: The First 60 Years, 1930–1990*. Sydney: ABC/Orca Publishing.

Doherty, A. (1998). Managing our human resources: A review of organizational behaviour in sport. *Journal of Sport Management*, 12(1): 1–24.

Dolles, H. and Soderman, S. (2013). The network of value captures in football club management, in S. Soderman and H. Dolles (eds). *Handbook of Research on Sport and Business*. Cheltenham, UK: Edward Elgar, pp. 367–395.

Downward, P. and Dawson, A. (2000). *The Economics of Professional Team Sports*. London: Routledge.

Dressler, G. (2003). *Human Resource Management*. Upper Saddle River, NJ: Prentice Hall.

Drucker, P.F. (1990). Lessons for successful non-profit governance. *Non-profit Management and Leadership*, 1: 7–14.

England Netball. (2007a). *Student Pack*. Hertfordshire, UK: England Netball.

England Netball. (2007b). *Annual Report 2006–2007*. Hertfordshire, UK: England Netball.

Euchner, C. (1993). *Playing the Field: Why Sports Teams Move and Cities Fight to Keep Them*. Baltimore: John Hopkins University Press.

Evens T., Iosifidis, P. & Smith, P. (2013). *The Political economy of television sports rights*. London: Palgrave Macmillan.

Fan Hong. (1997). Commercialism and sport in China. *Journal of Sport Management*, 11: 343–354.

Ferkins, L., Shilbury, D. and McDonald, G. (2009). Board involvement in strategy: Advancing the governance of sport organizations. *Journal of Sport Management*, 23: 245–277.

Ferkins, L. and Shilbury, D. (2012). Good boards are strategic: What does that mean for sport governance? *Journal of Sport Management*, 26: 67–80.

Ferkins, L. and Shilbury, D. (2015). Board strategic balance: An emerging sport governance theory. *Sport Management Review*, 18: 489–500.

Ferrand, A. and Stotlar, D. (2010). Introduction: New perspectives in sport event marketing. *International Journal of Sport Management and Marketing*, 7(3–4): 145–155.

Fiedler, F.E. (1967). *A Theory of Leadership Effectiveness*. New York: McGraw-Hill.

Fielding, L., Miller, L. and Brown, J. (1999). Harlem Globetrotters International, Inc. *Journal of Sport Management*, 13(1): 45–77.

Fletcher, K. (1999). Four books on non-profit boards and governance. *Non-profit Management and Leadership*, 9: 435–441.

Football Association (FA). (2008). *The FA's Vision 2008–2012*. London: FA.

Football Governance Research Centre. (2004). *The State of the Game: The Corporate Governance of Football Clubs 2004, Research Paper 2004 No. 3*. Birkbeck: Football Governance Research Centre, University of London.

Fort, R. (2011). *Sport Economics*. 3rd edn. Upper Saddle River, NJ: Prentice Hall/Pearson.

Foster, G., Greyser, A. and Walsh, B. (2006). *The Business of Sports: Text and Cases on Strategy and Management*. Mason, OH: Thompson South-Western.

Friedman, M., Parent, M. and Mason, D. (2004). Building a framework for issues management in sport through stakeholder theory. *European Sport Management Quarterly*, 3: 170–190.

Frisby, W. (1986). The organizational structure and effectiveness of voluntary organizations: The case of Canadian national sport governing bodies. *Journal of Park and Recreation Administration*, 4: 61–74.

Frontiera, J. (2010). Leadership and organizational culture Transformation in professional sport. *Journal of Leadership & Organizational Studies*, 17: 171–186.

Frosdick, S. and Walley, L. (eds) (1997). *Sport and Safety Management*. Oxford: Butterworth Heinemann.

Gardiner, S., Parrish, R. and Siekman, R. (2009). *EU, Sport, Law and Policy*. The Hague, Neth: Asser Press.

Goffee, R. and Jones, G. (1996). What holds the modern company together? *Harvard Business Review*, 74(6): 133–149.

Goldman, R. and Papson, S. (1998). *Nike Culture*. Thousand Oaks, CA: Sage.

Gomes. S., Kase, K. and Urruria, I. (2010). *Value Creation and Sport Management*. Cambridge, UK: Cambridge University Press.

Graaff, A. (1996). Service quality and sport centres. *European Journal for Sport Management*, xx/2.

Gratton, C. and Taylor, P. (1991). *Government and the Economics of Sport*. London: Longman.

Grattton, C. and Taylor, P. (2000). *Economics of Sport and Recreation*. Milton Park, UK: Taylor and Francis.

Green, M. (2006). From 'sport for all' to not about 'sport' at all: Interrogating sport policy interventions in the United Kingdom. *European Sport Management Quarterly*, 6(3): 217–238.

Green, M. and Houlihan, B. (2005). *Elite Sport Development*. London: Routledge.

Greenfield, S. and Osborn, G. (2001). *Regulating Football; Commodification, Consumption and the Law*. London: Pluto Press.

Grix, J. (2009). The impact of UK sport policy on the governance of athletics. *International Journal of Sport Policy*, 1: 31–49.

Grix, J. and Dennis, M. (2012). *Sport Under Communism: The East German Experience, Global Culture and Sport Series*. Basingstoke: Palgrave Macmillan.

Hall, J. (2016). *Governance Review for the British Judo Association*. Loughborough: British Judo Association.

Halpern, D. (2005). *Social Capital*. Cambridge, UK: Polity Press.

Hamil, S., Morrow, S., Idle, C., Rossi, G. and Faccendini, S. (2010). The governance and regulation of Italian football. *Soccer & Society*, 11: 373–413.

Hanlon, C. and Cuskelly, G. (2002). Pulsating major sport event organizations: A framework for inducting managerial personnel. *Event Management: An International Journal*, 7(4): 231–243.

Hart, L. (2006). *Accounting Demystified: A Self Teaching Guide*. New York: McGraw-Hill.

Harvard Business Review. (1998). *On Measuring Corporate Performance*. Boston: Harvard Business Review Press.

Heimovics, R.D. and Herman, R.D. (1990). Responsibility for critical events in non-profit organizations. *Non-profit and Voluntary Sector Quarterly*, 19: 59–72.

Henry, I. and Lee, P.C. (2004). Governance and ethics in sport, in J. Beech and S. Chadwick (eds). *The Business of Sport Management*. England: Prentice Hall.

Henry, I. and Uchium, K. (2001). Political ideology, modernity, and sport policy: A comparative analysis of sport policy in Britain and Japan. *Hitotsubashi Journal of Social Studies*, 33(2): 161–185.

Herman, R.D. and Heimovics, R. (1990). The effective non-profit executive: Leader of the board. *Non-profit Management and Leadership*, 1: 167–180.

Herman, R.D. and Heimovics, R. (1994). Executive leadership, in R.D. Herman and Associates (eds). *The Jossey-Bass Handbook of Non-profit Leadership and Management*. San Fransisco: Jossey-Bass, pp. 137–153.

Herman, R.D. and Renz, D.O. (1997). Multiple constituencies and the social construction of non-profit organizational effectiveness. *Non-profit and Voluntary Sector Quarterly*, 26: 185–206.

Herman, R.D. and Renz, D.O. (1998). Non-profit organizational effectiveness: Contrasts between especially effective and less effective organizations. *Non-profit Management and Leadership*, 9: 23–38.

Herman, R.D. and Renz, D.O. (2000). Board practices of especially effective and less effective local non-profit organizations. *American Review of Public Administration*, 30: 146–160.

Hersey, P. and Blanchard, K. (1977). *Management of Organizational Behaviour: Utilizing Human Resources*. Englewood Cliffs, NJ: Prentice-Hall.

Hess, R., Nicholson, M., Stewart, B. and de Moore, G. (2008). *A National Game: The History of Australian Rules Football*. Melbourne: Viking/Penguin.

Hess, R. and Stewart, R. (eds) (1998). *More Than a Game: An Unauthorised History of Australian Football*. Melbourne: Melbourne University Press.

Hill, L.A. (2008). Where will we find tomorrow's leaders? *Harvard Business Review*, 86(1): 123–129.

Hillary Commission. (2000). *The Growing Business of Sport and Leisure: The Impact of the Physical Leisure Industry in New Zealand*. Wellington, New Zealand: Hillary Commission.

Hilton, K. and Bramham, P. (2008). *Sports Development: Policy, Processes and Practice*. London: Routledge.

Hindley, D. (2003). *Resource Guide in Governance and Sport*. Learning and teaching support network in Hospitality, Leisure, Sport and Tourism at www.hlst.ltsn.ac.uk/resources/governance.html.

Hockey Canada. (2007). *Annual Report 2007*. Calgary, CA: Hockey Canada.

Hoehn, T. and D. Lancefield (2003), 'Broadcasting in Sport', *Oxford Review of Economic Policy*, 19 (4), 552–68.

Hofstede, G. (1991). *Cultures and Organizations: Software of the Mind*. London: McGraw–Hill.

Hofstede, G. (2001). *Culture's Consequences: Comparing Values, Behaviors, Institutions and Organizations Across Nations*. Thousand Oaks, CA: Sage.

Hofstede, G., Neuijen, B., Ohayv, D. and Sanders, G. (1990). Measuring organizational cultures: A qualitative and quantitative study across twenty cases. *Administrative Science Quarterly*, 35: 286–316.

Hoggett, J., Edwards, L. and Medlin, J. (2006). *Accounting*. 6th edn. Milton, Qld: Wiley.

Horne, D. (1964). *The Lucky Country*. Ringwood: Penguin Books.

Houle, C.O. (1960). *The Effective Board*. New York: Association Press.

Houle, C.O. (1997). *Governing Boards: Their Nature and Nurture*. San Francisco: Jossey-Bass.

Houlihan, B. (1997). *Sport Policy and Politics: A Comparative Analysis*. London: Routledge.

Houlihan, B. and White, A. (2002). *The Politics of Sport Development: Development of Sport or Development Through Sport?* London: Routledge.

House, R.J. (1971). A path-goal theory of leader effectiveness. *Administrative Science Quarterly*, 16: 321–338.

House, R.J., & Mitchell, T.R. (1974). Path-goal theory of leadership. *Contemporary Business*, 3, Fall: 81–91.

Howard, D. and Crompton, J. (2004). *Financing Sport*. 2nd edn. Morgantown, WV: Fitness Information Technology.

Howard, L. (1998). Validating the competing values model as a representation of organizational cultures. *International Journal of Organizational Analysis*, 6(3): 231–251.

Hoye, R. and Cuskelly, G. (2003). Board-executive relationships within voluntary sport organisations. *Sport Management Review*, 6(1): 53–73.

Hoye, R. and Inglis, S. (2003). Governance of non-profit leisure organisations. *Society and Leisure*, 26(2): 369–387.

Hoye, R. and Cuskelly, G. (2007). *Sport Governance*. Oxford: Elsevier Butterworth-Heinemann.

Hoye, R., Nicholson, M. and Houlihan, B. (2010). *Sport and Policy: Issues and Analysis*. Jordon Hill, UK: Elsevier/Butterworth Heinemann.

Hoye, R., Nicholson, M. and Smith, A. (2008). Unique aspects of managing sport organizations. In C. Wankel (ed). *21st Century Management: A Reference Handbook*. Thousands Oaks, CA: Sage, pp. 499–507.

Hughes, H. (1981). *News and the Human Interest Story*. London: Transaction Books [reprint of the 1940 University of Chicago Press edition].

Human Kinetics National Intelligence Council. (2000). *Global Trends 2015: A Dialogue About the Future with Non Government Experts*. Washington, DC: National Foreign Intelligence Board.

Hums, M. and Maclean, J. (2009). *Governance and Policy in Sport Organisations*. 2nd edn. Scottsdale, Arizona: Holcomb Hathaway.

Hylton, K. and Bramham, P. (eds) (2007). *Sports Development: Policy, Process and Practice*. 2nd edn. London: Routledge.

Hylton, K., Bramham, P., Jackson, D. and Nesti, M. (ed.) (2001). *Sport Development*. London: Routledge.

Institute for Volunteering Research. (2008). *Management Matters: A National Survey of Volunteer Management Capacity*. London, UK: Institute for Volunteering Research.

Institute for Volunteering Research and Volunteering England. (2008). *A Winning Team? The Impacts of Volunteers in Sport*. London, UK: Institute for Volunteering Research.

International Monetary Fund. (2000–2005). *Globalization: Threat or Opportunity?* Retrieved March 1, 2005 from www.imf.org/external/np/exr/ib/2000/041200.htm

Jaggard, E. (2006). *Between the Flags: One Hundred Summers of Australian Surf Lifesaving*. Sydney: UNSW Press.

Jarzabkowski, P. and Spee, P.A. (2009). Strategy-as-practice: A review and future directions for the field. *International Journal of Management Reviews*, 11: 69–95.

Jensen, R. (1999). *The Dream Society*. New York: McGraw-Hill.

John, G. and Sheard, R. (1997). *Stadia: A Design and Development Guide*. Oxford: Architectural Press.

Johnson, G., Langley, A., Melin, L. and Whittington, R. (2007). *Strategy as Practice: Research Directions and Resources*. New York: Cambridge University Press.

Johnson, G. and Scholes, K. (2002). *Exploring Corporate Strategy*. 6th edn. London: Prentice-Hall, pp. 4–11.

Johnson, G., Scholes, K. and Whittington, R. (2008). *Exploring Corporate Strategy*. 8th edn. London: Prentice-Hall.

Jung, T., Scott, T., Davies, H.T.O., Bower, P., Whalley, D., McNally, R. and Russell, M. (2009). Instruments for exploring organizational culture: A review of the literature. *Public Administration Review*, 69(6): 1087–1096.

Kahle, L. and Close, A. (eds) (2011). *Consumer Behavior Knowledge for Effective Sports and Event Marketing*. New York: Taylor & Francis.

Kaplan, R. and Norton, D. (1992). The balanced scorecard: Measures that drive performance. *Harvard Business Review*, January–February: 71–79.

Kaplan, R. and Norton, D. (1996). *The Balanced Scorecard*. Boston: Harvard University Press.

Kikulis, L.M., Slack, T. and Hinings, B. (1992). Institutionally specific design archetypes: A framework for understanding change in national sport organizations. *International Review for the Sociology of Sport*, 27: 343–367.

Kikulis, L.M., Slack, T. and Hinings, B. (1995). Toward an understanding of the role of agency and choice in the changing structure of Canada's national sport organizations. *Journal of Sport Management*, 9: 135–152.

Kikulis, L.M., Slack, T., Hinings, B. and Zimmermann, A. (1989). A structural taxonomy of amateur sport organizations. *Journal of Sport Management*, 3: 129–150.

King, N. (2009). *Sport Policy and Governance: Local Perspectives*. Jordon Hill, UK: Elsevier/Butterworth Heinemann.

Kotter, J.P. (1990). *A Force for Change: How Leadership Differs from Management*. New York: The Free Press.

Kouzes, J.M. and Posner, B.Z. (2006). *A Leader's Legacy*. Hoboken: Jossey-Bass.

Leisure Industries Research Centre. (2003). *Sports Volunteering in England 2002: A Report for Sport England*. Sheffield, UK: Leisure Industries Research Centre.

Lewis, G. (1993). Concepts in strategic management, in G. Lewis, A. Morkel and G. Hubbard (eds) *Australian Strategic Management: Concepts, Context and Cases*.Sydney: Prentice-Hall, pp. 5–38.

Li, M., Hofacre, S. and Mahony, D. (2001). *Economics of Sport*. Morgantown: Fitness Information Technology.

Locke, E.A. (1991). *The Essence of Leadership: The Four Keys to Leading Successfully*. New York: Lexington Books.

Lyons, M. (2001). *Third Sector: The Contribution of Non-profit and Cooperative Enterprises in Australia*. Crows Nest, NSW, Australia: Allen & Unwin.

Lyras, A. and Welty Peachey, J. (2011). Integrating sport-for-development theory and praxis. *Sport Management Review*, 14(4), 311–326.

MacLean, J. (2001). *Performance Appraisal for Sport and Recreation Managers*. Champaign, IL: Human Kinetics.

MacLean, J. (2009). Auditing performance management practices: A comparison of Canadian Sport Organisations. *International Journal of Sport Management and Marketing*, 5(3): 295–309.

Mannell, R. and Kleiber, D. (2013) Psychology of leisure, in T. Blackshaw (ed). *Routledge Handbook of Leisure Studies*. London: Routledge.

Mason, D., Andrews, D. and Silk, M. (eds) (2005). *Qualitative Methods for Sports Studies*. Oxford: Berg.

McCarthy, J. (2007). The ingredients of financial transparency. *Non-profit & Voluntary Sector Quarterly*, 36(1): 156–164.

McDonald, I. (2011). High performance sport policy in the UK, in B. Houlihan and M. Green (eds). *Routledge Handbook of Sport Development*. London: Routledge.

Mechikoff, R. and Estes, S. (1993). *A History and Philosophy of Sport and Physical Education*. Madison: Brown and Benchmark.

Miles, R.E. (1975). *Theories of Management: Implications for Organizational Behaviour and Development*. New York: McGraw-Hill.

Miller, T., Lawrence, G., McKay, J. and Rowe, D. (2001). *Globalisation and Sport*. London: Sage.

Muller,C., Lammert, J. and Hovemann, G. (2012). The financial fair play regulations of EUFA: An adequate concept to ensure the long term viability and sustainability of European club football. *International Journal of Sport Finance*, 7: 117–140.

New, B. and LeGrand, J. (1999). Monopoly in sports broadcasting. *Policy Studies*, 20(1): 23–36.

Nichols, G., Ferguson, G., Grix, J. and Griffiths, J. (2013). *Sport Makers: Developing Good Practice in Volunteer and Sports Development*. University of Sheffield.

Nicholson, M. (2007). *Sport and the Media: Managing the Nexus*. London: Elsevier Butterworth-Heinemann.

Nicholson, M., Kerr, A. and Sherwood, M. (2015). *Sport and the Media: Managing the Nexus*. 2nd ed. London: Elsevier Butterworth-Heinemann.

Norman, W. and MacDonald, C. (2004). Getting to the bottom of 'triple bottom-line accounting'. *Business Ethics Quarterly*, 14(2): 243–262.

Northouse, P.G. (2010). *Leadership: Theory and Practice*. 5th ed. Thousand Oaks, CA: Sage.

O'Brien, D. and Slack, T. (2003). An analysis of change in an organizational field: The professionalization of English Rugby Union. *Journal of Sport Management*, 17(4): 417–448.

Ogbonna, E. and Harris, L.C. (2002). Organizational culture: A ten year, two-phase study of change in the UK food retailing sector. *Journal of Management Studies*, 39: 673–706.

Organisation for Economic Co-Operation and Development. (2004). *Principles of Corporate Governance*. Paris: OECD.

Oriard, M. (1993). *Reading Football*. Chapel Hill: University of North Carolina Press.

Parent, M., O'Brien, D. and Slack, T. (2003). Strategic management in the context of sport, in L. Trenberth (ed). *Managing the Business of Sport*. Palmerston North, New Zealand: Dunmore Press, pp. 101–122.

Pattavino, P. and Pye, G. (1994). *Sport in Cuba: The Diamond in the Rough*. Pittsburg: University of Pittsburg Press.

Perryman, M. (ed.). (2001). *Hooligan Wars: Causes and Effects of Football Violence*. Edinburgh: Mainstream Publishing.

Pettigrew, A.M. (1979). On studying organizational cultures. *Administrative Science Quarterly*, 24: 570–581.

Pfeffer, J. and Salancik, G. (1978). *The External Control of Organizations: A Resource Dependence Perspective*. New York: Harper & Row.

Pitt, L., Parent, M., Berthon, P. and Steyn, P. (2010). Event sponsorship and Ambush marketing: Lessons from the Beijing Olympics. *Business Horizons*, 53: 281–290.

Porter, M. (1980). *Competitive Strategy*. New York: Free Press.

Porter, M. (1985). *Competitive Strategy: Creating and Sustaining Superior Performance*. New York: Simon & Schuster.

Porter, M. (1996). What is strategy? *Harvard Business Review*, November–December: 61–78.

Productivity Commission. (2003). *Social Capital: Reviewing the Concept and Its Policy Implications*. Canberra: Commonwealth of Australia.

Productivity Commission. (2010). *Contribution of the Not-for-Profit Sector*. Canberra: Commonwealth of Australia.

Putnam, R. (2000). *Bowling Alone: The Collapse and Revival of American Community*. New York: Simon and Schuster.

Quinn, K. (2009). *Sports and Their Fans: The History, Economics and Culture of the Relationship Between Spectator and Sport*. Jefferson, NC: McFarland and Co..

Quinn, R. and Rohrbaugh, J. (1983). A spatial model of effectiveness criteria: Towards a competing values approach to organizational analysis. *Management Science*, 29: 363–377.

Quirk, J. and Fort, R. (1992). *Pay Dirt: The Business of Professional Team Sports*. Princeton: Princeton University Press.

Rein, I., Kotler, P. and Shields, B. (2006). *The Elusive Fan: Reinventing Sports in a Crowded Marketplace*. New York: McGraw-Hill.

Rigauer, B. (1981). *Sport and Work*. New York: Columbia University Press.

Riordan, J. (1977). *Sport in Soviet Society*. Cambridge: Cambridge University Press.

Riordan, J. (ed.) (1978). *Sport Under Communism: The USSR., Czechoslovakia, The GDR., China, Cuba.* Canberra: Australian National University Press.

Robbins, S. (1990). *Organization Theory: Structure Design & Applications.* Upper Saddle River, NJ: Prentice Hall.

Robbins, S. and Barnwell, N. (2002). *Organisation Theory.* Frenchs Forest: Pearson Education Australia.

Robbins, S.P., Bergman, R., Stagg, I. and Coulter, M. (2004). *Management.* 3rd edn. Sydney, Australia: Pearson Education.

Robbins, S.P., Judge, T., Millett, B. and Boyle, M. (2010). *Organizational Behaviour.* 6th edn. Sydney, Australia: Pearson Education.

Robinson, L. (2004). Human resource management. In L. Robinson (ed). *Managing Public Sport and Leisure Services.* London: Routledge.

Rowe, D. (1999). *Sport, Culture and the Media: The Unruly Trinity.* Buckingham, Philadelphia: Open University Press.

Rowe, D. and Callum, G. (2010). Sport, media, and consumption in Asia: A merchandised Milieu. *American Behavioral Scientist,* 53(10): 1530–1548.

Sandy, R., Sloane, P.J. and Rosentraub, M. (2004). *The Economics of Sport: An International Perspective.* Basingstoke: Palgrave Macmillan.

Sashkin, M. (1996). *Organizational Beliefs Questionnaire: Pillars of Excellence.* Amherst, MA: Human Resource Development Press.

Schein, E. (1984). *Coming to a New Awareness of Organizational Culture.* San Francisco: Jossey-Bass.

Schein, E. (1985). How culture forms, develops and changes, in R.H. Kilman, M.J. Saxton, R. Serpa and Associates (eds). *Gaining Control of the Corporate Culture.* San Francisco, CA: Jossey-Bass, pp. 17–43.

Schein, E. (2004). *Organizational Culture and Leadership.* 3rd edn. San Francisco: Jossey-Bass.

Schein, E. (2010). *Organizational Culture and Leadership.* 4th edn. San Francisco: Jossey-Bass.

Schermerhorn, J.R., Hunt, J.G. and Osborne, R.N. (1994). *Managing Organizational Behaviour.* 5th edn. Brisbane: John Wiley & Sons, Inc.

Schroeder, P.J. (2010). Changing team culture: The perspectives of ten successful head coaches. *Journal of Sport Behavior,* 33(1): 63–88.

Schudson, M. (1978). *Discovering the News: A Social History of American Newspapers.* New York: Basic Books.

Schulenkorf, N., Sherry, E. and Rowe, K. (2016). Sport for Development: An Integrated Literature Review. *Journal of Sport Management,* 30: 22–39.

Senge, P. (1990). *The Fifth Discipline.* New York: Currency Doubleday.

Shibli, S. and Wilson, R. (2012). Budgeting and budgetary control in sport, in L. Trenberth and D. Hassan (eds). *Managing Sport Business: An Introduction.* London: Routledge, pp. 185–208.

Shilbury, D. and Ferkins, L. (2015). Exploring the utility of collaborative governance in a national sport organization. *Journal of Sport Management,* 29, 380–397.

Shilbury, D., Quick, S. and Westerbeek, H. (2003). *Strategic Sport Marketing.* 2nd edn. New South Wales: Allen & Unwin.

Shilbury, D., Westerbeek, H., Quick, S. and Funk, D. (2009). *Strategic Sport Marketing.* 3rd edn. Sydney: Allen & Unwin.

Shropshire, K. (1995). *The Sports Franchise Game.* Philadelphia: University of Pennsylvania Press.

Shropshire, K. and Davis, T. (2008). *The Business of Sports Agents.* 2nd edn. Philadelphia: University of Pennsylvania Press.

Slack, T. (1997). *Understanding Sport Organizations: The Application of Organization Theory.* Champaign, IL: Human Kinetics.

Slack, T. and Parent, M. (2006). *Understanding Sport Organizations: The Application of Organization Theory.* 2nd edn. Champaign, IL: Human Kinetics.

Slesinger, L.H. (1991). *Self-Assessment for Non-profit Governing Boards*. Washington, DC: National Centre for Non-profit Boards.

Smit, B. (2007). *Pitch Invasion: Adidas, Puma, and the Making of Modern Sport*. London: Penguin Books.

Smith, A. (2008). *Introduction to Sport Marketing*. Oxford: Elsevier Butterworth-Heinemann.

Smith, A. and Shilbury, D. (2004). Mapping cultural dimensions in Australian sporting organizations. *Sport Management Review*, 7(2): 133–165.

Smith, A. and Stewart, B. (1999). *Sports Management: A Guide to Professional Practice*. Sydney: Allen & Unwin.

Smith, A. and Stewart, B. (2010). The special features of sport revisited. *Sport Management Review*, 10(1): 1–11.

Smith, A. and Stewart, R. (2013). The special features of sport: a critical revisit, in S. Soderman and H. Dolles (eds). *Handbook of Research on Sport and Business*. Cheltenham, UK: Edward Elgar, pp. 526–547.

Smith, A., Stewart, B. and Haimes, G. (2011). *The Performance Identity: Building High-Performance Organizational Cultures in Sport*. New York: Nova Science Publishers.

Soares, J. and Correia, A. (2009). Factors and focuses in the strategic decisions of sporting organisations: Empirical evidence in Sports Associations. *International Journal of Sport Management and Marketing*, 5(3): 338–354.

Sport England. (2011a). *Clubmark Factsheet*. London, UK: Sport England.

Sport England. (2011b). *Sport Makers Factsheet*. London, UK: Sport England.

Standing Committee on Recreation and Sport Working Party on Management Improvement. (1997). *Report to the Standing Committee on Recreation and Sport July 1997*. Canberra, Australia: Standing Committee on Recreation and Sport Working Party on Management Improvement.

Statistics Canada. (2004). *Cornerstones of Community: Highlights of the National Survey of Non-profit and Voluntary Organizations*. Ottowa, Canada: Statistics Canada.

Statistics Canada. (2008). *Sports Participation in Canada, 2005*. Ottowa, Canada: Statistics Canada.

Stebbins, R. (2007). *Serious Leisure*. New Brunswick: Transactions Publications.

Stensholt, J. and Thomson, J. (2005). Kicking goals. *Business Review Weekly*, 10–16 March: 38–42.

Stevens, J. (2006). The Canadian Hockey Association merger and the emergence of the Amateur Sport Enterprise. *Journal of Sport Management*, 20: 74–101.

Stewart, B. (2007a). *Sport Funding and Finance*. Oxford: Elsevier Butterworth-Heinemann.

Stewart, B. (ed.) (2007b). *The Games Are Not the Same: The Political Economy of Football in Australia*. Melbourne: Melbourne University Press.

Stewart, R. (1989). The nature of sport under capitalism and its relationship to the capitalist labour process. *Sporting Traditions*, 6(1): 43–61.

Stewart, R., Nicholson, M., Smith, A. and Westerbeek, H. (2004). *Australian Sport: Better by Design? The Evolution of Australian Sport Policy*. London: Routledge.

Stewart, R. and Smith, A. (1999). The special features of sport. *Annals of Leisure Research*, 2: 87–99.

Stoldt, C. (2013). 'College Athletics Communications', in P. Pedersen (ed.). *Routledge Handbook of Sport Communication*. London: Routledge.

Surf Lifesaving Australia. (2010). *Annual Report: 2009–2010*. Sydney: Cheltenham, UK.

Szymanksi, S. (2009). *Playbooks and Chequebooks: An Introduction to the Economics of Modern Sport*. Princeton, NJ: Princeton University Press.

Szymanski, S. and Kuypers, T. (1999). *Winners and Losers: The Business Strategy of Football*. London: Viking.

Taylor, T., Doherty, A. and McGraw, P. (2008). *Managing People in Sport Organizations: A Strategic Human Resource Management Perspective*. London: Elsevier Butterworth-Heinemann.

Theodoraki, E.I. and Henry, I.P. (1994). Organizational structures and contexts in British national governing bodies of sport. *International Review for the Sociology of Sport*, 29: 243–263.

Thibault, L., Slack, T. and Hinings, B. (1991). Professionalism, structures and systems: The impact of professional staff on voluntary sport organizations. *International Review for the Sociology of Sport*, 26: 83–97.

Thomas, R.J. (2008). *Crucibles of Leadership*. Boston: Harvard Business School Publishing Corporation.

Tonazzi, A. (2003). Competition policy and the commercialization of sport broadcasting rights: The decision of the Italian competition authority. *International Journal of the Economics of Business*, 10(1):17–34.

Tricker, R.I. (1984). *Corporate Governance*. London: Gower.

Tricker, R.I. (1993). Corporate governance – The new focus of interest. *Corporate Governance*, 1(1): 1–3.

UEFA. (2007). *Financial Report 2006–2007*. Nyon, Switzerland: UEFA.

Van der Post, W. and de Coning, T. (1997). An instrument to measure organizational culture. *South African Journal of Business Management*, 28(4): 147–169.

Vezina, M. and Crompton, S. (2012). *Volunteering in Canada*. Ottawa: Statistics Canada.

Viljoen, J. and Dann, S. (2003). *Strategic Management*. 4th edn. Frenchs Forest, NSW, Australia: Prentice Hall.

Volunteering Australia. (2004). *Snapshot 2004: Volunteering Report Card*. Melbourne, Australia: Volunteering Australia.

Ward, T. (2010). *Sport in Australian National Identity*. London: Taylor and Francis.

Westerbeek, H.M. and Smith, A.C.T. (2003). *Sport Business in the Global Marketplace*. London: Palgrave Macmillan.

Westerbeek, H.M. and Smith, A.C.T. (2005). *Business Leadership and the Lessons from Sport*. London: Palgrave Macmillan.

Wexley, K.N. and Yukl, G.A. (1984). *Organizational Behaviour and Personnel Psychology*. Revised edn. Homewood, IL: Richard D. Irwin, Inc.

Whitson, D. (1998). Circuits of promotion: Media, marketing and the globalization of sport, in L. Wenner (ed). *MediaSport*. London: Routledge, pp. 57–72.

Wicker P., Breuer, C. and Pawlowski, T. (2010). Are sports club members big spenders? Findings from sport-specific analysis in Germany. *International Journal of Sport Finance*, 6: 155–169.

Williams, R. (1998). *Performance Management: Perspectives on Employee Performance*. London: Thomson Business Press.

Zimbalist, A. (2006). *The Bottom Line: Observations and Arguments on the Sports Business*. Philadelphia, PA: Temple University Press.

Index

Note: Page numbers in *italics* indicate a figure and page numbers in **bold** indicate a table.